CULTURE, SOCIAL MOVEMENTS, AND PROTEST

To my mother and father

Culture, Social Movements, and Protest

Edited by

HANK JOHNSTON
San Diego State University, USA

ASHGATE

Published by
Ashgate Publishing Limited
Wey Court East
Union Road
Farnham
Surrey GU9 7PT
England

Ashgate Publishing Company
Suite 420
101 Cherry Street
Burlington, VT 05401-4405
USA

www.ashgate.com

British Library Cataloguing in Publication Data
Culture, social movements, and protest
  1. Social movements 2. Political culture
  I. Johnston, Hank, 1947-
  303.4'84

Library of Congress Cataloging-in-Publication Data
Culture, social movements, and protest / by Hank Johnston.
    p. cm.
  Includes index.
  ISBN 978-0-7546-7446-7
  1. Social movements--Cross-cultural studies. 2. Culture. I. Johnston, Hank, 1947-

HM881.C86 2008
303.48'40723--dc22

2008030282

ISBN 978-0-7546-7446-7

Mixed Sources
Product group from well-managed forests and other controlled sources
www.fsc.org Cert no. SA-COC-1565
© 1996 Forest Stewardship Council
FSC

Printed and bound in Great Britain by
MPG Books Ltd, Bodmin, Cornwall.

Contents

List of Figures and Tables

Figures

Tables

Notes on Contributors

Colin Barker is retired from the sociology department at Manchester Metropolitan University. He remains an active scholar and socialist. He organizes the annual Alternative Futures and Popular Protest Conference at Manchester Metropolitan University. His books include *Festival of the Oppressed: Solidarity, Reform and Revolution in Poland*, and *Revolutionary Rehearsals*.

Donatella della Porta is Professor of Sociology in the Department of Political and Social Sciences at the European University Institute. Among her recent publications are *The Global Justice Movement* (with Massimiliano Andretta, Lorenzo Mosca and Herbert Reiter), *Globalization from Below* (with Abby Peterson and Herbert Reiter), and *Policing Transnational Protest*.

Gary Alan Fine is John Evans Professor of Sociology at Northwestern University. He received his PhD in social psychology from Harvard University. He has written on how activists shape political reputations by serving as reputational entrepreneurs. He is the author of *Difficult Reputations: Collective Memories of the Evil, Inept and Controversial*.

Sebastian Haunss is Assistant Professor in Political Science at the University of Konstanz, Germany. He has published on processes of collective identity and social movements and on forms and repertoires of protest. Currently he is researching conflicts about intellectual property claims.

Gabriel Ignatow is an Assistant Professor of Sociology at the University of North Texas. His research interests are mainly in the areas of cultural sociology, globalization, and social movements. He has written numerous articles and book chapters, and the book, *Transnational Identity Politics and the Environment*.

Hank Johnston is Associate Professor of Sociology at San Diego State University. His research focuses on nationalist movements, state repression, framing theory, and cultural approaches to mobilization. He is founding editor and publisher of *Mobilzation: An International Quarterly*.

Sveta Klimova taught at University of Strathclyde, Glasgow, Scotland, and is currently Honorary Research Fellow at the School of Social Sciences, University of Birmingham, England. Her research interests include normative aspects of social conflict, discourse analysis, communicative action, hermeneutics, and social movements.

John Krinsky is Associate Professor of Political Science at the City College of New York. He is the author of *Free Labor: Workfare and the Contested Language of Neoliberalism*, and several articles on welfare reform and workfare in New York City. A sociologist by training, he is currently studying changes in public sector labor-regulatory regimes, theories of political cognition and strategy, and developing a broader Marxist perspective on social movements.

Darcy K. Leach is currently a Visiting Assistant Professor at Boston College. Her research focuses on the viability of non-hierarchical organizational forms, oppositional ideologies and countercultures, and social change in advanced capitalist democracies. Her dissertation compared the impact of ideology on the organizational practices of the German nonviolence and autonomous movements. She has recently begun a study of how collectivist democracy became an established feature in German social movements but has not proved sustainable in the US.

David S. Meyer is Professor of Sociology, Political Science, and Planning, Policy, and Design at the University of California, Irvine. He has written on the development and impact of social movements. His most recent book is *The Politics of Protest: Social Movements in America*.

Ingrid Miethe is Professor for General Education at the Protestant University of Applied Sciences in Darmstadt. She has written on the women' movement and political opposition in East Germany, including her book, *Frauen in der DDR-Opposition*. Her research interests include social movements, education and social inequality, qualitative methods, and biographical research.

Francesca Polletta is Associate Professor of Sociology at the University of California, Irvine. She is author of *Freedom is an Endless Meeting* and *It Was Like a Fever*. She is also coeditor of *Passionate Politics: Emotions and Social Movements*.

PART I
The Cultural Analysis of Social Movements

Chapter 1
Protest Cultures: Performance, Artifacts, and Ideations

Hank Johnston

In the study of social movements and protest, research from a cultural perspective began in earnest a little over two decades ago. Prior to that time, a cultural focus was mostly latent, kept in suspended animation by scholars assuming the role of beliefs, attitudes, and ideologies in social movements. It was via the notion of framing as an element in recruitment and participation, first through of social psychology (Gamson, Fireman, and Rytina 1982) and then symbolic interactionism (Snow, Rochford, Worden, and Benford 1986), that the systematic treatment of cultural factors established roots in the field. For quite some time thereafter, the framing perspective, especially in the elaborations of David Snow, Robert Benford, and colleagues, and an interest in the role of collective identity, which was kindled by European research in new social movements, were the main carriers of cultural analysis. This was the general lay of the land regarding culture in social movement studies until the publication of *Social Movements and Culture* (Johnston and Klandermans 1995), which brought together US and European perspectives to present several new analytical approaches from various social science fields: rhetorical analysis, sociology of culture, narrative analysis, social psychology, and cognitive science. Since that time, there have been important additions to the cultural cannon: Jasper (1997), Rochon (1998), Steinberg (1999); Davis (2002); Young (2002); Stryker, Owens, and White (2000); Ewick and Silby 2003; Goodwin and Jasper (2004), Johnston and Noakes (2005), Polletta (2006), to name a few. This volume of theoretical essays and empirical research is intended to move our understanding yet another step ahead, extending the scope of how a cultural perspective can inform protest analysis.

It is fair to say that, until recently, the framing perspective has been the primary vehicle of culture in protest studies. Its focus on how organizations use values, beliefs, and general cultural trends to their advantage, nicely synchronized with the instrumental-structuralist focus of political process and opportunity structure models that dominated the field. An important insight of frame analysis was that leaders and organizations strategically craft their messages so that they have the widest impact or present events in the best possible light. A large body of research has considered how social movements and their constituent organizations do this (Gerhards and Rucht 1992; Benford

1993a; Noonan 1995; Rothman and Oliver 2002; Hewitt and McCammon 2005; Kenney 2005; Valocchi 2005; Ferree, Gamson, Gerhards, and Rucht 2002, among others). Strategic framing is a compelling fact of life when one looks at contemporary politics (e.g., Lakoff 1996) and large, professionalized social movement organizations (Dalton 1994). Clearly, politicians, their handlers, and their campaign consultants, do a lot of framing, just as do the leaders of social movements and protest campaigns—for their members, potential members, opponents, and the media. It is not surprising, then, that a large majority of social movement research falling under the cultural rubric has been about how movements and/or movement organizations frame issues, with the implicit dependent variable being some form of mobilization success. Other cultural foci such as narratives, cultures of resistance, cultural performance, the place of music, art, and theater, while representing important avenues of research, comprise much smaller proportions. The goal of this volume is to present cutting-edge empirical research that demonstrates the centrality of a different set of cultural processes in explaining protest movements and their development. An underlying theme of many chapters is how these new approaches engage the framing perspective, but all either enter new territory in cultural methodology or allow us to recognize cultural patterns in new ways.

Culture and Protest Movement Research

When we refer to culture in everyday parlance, we recognize that different groups of people make different assumptions about the world, categorize it in different ways, and adhere to different values and beliefs, all of which significantly shape behaviors and ways of thinking. This commonsense notion of culture can be applied readily to social movements insofar as participants often hold values, attitudes, beliefs, and ideological orientations that are often quite distinct from the broader culture and that shifts in beliefs cause social change. There is an extensive body of research in sociology and political science that is based upon this commonly held and uncontroversial view of cutlure (Inglehart 1990, 1997; Wildavsky 2006; Rochon 1998; Jasper 1997). But the concept as it is often encountered in today's academic discourse is frequently more complex and fluid than this (see Baldwin et al. 2006: x). Over the past thirty years, as different fields in the social sciences have come to embrace diversity and contestation in culture, the use and application of the term also has become increasingly contested—appropriated by different academic discourses and used as a tool for different theoretical projects—in sociology, anthropology, political science, social psychology, communications, cognitive sciences, literary studies, and numerous subdisciplines, including protest studies.

    The view of culture that predominated thirty years ago stressed the inter-connectedness of symbols, categories, and beliefs. Culture was a vast net and social actors were entangled in it, its influence seen in various ritualized as well as everyday behaviors. This view was built upon a "myth of cultural integration" (Archer 1996: 2) that highlighted consistency of ideational orientations in social groups, specifically ones that speak the same language. Two generations of social scientists, nourished by Durkheim, Kroeber, Boas, Benedict, and Parsons, mostly adhered to this view of a uniform cultural fabric. More recently, this cloth has been torn apart, politicize, contexualized (and textualized), relativized, schematized, diversified, iterated, elaborated, narrated, and—some may say—obfuscated. Archer's observation made over a decade ago holds to this day: "What culture is and what culture does are issues bogged down in a conceptual morass from which no adequate sociology of culture has been able to emerge" (1996: 2).

Narratives, text, discourse, metaphor, rituals, actors, and performances, all these key themes of contemporary cultural analysis have not been widely employed to explain how social movements come into being and develop. In her manifesto about cultural analysis of politics, Ann Norton states, "Culture is not a 'dependent' or 'independent' variable. Culture is not a variable at all" (Norton 2004: 2). Her position is that because nothing is outside of culture, any given society, social process, social institution, or social movement organization cannot have more or less culture. Although a researcher may identify and describe in detail important cultural processes that shape behaviors, culture, being the medium of social life and meaning, cannot vary in its presence. In the absence of factors that vary in their causal influence, there is little for the social scientist to do but "describe, describe, and describe," as Norton reports (2004: 90). The rest of the statement, which she attributes to Theodore Lowi, is, "and then you have *explained* it." As important as description is in the building of knowledge, the most thorough and detailed description will not result in the kind of generalizable explanation that many social scientists typically seek. Regarding social movement research, given the instrumentalist-structuralist lens through which many issues of the field are seen, the search for causes of movement success and the variable development of movement trajectories, protest events, and state responses is not something that will be easily foregone.[1]

What is the theorist of protest movements to do in this situation? How can we view protest mobilization in ways informed by three decades of theoretical work that redefines culture processes as ubiquitous and relativizing, yet diverse, fragmented, variable, and inconsistent in their use? First we have to recognize that descriptions of cultural processes *can* lead to explanations, but not in the way that Lowi may have meant it. Polletta's work on narratives and story telling (2006; see also Chapter 2) is informed by a cultural focus on narrative structure and the use of metonymy, synecdoche, and metaphor. The result

---

1   Social psychologists have long known that the attribution of cause is a basic cognitive process. Human beings do it—every day. Because it is fundamental to how we make sense of the world, it a safe assumption that the quest for causal explanations is not going away.

is to identify possible ways that stories that are more powerful in mobilizing participants can be identified. This is an example of how culturally informed description of basic cultural processes can lead to explanation of recruitment and mobilization. Many of the chapters in this volume are descriptions of cultural processes in social movements—the use of speech acts, metaphors, narratives, deep grammars—that point to directions whereby mobilization success and recruitment can be explained, not just described. Movement success remains the explanandum at the heart of our discipline, but a cultural factor, narrative structure, is causative depending on its application according to normative prescriptions of a good story.

Second, we have to recognize that cultural factors, while different from more easily quantifiable measures such as fund raising, size of collective action events, or police presence, still can be grouped, counted, and their influence analyzed. For example, Hewitt and McCammon's work on framing strategies of the woman suffrage movement (2005) shows how framing categories can be devised from common factors, ones that could be easily recognized by panel of judges, and then tested for their effects on movement participation. Gerhards and Rucht (1992) have categorized frames according to interrelatedness and scope and show how they better mobilize participants. Several studies have shown the importance of frame consistency and resonance with the dominant culture for mobilization success (Williams 1995; Diani 1996; Williams and Kubal 1999). The coding of newspaper reports, movement documents, and archival records that go into these reports is surely cultural work, and some cultural theorists tell us that it is by our own symbolic actions we parse this world into meaningful chunks, but this critique overlooks that our coming to terms with the world is not free-form, but rather is guided by: (1) characteristics of the way the empirical world actually is; and (2) by shared cognitive processes shared that impose structure onto the world because of how the human brain works. The point is that the analytical categories of cultural analysis, while social constructions, are not arbitrary but rather guided by how we as human beings put together a world that, at some level, we all share.

Third, even though culture is everywhere, it is important to approach it systematically and parse it into categories that are empirically verifiable. These are methodological decisions and practical ones. On the one hand, some cultural categories make more sense than others. As Gabirel Ignatow shows in his chapter, one way to verify a cultural category is to count the number of occurrences, in his case, of different metaphors in organizational speech. On the other hand, if culture is everywhere and ongoing, it is practically necessary to freeze frame, so to speak, in order take a snapshot of the cultural processes, as Johnston does in his chapter, looking at strategizing of Islam at critical junctures in the trajectory of the Chechen national movement.

A common theme in many studies over the years is that there are three basic categories of cultural factors: ideations, artifacts, and performances. Ideations are the traditional stuff of culture such as values, beliefs, mentalités, social representations, habitus, ideologies, or more specific norms of behavior, including normative forms of speech. We can also include here recent cognitive reformulations of these concepts, such as frames, schemata, algorithms, and grammars (DiMaggio 1997). Artifacts are cultural objects produced either individually or collectively, such as music, art, and literature, which stand alone in their materiality and are available to others after the initial (cultural) behavior that produced them. Performances can be defined as actions that are symbolic because they are interpreted by those also present at the action, the audience. Performances are locations where culture is accomplished (Alexander 2006: 32–4).

All three categories exist in reticulated relationships with each other. Social performances (or praxis, or pragmatics) are the most fundamental because they are where human agency is located, constituting the ontological basis culture—its nodes, so to speak, where culture gets accomplished. Artifacts are not only materially constructed but also socially constructed. Even though they may be individually produced, their creation too is, in a sense, a social performance because the audience is always in the artist's mind. Because of their permanence, cultural artifacts can serve as the focus of numerous other performances after their creation.

Both social performances and artifact-based performances, however, are closely linked to the ideations. There are tendencies in cultural studies to de-emphasize the mental life of individual actors (Wuthnow 1989), but it is axiomatic that intentional behavior does not take place without an idea preceding it. Traditional definitions of culture have always included ideational elements: norms, values, beliefs, and traditions; and although today these represent a superficial view of culture, everyone would agree that they have an intuitive quality and represent *something* related to culture (in some way). Goodenough (1964: 11) went so far as to suggest that culture could conceptualized as all that an actor needs to know to function appropriately in a society. "It's the form of things that people have in their mind, their models for perceiving, relating, and otherwise interpreting them." Most analysts today take as cannon that culture is not simply the sum total of these individually held beliefs, values, and understandings, but rather is how they are played out in social performance or social action, stressing the agentic and collective aspects of culture. Recognizing this, however, raises the question of what exactly do we do, analytically, with the ideas that precede performances—that initiate them and guide them—at least through initial stages.[2] Performances are interpreted and reinterpreted by ideations, being accessed,

---

2   It is a view that also privileges behaviors that give rise to discrepant and/or contested interpretations over those which are interpreted, not precisely but almost exactly, as they were intended. Symbolic behaviors that do not cause great breaches in the ongoing flow of interaction, that for the most part unproblematically represent what they were intended to be, according to an existing mental schema of the actor, constitute most of everyday interaction.

applied, and reformulated as cognitive schemata (D'Andrade 1995). Cognitive research suggests that how representations and interpretations are made affects how they are stored in memory, the ease and intensity with which they are invoked and applied, thus affecting subsequent social action (Schön 1979; Fernandez 1991; Johnson and Taylor 1981).

In looking the at role of culture in protest movements, I will organize the discussion in terms of performances, artifacts, and ideations, but always bearing in mind that they occur within a complex and dense network of social action, imparting an interrelated and recursive quality that makes it difficult to speak of one without invoking elements of the others. In fact, this network image—I prefer the term "matrix" to avoid overemphasizing structural elements—is one I will use often. It captures the complexity, diversity, and sociality of cultural elements (Norton 2004: 1–2). It carries with it Geertz's metaphor of culture as a web of meaning that covers us (1973: 89), but also stresses that the meanings are not as uniform because they are embedded in social relations where agency, diversity, and opposition enter in. These relations in the cultural matrix include the agent and the ideations the agent brings to a performance or the creation of an artifact. It then includes all the other audiences in the situated performance, and the cultural knowledge they bring to make sense. Finally, it encompasses the interaction itself, whereby a network of people perceive and interpret artifacts and performances, creating their own social representations of the world the live in, jointly within a structure social encounters (Mische 2003). Yet this buzzing world of complexity and interrelatedness is so general that it begs the next step of pointing where we go analytically. A good place to start is with performances and how to analyze them.

Opposition, Performance, and Strategy

The cultural perspective that this chapter develops conceptualizes social movements, first and foremost, as performances. Demonstrations, marches, protests, press conferences, presentations, and violent confrontations can all thought of as performances of collective actors geared to a variety of audiences—the media, authorities, counter-movements, the public. These are movement performances at a broad level of analysis, but the specific workings of movements also have performative aspects, such as internal discussions and debates, planning sessions, conflicts among members, and narrative performances, all of which have their own internal audiences. When the analyst focuses on the actions of these various parties and how they are connected, the theatrical metaphor is not only apt but, more importantly, locates culture where it is actually taking place, in the interaction among participants, firmly grounding culture in its collective enactment.

The performative approach to culture is emphasized by several strands of cultural theory, including Goffman's interactional cynicism (1956), Bauman's performance-oriented approach to folk-norms (1986); and, in linguistics analysis, Hymes's and Austin's pragmatic approaches to speech performance (Hymes 1964; Austin 1962). Swidler's toolbox metaphor (1995), from which stories, symbols, values, and scripted behaviors are taken from a widely shared cultural stock and used to the movement's advantage, clearly brings to the foreground the performative perspective common in contemporary social movement analysis. The strategic approach to framing that focuses on how leaders and activists craft public messages to attract public attention, influence public opinion, and draw members to a movement has a strong performance-oriented emphasis.

But social movements are special kinds of performances. They are oppositional performances and part of the diversity and conflict inherent in a broad cultural matrix. All cultures, writ large, contain their own internal critiques in varying degrees. Research in social movements has for some time recognized that there are free spaces (Polletta 1999b), half-way houses (Morris 1984) and oppositional subcultures (Johnston and Mueller 2001) that carve out islands of freedom and resistance in the dominant society and from which social movements emerge. Billig (1995) and Johnston (2005) have pointed out in their research that the inherent oppositional quality of culture is also apparent at the microsociological level, present in the prevailing discourses and in oppositional speech acts in institutional settings. There is an inherent, formal, antithetical quality to all cultures in that the very act of defining something as meaningful invokes its opposite by implying too what it is not (Levi-Strauss 1963). Whether referring to a fundamental binary oppositions such as raw and cooked or sacred and profane, or more complex ones like Regan Republicans versus latté liberals, pro-life versus pro-choice, or socialism versus capitalism, oppositions are fundamental to culture, to the production of new meanings, and the elaboration of old ones. Social movements become phenomena of study because they represent a clustering of certain critiques imparting to them a broader collective scope than those which, otherwise, are simply everywhere. By performing together their critiques—sometimes broader, sometimes deeper, sometimes more frequently than the commonplace ones—members come to see themselves as members a movement—as do outside observers. Mario Diani and others have long argued for the network basis of social movements (Diani 1992, 1996; della Porta and Diani 2005), to which a culturalist perspective might add that a network of oppositional meanings and symbolism overlays and animates the performances of these network relations, being read not only by network members but also by outside observers, namely, members of the larger cultural martrix who also impart meaning to the relations. There are two sides to the social movement performances: the collective action that constitutes the opposition and the reading of it by the audience. Together they constitute the creation of social movement culture.

The inherent oppositional quality of culture penetrates to the heart of the protest studies field. Every social movement is not only a creation and affirmation of its own ideoculture, but also the creation of the larger culture in which it is embedded. It should not be surprising, then, that observers note that we live today in a social movement society (Meyer and Tarrow 1998; Soule and Earl 2005) in which, by virtue of open political channels, numerous media outlets, and relative freedom of information flow, the fundamental contradictoriness of culture blossoms and becomes institutionalized. Offices of ombudsmen, public relations firms, congressional liaison offices, and professionalized movements with marketing departments all reflect the oppositional nodes that are integral parts of the broader cultural matrix. This pervasive contentiousness is nothing new. Past repertoires of contention are the concrete manifestations of a culture's internal opposition specific to a historical time and place. Charivaris and social banditry were meaningful form of opposition in pre-industrial Europe but not in the modern cultures (Hobsbawm 1963; Tilly 1995).

Oppositional Performances

Another reason for culture's inherent self-opposition is that cultural performances are played out by individuals who experience and produce meanings that they almost always perceive as incomplete in comparison to the community's templates (Norton 2004: 60). A culture is always community of outsiders—in varying degrees. This helps explain new social movements—ecology, animal rights, gay rights, autonomen—whereby agents of resistance are created by virtue of alienation from aspects of the dominant culture and through their own self-affirmation. We see these principles in Chapter 11, where Leach and Haunss describe the role of urban "scenes" as sites of political and lifestyle resistance, which are then embedded within the larger cultural networks: the Hamburg scene within a German autonomen scene within a European scene. The same can be said of Johnston's analysis of Chechen resistance against Russian communists (Chapter 10) where the nesting of one cultural matrix within the other was characterized by a great deal of tension and opposition, not only socially and politically, but also in terms of conflicting personal identities of Chechen, party member, kinship, and adept in Sufi Islamic brotherhoods. Finally, we see them in della Porta's study of social forums. These are composed of diverse and innovative oppositional clusters. Indeed, they can be aptly conceptualized a dense matrices of performance and experimentation in deliberative democracy as a counter-hegemonic form of organization and cultural practice.

The innovation and creativity characteristic of social movements comes in part from how human agency is accomplished through the playing out of multiple identities by which the actor bridges more or less institutionally embedded performances in their own lives. Social psychologists have long recognized that there is a social component to self-identity (Tajfel 1981; Turner 1987), built up through memberships in groups upon fundamental psychological foundations of in-group identification that is cognitively contrasted with out-groups. Cultural theorists have extended this view by pointing out that each person has numerous identities which are performed in different settings and which all have a collective component. This is obviously true in diverse and complex national cultures like the UK or the US, but equally true in the minority-national cultures, Basques, Québécois, or Chechens, or the ideoculture of the Black Bloc. The integration of individual movement members is never complete because they occupy other institutional settings and have other self-identities. A movement identity is never total. Moreover, della Porta's respondents reported that the dense matrix of social forum groups provide opportunities for performing the complex subidentities within the global justice movement. In the words of one activist, "One day I'll go and take the Tobin Tax stand, another I'll go with the Lilliput network, or I'll put on white overalls. The strength of the movement is ... you can join one time, twenty percent or thirty percent." Since the May 1968 protests in Europe, researchers have recognized that these multiple collective identities—their articulation and confirmation—haves become a central focus of some movements, and movement performances take up significant clusters of a member's identity. Although it has been noted that collective identity has always been present in social movements, the prevalence of identity-based movements suggests that other social forces are at work in the postmodern period—the multiplication of identities, as Alberto Melucci (1989, 1994, 1995) has pointed out. Numerous research projects theorizing essays have explored aspects of collective identity in both European and North American contexts, its relative emphasis, its "newness," its social construction, role in mobilization, and movement solidarity (Cohen 1985; Offe 1985; Melucci 1989, 1994, 1995; Johnston, Laraña, and Gusfield 1994; Kriesi, Koopmans, Duyvendak, and Giugni 1995).

The point here is that collective identity is both an aspect of group culture, embedded in the matrix of interactions and meanings that confirm and define the group, and also an integral part of self identity, which, in varying degrees, coincides and overlaps with other collective and institutional identities. During movement performances, these other embedded identities do not cease to be part of one social self, but rather exists as part of as self-schema or frame that is complex, connected, and available for interpretation. It not only helps define what it means to be a member of the movement group but also offers unique perspectives to social action within it. is In other words, there is a cognitive basis of the cultural tool box partly linked with different aspects of the self and how they are managed by each social actor. Movement participants bring this richness of identity to movement performances, make their unique contributions to the collective definition of identity through their actions, and also contribute their own unique perspectives on strategy, goals, and behaviors. These different perspectives on courses of action are important sources of innovation, experimentation, and opposition, as della Porta's social forum participants are fully aware.

We see this when movements use the raw materials of the dominant culture in creative ways. During Poland's opposition to the communist rule, a protest group called the Orange Alternative used an anniversary celebration of the

Civic Militia to mock the regime. They carried signs and shouted, "Long live the military" and "Democracy is Anarchy," and "Youth is with the Party." Similarly on anniversaries of the October revolution, they marched in the streets, shouting "Lenin is with us" and "We love the police" (Uncensored Poland News Bulletin 1988: 3).[3] In a widely cited piece, Noonan (1995) observes how elements of patriarchal culture, such as the official exultation of traditional motherhood, were seized and transmuted into elements of women's opposition to the Pinochet regime in Chile. Similarly, Steinberg's (1999) analysis of the class interests and social change among early nineteenth-century English weavers shows how the dominant discourses of early capitalism were used by workers to come to terms with the injustices they faced. This influenced their collective action, which, in turn, recursively influenced their subsequent discursive production. Much like Noonan's study, Steinberg shows how the weapons of the weak are taken from the discursive armamentarium of the dominant culture. A different perspective is provided by Klimova's research (Chapter 5 in this volume) that shows the underlying embeddedness of movement discourse in the broader cultural matrix. She shows this by tracing the shared moral understandings in speech acts of three Russian movements.

There are other sources of strategic innovation of movement performances. Krinsky and Barker present one approach to strategic innovation based on the work of Lev Vygotsky (1978; 1986), which is called cultural-historical activity theory. Their focus is mainly on how individuals bring past experiences from the same movement to collective recalculations of strategy and goals, but participants also may bring experiences derived from multiple collective identities in other spheres of activity, and apply them with creative modifications. By applying experiences from other situations creatively to the problem at hand, actors can see alternatives and new possibilities, which are the heart and soul of culture's self-oppositional character. Lévi-Strauss's idea of bricolage (1966) is a similar way of thinking about strategic innovation. Bircolage which is the work done by the French jack-of-all-trades handyman, the *bricoleur*. He is a workman, a tool user, but also an innovator in that he uses what's available to him to make a repair. The demands of the moment drive his creativity to make the best use of the tools and materials at hand. Neither view is exclusive of identity-based approaches or a cognitive perspective whereby mental templates for other situations or role scripts can be applied creatively elsewhere. In all cases, the actor has sown the seeds of cultural change that germinate as other participants acquire the practice and confirm its new application.

---

3   Colin Barker (Chapter 9) kindly provided information about the activities of the Orange Alternative.

Stories and Narrative Performance

Narratives performances are common elements of culture. Indeed, some scholars see them as primary vehicles of meaning creation (Polkinghorne 1988). In traditional societies narratives often take the form of ritual performances that invoke aspects of group history, affirm and reinforce fundamental beliefs, and define collective identity. The ritual performance of a narrative emphasizes not only the content of the story, but also the form it takes, and the normative understandings about its delivery, location, length, and time of performance. Contemporary narratives have all these properties in varying degrees, but its ritual quality becomes an empirical question (as it always was) anchored in the details of the specific performance. In contrast to traditional anthropological accounts of verbal performance (e.g., Frake 1964), contemporary narrative analysis has come to recognize the creativity of the speaker and the active participation of the audience in interpretation.

There has been a great deal of social science interest in narratives, stories, and their structures, but until the last decade, this interest has not strongly informed the study of protest movements. Part of the reason is that, in social movements, narratives are often about biographical elements of self-understanding, group affiliation, and identity formation. They typically give explanations of choices and behaviors, such as why a person joined a movement, or left a movement (see Ingrid Meithe's Chapter 6 in this volume), which are more circumscribed questions than why a movement succeeded or why it changed its strategy. Gary Fine and Francesca Polletta, two contributors to this volume, played primary roles in showing how narratives figure into basic mobilization processes: creating collective identity, collective memories, and organizing relations. Polleta's chapter (2) shows the power of narratives in movement processes. Both Fine's chapter (3) and Gabriel Ignatow's chapter (7) depict how narratives can be used strategically in a straightforward political sense. Sveta Klimova's chapter extends these observations by showing how, seen through the lens of speech act theory, narratives and other movement texts are used strategically to accomplish actions such as making accusations, demands pleas for help, declarations, and other "performatives." This volume offers several chapters that plumb the narratives of movement participants to gain insight into the cultural dimension of mobilization and contention. It is becoming increasingly recognized that narrative analysis is an important methodological tool for social movement research (Davis 2002; Johnston 2002).

The analysis of narratives draws upon linguistic insights about the forms and permutations fundamental narrative structures as well as literary insights about what makes a powerful performance. We know that narratives are recapitulations of past experiences and events (Labov 1972: 359), given a temporal order (Ricoeur 1981: 52), in which a change of conditions is essential (Barthes 1977: 94)—these elements comprise the basic template. Narratives are reports of sequential and emplotted events, often of a conflictual or dilemmatic nature. Beyond this, we know that sequencing occurs according to certain principles of story grammar that provide a global schematic form (Abbot 1995), in some narratives there seems to be a typology of actors; and that there is a substructure to narratives that can be analyzed according to functions (Labov 1972: 370). Events are presented teleologically in that a narrative' ending clarifies its sequencing and selection of events. Up until that point, understanding is tentative without the narrative's moral ending (White 1981). Successful narratives presume a degree of identification between the teller and the audience, and their moral point assumes shared norms and values, as Klimova shows in her chapter (5) Also, they build upon presuppositions held by the audience that allows the teller to lead them to intended conclusions. These structural and functional elements of narratives may help the social movement analysis determine what makes a compelling story, but formal structure alone does not capture the performative aspects of narratives—on the part of both the speaker and hearer.

An important insight that has developed from the literary analysis of stories is the narrativity of the audience. At the heart of this concept is a certain degree of ambiguity is necessary in the telling of a narrative. Benford (2002) points this out ambiguity is often present in the what he calls the "controlling myths" of social movements, stories that attract participants and maintain solidarity. Not only do these stories accommodate ambiguity to cast a wide net of adherence, but also ambiguity allows members to construct their own interpretations, in effect, making them participants in the narrative too. Not limited to participants, Klimova (Chapter 6) demonstrates the joint participation of authorities and bystander publics in social movement narratives. She analyzes the normative presumptions of several types of social movement speech acts to lay bare the relational basis of all claim making.

Narrativity specifically refers to the ways that the audience is given room to make connections that are left out of the story's telling, allowing space for the hearer's participation and creativity (Leitch 1986). Polletta draws on these insights in Chapter 2 as she traces how the stories in her data are joint accomplishments. She shows how the narrator creates a tension at the story's climax created by a gap in the reasoning that the auditors of the story must fill. This gap requires that those hearing the story make the meaningful connections themselves, which, as narrativity theory holds, is central to what makes a good tale. In one instance, Polletta describes a narrator who had been in an abusive relationship and contemplated suicide. Her story tells of a beating at the hands of her boyfriend, and at a climactic point, "choosing life instead of death," which, in this tale, led to her seizing knife and attacking him. While the story itself is dramatic, the central tension comes from how her critical decision is simply offered up without explanation or analysis, necessitating that the auditor make the connections, in a sense, making the story his or her own. Such narrative tropes allow listeners to cognitively appropriate the story in ways we don't yet fully understand, but which seems to ride on their own agentic imputation of meaning. Without the creativity of the listener, what we are often left with is a boring moral lecture, which rarely motivates people to action. Or, if given too much information, it becomes obvious where the story is headed and listeners feel manipulated.

Clearly, in addition to these elements of narrative structure there are other factors in movement participation, such as availability, network connections, and past participation. Moreover, some tales are so compelling that they seem to have their narrative tension built into the very sequence of events, say, the nuclear meltdown at Three Mile Island or Chernobyl, or a loss of a child to a drunk driver. In these cases, there is a gap derived from and unanswered why question: Why did this happen? Where is fairness in the world? It is likely that, in these cases, even a bad storyteller can move the listeners with the raw narrative. Still, Polletta's research on narrativity holds promise in social movement research, not only for analysis of the strategic use of narratives, but also because it points to a more general principle that movement culture is also jointly accomplished, even at the microlevel of narrative performance. The audience's joint participation allows their "cognitive praxis" in the narrative, providing a consciousness raising function that may essential for mobilization at all levels of risk, but perhaps even more for high-risk activism (McAdam 1982). By describing a situation that allows the audience to see things differently, breaking the old cultural templates of quiescence and making new connections, we have what has variously been called persuasion, resonance, diagnostic framing, conversion, and so on, with the end result being new participants coming to a movement or a protest campaign. This is partly why close narrative analysis is so important for the study of social movements, but we are beginning to understand that speech that brings about consciousness raising or new collective action frames must function according to various rules about the use of metonymy, synecdoche, simile, and metaphor to bring the listener into meaning production. To the new student of culture, I would emphasize that these are more than just obscure terms. They have clear rhetorical functions, some of which we know are tied to memory and other cognitive functions (see Ignatow's Chapter 7) that are related to the communicative power of an idea, not just a function of its substance or a reflection of rational interest.

Culture as Artifact

Artifacts are the results of performances, the products that—usually intentionally, but sometimes unintentionally—become available as the foci and/or the raw materials for subsequent performances. Although embodied in concrete form, artifacts are no less social than the original performances that created them and which they often represent. Building on Latour's discussion of technical artifacts (1988), they are: (1) created by social actors; (2) constitute sources of meaning, which allow them to stand in for human actors in specific situations;

(3) shape action themselves by carrying with them a prescribed range of appropriate responses; (4) often require the active complicity of other social actors to engage their oppositional meaning.

Regarding social movements, a good place to begin is with the "high cultural" artifacts, such as the plastic arts, poetry, literature, theater, music, opera, which often inspire and confirm protest themes. Nineteenth-century movements of nationalism often gave rise to music and literature of this sort. Then, there are the counterparts in popular culture: rhymes, graffiti, folksongs, logos, popular music, iconic images such as Che's ubiquitous countenance, to name a few. Protest researchers frequently recognize these as factors in mobilizing people to action, but often relegate them to a secondary role. Yet, the songs of the civil rights movement and the labor movement (Eyerman and Jamison 1998), and, I might add, the role of music in various nationalist movements across the globe (the Estonian national movement against the Soviets was called "the singing revolution") are important components of mobilizing people to action, as are other artifacts. The strong and chiseled images of workers socialist and communist posters, the ubiquitous graffiti of the South American Left, these stylistic elements of social movements are commonly seen as symbolic—which of course they are—but symbolic in the sense that they represented something else that is more important, namely the movement ideologies and shared injustices that animate their production.

One of the important insights that cultural sociology offers protest studies is that such artifacts have their own place in the matrix of a social movement, one that is more than merely representations of key political themes and ideologies. The producers of these cultural artifacts, the social embeddedness of the artifacts themselves, and their effects, are all elements in the progress of mobilization trajectories. I have in mind the way symbols are often placed in public places. I have heard tales of various nighttime excursions of activists in Barcelona, Spain or Tallinn, Estonia, two cities where I have done field research but representative of many other locales, in which oppositional statements were painted on the sides of buildings or national flags—powerful artifacts in themselves—were hung in prominent places. The planning and clandestine execution of these actions by small groups were movement performances that shaped the activists and their groupings, but also performances that left oppositional artifacts for many to see on their way to morning work, before authorities took them down or cleaned them up. And then the artifacts became the fodder of oppositional microperformaces as bystanders discussed them among themselves, commenting on their meaning and audacity. Although these examples are quite fleeting, they represent how artifacts are appropriated, discussed, modified in their retelling, amplified, and expropriated for further actions, giving them a life beyond their relatively short-lived material existence. And this is only part of the story, as we will see in how music is used in protest movements.

Music in Protest Movements

Compared to other examples of high-cultural and pop-cultural artifacts, music is probably the most widely studied. It has been a factor in many major movements, such as the labor movement, the civil rights movement, socialism in Chile, various ethnonationalist movements, and, of course, the aggressive, anarchist punk scene (Denisoff and Peterson 1973; Eyerman and Jamison 1998; Halker 1991; Rosingo and Danaher 2004). There are cases where music and/or the symbolic stature of a musician or a musical group, become important players in the trajectory of a movement, such that seeing music as *just* an artifact of the movement, that is, once removed from the real forces of change, or *just* a resource to build solidarity, misses the point. Following Eyerman and Jamison (1998: 162), music not only can function as a resource to build collective identity, or to pass information, or preserve a tradition, but also can be integral in the unfolding performance of the movement itself, constituting it by the way songs bring people to participation, by the meaning the songs come to assume, and by the meaning the opponents come to attribute it.

We can see this last point in the Czechoslovak democracy movement (1968–1989) and the songs by its emblematic rock band, the Plastic People of the Universe. In the early years of the movement, the post-Prague Spring period, the band's songs served as the catalyst for dissidents and mass opposition, which was mostly underground and unobtrusive. This role derived not so much from contentious or political of the band, but from the response towards them by the hard-line communist regime, which imparted an oppositional significance to the band and its songs which otherwise would not have emerged. During the band's career, which spanned twenty years, only one song in their repertoire might be considered overtly oppositional or political. In the words of the band's manager, "We were just a band of freaks, playing rock and roll …. It was the problem of the communist government and the party that they didn't like us. They didn't like our aesthetics because it was something from the West—longhairs, capitalism" (quoted in Pareles 2007).

The state prevented the band from playing public concerts, which drove them underground and increased their word-of-mouth popularity. Later, a band member was arrested and tried for "organized disturbance of the peace." During the trial, well known dissidents came to support the band members. Until then, the intellectuals of the Czech dissident groups tended to see the Plastics (as the band was known) as uncommitted and irrelevant hippies and dropouts. New oppositional meanings for the band and its music were forged, by movement actors, by the government agents, and by the interactions among them all, with the band often playing a secondary role. Vaclav Havel, playwright, dissident activist, and later president of Czechoslovakia, supported the band, and one its albums was recorded at his farm. We see in this story the intertwining of elements of the movement's cultural matrix—with dissidents, students and young people, police agents, party members, and the band's own creative agency—all attributing meanings for music such that it became iconic of the opposition. This occurred not by a movement group plotting mobilization strategies, but by the responses of other actors in the cultural matrix.

Nevertheless, it is fair to say that the Plastic's music was only part of the Czechoslovak democracy movement, which was about political rights, not musical freedom. In fact, most protest scholars would agree that popular cultural elements in movements (music, art, theater) are usually never center stage, and therefore are often included as part of "movement culture," a term which—used in its superficial sense—implies the secondary status of cultural artifacts. Yet there are cases when "movement culture" and its artifacts are central, taking an equal place alongside the elements of contentious politics. For example, punk subculture accords music a focal role in the way it merges anti-establishmentism, anti-racism, anarchism, lifestyle, and community for social change ends (Moore and Roberts 2007; Haenfler 2006; Duncombe 1997). In contrast, music plays an insignificant role in the US abortion-rights movement, and a minor role in the Brazilian landless workers movement, the MST.

It also seems the role of popular cultural elements takes on greater significance depending on the stage of mobilization and state responses (Johnston and Mueller 2001). Czech theaters, for example, were also identified with the opposition via linkages with the dissident community. Theaters were focal points for organizing the Civic Forum, the main dissident group that authored Charter 77 (Goldfarb 1980). Plays used oppositional language that was "clear to sympathetic spectators but unintelligible to the totalitarian watchdogs of culture" (Oslzly 1990: 99). Especially among ethnic nationalist movements, such as in Quebec, Catalonia, the Basque region, Armenia, and Georgia (under the USSR), high culture and popular culture elements often embodied political aspirations. This was evident in the songs of Gilles Vigneault, Claude Léveillée and the other *chansonniers* (Quebec), Raimón and Lluis Llach (leaders of the *nova cançó* in Catalonia), and the nationalist punk music of Negu Gorriak (Basque region),[4] but usually in the early stages of movement development. When repression is heavy, artistic production constitutes a significant proportion of the oppositional culture. As repression eases or in countries where it is less obtrusive, artifactual production tends to take textual form because language is better adapted to represent complex ideas. In general, under repressive regimes artistic and intellectual production often are sites of oppositional meaning, first, because creativity and artistic freedoms are so much at odds with authoritarian control; second, because the state go to such lengths to repress them; and, third, because ambiguity of the message and popularity of the artists often make a costly strategy compared to repressing political activism. Important and provocative topics of future research will be

---

4   Negu Gorriak (Hard Winter in the Basque language) is an interesting case that mixes oppositional representations of both ethnic-national opposition and the anti-establishmentism of punk. See Lahusen (1993).

how patterns of how of movement culture and artifactual production correlate with movement focus, timing, and regime type.

Text as Artifact

Like music, the linguistic production of a movement—its texts—are also powerful artifacts that have lives long after their initial production. The "linguistic turn," in the social sciences came to recognize the importance of texts as a methodological focus to empirically ground cultural analyses, but the turn was slow to course its way into the study of protest movements. Among the early research, Wuthnow (1989) looked at the texts of the Reformation, the Enlightenment, and European socialism to trace the broad contours of discursive communities. Johnston (1991), in contrast, took a microscopic approach by analyzing the movement stories and tracts from linguistically informed perspectives. In both cases, the artifactual element was captured by focusing on representative texts, such as Luther's writings for the Reformation, widely distributed calls for protest against the regime, or documents that capture key movement issue, for example, Steinberg's close analysis of the Wages Protection Act (1999: 114–17).

Used in these ways, texts give insight into a group's communicative repertoire, or its discourse—the symbolic space and structure of that repertoire. Discourse, simply stated, is what is said in a group, how it's said, and how it's interpreted. It is the connective tissue of a group's cultural matrix. In this broad sense, the totality of a group's words and meanings can itself be understood as a text performed by the participants. Cultural theorists often point to the interconnectedness of symbolic action and how it is "read" by participants to portray the entirety of culture as a text or discourse (Alexander, Giesen, and Mast 2006: 15; Norton 2004: 22). In these cases, the "text" of a culture is often taken as the sum total of performances guided by participants' symbolic understandings. While these are not themselves artifacts in the concrete, material sense that I am using the term, the methodological reliance on written texts to capture the essential elements of group discourse means that a few words about discourse and discursive analysis are warranted.

In practical terms, discursive analysis takes as it object of study the pamphlets, manifestos, minutes or recollections of meetings and strategy sessions, slogans, speeches, media coverage, public statements of leaders, organizational records, actions of political demonstrators, in other words, the written and spoken text of a movement. At the broadest macrolevel, there are world-historical discourses (*mentalités, Zeitgeist*) such as the Enlightenment, Islamism, eighteenth-century liberalism and twenty-first-century neoliberalism. Here the principle of representativeness is usually implied, as we discussed regarding Wuthnow's expansive study, *Communities of Discourse* (1989). These are broad discourses that influence and shape movement-specific discourses, such as feminism, liberation theology, or ecology. Rochon (1998) points out that the movement level often reflects these broad discursive elements that resonate among the larger populace. Showing this nesting phenomenon in which subordinate mesolevel discourses draw upon and reflect the essential elements of broader macrolevel ones, is a common research goal of discourse studies.

At the mesolevel, discourse analysis can focus on a movement's textual production. It is common that the discourse produced by intellectuals and movement leaders is taken as representative of organizational discourse. When a movement is structured according to different SMOs, their textual production forms part of the polyphonous voice of a movement's discourse, typically reflecting the conflicts, struggles, and political cleavages of the broader social and cultural environment. Discursive analysts often use the plural form, *discourses*, to emphasize that what is being discussed and acted upon is never unanimous, but frequently challenged and negated by opposing groups, a focus that reflects the overlapping and intersecting of numerous cultural submatrices. Contemporary discursive perspectives also stress the emergent and agentic character of textual production, variably called the discursive/ rhetorical approach (Billig 1995, 1992), the rhetorical turn (Simon 1990), or the dialogic perspective (Steinberg 1999), such that all meaning is context-specific, multifaceted, ever evolving, and contested.

At the microlevel, the researcher analyzes the individual production of text and speech by participants and activists, the narratives of social movement participation. Narratives and stories, which I have discussed earlier, are specific examples of text. As we saw, they are often important, not because they are representative, but because they are powerful, which demands a different strategy for sampling narrative texts. Narratives span the divide between textual artifacts of a movement culture and the performances that constitute its discourse (as we discussed them earlier). When they are told, they are performed, and their impact is highly contextual. When they are written, they are the artifacts of a movement culture, and can become the subject matter of subsequent performances. These too are contextual, but compared to spoken narratives and stories, typically less so because the actual text can be invoked for "correct" interpretations by "specialists," say, people present at previous invocations. Important narratives are told and retold (or read and reread), often in ways approaching ritual, and in so doing, strategic choices are made and justified, movement actions enshrined, and individual participation rendered a collective behavior (Polletta 2006). When these are audio-recorded and transcribed, they are "artifactualized" for the analyst, bringing the researcher into the cultural submatrix of the movement.[5] Today, caught on a cell phone and uploaded to YouTube or My Space, we

---

5 A process long-recognized by qualitiative reseachers, who nevertheless tend to hold that objectivity can still be approached, in contrast to some cultural studies perspectives. Researcher involvement in a social movement was embraced fully by Touraine and associates with their method of sociological intervention (Touraine 1981; Dubet and Wieviorka 1996).

encounter both the artifactualization of performances that in the past would have been fleeting and their dispersion far beyond the immediate audience of their creation—possibly for millions to see. But the key here is that these artifactualized performances become available to the researcher for analysis, and not just YouTube videos, but a range of preserved performances that are represented by the various research foci in this volume. The recording of spoken narratives, stories, and texts gives snapshots of cultural performances, without which analysis would often be impossible. By examining the snapshots of texts at different points in time, the analyst can plumb how the meaning systems of movement groups evolve.

Culture and Ideation

I share the perspective of Paul DiMaggio (1997, 2002), Karen Cerullo (2002), Roy D'Andrade (1995), and others, that culture is *both* socially performed and cognitively based. Participants in social movements bring values, norm, attitudes, beliefs, and ideological orientations to movement performances. When they leave those performances, they take the social experiences with them, stored in memory, to be invoked again in subsequent encounters, in ways cognitive scientists are beginning to understand more completely (for a review of this research, see DiMaggio 1997, 2002). There are many ways that a broad cultural focus is related to cognitive processes in sociology and political science: collective memory, the social construction of categories, social discrimination, and—especially relevant to the social movement field—frames and framing processes. In the study of social movements, although frames are often conceived as socially produced cultural effects, it is also widely recognized that frames are cognitive schemata that help actors navigate the world and give it meaning (Goffman 1974; Oliver and Johnston 2005).

Traditional approaches to culture in protest studies and political science have stressed the ideational elements, especially norms, values, beliefs, ideologies, political predispositons and creeds, value orientations, and collective identities, for example and Almond and Verba's civic culture (1963, 1989), Inglehart's political culture (1990); Fantasia's movement cultures (1988), and Rochon's elite-driven analysis of cultural change (1998), to name just a few. This is also true for protest scholars working from the perspective of social psychology (Klandermans 1997; Klandermans and Smith 2002; Ferree, Gamson, Gerhards, and Rucht 2002). While in varying degrees the collective basis of these concepts is either overtly recognized or taken for granted, in practice, these views also presume that culture is in the heads of participants, especially when survey questionnaires are used to gauge cultural orientations or cultural change. The same is true of framing studies that use questionnaires or interviews to elicit responses from movement participants (Caroll and Ratner 1996), or historical texts that are produced by activists (McCammon et al. 2001; Hewitt and McCammon 2005). Although no one disputes that individual actors have something in their heads, the key question is, are these mental representations cultural? Talking about the consistency and sharedness of beliefs, values, and norms seems almost quaint and outdated in contemporary cultural discourse. However, if it makes sense to speak, for example, of the degree of sharedness of a belief or attitude—that is, if researchers agree that such a construct somehow captures a social fact, then such discussions bring the study of culture full circle by locating part of cultural production back in cognition. Once accomplished, we must then bear in mind that this information is not stored inertly in memory, nor uniformly shared among group members, but cognitively based in different ways among different participants, organized in relation to other stored experiences and typical situations, sometimes in connected schemata, sometimes in autonomous models.

When we consider the interlinked cultural matrices described in this chapter, mental representations come to play as individuals enter performative situations where social action is produced. There are two ways of thinking about what participants bring to the interaction. First, they bring cultural content, that is, past experiences of collective life, stored in memory, that shape subsequent interpretations and actions. In my reading, this is the way that Goffman conceived his original concept of a frame, as a cognitive schema produced by social interaction and experience, which is used to interpret "what's going on here." His formulation of everyday experience was, in this way, thoroughly social, which is to say, cultural, as well as cognitively anchored (Goffman 1974). The second way to conceptualize mental representations is a focus on how we think. This includes research in cognitive psychology and cognitive sociology that traces both the processes of storage and retrieval of information and how these may affect how we think about "what's going on here"; and research on "social mindscapes" (Zerubavel 1997) about how the organization of social life affects cognitive processes, which again affects how we process experience (DiMaggio 2002).

There is a body of research that indicates that a "cognitive twist" in the "cultural turn" may be warranted, or if not a twist, then perhaps a "pathway" that allows us to at least consider aspects of mental life as part of culture. Paul DiMaggio, who too advocates this cognitive approach, reviews the relevant research (1997, 2002) and sums up the key points in this perspective. They are as follows:

First, research in cognitive science supports the "tool kit" metaphor (Swidler 1986; 2001), which we discussed earlier in terms of the strategic and innovative nature of many cultural performances, especially those in social movement settings. Cognitive research supports Swidler's observation that "people know more culture than they use," in that we store away multiple facts and opinions from varied sources without expending much effort to check their plausibility. These are the available tools to the cultural handyman (the *bricoleur*), and only when the tools break or prove to be impracticable or less useful than others are they discarded.

Second, psychologists have shown that much of this knowledge is organized into schemata, scripts, algorithms, or categories. D'Andrade (1995) reviews research that strongly points to the existence of these mental models.

Third, DiMaggio points out that these mental structures are rich in substantive content and quite complex, which reflects cognitive research on the complexity of memory storage, retrieval, and organization according to different mental "domains." Also, what we are learning about the complexity and domain-specific nature of memory storage suggests explanations for how individuals juggle multiple cultural roles, and move in and out of cultural traditions, because these are stored in autonomous (and dispersed) ways, which facilitates this kind of multiple functioning. Organization of cultural knowledge by domains provides an especially rich and varied toolbox for bricolage. It also helps explain what we observed earlier as the inherently oppositional nature of the cultural matrix, as actors bring multiple perspectives that are far from uniform, opening possibilities for new and divergent group behaviors and representations.

These findings are important for protest studies because so much of culture comes to the field via the framing perspective (see Snow 2004 for a comprehensive review), and frames are cognitive schemata. Goffman originally defined frames as mental constructs, socially received and therefore part of culture, that organize perception and interpretation "in accordance with principles of organization which govern events—at least social ones—and our subjective involvement in them (Goffman 1974: 10). Ableson (1981: 717) describes frames as "structures that, when activated, reorganize comprehension of event-based situations .... In a strong sense, [they involve] ... expectations about the order as well as the occurrence of events." The basic premise of Goffman's *Frame Analysis* is that we encounter daily life through frames, and, indeed, we are helped through our daily lives by the cultural work already done by others, by the understandings received from them. He describes how frames are invoked when giving mail to a letter carrier, talking informally with an acquaintance, and getting into a car to go to work. Frames "selectively punctuate and encode objects, situations, events, experiences, and sequences of actions within one's present and past environment" (Snow and Benford 1992: 137). Simply put, frames (or schemata) are always being invoked, everywhere, everyday. They are precisely a species of mental schemata that, in seeking the cognitive processes that enable quotidian experience, the research mentioned above has confirmed.

Yet, if frames are used everyday, then, for movement activists, part of their everyday activities consists of understanding "what's going on" in the social movement. And more importantly, for quiescent bystanders, part of mobilizing them for action must be changing their understanding of "what's going on," so that they are moved from complacency to activism. In terms of cognition, this involves the addition of new elements to relevant schemata—overriding old ones or placing them in separate domains—so that new ways of seeing and understanding can be achieved, a process that is achieved socially. Goffman discusses the shared nature of some templates in terms of a group's primary framework. They "constitute a central element of [a group's] culture, especially insofar as understandings emerge concerning principle classes of schemata, the relations of these classes to one another, and the sum total of forces and agents that these interpretative designs acknowledge to be loose in the world" (Goffman 1974: 27). Elaborations of the framing perspective by Snow, Rochford, Worden, and Benford (1986) and Snow and Benford (1988, 1992), have built upon this social perspective, one that is strongly informed by symbolic interactionism, by emphasizing the social processes in restructuring these schemata, and especially the group and organizational behaviors by which new and resonant frames emerge for collective action.

But in his *Frame Analysis*, Goffman also recognized that frames were not 100 percent social. In Chapter 6, Ingrid Miethe draws upon several concepts in *Frame Analysis* overlooked by protest researchers to discuss how social movement participation and commitment can be seen in terms of both individual and collective frames. She traces Goffman's concept of keying, which is the construction of frames through both individual experience and group participation. Keying is how individual frames are built up to produce the frames's rim. The rim of a frame is what guides and individual's behavior in a group most of the time without reference to the keying process that built the frame. Miethe shows that the keying process is deeply biographical. To recast Goffman's eccentric lexicon into something more recognizable, we might say that, even though frames (or schemata) are received and reformed through social action, they are processed and stored through the cognitive and emotional idiosyncrasies of the individual as well as through the individual's unique biography (which is also organized and stored schematically).

Given the theoretical orientation of much of Goffman's work, as well as the theoretical roots of frame analysis as applied to social moments, these insights can also be recast in the terminology of symbolic interactionism: Our understandings of the world are forged in ongoing and emergent social interaction (performances). This is where meaning is created. Meaning is thoroughly social. These meanings are then organized and interpreted through the lens of the social self. I invoke symbolic interactionism because, first, many of its insights run parallel with the emergent and reticulated view of cultural representations characteristic of cultural studies; and, second, because cognitive psychologists have explored the role of self-schemata and their central relation to different domains of organizing experience (DiMaggio 1997: 279). DiMaggio observes that understandings of the self seem to be embedded in an "emotionally supersaturated cluster of schemata." While his review suggests that empirical research in these topics is just beginning, it is relevant for protest studies in that self-related cognitions may be linked with "hot cognitions" that are essential for mobilizing people to action and taking risks.

To summarize, in my reading of Goffman—and Meithe's too—frames are both social *and* individual. Participants in cultural performances bring their own cognitive life—their frames or schemata—to the table of interaction, which, for a moment, help them make sense of "what's going on here." Collectively, if enough participants share similarities in the "rims" of their frames—the frame's superficial orienting principles—the action will appear to be more or less coordinated, at least initially, and thereby just the kind of phenomena that social scientists have traditionally been interested in.[6] However, there are cases where, as the performance progresses, the meaning making from the individual's perspective, *takes its own course*. We know well from social psychological research that this can take the form on conformity, in which the experience of group pressure overrides individual tendencies. But we also know that, collectively the result a performance may be *going in new and creative directions*, perhaps a more frequent experience in the postmodern world than in traditional societies. Recognition of this has given rise to a view of cultural production as complex and recursive. This recognition also has repercussions for social science research because it suggests that the salience of preconceived ideations may not be very helpful in understanding some forms of social behavior. Different data may be necessary, and different kinds of research questions may be posed, questions that move away from the whys of explanation and from aggregations of individual states that capture the sharedness of frame rims, and towards deep descriptions of diversity, conflict, recursiveness, and cultural innovation.

In a complex social world, I would suggest, both approaches remain relevant. Determining which one is appropriate for what situation is an empirical question that should be answered by the nature of the performances under consideration. Moreover, whether we are looking at performances that tend to cluster towards the coordinated pole, that is, ones with a more ritualistic quality, or we are looking at creative and innovative bricolage, in both cases there will always be *a* moment when the ideations of the participants are relevant data, that is, the moment of engagement and initial unfolding of the performance.

There is no way of knowing for certain how a performance or engagement will develop. The researcher might look similar situations to make an informed judgment, but probably the best predictor is the constellation of relevant schemata that each participant brings to the table. This, of course, is a fundamental social science method and follows the logic of a long tradition of survey methods in political research, and—in a more restricted sense—in social movement research as well (Klandermans 1997; Klandermans and Smith 2004). Gamson, Fireman, and Rytina's seminal research on framing (1982) used both approaches. Anticipating emergent group discussions about a perceived injustice, they videotaped the interaction to look for processes of reframing a legitimate focus group into one where unjust authority was being exercised. They

---

6 Setting aside that the researcher is engaged in meaning making too, in the name of science.

also gathered background information on the participants beforehand to help explain why some groups successfully were able to build an injustice frame that their rebellion was based upon and others did not. Rebellious groups often had participants with past experiences (or schemata) in community activism or social movements. A related strategy is to capture the ideational content, by surveys or content analysis of documents, at one point in time with the recognition that there will be emergence and bricolage as the movement develops, which is then captured by taking measures of cultural production again at a later point (Johnston 2005). Either way, data on ideational content remain important for under-standing and explaining social phenomena.

Conclusion

This chapter has discussed the cultural analysis of protest movements in terms of three broad categories: performances, artifacts, and ideations. It has traced some of the reasoning and literature that lay behind each category, demonstrated insights that each focus offers, and drawn links with the chapters that follow.

Of the three categories, cultural performance is the most fundamental. Performances, bound into broad matrices through overlapping participation of social actors, are the primary loci of culture. Performances are encounters to which social actors bring their ideas about how the world is or should be, offering them up to social discussion, scrutiny, and vetting, and, then, act. In the process they appropriate the collective wisdom (or foolishness) that results from the resulting social practice. In numerous performances such as these, culture is created and affirmed, changed and fortified, nudged along and tied to past practices. For researchers interested in understanding social movements and protest campaigns, change-oriented performances and/or conservative-oriented ones (for counter-movements and state agencies) comprise the subject matter of the discipline. Detailed descriptions of organizational processes, actors strategizing to make their claims, confrontations with the opposition, and the actual protest performances in public places, are the best way to untangle cultural processes at work in protest mobilization. Most of the time, these performances are accomplished with words, in stories, narratives, debates, presentations, and proposals, embedded in larger discourses, which privileges the linguistic focus in cultural analysis. Of the chapters in this volume, three collected the next section and three in the section that follows specifically analyze narrative performances, either by individual or collective actors.

However, for a full social science of social movements and protest campaigns, the other two categories of cultural artifacts and ideations are fundamental too. In fact, they are *sine qua non* for the kinds of explanations that, given the strategic-structural focus of the field, many researchers seek. There are numerous cases where performances are artifactualized to become the focus of subsequent social action. We discussed how narratives often span the categories of performances and artifacts when they are recorded and preserved. In the past, performance narratives were commonly captured as they were written down and reproduced in newspapers, say, a major speech by a prime minister or by a candidate for office. Also, through the minutes of meetings or printing of ideological tracts—perhaps the result of intense discussion and debate—the immediate moment of verbal performance was preserved (never perfectly—always changed in the act of recording) to become the foci of subsequent culture making as they were reread and interpreted. Today, audio/video recording is a technology that presents opportunities for widely dispersed performance artifactualization. YouTube videos are seen by millions and discussed by media commentators, citizens, and activists, making them available for new categories of culture making.[7] Regardless of the form which artifactualized performances take, their original production occurred in contexts different from when their subsequent reading and/or playback become the focus of new performances, giving rise to different interpretations. An artifactualized performance has a cultural life different from the original, and invokes the active cultural practice of subsequent participants.

There is a long and established history in the social sciences of taking performances-as-artifacts as primary data. There is a sense in which this applies to some archival data when collectively produced documents are analyzed to reconstruct mobilization processes. It also applies when researchers rely on newspaper reports of meetings and protests to reconstruct organizational processes. Certainly it is true with qualitatively focused research. In the present volume, several chapters follow these research strategies: narratives preserved in newspaper accounts and archives (Fine's Chapter 4 and Meyer's Chapter 3); verbal performances recorded in documentary videos (Polletta's Chapter 2), transcribed deliberations of strategy meetings (Ignatow's Chapter 7) and public meetings (Klimova's Chapter 5). Then, there is the category of data in which recorded performances have the researcher as part of the audience or, if assuming the role of interviewer, as an active participant in the narrative production (Miethe's Chapter 6). In all cases, the context of the narrative production as well as the context of their interpretation are issues that the researcher must confront. There is a long tradition of social science methodology that offers strategies to deal with issues of context and interpretation, in effect, recognizing

---

7 As I write during the 2008 election year in the US, this has occurred many times, with two noteworthy instances. First, it occurred with Barak Obama's candidacy when the YouTube video of his church's pastor, Jeremiah Wright, was posted on the internet and became fodder for many media commentaries. Second, John McCain's words that "the economy was in fundamentally good shape", recorded by ubiquitous news and cell-phone cameras were repeatedly played back on television and the internet as banks and stock markets crashed. These examples will fade from popular memory long before this book goes out of print, and the reader, no doubt, will be able to think of more current examples.

what a culturalist perspective on methodology proposes as axiomatic, namely, that doing social science too is cultural performance.

Finally, regarding ideations, taking them as primary data also has a long and established history in the social sciences. This is the methodology of a huge quantity of survey research that relies on the logic that ideations precede actions, and that gauging attitudes, beliefs, and predispositions is a good way to explain and predict behavior. Della Porta's chapter is an excellent example of this logic applied to cultural themes. It is thorough social science using the combination of several methodologies, all based on the premise that a shared ideal—deliberative democracy—animates the creation of new settings and innovative practices in the social forum movement. I am aware that viewing aspects of culture as located in one's mind and that asking survey questions to get at them (or focus groups to discuss them) contradict the commonly accepted view that the cultural fabric, in its entirety, is a collectively enacted enterprise and that individual thoughts and orientations are not culture. Moreover, cultural theorists typically reject survey methodology because they see its design, execution, and analysis as proceeding without recognition of the cultural production surveyors engage in (while the same, perhaps, cannot be said about some focus-group methodologies). Both these criticisms are too parochial, in my judgment. On the one hand, they preclude a robust definition of social science, one that recognizes it as a cultural enterprise itself, complete in its diversity, multifaceted praxis, and inherent oppositional quality. On the other, criticisms along these lines typically fail to recognize their own cultural performance, the pot calling the kettle black, so to speak.

It is paradoxical that explanatory social science, and by implication, the structuralist-instrumentalist focus of the social movements field, are often criticized for being unreflexive about their cultural embeddedness. While this may be true at one level, namely, there is not an ongoing reflexivity about one's own performance, it is clear that in other ways it is not the case at all. First, methodological concerns are part of the institutional culture of social science, which impart a great deal of reflexive awareness about how the performance of data gathering is accomplished. Second, every scholar knows that there is a culture that engulfs the production and consumption of academic research generally, and publication and citation within their discipline specifically. These considerations guide many decisions, from definitions of research questions to what journal to publish in. Third, every scholar is aware of the inherently oppositional quality of the cultural matrix they move in: every research project has it critics, every finding its naysayers. It should not come as a surprise, then, that all which was said earlier about culture's ubiquity and inherently oppositional quality applies to the practice of social research as a cultural endeavor. While this realization may impart a degree of equanimity to the disengaged observer, when one is in the middle of the fray, the disputes are very real. The winding and snarling debates in the field of protest studies, as in social science in general, over theory, methods, measurement, and findings matter to the participants (performers) because they are meaningful to them. This is partly true because identities and reputations are based on them. But also these elements are so contentious because they comprise the cultural text of our world we live in, the glue of our networks, the vocabulary of our narratives, and there is no way to extricate ourselves—nor would we want to. The bottom line is that, embedded as we are in this matrix of social science, there is little to do but get to work and let the fray begin.

PART II
Narratives and Stories in Social Movements

Chapter 2
Storytelling in Social Movements

Francesca Polletta

Activists, like prophets, politicians, and advertising executives, have long recognized the power of a good story to move people to action. The tale of a chosen people's wanderings that end in the promised land becomes a clarion call to revolution. A political official is reimagined as an emperor without clothes and dissent that was only whispered becomes voluble. An ordinary man recounts the moment at which he cast off years of fear and shame to acknowledge publicly his homosexuality and members of his audience resolve that they too will come out.

But what is it about stories that render them more politically effective than other discursive forms? Just as important, are there political risks to telling stories—especially for groups challenging the status quo? If you are a feminist charging sex discrimination in hiring, are you better off documenting statistical disparities in the promotion rates for men and women or having a few women testify to their stifled aspirations? If you are an adult survivor of child abuse, does telling your story of pain and humiliation motivate others with the same experience to step forward? Or does it alienate people who are unwilling to see themselves as victims?

In this chapter, I draw on cases ranging from nineteenth century abolitionism to twentieth century movements around AIDS, abortion, child molestation, desegregation, and domestic abuse to support two non-intuitive arguments. One is that stories' power comes not from the clarity of their moral message but from their allusiveness, indeed, their ambiguity. The other is that activists' ability to tell effective stories is shaped as much by the norms of stories' use and evaluation as by the norms of their content. In this sense, culture may curb challenge less through the canonical limits on what kinds of stories can be imagined than through the social conventions regarding when and how stories should be told.

My aim in this chapter is not only to assess the mixed political benefits of telling stories but to make a case for studying storytelling as a form of movement culture. I argue that analyzing the stories told in and about movements can help us to gain purchase on a question that has been difficult to answer. How are activists constrained in their ability to use culture effectively? Presumably, activists hew to dominant cultural norms where it serves them and challenge those norms where it does not. Yet, that calculus is never transparent. Activists, like the rest of us, are risk-averse. And they struggle to master the norms of cultural expression at the same time as they decide whether to defy them. Paying attention to storytelling, and especially to how activists strategize in their use of stories in different institutional arenas, can shed light on the cultural constraints that activists face and why they only sometimes succeed in overcoming them.

Let me begin, then, by defining narrative and making several claims for its virtues as a window onto broader cultural processes.

Why Stories?

Although scholars have drawn on an array of concepts to capture the role of culture in movements, among them, ideology, discourse, schema, identity, rhetoric, and belief, the concept of collective action "framing" has held pride of place (for a good overview, see Snow 2004). Frames are sets of beliefs that "assign meaning to and interpret relevant events and conditions in ways that are intended to mobilize potential adherent and constituents, to garner bystander support, and to demobilize antagonists" (Snow and Benford 1992: 198; Benford and Snow 2000: 614). What makes a frame successful in doing those things? Scholars have drawn attention to features of the frame itself and to features of the group that is targeted. With respect to the first, frames that are clear, coherent, and consistent are more likely to persuade people to join and support the cause. The diagnostic, prognostic, and motivational components of the frame should be richly developed and interconnected (Snow and Benford 1992: 199). There should be a clear "we"—those to whom the injustice is done—and an obvious "they" who are responsible for the injustice (Gamson 1992; Stoecker 1995). Effective frames are "empirically credible," that is, they are consonant with what their audiences know to be true (Benford and Snow 2000). Those who articulate the frame should be credible too (Benford and Snow 2000).

Effective frames are "salient" to their audiences. That is, they call on beliefs that are already strongly held. Of course, people's beliefs are multiple and diverse (Gamson 1988). Still it is possible to identify a hierarchy of popular salience (Gamson 1988; Snow and Benford 1992: 205). For example, many people believe that animals should be taken care of but believe more strongly that medical researchers should be given as much freedom as possible if their research might generate cures for diseases. In addition to being credible and salient, frames should be "experientially commensurable" (Snow and Benford 1992: 208; Benford and Snow 2000). They should resonate with people's everyday experiences. Finally, frames should be characterized by "narrative fidelity" or "cultural resonance." They should accord with familiar "stories, myths, and folktales" (Snow and Benford 1992: 210; Gamson 1988).

Framing theories talk about narrative in two ways. Effective frames accord with dominant cultural narratives (Snow and Benford 1992; Gamson 1988). And frames often make use of stories as a powerful rhetorical device (Benford 1993; Gamson 1992). Both claims are plausible. However, I argue that fuller attention to storytelling, drawing on the insights of a multidisciplinary body of scholarship on storytelling, can respond to several problems in framing theory, specifically with respect to its account of how and when frames are successful.

One problem centers on framing theorists' contention that effective frames are clear, coherent, and consistent. These claims have been more asserted than empirically tested. We simply do not know whether clear frames are more effective than ambiguous ones; whether frames with consistently related diagnostic, prognostic, and motivational components are more mobilizing than those without; whether effective frames do delineate adversaries sharply. Given the fact that, as framing theorists themselves have pointed out, most ordinary people's beliefs are vague, shifting, diverse, and internally contradictory (see also, Merelman 1998; Billig et al. 1988), why should we expect that people will put a premium on clarity and consistency in the messages they attend to and believe? We need a better understanding of how persuasion works than framing theory has yet provided. We need to grasp how combinations of words (and images) work to garner attention, establish authority, provoke new ways of thinking, and spur action.

The second problem in framing theory's calculus of frame effectiveness is a limited understanding of how frames are shaped by their audiences. Certainly, framing theorists have always acknowledged that there are multiple audiences for movements' framing efforts. Although early work concentrated on potential recruits, researchers since then have studied activists' framing to reporters, in court, and on television talk shows. They have drawn attention especially to the conflicts created by the generally moderate messages that are required by the public and the more radical ones that resonate with movement participants (Ferree 2003; Whittier 2001). However, to talk about the different audiences to which activists must appeal risks suggesting that frame success is just a matter of resonating with the personal beliefs of the people who have power within a given institutional arena. It misses the specifically institutional demands of claimsmaking. These demands often center less on the substance of groups' claims and justifications than on their form. For example, in court, activists may be discouraged from giving the kinds of personal accounts that are familiar in everyday life but considered inappropriate in the law (Conley and O'Barr 1990). On a television talk show, they may be discouraged from providing statistical evidence rather than purely personal accounts. In short, to understand why particular frames succeed or fail, we need to know more about how institutional and popular norms of cultural expression shape what activists can say.

The third problem in theorizing about the conditions for frames' effectiveness is an assumption that culture, understood as beliefs, values, myths, and worldviews, is separate from experience. This assumption is evident in the idea that frames' "empirical credibility" and their "experiential commensurability" (Benford and Snow 2000) can be appraised separately from their resonance with cultural myths. Surely, however, people's personal experiences are shaped by their cultural beliefs, values, and perceptions. In this sense, the challenge for activists is not only to frame persuasive claims but also to frame intelligible ones. Activists must challenge not only people's formal beliefs but also their common sense. To give an example that I will take up again later, a judge may believe firmly in women's equality with men. And yet he may hand down rulings that systematically disadvantage women, not because his professed egalitarianism is a lie but because he understands gender equality in the context of a whole cluster of assumptions about men and women and difference and biology and preferences. Activists often find themselves struggling to craft a frame capable of debunking symbolic associations that are difficult to even name. As analysts, we need tools to get at this background common sense with which activists must contend.

Moreover, activists themselves are vulnerable to the cultural constructions that pass as common sense. That statement may raise a red flag by suggesting that activists are falsely conscious, somehow blind to their own best interests. Of course, individual activists, like all of us, have blind spots and superstitions. The challenge, however, is to show how those blind spots and superstitions are widespread and powerful enough among activists to systematically foreclose strategic options. What we need then, is a fuller understanding of the mechanisms that make certain claims risky.

In sum, theories of collective action framing have been limited by their failure to probe the rhetorical vehicles of framing, the institutional norms that delimit appropriate ways of talking, and the underpinning common sense in terms of which frames are understood. Why should an analysis of narrative help us to do all these things? Define a narrative, uncontroversially, as an account of a sequence of events in the order in which they occurred so as to make a point (Labov and Waletsky 1967). Formally, narratives are composed of (a) an orientation, which sets the scene, (b) a series of complicating actions (implicit "and then ..." clauses) ending with one that serves as dénouement, and (c) an evaluation, which can appear at any point in the story, establishing the importance of the events related (Labov and Waletsky 1967).

Thanks to a substantial literature on narrative in diverse fields, we know a great deal about how narrative achieves its rhetorical effects. What makes a story believable, persuasive, resonant? First, the fact that narratives integrate description, explanation, and evaluation. Think about how we hear or read a story. We tack back and forth from the events that are described to the larger point that they add up to. We assume that later events in the story will make sense of earlier ones and that details that are irrelevant to the story's point will be omitted. Depending on how dramatic the story is, we experience the events' resolution as a veritable release of psychic energy; we talk about a story's "climax." We also expect that the resolution of the story will be moral. It will project a desirable or undesirable future. Of course, some stories moralize more explicitly than others. But all have what linguists William Labov and Joshua Waletsky (1967) call an *evaluative* component specifying why the story is important to tell. Storytellers rarely say explicitly to their audiences, "and the moral of the story is …." Rather, the story's larger meaning seems to be given by the events themselves. The final events in the story resolve the problems raised by earlier events in a way that tenders a more general normative point.

Framing theorists argue that effective frames tightly link diagnostic, prognostic, and motivational elements. Stories do exactly that. However, they do so the basis of a narrative logic rather than a formal one. Developments in a story make sense because we have heard (something like) them before. Stories depend on plots, on a limited number of structures that configure events and their meaning. Certainly, as Patricia Ewick and Susan Silbey observe, "Narratives are fluid, continuous, dynamic, and always constructed interactively—with an audience and within a context—out of the stuff of other narratives" (2003: 1343). Still, most theorists agree that there is a cultural stock of plots. Stories that draw on plots outside that sock or that are incompatible with "the stuff of other narratives" risk being seen as bad stories or as incomprehensible ones.

However, if stories must hew to familiar plotlines, a story that was so familiar as to be entirely predictable would be no story at all. It would be the moral without the story. Social psychologists have shown that stories in which the normative message is too pronounced are unlikely to persuade their readers (Slater and Rouner 2002). As literary theorist Wolfgang Iser writes, "It is only through inevitable omissions that a story will gain its dynamism" (1972, 285). Stories require our interpretive participation. They require that we work to resolve ambiguities as events unfold, to anticipate the normative conclusion to which the story is driving. Indeed, the closure stories promise may never be fully realized. The story's meaning remains elusive. Stories are thus distinctive in their openness to interpretation. This is not to say that other forms of discourse are not interpretable. To the contrary, analyses as much as narratives can be plumbed for multiple meanings. So can arguments, descriptions, and formal mathematical proofs. But we *expect* to have to interpret stories. By contrast, we tend to see ambiguity in logical arguments as imprecision or error. We are less likely to do the work necessary to make sense of an allusive passage or what appear to be contradictory developments.

For my purposes, these features of narrative suggest, first, that stories may be mobilizing on account not of their clarity but their engaging ambiguity. In this vein, J. Hillis Miller (1990) maintains that stories' meaning hinges on a key gap at the story's center, an ellipsis in which the reader or listener is forced to fill in meaning. That process can prove mobilizing. In the stories told by black student sit-inners in 1960 and budding feminists in 1970, an ellipsis (often literally three dots; "…") captured the point in their stories at which individuals became a collective and acquiescence turned to action, and did so in a way that demanded more stories, and more actions to recount (Polletta 2006). Another way in which stories may persuade more through their ambiguity than their consistency lies in their use of point of view. Point of view is the perspective from which the story is told. That perspective may shift among characters during the course of the story; it may transcend the characters (the omniscient narrator); it may be obvious or opaque. Indeed, authority may be created by selectively revealing and concealing point of view in stories; that is, by rendering "we" and "they" obscure rather than clear (Polletta 2006).

A second implication of stories' form is that, to put in the language of framing, stories' empirical credibility and experiential commensurability may both be a *product* of their narrative fidelity. Stories may seem resonant because they are familiar but they may also seem empirically *true* because they are familiar; because they conform to stories that we have heard before (White 1980). In a related vein, social psychologists have shown that people are likely to report information that they know to be invented as true if they hear it in a story. Apparently, their absorption in the events recounted in the story diminishes the likelihood that they will hear facts critically (Green and Brock 2000). So, the information contained within a story may be credible because it is presented in story form and because it is familiar from previous stories.

Stories conform to familiar plots. But that statement is problematic: it suggests that there is a single canon, one set of tellable stories that together impart a coherent moral canon. That is clearly not the case. For every story that enjoins us to turn the other cheek when insulted, another instructs us to let no assault on our dignity go unavenged. Stories attesting to the power of the unencumbered individual are countered by stories about the power of loyalty to the group. Instead, then, consider this possibility. Stories' power comes less from the explicit moral instruction they provide than from the normative possibilities that are excluded from the pattern of their interrelationship. The argument, which goes back to Claude Levi-Strauss's (1963) structuralist analysis of myth, is that culturally resonant stories chart in similar fashion the relations between the privileged and denigrated poles of familiar cultural oppositions For example, we grasp what reason is by telling stories that thematize not only reason's difference from passion, but its similarity to men's difference from women, and culture's difference from nature, and so on. What poststructuralist theorists add is the insight that it takes active *work* to ensure that alternative relations—and alternative meanings— are ruled out (Derrida 1978; Scott 1994). To continue with the example, our understanding of reason requires that people make emotional performances of reason, that they demonstrate in their speech, tone, and gesture the seeming lack of affect that passes for reason—while at the same time maintaining that emotion and reason are opposed. The stability of legal, political, and other institutions, to extend the argument, depends on their promotion of stories that thematize familiar opposition. Such stories are powerful not because they are told over and over again in identical form but rather because they mesh with other familiar stories that navigate similarly between the poles of well-known oppositions (see Polletta 2006, ch. 1 for a fuller development of this argument).

In addition to the fact that it is easy to identify narratives in discourse, and that we can draw on a body of scholarship on how narratives work rhetorically to produce a fuller, and in some ways, counter-intuitive understanding of how persuasion works, narrative has a third virtue. It is a folk concept. Unlike frames, ideologies, and discourses, all of whose referent is defined by analysts rather than the people who produce or act on them, most people know when they are telling a story. They know how to construct a story, and when and why they should tell stories, and how to respond to a story. Some conventions of storytelling are formalized as are, for example, those in courtroom testimony. Other conventions are not formalized and can be gleaned rather from stories' distribution across settings and speakers and topics of discussion. People often reflect openly on what they see storytelling as good for and where they see its limitations. From there, we can begin to determine the work that popular theories and conventions of storytelling do in sustaining institutions and in shaping strategies for transforming them.

To study narrative sociologically, then, is to study not only stories but also stories' performance. It is to study not only the conventions of narrative's form, but also the conventions of its use, interpretation, and evaluation. It is to study not only meaning but also the social organization of the capacity to mean effectively.

Strategy and Storytelling

One can use the concept of narrative that I have outlined above to shed light on a variety of movement processes. For example, the fact that we can isolate narratives in discourse and can isolate different versions of the same narrative makes it possible to trace the careers of particular stories, exposing the political processes by which they come to be tellable or authoritative but also the dynamics by which newly legitimated stories produce new modes of action and new terrains of contention (Polletta 2006, ch. 1; Davis 2005). The stories told by people in fledgling movements provide insight into individuals' decision to participate rather than free ride on the efforts of others (Polletta 2006, ch. 2). The stories told about movements provide a measure of movements' impacts (Polletta 2006, ch. 6).

In this essay, however, I want to focus on activists' strategic use of stories to persuade. Their persuasive efforts go beyond recruitment, of course. Activists seek to persuade funders to support their efforts; reporters to cover their demands; judges to hand down favorable decisions; Congressional subcommittees to press for legislation; ordinary citizens to think differently about their everyday practices. It is easy to see the appeal of stories in all these tasks. Personal stories, especially, make the abstract real and the political personal. Told in court, to the press, in the halls of Congress, and at the head of marches, they turn shadowy institutional forces into heroes and villains, and turn complex goals into moral imperatives. Sometimes, they expose the bias in governmental policies by showing that supposedly universal categories and neutral standards embed the experiences of only some people. Personal stories compel their audiences to sympathize and, occasionally, to act.

On the other hand, progressive activists, and especially feminists, have been keenly aware of the dangers of telling personal stories. They worry that stories of injustice and exploitation, of hurt and humiliation, require that their tellers trade agency for passivity. Surely representing oneself as a victim, and as powerless, pitiable, and generic, cannot but diminish one's own capacity for action (Bumiller 1988; Kaminer 1993; Minow 1993). Surely casting women or gays or lesbians as victims rather than as proud challengers worthy of respect and power will repel rather than attract potential recruits (Wolf 1993; Roiphe 1993; D'Emilio 1992; Epstein 1996). And even if successful in gaining the sympathy of the powerful, surely such stories will translate into protection at the expense of power (Wolf 1993; Kaminer 1993).

These concerns are certainly legitimate. But they are by no means intrinsic to the form. It has been possible, at other times, to conceptualize victims differently. And this is in part because people have conceptualized *storytelling* differently. They have operated on a different theory of narrative and knowing, a different set of expectations about how stories affect their audience's understanding and emotions. Consider the stories told by antebellum abolitionists who were former slaves. In these stories we might well expect to see victims as we commonly think of them: passive rather than active, to be helped rather than emulated. However, that was not the case. As Kimberly Smith (1998) has shown, slave narratives were modeled on Christian conversion narratives. These were familiar to many Americans and they were typically told by people petitioning for membership in congregations. In eliciting sympathy on the part of congregation members, the petitioner successfully demonstrated his understanding of God's glory and his suitability for membership in the church. But the sympathy listeners experienced was thought to lead to their own enlightenment. On that model, slave narratives sought not to elicit their audience's pity. Rather, they sought to produce a sympathetic identification, to make the audience feel about slavery as the slave did. This helps to explain a peculiar feature of the slave narratives: they did not spend much time making a case against the institution of slavery. The assumption was that the story itself would educate the moral intuitions of readers in a way that would compel right action. On the template of the Christian conversion narrative, then, slave narrators were victims but also moral guides. Victims were seen differently than they are now because stories were heard differently.

Since then, activists have continued to tell stories of their suffering in ways that have highlighted their fortitude and insight. In the consciousness-raising groups of the women's movement, women told personal stories to prove that they knew better than any expert the sources of and solutions to their problems (Echols 1989). "Coming out" stories have inspired others to proudly declare themselves gay (Plummer 1995). Stories of abuse "survivors" have emphasized the victim's recovery (Dunn 2005; Loseke 2000). So, conceptions of the victim as moral guide, expert, and survivor have existed alongside side that of the victim as a passive object of pity. Yet, activists have often found it difficult to gain acceptance for these conceptions outside the movement. They have tried and failed to get victims seen as people struggling against constraints rather than as people who are entirely powerless. They have tried and failed to get victims seen as heterogeneous, united only by their common experience of hurt rather than as homogenous.

The fault lies less with movements' bad strategy than with the institutional settings in which they operate. In her study of activism by adult survivors of child abuse, Nancy Whittier (2001) found that when survivors gathered in movement conferences and at marches, speakers told stories of personal fortitude and of fear ceding to pride. With titles like "Sing Loud, Sing Proud," and "Courageous—Always Courageous," movement magazine articles and workshops encouraged participants to emphasize their recovery rather than the details of their abuse. When survivors appeared in court to seek compensation as crime victims, however, the stories they told were different. Survivors described the fear, grief, shame, and hurt produced by their abuse but made no mention of their subsequent and anger and pride. These kinds of emotional performances were required in order to prove that the survivor was a victim deserving of compensation. Articles in movement magazines warned that going to court was a demeaning experience and that survivors should find outlets to tell other parts of their stories—but that betraying their anger in court would hurt their case.

On television talk shows, another place in which child abuse activists appeared frequently in the 1980s, survivors told stories of abuse and enduring trauma. Guests often cried while clutching stuffed animals or speaking in childlike voices. They were usually joined by therapists who interpreted their stories to the audience, further reinforcing an image of them as childlike. Whittier points out that that image may well have repelled others suffering from abuse, who instead might have been mobilized by stories of focused anger and personal overcoming.

Certainly, one can challenge the conventions of narrative performance. Survivors could have told stories of anger on talk shows and could have recounted moving from shame to pride in courtroom hearings. But doing so would have been risky. Culture shapes strategy in the sense that abiding by the rules of cultural expression yields more calculable consequences than challenging them. This is clear in the case of women who challenged workplace discrimination in court in the 1970s and 1980s. Judges sometimes explicitly encouraged plaintiffs to put women on the stand who could testify to their experience of aspiring to a higher paying but traditionally masculine job and not getting it. This was in spite of the fact that providing a few such stories could not, on its own, demonstrate *patterns* of disparate treatment. Presumably, some women were interested in the higher paying jobs and some were not, just as some men were and some were not. What such witnesses could not do was prove that they were representative of the larger pool of eligible workers. Only statistical evidence of gender disparities in hiring and promotion could do that. Plaintiffs could have refused to frame their claims in terms of individuals' experience of discrimination. But when they did, they were much more likely to lose their cases (Schultz 1990).

Why? Because judges wanted something like a liberal storyline to counter the congery of stories that stood behind the conservative argument. Employers' argument that women did not want the higher-paying jobs, which were intrinsically "heavy" and "dirty," was convincing because it squared with countless familiar stories about little girls liking to be clean and little boys to be dirty and women being different from men. That women preferred not to do masculine jobs was a matter of common sense, as conservative courts often put it. Against that common sense, plaintiffs only argued that women's preferences were not fundamentally different from men. But that claim suppressed gender differences rather than accounted for them. This was why it was so important for plaintiffs to produce witnesses who could testify that they had wanted non-traditional jobs. Although such witnesses could not prove that their experiences were representative of the larger pool of workers, they could tell something like a liberal story of women who, but for their sex, were exactly like men and therefore entitled to the same jobs.

So what was the harm in plaintiffs' producing those victims? By corroborating the storyline expected of them by liberal judges, Schultz shows, plaintiffs ended up challenging only *some* of employers' discriminatory practices, leaving others intact. By hewing to the liberal storyline, in which work preferences were formed through socialization processes outside the labor market, they were ill-positioned to show that workers' preferences themselves were influenced by employers' practices. Why would women want a job that was advertised and described through word of mouth as a man's job? This question was not asked.

The problem for women charging sex discrimination was not only that they were forced to style themselves generic victims. The deeper problem was that in the absence of a compelling story of how women came to forge their job preferences, women effectively ceded terrain to conservatives, who did have such an account. The conservative story was detailed, variegated, and meshed with countless stories told in other settings about gender differences and socialization processes. The liberal account, which was made up of dry abstractions and denials of a causal chain rather than the assertion of one, was no match for the conservative story, and for the countless other stories against which—in terms of which—it was heard. I want to underscore the last point. Narratives are hegemonic not because there is a single story that is told over and over again but rather because stories mesh with other familiar stories that navigate similarly between the culturally privileged and denigrated poles of well-known oppositions.

Could plaintiffs have told an effective story? Could women working in lower wage jobs have described how the higher paid jobs they heard about were represented as inappropriate for them, with their descriptions bolstered by social scientists explaining how preferences are forged in the labor market rather than prior to it? Would telling this admittedly more complex but also truer story have worked? We do not know. But we can see how women's more complex stories fared in a different area of the law. Women who are abused by their partners and who strike back against them, wounding or killing them, should be able to plead innocent by reason of self-defense. They acted to save their own lives. And yet in the early 1990s, only a quarter of the battered women who pleaded self-defense in homicide cases were acquitted (Trafford 1991). More significant, convictions of battered women who pled self-defense were overturned on appeal at a substantially higher rate than were convictions in other homicide cases (40 percent compared to 8.5 percent [Maguigan 1991]). Clearly, there were problems in how such cases were being tried.

One problem lay in popular expectations about what true stories sound like. As Kim Scheppele (1992) points out, women who have been the victims of domestic abuse, as well as those who have been the victims of rape, incest, and other forms of sexualized violence, often delay in recounting their experiences. When they do tell their stories, their narratives often have a fragmented character. Their accounts change over time as they piece together what happened and begin to retreat from their initial impulse to normalize their experience. But judges and juries operate on the assumption that true stories are told immediately and stay the same over time. The stories that women tell later are often heard suspiciously. A prevailing narrative epistemology has thus operated to discredit women's accounts of their abuse.

Battered women's activists' success in making expert testimony admissible in court should have helped in this regard. Experts could account for the discrepancy between the victim's earlier and later stories by citing the effects of post-traumatic stress disorder. In addition to strengthening the battered woman's credibility, activists believed, experts would describe both the psychological mechanisms that prevented women from leaving abusive relationships and the economic and cultural ones: the lack of support services; the norms that expected women to keep families together at all costs, and so on. Experts would also help to expose the real possibility faced by the abused woman that she would be hunted down and attacked by her abuser if she left. Experts would show that the defendant's apprehension of imminent danger and great bodily harm was reasonable.

Yet, the introduction of expert testimony has not been enough to secure abused women equality in their legal defense. This was the other problem facing battered women defendants: often, their own defense attorneys did not think them capable of meeting the standards of reasonableness necessary for a self-defense claim (Schneider 2000). The problem was not, as some scholars maintained, that the legal standards for pleading self-defense—imminent danger, proportionality, and the duty to retreat—were inherently biased against battered women. Most jurisdictions did not impose a duty to retreat before using force, and those that did usually exempted a person attacked in her home. No jurisdiction prohibited the use of a weapon against an unarmed attacker. Standards for self-defense were just as capable of handling violence in which parties were intimates and where the imminence of danger extended over a substantial period. The problem was not the legal standards but the fact that judges, juries, and lawyers were unwilling to see battered women's use of deadly force as reasonable under those standards (Schneider 2000; Maguigan 1991). Familiar stories of the soldier on the battlefield, the man defending his home against an unknown intruder, and the barroom brawler continued to shape legal decision makers' thinking about what constituted legitimate self-defense. Against the backdrop of those stories, it was difficult for legal professionals to imagine that women were acting reasonably when they assaulted their partners.

The challenge was to see women as victims *and* as rational agents. As Martha Mahoney writes, in our society the two are seen as unalterably opposed: "[A]gency does not mean acting for oneself under conditions of oppression; it means *being without oppression*, either having ended oppression or never having experienced it at all" (Mahoney 1994: 64; see also Dunn 2005; Loseke 2000). When the battered woman has killed her abuser, emphasizing her victimization undermines her claim of rational agency. That, in turn, has made it tougher to meet the standard of reasonableness necessary to claim self-defense. In this respect, advocates' victory in gaining the admissibility of expert testimony has been mixed in its effects. Lawyers for battered women have encouraged experts to testify to the defendant's so-called learned helplessness rather than the fact that she acted to save her own life. Battered women's syndrome has become a popular term and is often used simply to indicate the existence of a battering relationship. But its connotation of an impaired mental state has made it difficult for lawyers, judges, and juries to comprehend the reasonableness of the woman's act. Instead, women have been encouraged to register pleas of insanity or manslaughter; both clearly less serious than homicide but still quite different from a plea innocence by reason of self-defense.

The woman who has killed her abuser faces two equally unacceptable options. She can assert her agency, telling a story of her actions in which she appears composed and in control of herself. But then she may not be seen as victimized at all. Or, she can emphasize her victimization. But then her actions risk being seen as unreasonable. They are to be excused through an act of judicial solicitude rather than justified by her experience of abuse. If she departs from the stock image of the victim, moreover, if she is too angry, aggressive, or insufficiently remorseful, she may not be seen as a victim, no matter what she says.

So, does telling stories work for battered women? Lawyers, judges, and scholars hear the stories that battered women tell. But they hear them through familiar plotlines with stock characters. On one side are stories of the soldier on the battlefield, the man defending his home against an unknown intruder, and the barroom brawler, stories that have defined what counted as legitimate self-defense. And on the other side are stories of mad women who are victims and bad women who are not.

Activists use stories strategically. But they are up against at least two obstacles. One is that their stories are heard against more familiar stories. To achieve equality, women need to reject both poles of the dichotomies I have described. Women are like men in some respects and unlike them in others. Women in some situations are victimized *and* agentic. They are autonomous *and* dependent, to note another opposition that has limited women's legal remedies (Fineman 1995). But what makes it so hard to challenge such dichotomies is that they are reproduced in many *different* narratives, appearing in movies and magazine articles, political speeches and news stories, in self-help books and television commercials. The credibility of such narratives comes from the fact that they are both ubiquitous and diverse: coming in innumerable versions, they seem to capture a reality that is complex. A story that is palpably at odds with those stories is easily discounted as unbelievable, idiosyncratic, or simply unintelligible.

The other obstacle lies in prevailing beliefs about what makes some stories and storytellers credible. Such beliefs are historical, as I noted. They are also at once institutional and popular. A complainant in small claims court who tells an otherwise credible story of having been bilked by his employer loses his case because his story fails to specify the unambiguous chain of causality that is expected of testimony in court. A woman who tells the story of her rape loses her case because, like many victims of trauma, she has filled in missing parts of the story as she has retold it, and now she violates the jury's expectation that true stories remain identical in their retelling. The small claims complainant is hurt by beliefs about narrative that are peculiar to the institution of American small claims court. The rape victim is hurt by popular beliefs about narrative that operate within legal settings but extend beyond them.

When encountered by activists, these kinds of cultural constraints are practical. They are not attributable to activists' false consciousness or their inability to perceive alternatives. Rather, they reflect the institutional rules of the game that those wanting to effect change must play. But, without accusing activists of false consciousness, it is hardly surprising that they sometimes fail to anticipate fully the costs of playing by the rules.

Telling Non-Canonical Stories

Is there any solution? Are activists' stories fated to meet with disbelief or incomprehension, capable of producing emotional catharsis but not practical action, effective only where they affirm rather than challenge popular cultural beliefs? No. I want to conclude by showing how activists have put features of narrative's form and the conventions of its evaluation to surprisingly effective use.

I argued earlier that narrative's allusiveness—the fact that it compels its audience to fill in the gaps, and indeed, that its meaning is always provisional—accounts in part for its role in engaging audiences' attention. I want to suggest now that that feature of narrative can do more: it can help audiences to hear non-canonical stories, stories that refuse the antinomies that are responsible for policies' uneven benefits. Let me turn again to legal defense of abused women. As I said, the hurdle has been to get legal decision makers to see battered women who kill or wound their abusers as both victimized and rational. In 1989, as part of a Maryland campaign to gain the admittance of expert testimony, battered women's activists made a film in which four women in prison for their offenses told their stories (Public Justice Center, 1990). The film was shown to legislators, the governor, parole commission officers, activists, and the public. And remarkably, where past efforts had failed to gain traction, this one succeeded in securing public officials' support and then action.

In some ways, the film seems to reproduce the problem. The film is organized around the observations of an expert, Lenore Walker, who describes the successive phases of a battering relationship, from the early days of intimacy, to increasingly more severe abuse, to the woman's desperate act of violence. Excerpts from interviews with the four women are intercut to illustrate Walker's points. Then former assistant attorney general Benjamin Civiletti summarizes the relevant law and makes a case for reform.

The women are not named until the very end of the film and their testimony always follows Walker's descriptions of the stages of a battering relationship, matching them closely enough to justify Walker's references to "the" battered woman and to a generic battering relationship. The women seem not only generic but helpless, so incapacitated as to have been unconscious of their actions. After describing the escalating violence to which they were subjected, three of the four narrators say that they do not even remember taking the action that killed their partner. "I didn't feel my hand pull the trigger. I don't remember shooting him. All I remember was handing him the weapon and him grabbing it and I remember it going off." said one. Another: "I don't recall stabbing him no twenty-two times with no scissors." And a third: "My daughter said that I loaded the gun, and it will be five years this September, and I still don't remember loading that gun." Such actions seem the opposite of reasoned and the women responsible for them the opposite of agentic.

Yet in other important ways, the film undercuts this image. The women come off as victimized and agentic, in pathological relationships but not pathological themselves, unable to recount the details of their murderous actions but compelling in their candor and insight. How do they do this? By way of the stories they tell and the literary tropes they rely on, tropes that are familiar to literary critics but less so to social scientists: shifting point of view, irony, and antithesis. Each trope, notably, highlights the ambiguity of meaning. I am not arguing that the abused women or the activists who put their stories on film were conscious of the sophisticated literary tropes they relied on. Rather, some women knew how to tell evocative stories, the film's director knew how to choose evocative stories, and the film's editor knew how to present and combine evocative stories. Let me rehearse in some detail how they did so.

Although some portions of the women's stories are rendered vividly, one never loses the sense that events are being related by a narrator. Yet, rather than a clear, obvious "I" who is recounting events, the point of view in each woman's story shifts repeatedly: between the narrator now, who is trying to understand at the same time as she relives the experience of her abused self, and the narrator then, who is that woman. We get two points of view and two images: the women as insightful and naïve; rational and victimized.

The narrators display not only distance from the events they describe but also a rueful irony with respect to them. One woman says, "He would hit me with anything. He would bite me all over. Pick up things and throw them at me and hit me with them. But I never went to the hospital for anything. It was too embarrassing. I was so determined that this was going to work if I would just stop and just make him happier." She sounds bemused: that even as she was abjectly victimized, she was convinced of her own power to make the relationship work. The strangeness is the idea that a relationship in which violence is kept at bay by the wife's unrelenting effort can be said to be working. Another woman recounts, "Soon after we started dating I had noticed that he was kind of possessive and he was very jealous. But I didn't really count it as out of the ordinary; it kind of flattered me to be honest. I kind of thought, well, he loves me this much that he cares, he don't want me speaking to this one or he don't want me going there without him. And I kind of thought that was really kind of nice, so I must have been something really special."

Drawing out the word, "special," the woman highlights her own confusion of possessiveness and caring. The irony is that her dehumanizing abuse began, in her mind, as the recognition that she was special.

An ironic stance is even clearer when a third speaker recounts her response to her boyfriend's suggestion that he quit her job: "I was like, girl, my boyfriend told me I don't have to work, he's going to take care of me so I don't have to go to work nowhere." She goes on, "I didn't know he was in the process of putting me in his own little prison." Here, as in the previous account, the woman mocks her misinterpretation of her partner's blandishments. But in doing so, she exposes the societal norms that make such misinterpretation easy. The real ironies, in other words, are that pathological possessiveness in our society is taken as a sign of romantic passion; that the line between violent relationships and ones that are thought to be "working" is so thin; and that women fantasize of rescue from the world of work. We, the audience, may begin to recognize that the narrator was trapped by powerful social norms as much as by a violent man.

The women also defy an image of themselves as passive victims by telling an altogether different story than the experts relate, one that relies on surprising gaps and discordant elements. The story is not about women so brutalized and degraded that the only option they see, "rightly or wrongly"—as the film's narrator puts it— is to kill their abusers. It is not about their progressive loss of will but about their assertion of it. The climax of the story is not the point where the woman strikes back at her abuser but rather earlier, when she decides that she wants to live. In each case, however, that moment is rendered strangely. I want to rehearse in some detail the segment of the film, occurring two thirds of the way through, in which these transitions occur. One woman describes believing that her boyfriend would kill her and not caring. She wouldn't be leaving children, she explains, and she hadn't even come from a loving family, she says in what sounds like a kind of obituary. Then she describes her boyfriend beating her in the kitchen as her boyfriend's friend looked on. "But right in mid-stream, as he was beating me and as I was sliding down my refrigerator, something inside me was like: I wanna live. You know, I have something to live for. Something is out there for me and I'm going to get it. And I'm not gonna die, and I'm not gonna let him kill me in here with his friend watching. I meant that." She decides she wants to live when she is "sliding down my refrigerator"—an odd image. And she vows to herself that she will not die with her boyfriend's friend watching. It is the idea of someone watching her own murder that is repugnant to her.

The absurdity of the situation is gripping; and it is the narrator's recognition of the absurdity of the situation that moves her from passivity to action—we surmise. For in a way that is characteristic of stories, the central transition, the key causal relation, is represented but not explained. That gap—between passivity and self-assertion—is what engages us. "But right in mid-stream, as he was beating me and as I was sliding my refrigerator, something inside me was like: I wanna live." This is the climax of her story. Its importance is suggested by the fact that this is in fact the second time we hear her say it. Her statement, "But right in mid-stream, as he was beating me and as I was sliding down my refrigerator ..." opens the film as a voiceover to images of a police officer knocking on a door; a woman being handcuffed; and a prison door being closed by a female guard. At the beginning of the film, the statement is easily ignored; when it is repeated, it becomes thematic, what the film is about.

When this woman describes not wanting to live any longer, she is the third to express the same feeling. The first woman, who has described her husband playing a sadistic game of Russian Roulette with her, says, "Because I kept thinking, when is the time, when is it going to be? We kept playing these little games with the gun up to my head, and I kept thinking, well one day, it's just finally going to be over. And I really can't wait until it's over." The film then cuts to a second woman who sighs loudly and says tiredly, "Many times I thought I would die. Many times I didn't want to live anymore. Because what was going on, I thought it would never end. I thought it wouldn't. I said, if he don't kill me, I'm sure I'll kill myself, because it was that painful." The third woman, whom I quoted a moment ago, begins, "And on the night that I stabbed my boyfriend ..." in a way that suggests her story follows on from that of the woman before. But her story takes a different turn: as her boyfriend's friend watches her slide down the refrigerator, she determines that she wants to live, and says so in a voice that is assertive and powerful, unlike the women who have preceded her.

The film now cuts back to the second woman who, crying, "I know I want to live. No, I don't want to die. I don't want to have anybody beat on me or threaten my life." She does not explain the change from her last statement about expecting to take her own life. It seems almost as if the preceding woman's story is her own—despite its strange particularity. "I want to live," she says, echoing the woman before. She has also shifted verb tense. She recounted her feelings of wanting to die in the past tense but her knowledge that she wanted to live in the present. According to sociolinguists, shifts from the past tense to the conversational historical present are generally used to introduce a new and critical segment of the story (Wolfson 1979). Here, "I know I want to live" expresses the key shift, the point at which the woman refuses to acquiesce to her abuse. That event, her determination to live, is the climax of the story—not her decision to strike back at her abuser.

At this point, the film cuts back to the first woman, who had recounted wanting the gun her husband put so often to her head to go off. Now, without any preliminaries other than an "ummm," she says, "So he went and got the gun. He loaded the service revolver. And I was on my knees begging him for life. And for a long time, he was taunting me. And I told him, I couldn't do this. Of all the things, I didn't want to die, I really didn't want to die." Again, the shift from wanting to die to wanting to live is not explained, only rendered, strikingly so.

When each of the four women describes picking up a weapon and attacking her abuser, it comes after the story's climax. The women seem genuinely not to remember what happened. But set against their clear and striking memory of the point at which they decided to save their own lives, it seems almost unimportant. The important point, and the one with which the viewer identifies, is the moment that each woman discovers her desire to survive.

The women's stories emphasize their choice to live far more than their decision to kill; indeed, recast their decision to kill as a determination to live. They do not explain that decision—for, in fact, can anyone explain a decision to live rather than die? The women tell a different story than the experts in another way. The experts repeatedly emphasize the limits on battered women's perception of the imminence of the threat they face. The narrator opens the film by describing battered women's syndrome and saying, "and in the darkest part of that trap, she reaches a point here she believes, rightly or wrongly, that to protect herself or to protect her children she must kill her abuser." The legal expert explains the doctrine of "imperfect self-defense" in which a person *believes* that his or her life is threatened. Lenore Walker describes the condition of learned helplessness and describes the expert witness's role as to "explain to the jury why *in her mind* it was reasonable for her to perceive that she was in imminent danger. And imminent danger is not just immediate danger for a battered woman. To understand the danger *that's in her heart and in her mind* all the time" (emphasis in the original). To talk about the danger "in her mind" suggests that the danger is imagined, not real.

The women interviewed in the film sometimes use the same phrases, or otherwise echo experts' view of their limited grasp on reality. One woman says, "it hurts knowing that, *in my heart*, I was protecting me and my children from abuse" (emphasis in the original). Another notes how hard it was to get others to understand why she had not left her abuser and then says, "it's a sickness." Yet, the women also make clear that they really *were* in mortal danger. The woman who said that "in her heart" she was protecting her children had described earlier an episode in which her husband had turned from beating her to choking her daughter. The danger clearly lie in more than her heart. The woman who said "it's a sickness" then repeated her husband's chilling threat; "if you leave me you're going to look behind your back, you better watch out." She continues, "And I believed him because I knew what he could do." Her thinking seems indicative not of a sickness but of common sense. Interestingly, immediately after this excerpt, Lenore Walker describes the phenomenon of learned helplessness. But she does so somewhat confusingly, in contrast to the clarity of her other comments: "When somebody develops learned helplessness, they lose the capacity to believe that what they do will really protect them. That their natural responses will make a response predictably that will be okay. So they only will—if they're in danger, they will only do something that has the most prediction of working." The psychological explanation seems inadequate.

Finally, at the very end of the film, in the last frame, the line between (rational) expert and (irrational) victim is erased. The film's narrator, who earlier had been identified as an education director at a battered women's clinic and had described herself as a battered woman, is shown to be even closer to the profiled women: it is revealed that she served five years of an eight year sentence for having attempted to kill her abuser.

The protagonists in these stories were pathologically dependent on abusive men, they lacked supportive friends and family, and they killed another human being. What made the women sympathetic was neither the sheer pathos of their stories (which would have elicited only audiences' pity) nor the fact that their stories made them seem just like their audience (which likely would have been impossible to do, leaving their acts still unfathomable). Instead, the profiled women used literary tropes to tell a different story than the one they were ostensibly telling, a different story than the one that an audience anticipates when the topic is husbands, wives, abuse, and murder. The women's stories shifted point of view in a way that combined an abject victim and a rational, insightful actor in the same person. They used irony to highlight the social norms that kept them with a violent man. And they used discordant images and ideas to draw the audience's attention to a different point in the story than the one it expected: not the moment when the woman decided to kill but the moment she decided to live.

Of course, I am speculating that the stories had these effects. In support of my interpretation, however, I offer not only the fact that, after viewing the film and meeting with the profiled women, Maryland's governor became a staunch advocate for the women's cause despite the fact that he had never before supported legislation to help battered women, but also how he explained his change of opinion. "This isn't something they made up," he told reporters. "A long history of abuse, terrible abuse ... So I felt that some of them, there was not any question in my mind, that they were in danger for their own life" (Lewin 1991a). The governor referred to the women's victimization but then made clear that the women were acting in self-defense. He eventually commuted the sentences of eight women convicted of killing or attempting to kill their abusers and pressed successfully for legislation allowing the introduction of testimony about a history of abuse and about the phenomenon of battered women syndrome. In subsequent news stories, his criticism of a justice system that made it difficult for abused women to plead self-defense was as prominent as his description of their horrific abuse (Lewin 1991b).

If the film was indeed partly responsible for these effects, this is not to say that the women "spun" their stories or misrepresented them. It is not to say that activists should stop themselves from recounting their experiences honestly and authentically. To the contrary, speaking from the heart probably means speaking in a more literary fashion than challengers have often done when they have concentrated instead on generating a simple, unitary message.

If activists have been able to capitalize on stories' allusiveness, they have also been able to capitalize on the institutional norms of stories' use and evaluation. I have described the dilemmas of telling personal stories to secure equality in court. By contrast, personal storytelling in the media has proven easier. A distinctively American skepticism of professional expertise has given ordinary people and grassroots groups a surprising presence and, indeed, voice in the mainstream American press (Ferree et al. 2002; Gamson 2001). Critics have tended to bemoan the media's focus on individuals over structures, a focus, they say, that makes it difficult for activists to press their case (Bennett 1996). But some activists have countered that since reporters want access to people affected by an issue, movement groups can supply not only the people but information on the larger issues that their experiences illuminate (see discussion in Polletta 2006, ch. 5). This insight is substantiated by recent social psychological research. When audiences hear or read news stories in which someone affected by an issue is profiled, they are likely to see that person's views both as widespread and as persuasive. This is true even if they are presented factual evidence to the contrary (Zillman and Brosius 2000). The well-placed person on the street may indeed serve to popularize the movement's views.

Finally, insofar as current conventions of storytelling do reproduce existing inequities, activists can make them the targets of challenge. They can turn a Congressional hearing into a speak-out or a courtroom appearance into a seminar. Indeed, one of the ways in which movements may have an impact is by gaining institutional purchase for new distributions of storytelling authority. For example, in the 1980s, AIDS activists succeeded in gaining formal representation on federal research review committees. But they also gained recognition for AIDS patients' personal accounts of their illnesses as authoritative knowledge in drug research (Epstein 1996). Challenging the institutional rules of storytelling can have powerful effect.

Conclusion

I have argued that paying attention to the stories that are told in and about movements can help us to grasp dynamics of mobilization that have been difficult to get at from a framing perspective. In particular, studying stories offers insight into how frames actually persuade; into the institutional norms that encourage some kinds of claimsmaking and discourage others; and into the underpinning common sense against which frames seem intelligible—or not. This can help us to do several things: to account for why people participate in collective action rather than free-ride on the efforts of others; to understand why some institutional practices come to be subject to contention when they do; to trace the consequences of social movements. In this chapter, however, I have concentrated on a different movement process. I have argued that paying attention to activists' strategic use of storytelling can shed light on the distinctly cultural obstacles that activists face in effecting change. Such obstacles are never insuperable, but like the distribution of financial resources or the structure of mainstream politics, they operate for the most part to support the status quo.

Culture does not constrain challenge only or even mainly by limiting what activists can aspire to. Just as much as the analysts who study them, activists are broad-minded in the options they perceive and canny in devising ways to pursue them. They use culture generally, and stories in particular, practically and creatively. The problems they face are twofold. One is that the stories that they tell cannot but seem thin and abstract compared to the multiple, diverse, and overlapping stories that are told in many media and in many forms and that together make up a common sense about an issue. To put it another way, hegemony operates not by way of a single canonical story repeated over and over again in identical form but rather by way of many stories that are quite different from each other but navigate similarly between the poles of familiar symbolic oppositions. Against that backdrop, stories that challenge those oppositions are either disbelieved or assimilated to more familiar stories.

The other problem lies in the norms governing how stories are heard and evaluated: when they are considered appropriate, believable, serious, and so on. I have argued that these norms are historical. Victims today are unlikely to be granted the moral authority they were in antebellum America to an audience that was familiar with Christian conversion narratives. Our assumptions about how stories affect their listeners are just different. Norms of stories' evaluation are also distinctive to particular institutions. In this respect, activists telling stories of their victimization have fared better in the media than in court. In the media, activists have been able to style themselves Everypersons, connecting their own experiences to a larger normative point. In court, by contrast, the expectation that true stories remain identical in their retelling has hurt women who have suffered sexual trauma and whose stories, as a result, have changed from the initial fragmented account they gave to police. Note, however, that beliefs about true storytelling are not specific to legal institutions. Rather, they form part of a popular theory of narrative and knowing, a theory which transcends and may, indeed, contravene institutional instructions.

So culture is stacked against those who would use it to effect change. Perhaps that is no surprise. In addition to shedding light on just *how* culture is stacked against challengers, I have pointed to ways in which challengers have overcome that disadvantage. In short, they have successfully exploited narrative's reliance on *ambiguity* and the *ambivalence* with which it is evaluated as a rhetorical form. With respect to the first, activists have used literary tropes such as irony, shifting point of view, and antithesis to craft appeals that manage to resonate while still being heard as truly different from what people have heard before. Activists have capitalized on audiences' assumption that a story will be allusive and their willingness to do interpretive work to make sense of it. With respect to people's ambivalence about story as a credible form, I have suggested that in institutions characterized by a popular skepticism of expertise, for example, media reporting, activists may be advantaged in their use of stories. Where that is not the case, activists may be served by challenging the hierarchies of credibility in terms of which rhetorical forms are heard. There may be strategic advantage to determinedly telling stories where statistics are called for and fighting for the admission of statistics where personal stories are deemed appropriate.

Chapter 3
Claiming Credit: Stories of Movement Influence as Outcomes

David S. Meyer

In tightly controlled polities, both mythic and real, political authorities control mass media to present coherent, consistent, and self- and state-serving narratives that ascribe responsibility and blame; such narratives might be revised frequently during leadership shifts (think about the Ministry of Truth in George Orwell's *1984*). In actual democracies the process is more complicated; all versions of causality and responsibility can be contested. Politicians try to take credit for whatever popular outcomes they can, knowing that critics, journalists, and their opponents might take them to task for straining credulity. The stakes are high, however, and the relative openness of debate generally rewards the bold.

The stakes for successfully claiming credit are similarly high for social protest movements. The civil rights movement of the 1950s and 1960s, for example, plays a central role in virtually all narratives of race in contemporary politics, and is portrayed as a successful and heroic struggle for equality for African Americans, in consonance with values expressed by the Declaration of Independence. The establishment of a national day commemorating Martin Luther King Jr, enacted under a Republican administration in the 1980s, marks the consolidation of the narrative's success. Of course, this isn't all. Virtually all of the Southern states in the United States now organize and promote "civil rights tourism," as does the National Park Service.[1] The civil rights struggles of the 1950s and 1960s have become every bit as accepted a part of the heroic American story as the American Revolution, even promoted—and distorted—by those who opposed the movement during its heyday.

If the civil rights movement represents one end of the continuum of credit claiming success, many other movements cluster at the opposite pole. Stories

---

1   On civil rights tourism, see a Debbie Elliot report, "Civil Rights and Tourism," on National Public Radio's "All Things Considered," broadcast July 4, 2000. Elliott reports that while Southern states were once ashamed of their role in civil rights history, they have discovered that it's a good source of tourism and money. Virtually every Southern State now promotes Black Heritage sites. The National Park Service offers an inventory of historic sites, and suggests that one has to consider a longer view of American history, including slavery, to understand the civil rights movement, and to consider the civil rights movement to understand any politics since. For example, see http://www.cr.nps.gov/ delta/heritage.htm.

that protest is ineffective or counter-productive are common in public discourse. Curiously, often the people who lead and animate the social movements of our time downplay the impact of their efforts. Smith (1996), asked key activists involved in the 1980s movement against US intervention in Central America to evaluate the impact of their efforts. For the most part, they were mercilessly self-critical, quick to acknowledge falling short of their goals, and to blame the media, conservative political culture and/or political apathy, and themselves.

To take a recent case in point, opponents of an American-led war against Iraq mobilized an unprecedented global campaign against military intervention, engaging millions of people in the full range of movement activities, from writing letters and emails to staging large demonstrations and civil disobedience actions. This movement changed the rhetoric and military strategy of the US, delayed the start of war, and engaged the UN (Arkin 2003), but these achievements seemed pale as tanks rolled across the desert. Still, a story that describes only the defeats is not only incomplete, but politically counter-productive. It provides no foundation for subsequent mobilization and reinforces a sense of futility among those who participated.

Regardless of how dispassionate and well-informed scholars may assess the causes of movement influence, the popular storyline about a movement's impact often does not line up with the scholarly consensus. The popular storyline, however, is far more likely to affect what happens next; the stories people hear about the past influence how they view future possibilities and, most significantly, their prospective role in making it. I pose an analytical challenge for social movement scholars to separate the question of assessing influence from that of establishing a narrative of influence. I argue that the emergent story of what happened is an important social movement outcome—but one generally neglected by researchers.

Social Movement Outcomes: You Can't Ever Get All You Want

The most obvious explanation for differential attributions of success is simple: some movements win more extensive responses than others, and broadly accepted reputations and stories of influence follow actual accomplishments. Although relevant, it is only part of the story. Without doubt, the civil rights movement changed the face of America, and the nature of racial politics to date. At the same time, widely articulated goals of equality and opportunity are belied by ongoing inequalities in education, employment, and elsewhere in American life. There is much the movement didn't win; but opponents, bystanders, and participants all recognize some accomplishments, even if viewing work to be done very differently.[2]

---

2   Additionally, as in the case of all movements, significant non-movement actors and concerns were involved in advancing civil rights. Architects of American foreign

On the other hand, there are real accomplishments veterans of the Central America Solidarity movement *could* claim. Although the Sandinista government fell in Nicaragua, it did so from an election, not foreign military invasion that seemed possible in the early 1980s. Smith (1996) makes a compelling case that multinational peace politics, particularly efforts by the United States government, were substantially influenced by the citizen movements of the 1980s. Although the outcomes were different from those activists sought, promoting procedural democracy and peace is hardly trivial. The absence of a movement narrative for what happened in Central America, however, left the Reagan administration to tell a largely uncontested tale in which it ousted the Sandinistas—over the objections of a misguided and diffuse American left. In a story of movement containment of American military and foreign policy, incremental achievements could be seen as a foundation for subsequent efforts; in the story of Reagan triumphalism, such incremental achievements appear, at best, as pale consolation.

There is no automatic relationship between actual and claimed or reputed achievements (Lang and Lang 1988). An ample supply of actual events and conjecture as raw material to allows partisans of most movements to tell tales of both victory and defeat. Challengers, opponents, and authorities construct competing narratives in a contest of narrative, meaning, and politics. The extent of movement influence and the means by which it is effected influences, but doesn't determine, which stories dominate.

Moreover, as students of social movements have noted, it is extremely difficult to assess causality reliably anyway, for the factors that give rise to social movements are often also those that give rise to policy change (e.g., Giugni 1998; Amenta, Dunleavy and Bernstein 1994). Social movements always struggle in circumstances of some adversity representing minority points of view or constituencies, or majorities that are structurally disadvantaged in conventional politics (Burstein 1999; Tarrow 1998). This is the case for all sorts of movements, and the critical questions are where to set the bar for success, and how to determine who was influential in achieving what. In addition to sorting out the influence of a movement, writ large, determining which movement elements or strategies were responsible for what outcomes is also an analytical and political challenge.

To examine social movement influence, scholars have generally set the bar for success rather low, following William Gamson's (1990) landmark study of challenging groups in the United States prior to World War II. Gamson assessed two distinct outcomes in regard to the state: a group can gain recognition as an actor; and/or a group can get some of its policy demands met. If any aim of the challenging group was achieved to any degree, the group was successful, even if it was not the only challenger advocating this reform; additionally,

---

policy during the Cold War, for example, were concerned with the damaging effects of racial segregation on the image of the United States abroad (Dudziak 2000).

the time horizon for success ranged up to fifteen years, even if the group had since disappeared, implicitly assuming that authorities might be responding to recently departed movements. Activists, of course, who necessarily live in the politics of the moment, are unlikely to set the bar so low. Organizers mobilize by systematically inflating goals, urgency, and the possibilities for success in the shorter term (Gamson and Meyer 1996; Benford and Snow 2000), and emphasizing the potential influence of each new recruit's efforts (Benford 1993b).

Subsequent attempts to assess the impact of social movements on public policy have generally offered less explicit comparison but provided more detail on particular policy issues, and have offered different theories of *how* movements might exercise influence. Piven and Cloward (1977), for example, emphasized *threat* and *disruption*, arguing that authorities sometimes provide poor people easier access to social welfare benefits in order to quell disruptive protest. In contrast, writing on New Deal era pension and social welfare policies, Amenta (1998) argues that political movements gave institutional reformers cover and incentive to pursue the spending policies they already wanted, identifying *mediation* as the primary mechanism of influence.

Looking at the protests against the war in Vietnam, scholars have argued that protests kept the issue of the war on the political agenda, constantly forcing elected officials to address the issue—but not mandating a particular policy choice; in this view, movements work primarily by *agenda setting* (Small 1988; McAdam and Su 2002). Of course, these mechanisms are not mutually exclusive, and vary across movements and over time. Nonetheless, how a movement exercises influence is likely to affect the ease with which authorities grant it credit. It seems far more likely for authorities to recognize the influence of moral suasion, new arguments, or evidence, on policy, than say, disruptive threat.

Claiming Influence In Politics and Culture

Even if movements get credit for enactment of a new policy responding to their concerns, the nature of the legislative and administrative processes guarantees compromises in execution—if not in goals. The nature of the legislative process in the United States essentially mandates both polemics outside government and compromise within institutions, such that most people involved are getting somewhat less than what they would want. At the same time, political pressures lead authorities to oversell any of the programs they propose, and any bits of legislation they had a hand in enacting (Edelman 1988).

Rhetoric about "ending welfare as we know it," fighting a "war" against drugs (after losing one against poverty), or adopting "zero tolerance" for crime or environmental pollution predominates. *There is a mismatch of a political discourse that emphasizes absolutes with a political process that prizes compromise and incrementalism.* Thus, the dynamics of contemporary American politics virtually mandate that *most people are going to be disappointed most of the time*, and ambitious reformers are going to be quicker to see defeats than victories. The growth of government activity since the 1960s, legitimating and encouraging more single-issue groups and social movements, exacerbates the dynamic of disappointment (Godwin and Ingram 1980).

Direct influence on the policy process is difficult to trace, but other important avenues through which movements can exercise influence are at least as difficult. Social movements can do much more than engage in the policy process, such that analysts need a multilevel framework for evaluating their outcomes, separating out influence on policy, organizations, and individuals (Meyer and Whittier 1994). Simply, social movements can affect the substance and/or process of policy, can affect the organizational structure, practice, and culture of challenging groups (e.g., Moore 1996), and can influence the individuals who participate in them (McAdam 1988; Whittier 1995), all in ways that alter the nature of subsequent social movements.

To establish narratives of influence as a social movement outcome, we need to extend the analytical frame of movement influence beyond specific policy outcomes. Here Rochon (1998), who contends that the arena in which movements have the greatest effect is cultural, is particularly helpful. Because cultural change appears to happen suddenly, simultaneously sweeping diverse and decentralized settings, often through relatively invisible actions, it is easy for movement influence to be obscured as credit is widely dispersed. Rochon contends that studying the movement of ideas helps delineate what processes are actually at work.

Broad cultural change begins with the creation of new ideas within "critical communities" (Rochon 1998: 22) that develop around particular social problems, analyses, or potential solutions.[3] Social movements carry these ideas to a broader audience. But social movements also draw ideas, values, and symbols from the dominant culture, operating in dynamic interaction with a larger social context that normally obscures them (Johnston and Klandermans 1995). As a result, it is at least as difficult to claim credit for promoting meaningful cultural change as in promoting policy reform.

As movements make claims on matters of policy, it is not necessarily the achievement of desired changes in policy that determines movement influence; there are also, often unclaimed, "spillover effects" (Meyer and Whittier 1994). The failure of the Equal Rights Amendment, which consumed a great deal of feminist effort during the 1970s, is a useful case in point. Despite the policy defeat, widespread cultural values and attitudes about women in politics and in the workforce changed dramatically (Mansbridge 1986). Oddly, then, we can imagine tales in which the movement failed to win ERA, and social and

---

3   Risse-Kappen's (1994) similar argument emphasizes the transnational movement of ideas.

cultural changes resulted from other, undefined, factors. In short, it's easy to edit the movement out.

When a movement extends its vision of an issue to a broader audience, its influence, and especially its capacity to claim influence, falters. Rochon (1998: 195–6) notes the irony,

> As the culture takes hold of a new idea, adaptation occurs to make the concept fit with existing cultural beliefs ... the critical community loses exclusive ownership of the issue—precisely because the new concepts are now part of the wider culture ... [p]eople outside the critical community begin to portray themselves (and be accepted by the media) as "experts" on the issue.

At such a time, movement activists are able to slip out of, or into, identification with a particular movement. People with no previous connection to the women's movement, for example, can claim to be feminists—or environmentalists or animal rights supporters or peace activists. In doing so, not only do they make explicit claims about their own identity, but also about the politics and identity of the larger movements.

As any movement is the product of a range of groups that cooperate, to varying degrees, for political gains, yet still differ among themselves (Rochon and Meyer 1997; Meyer and Corrigall-Brown 2005), the problem of identity and politics is particularly acute. In a relatively open polity such as the US, the lines separating activists within a movement from other sympathizers are difficult to draw, and movements only weakly police their own boundaries (Benford 1993a). Thus, one can claim to be an environmentalist and lobby for ratification of international agreements while sitting in redwood trees to protest logging *or* support drilling in Alaska and drive a sport utility vehicle on hunting and fishing trips. The label, "environmentalist," defines few strict boundaries. As political and cultural circumstances change, individuals can focus on different beliefs, relationships, or characteristics to make claims on the basis of a different identity (see Mische 2003). Whereas a more hospitable environment for women's rights, for example, might make it safer for some women to make claims on a gendered identity, it could also make the identity less problematic or salient for others.

To summarize, the scholarly literature on the impact of social movements has identified numerous problems in assessing influence, including: (a) the diversity of efforts within and around a movement pressing for change; (b) numerous possible outcomes of mobilization, some of which are unlikely to be explicitly targeted by activists themselves; and (c) disputes about the mechanisms by which influence is effected. To the range of possible movement outcomes, I want to suggest we add the story of movement influence. Most movements leave a trail of actions and statements that can provide the raw materials of a claim for credit, but that the translation of such raw materials into a compelling and broadly resonant claim only sometimes takes place. For help in figuring out why, I now turn to the broader literatures on reputation, social construction, and narratives.

Movement Influence as Reputation

Popular understanding of the extent and mechanics of a movement's influence comprise a large share of its reputation. Here, we can draw on scholarly consideration of the reputation of individual artists, political leaders, and activists. In looking at the reputation of etchers, Lang and Lang (1988) note that the volume and quality of an artist's work explain only a portion of his posthumous reputation. An artist's personal and professional networks, the quality of records about the work, and the persistence of posthumous promoters (often with a financial interest in the work) all influence reputation. Employing a similar constructionist approach to reputation, Gary Alan Fine has examined the construction of the reputations of political and cultural figures. In looking at the Warren Harding's reputation, for example, Fine (1996) argues that the president's record was sufficiently complex to provide a narrative of accomplishment—as well as the story of incompetence and corruption that came to dominate. Political entrepreneurs constructed a tale of Harding's failure to legitimate and promote their own agendas. Their success in doing so created a reputation that has outlived the agendas it was constructed to support. Similarly, Fine (1999) contends that radical abolitionists tied their cause to John Brown's dramatic and violent crusade against slavery, constructing a martyr by editing and repackaging Brown's life and actions in ways that would resonate with broader cultural values.

But successfully building and maintaining a reputation may entail editing out a substantial portion of a figure's career and concerns. Bromberg and Fine (2002) examine singer Pete Seeger's development into an icon of American folk music over time. Nothing that Seeger's long membership in the Communist Party could easily have disqualified him from honors such as designation as a "living legend" by the Library of Congress and a lifetime achievement award from the Kennedy Center. These awards, however, along with a Grammy and the Harvard Arts Medal, came rather late in Seeger's career, decades after being blacklisted for communist and anti-war activities. Outliving both enemies and his most controversial politics, however, Seeger has seen his popular reputation built around political commitments to less problematic causes, particularly environmental issues. At the same time, his acceptance as a kind of icon reflects a political cleansing that has stripped him of any power as a symbol of rebellion. Bromberg and Fine (2002: 1147) contend, "He is not dangerous, because he is not taken seriously. He is not fully heard, free to sing whatever he likes because this saintly old man can hardly be 'seriously' proposing rebellion. His reputation traps him." They argue that similar processes of cultivating acceptance for political heroes, including Abraham Lincoln and Martin Luther King, have meant the neglect of the more difficult and more radical politics those figures embraced (see also Schwartz 1996). Essentially, a "consensus hero" is of limited use to *any* cause.

These studies of individual reputations establish several important points useful in making sense of the development of popular understandings about social movements and political influence. First, tales of influence, like reputations, are constructed from the raw material of events and actors. Second, political or reputational entrepreneurs try to promote preferred understandings of the past in order to support their current agendas. Third, reputations or common understandings can be remarkably resilient and long-lived (see Schuman and Scott 1989), and can constrain as well as enable collective action. The impact of a particular understanding of a movement's history and influence is a function of how subsequent actors use that understanding to frame the possibilities of new collective action. In organizing for the future, activists must make sense of the events of the past, explaining previous triumphs and defeats by constructing narratives that resonate with popular beliefs and shared values even as they challenge them.

Constructing Causality and Telling Stories

Political figures of all sorts construct causal explanations. Recognition of this social construction is well established in the study of social problems (e.g., Best 1995; Holstein and Miller 2003; Spector and Kitsuse 2001), but not generally applied to narratives of social movement influence. The social movement literature has embraced a compatible approach in dealing with the problem of political mobilization. Organizers craft *collective action frames* to define both social problems and potential solutions that particular sorts of collective action can promote (e.g., Benford 1993; Benford and Snow 2000; Benford and Hunt 2003; Ferree et al. 2002; Gamson 1992; Gamson and Meyer 1996; Snow et al. 1986). But the framing literature is focused generally on mobilization within a social movement (e.g., Gamson 1995; Benford 2002).

Like frames, narrative is a distinct rhetorical tool that organizers use to mobilize, channel, and legitimate collective action. Also like "prognostic" frames, narratives explicitly make causal claims about the past and future. Unlike frames, however, narratives emphasize sequence in order to make causal claims and inspire action. Deborah Stone (1997: 189) contends that causality is asserted through "strategically crafted" stories, adorned with symbols and numbers, and pressed by "political actors who try to make their versions the basis of policy choices." Stories identify the factors relevant to an issue, defines which policy areas are amenable to human intervention, which claims and claimants are worthy, and which actors are politically significant (Schneider and Ingram 1997). As Gubrium and Holstein (1998: 147) explain, "A narrative assembles individual objects, actions, and events into a comprehensible pattern; telling a story turns available parts into a meaningful whole" (also see Griffin 1993).

Political actors are wise to construct simple stories that clearly and unambiguously identify problems, offer solutions, and concentrate blame—even if historical accounts and actual events offer a much messier picture. At any given time, numerous causal stories compete for primacy, finding support with different audiences. Stone cautions,

> The different sides in an issue act as if they are trying to find the "true" cause, but … [p]olitical conflicts over causal stories are … more than empirical claims about sequences of events. They are fights about the possibility of control and the assignment of responsibility. (1997: 197)

Numerous story elements are available in public events, including efforts of an activist group, changes in a policy, changes in political conditions, and speeches and public statements. A convincing story will draw from these elements, heavily editing, and adding plot. But crafting a story is only part of the larger struggle in promoting it. The effective storyteller is mindful of distinct audiences, their values, expectations, and likely responses to different narratives, as well as the demands of different settings in which stories are offered. Daily newspapers, for example, offer less space than longer-form journalism, and thus respond better to shorter chains of causality and simpler claims. Ultimately, widely accepted stories combine an edited version of available elements, consonant with accepted facts, perhaps supplemented with fictions that resonate with longstanding national myths, widespread cultural beliefs, or familiar plots (Tilly 2003).

As political actors compete to win adherents for their preferred story of influence, the factors that make one or another story predominate in politics, although influenced by credibility (Benford and Hunt 2003), are not limited by it. The advocates' vigor and skill is critical to their narratives' acceptance, for, as Stone notes,

> There is always someone to tell a competing narrative, and getting others to believe one version of events rather than another is hardly automatic…. . A causal story is more likely to be successful if its proponents have visibility, access to media, and prominent positions; if it accords with widespread and deeply held cultural values; if it somehow captures and responds to a natural mood; and if its implicit prescription entails no radical redistribution of power or wealth. (1997: 202)

Causal stories appear in both wholesale and retail forms, the former directed to broad audiences, the latter targeted to smaller distinct ones. We can trace the trajectory of mass-market stories in public documents, official speeches, commemorations, and in the popular textbooks for public schools. At the same time, the work of promoting meaning, like that of mobilizing, also must take place at a grassroots person-to-person level, through daily interactions (Holstein and Miller 2003). Within social movements, activists reinforce their preferred stories through sermons, speeches, songs, and slogans.

There is an inevitable tension in managing stories to win acceptance within a social movement community and to spread a message more broadly because social movements develop distinct internal cultures that distinguish them from mainstream society (Rochon 1998). Importantly, the more resonant a story is with conventional political and moral values, the more likely it is to be accepted; but such resonance comes at a price of limiting the sorts of claims made and the kinds of tactics employed. Activists always face a difficult balancing act in trying to stretch, but not transgress, the boundaries of legitimacy. There is also a consistent strain resulting from social movement dynamics that produce, at best, partial victories.

Recognizing that stories of social movement influence are constructed is not to suggest that this construction goes on in a vacuum, or that the skill of an organizer is the only factor determining a story's resonance and public acceptance. Activists, like other promoters of social problems, peddle their narratives in an environment mostly beyond their control even though it dramatically affects their prospects for success (Best 2003). The umbrella salesman on the corner of a busy city, knows that overcast skies can help sales even more than a vigorous or creative sales pitch. Organizers' skill and will to construct and promote stories of influence—in effect, their agency—is important, but it is not the only factor affecting the acceptance of stories.

Why Some Movement Stories Stick

We can identify a non-exclusive set of factors likely to affect movement actors' prospects for successfully claiming credit, including: the articulated goals of a movement, the survival of at least some of its component organizations, the institutional positioning of allies or sympathetic participants, the relative costs and risks of claiming victory, and the nature of the constituency the represented. All affect the propensity of activists to get their version of the story out beyond the boundaries of the faithful to broad audiences, and their capacity to do so. I ground this analysis in our understanding of the past, but this argument calls for empirical examination.

Movement Goals

Movements always target for more than they ultimately get, and some movement factions approach a campaign's focal point by making much broader claims. Because all victories are partial, it's important to figure out why some factions do better at claiming them. Both very limited and very broad expressed goals make victories harder to claim.

Goals that don't affect some substantial portion of the body politic are unlikely to resonate with a larger population. In recent years, activists have devoted a greater share of their efforts simply toward winning the rights to protest at specific places and in particular ways (della Porta 1999). That demonstrators may succeed in winning their desired space, or carry off the events they plan can be claimed as a victory for only a short time, and only among the already committed. In evaluating the counter-inaugural he helped organize, for example, Brian Becker, national coordinator of Act Now to Stop War and End Racism (ANSWER), claimed, "We think this is a significant achievement for the anti-war movement. We have bleachers, a stage, a sound system, and we're right along the parade route. We feel we have succeeded" (Jankofsky 2005).

Notwithstanding Becker's confidence, it's unlikely that many other opponents of President Bush's agendas felt so sanguine about their success as the president took the oath of office for a second term. While some activists may get tremendous satisfaction in, say, staging a large demonstration and hearing good speakers and music, such satisfaction isn't likely to spread beyond the faithful, nor is it likely to last.[4] For the larger public and for most participants, the successful demonstration or protest event is also a means to some other end. Similarly, although we know that social movements can change individual lives and build new organizations, activists rarely mobilize for these ends—save as a means to larger goals.

In contrast, groups seeking broader collective goods (Amenta and Young 1999; Cooper 1996) easily meet the challenge of significance, but face stronger competitors in claiming credit. Although a movement may seek collective goods from the margins, as it approaches some policy impact, its claims will be taken up, albeit in some kind of dilute fashion, by more mainstream political actors. The general benefits of such policy reforms, be it cleaner air or more thoroughly labeled food packaging, will be claimed not only by the movement, but by more powerful institutional actors, with immediate credibility in mass media, permanent staffs to manage public relations, and perpetual campaigns in which they will have opportunity to retell the story of their achievements. Because the benefit is diffuse, it is not only harder for a movement actors to claim credit, but also less likely that some distinct constituency will feel the same stake in the goal's achievement. The cause of clean air, for example, might be taken up by anyone, and longtime activist groups are hard-pressed to discredit the efforts of a movement's late converts, particularly if the newly recruited are better positioned to affect policy.

For movements that win on anything, there is also the problem of what might be called a *moving finish line*. When the modern environmental movement emerged in the 1960s, an initial focus on pesticides quickly generated real victories. Of course, environmentalists tried, and continue to try, to build upon

---

4 It is telling that in his analysis of varieties of movement narrative, Fine (1995) provides no stories of movement influence. Even "happy stories" are about personal growth, safety, or new allies, not policy change.

such policy achievements and move further, pressing new "policy frontiers" (Gornick and Meyer 1998). As the movement succeeded in gaining some recognition and influence, participating organizations constantly sought new related issues on which to make claims (Rucht 1999), both to achieve their goals and to maintain their support. The work never done, organizers generally focus on the greatest threat or most salient current issue, leaving any past victories for others to claim.

Organizational Survival and the Politics of Coalitions

Like Coleridge's "Ancient Mariner" or Melville's Ishmael, someone must be around to tell the story. Although organizations that do not focus on sustaining themselves may have substantial impact (Piven and Cloward 1977), they are poorly positioned to take credit for their influence. Outliving the opponents and continuing visible action enhances the prospects of wining credit for the past—as we saw in the tale of Pete Seeger's installation as an American legend fully forty years after the height of his popularity as a musician (Bromberg and Fine 2002). But activists, professional organizers, and groups move on to other issues and other organizations, often shifting the emphasis of their political concerns. The movement against nuclear power was antagonistic to developing formal and permanent leadership structures (Dwyer 1983), and individual activists drifted in and out of participation. The movement faded after the Three Mile Island accident in 1979, along with licenses for new nuclear power plants, a victory no one was around to claim (Jasper 1990; Joppke 1993). To be sure, supportive groups, like the Union of Concerned Scientists survived, but did so by turning to more salient issues such as nuclear weapons. No group enjoyed sufficient capacity and interest to issue press releases, return reporters' queries, or constantly correct competitors' explanations for policy change.

In the U.S., contemporary social movement politics *are* coalition politics, the product of organizations and individuals who affiliate in the service of particular campaigns and causes, but maintain their own visions of justice, repertoire of tactics, independent organizational needs, and distinct, yet often overlapping, constituencies (Rochon and Meyer 1997; Meyer and Corrigall-Brown 2005). Social movements succeed when the efforts of distinct organizations have a synergistic effect, even if some groups are short-lived. *Their* version of events, claims to effectiveness, and vision of what is to be done—in short, their story—disappears, particularly when other groups survive. Thus, in contemporary politics, the NAACP (National Association for the Advancement of Colored People), and to a lesser extent, the SCLC (Southern Christian Leadership Council) are far better positioned to explain the influence of the civil rights movement than is SNCC (Student Nonviolent Coordinating Committee), which imploded more than thirty years ago. While SNCC's direct action campaigns were critical, narratives about more reformist politics predominate, with a focus on moral suasion more than political disruption. Similarly, the radical edge of the labor movement has its story told by academics far more than by organizers, and to much smaller audiences than its more mainstream allies. Because more moderate organizations are most likely to survive (Wilson 1995), popular stories about social movement influence tend to emphasize more institutional routes to effectiveness, downplaying the grassroots activity and mass mobilizations that animates movements.

The Risks of Victories

Claiming credit also entails risks for social movements. Movements recognized as successful can provoke their opponents (Meyer and Staggenborg 1996) and risk complacency among supporters. For many interests, risk and threat rather than support from government generates mobilization of activism and financial contributions. In abortion politics, for example, Supreme Court decisions are typically followed by press conferences in which groups on both sides of the issue claim defeat; activists want to heighten urgency, keep the faithful engaged, and solicit financial contributions. The abortion issue also illustrates the politics of compromise and partial policy resolutions. Although abortion has remained legal in the US since 1973, movement organizations continually battle on a broad range of issues, ranging from explicit discussion of abortion to regulation of particular procedures to parental or spousal notification to the size of a buffer zone separating anti-abortion protesters from clinics; there are always potential threats.

Given the nature of social movement politics, stories of optimism or achievement are risky. Journalist Gregg Easterbrook (1995), a self-described liberal seeking to vindicate government action, argues that federal government action, prompted by the environmental movement, made huge progress in improving air and water quality. In his story, however, the environmentalists are whining winners. "Enviros won the last 20 years of political battles by a wide margin," Easterbrook (1995: 381, 383) writes, "but you'd never know it from their public statements .... As environmentalists have become effective lobbyists they have learned the negative tools of the trade: bluster, veiled threats, misrepresentation." The pressures of direct mail fundraising, he argues, lead environmentalists to employ hyperbole and distortion in order to continue to raise money. To generalize, a group that claims success risks forfeiting its capacity to mobilize, either to sustain networks and organizations and employment that it has developed, and also in terms of lodging subsequent claims.[5]

---

5   Unsurprisingly, a result of both politics and the moving finish line, Easterbrook's book encountered negative reviews from environmentalists. Reilly, Shabecoff, and Davis (1995: 366a) took Easterbrook to task for "tak[ing] the remaining environmental problems too lightly. The global environment may have improved but the fact remains that these problems are very serious and that there should be no letup in efforts to address them."

There are good reasons *not* to proclaim victory. Politically, acknowledging victory risks lessening urgency and ceding what is always a limited agenda space (Hilgartner and Bosk 1988) for issues to other causes and claimants; there is always more important work to be done. Organizationally, declaring a win risks embracing identification with mainstream allies and politics and forfeiting the urgency of their claims on supporters. Paradoxically, a well-heeled group best positioned to get its claim of victory out risks the most in doing so.

In the case of the civil rights movement, even as the public policies and social changes activists won were far less than the goals they articulated, activists did succeed in making it politically costly to attack the goals of inclusion. Opposition to civil rights is no longer articulated as a social good in polite society or mainstream politics. Such talk, if not belief, has been banished to the marginalized political netherworld of segregationist politics. Articulating support for the broad goals of racial integration and equality is low risk politics, tied to no definite position in contemporary contested political debates. This was not always the case for advocates of civil rights for ethnic minorities, nor is it for those who express sympathy with gay and lesbian rights. Vanquishing the explicit opposition makes it easier to claim credit.

Marching into and through Institutions: Constituencies and Claimants

The relative positions and power of claimants have a great deal to do with what stories get out, and how they are received (Stone 1997). Movements that make inroads into established institutions, particularly winning elective office, produce individuals with both the stake and status to make claims about movement influence. To the extent that someone representing a social movement stands beside candidates for office, makes speeches in the House of Representatives, and represents movement positions in policy debates, that person shows one aspect of movement influence. Increased capacity to make claims of influence, however, comes with constraints and somewhat different incentives.

The non-debate about the end of the Cold War provides a good illustration. Most peace movement organizations had begun to fade in the middle 1980s, as deployment of new missiles they vigorously opposed began (Edwards and Marullo 1995); their opponents were far better positioned to interpret the restoration of arms control in the later 1980s and the fall of communism in 1989. Pundits, politicians, and well-sponsored academics claimed that the threat of an eventual ballistic missile defense system, popularly known as star wars, or just general toughness and spending during the 1980s, wore the Soviet Union down. Democratic allies of the peace movement in congress claimed, instead, that forty years of bipartisan containment policy achieved these ends. In short, politicians in both major political parties used the remarkable events of 1989 as grist for retelling old stories supporting their preferred policies and their political futures.[6]

Empirical evidence supporting these positions is very weak. Risse-Kappen (1994), tracing the transnational movement of ideas, and Knopf (1998), looking at changes in U.S. national security policy, convincingly demonstrate the impact of the peace movement on the end of the Cold War. Recently opened archives provide additional evidence to counter the dominant narratives. Evangelista (1999), using newly available Soviet documents, makes a compelling argument that moderation from the West, particularly the United States, rather than hard line policies, produced and accelerated reform in the Soviet Union.

Activists who made these arguments earlier (e.g., Cortright 1993), however, got little attention. Neither academics nor activists enjoyed much capacity to promote alternative explanations for the end of the Cold War. Activists whose organizations had been crippled years before were poorly positioned to make claims of influence and credit, and indeed focused most of their attention on new, now more promising, issues. In effect, they were willing to accept stories from those they believed had defeated them. At the same time, one-time allies of the movement ditched that affiliation in favor of others that appeared more fruitful; members of Congress who had eagerly portrayed themselves as peace activists in the early 1980s retrospectively donned the mantle of containment.

Policies cannot speak for themselves. When a movement is about the treatment of identifiable and distinct groups of people, for example, African-Americans, women, gays and lesbians, individual careers can readily be seen as social movement successes. Appointment or election to government positions, or anointment by the mass media, enables them to claim credit for partial victories, even if those so advantaged are not hardcore movement activists, or represent a more moderate wing of movement.

Paradoxically, individuals who win elected office, even veterans of radical organizations, such as John Lewis from SNCC, or Tom Hayden from the Students for a Democratic Society (SDS), by virtue of their hard-won careers in mainstream politics, can't help but emphasize the importance of institutional politics. Winning access to such positions becomes both a movement triumph and the signal for a shift toward institutionally oriented politics. Polletta (1998b) examined narratives of the civil rights movement employed by members of Congress on the floor of the House or Senate, and found that the stories were most likely to be told by African-Americans, confined almost exclusively to commemorative occasions, and stressed an individual connection to Martin Luther King—or his dream. She notes that "Speakers are clear that their own careers were made possible by the travails of an earlier generation of movement activists .... Their own careers become *the next stage* in a saga of African

---

6   Meyer and Marullo (1992) provide more detail about the debate immediately following the end of the Cold War.

American struggle" (Polletta 1998a: 435, emphasis added). Polletta recognizes an irony in the deployment of a movement narrative focusing on the action inside mainstream political institutions. Here, one-time activists gaining access to political institutions win the capacity to get a movement story out, but it is a story fixed in the past, emphasizing conventional politics for the future.

In contrast, individuals who win access through policy-focused movements have a more difficult time claiming credit for their movement; indeed, exercising influence within policymaking circles frequently entails disavowing movement connections. The peace activist who takes an appointment in the Arms Control and Disarmament Agency or the environmentalist who works for the Environmental Protection Agency, as examples, disavow activist identification as part of the bargain. Even if they do not, activists in the street would quickly disavow them for excessive moderation. For some movements, winning access to political institutions essentially means slipping an identity, something people identified by characteristics beyond belief cannot easily do.

Middle-class movements (Parkin 1968; Kann 1986) mobilizing on issue positions distinguish their participants from the society they challenge primarily on the basis of beliefs, although they may share norms of presentation, styles, and conversation. Indeed, seeking public support, they often emphasize how much like a non-mobilized and mainstream audience they are. When their ideas are accommodated, however, at most some portion of style or of belief is incorporated into governance, generally carried by an elected official or appointee. The connections between government employees, seeking credibility, and the movements that supported them, seeking viability, operate to attenuate connections between the margins and the mainstream.[7] The elected official presents ideas as her own, even if claiming identification with the movement.

Movements based on providing targeted advantages to an identifiable constituency are thus better positioned to claim credit than those that build support on the basis of belief. Whereas skin color, gender, ethnicity, or even sexual orientation, are relatively "sticky" identities, movements based on belief are far more "slippery," although how slippery an identity is may change over time. Women in mainstream politics can now sometimes ignore the impact of the feminist movement (Sawyers and Meyer 1999), African-Americans who try to shed this identity have it thrust back upon them by mainstream politics.

In discussing identity, organized labor in the US provides a particularly interesting case. Whereas in Western Europe an individual's identification with labor—and indeed, the working class—has historically been a sticky and longlasting one, this is not the norm in the US. As organized labor in America suffered under Taft-Hartley and red-baiting after World War II (Goldfield 1987), its members encountered increasing opportunities and incentives for shedding their identification with the larger movement, making individual, rather than

---

7   At the same time, activism in the streets can enhance the leverage and influence of people making more moderate claims inside institutions (see Raeburn 2004).

collective goals, the primary focus of even collective efforts. Further, US workers were further divided along ethnic, religious, and neighborhood lines, so that additional (and alternative) identities were always readily available (Katznelson 1981), and became even more accessible if an individual was promoted out of the working class. This compounds the difficulties that leaders who earn large salaries and do not work on the shop floor face in maintaining credible connections with a broader—and divided—working class.

By the end of the 1960s, the New Left would disparage and dismiss all the achievements of the labor movement. As example, in his popular analysis of organized labor, first published in the early 1970s, Aronowitz opined that the organized left in Western Europe and the US had helped

> consolidate the power of capital over workers in two ways: it assisted in the organization of unions that have increasingly been instruments for the disciplining and control of workers; and it fought for reforms that strengthened the power of the capitalist state to organize and rationalize the most chaotic features of the socioeconomic system and secure the dependency of larger segments of the underlying population on state welfare measures. (1974: 14)

In emphasizing labor's shortfalls and disappointments, the critic simultaneously slighted real accomplishments. With such beliefs widespread, organizing new workers became a struggle up an even steeper hill.

The Significance of Story

The actual influence of a movement or any other actor, difficult to determine in any case, is only one factor determining the content of a story and the nature of the audiences who accept it. Nonetheless, the dominant narrative about the trajectory of a movement, or of the origins of a policy, becomes part of the culture in which movements arise (or not), legitimating certain kinds of claims, actors, and tactics, while undermining others. A story that emphasizes effective and purposive efforts by citizens legitimates social protest and simultaneously reinforces the political significance of interested actors outside government. In contrast, a story that emphasizes broad historical forces or the efforts only of committed individuals within government, works to delegitimize and demobilize potential citizen movements. Similarly, as Polletta (1998a) notes, stories that emphasize accident, contingency, and spontaneity, belie the important work of organizing, portraying movements as almost magical.

Who succeeds in claiming credit matters. The old axiom that history belongs to the winners might properly by rephrased: *those who win in the writing of history shape the future*. A dominant story about the influence of a citizens' movement on politics and policy legitimizes extra-institutional mobilization on particular issues, provides a "demonstration effect" (Freeman 1983), and is a resource for mobilization in the future. Indeed, as Voss (1998) notes in comparing American and British labor at the start of the twentieth century, a story that tells of a movement's defeat, but offers an explanation of why and strategies for improvement, can also be a resource for subsequent mobilization. In contrast, a dominant story that emphasizes the power of institutional actors to do what they want, for good or evil, robs incipient movements of a residuum of efficacy that makes sustained mobilization possible.

Organizers can use narratives of movements of the past to spur or support new efforts, as Polletta (1998a) notes in her study of stories from the civil rights movement. Narratives of past influence can maintain the enthusiasm of the faithful, mobilize new activists by providing a script for contemporary actions and make sense of current political challenges. That the civil rights movement is broadly accepted as a cause for significant improvements in the treatment of African Americans, both by the state and by individuals, has been a source of inspiration for other social movements—on the right as well as the left—providing a sense that the proactive efforts of individuals in the service of a moral cause against great odds was worthwhile. It has also spurred imitators in terms of both tactics and language. That demonstrations, marches, and civil disobedience were part of an *effective* repertoire of contention vindicates movement strategies—at least sometimes. In contrast, that the sanctuary and non-intervention movements are viewed by those who initiated them as costly, and ultimately futile, has obvious bearing on the prospects for launching subsequent challenges on matters of foreign policy.[8]

In looking at the stories of influence told by social movement activists and their competitors, we can identify the implicit negotiations in constructing accepted narratives of influence. Perhaps the most successful case, that of the civil rights movement for African-Americans, demonstrates both the extent and limits of success claimed. Although the movement is widely given credit for winning basic civil rights, its popular image emphasizes charismatic leadership, rather than political organizing, most notably in the eventual inclusion of Martin Luther King Jr in the pantheon of national heroes. The frequently told story of Rosa Parks's civil disobedience on a bus in Montgomery in December 1955 is decontextualized and depoliticized. Parks is remembered as a tired old lady, with rarely a mention of her connections to long-standing organizations like the NAACP and the Highlander Folk School's leadership programs. Ironically, her heroic reputation is based on editing out the training and organizational infrastructure that supported her heroism. Dramatic disobedient action, such as the sit-in movement which catapulted to national attention in Greensboro,

---

8   Smith (1996) notes that many of these activists viewed their efforts in terms of moral witness. Demonstrating efficacy was less important, in this view, than moral and spiritual commitments. While some people, often those with strong religious commitments, will take on a sort of martyrdom independent of likely efficacy, the number is likely to be extremely limited.

North Carolina, in 1960, is treated similarly, as a spontaneous eruption (Polletta 1998a), although the sit-in was a well-established, and intensively organized, protest technique that had circulated throughout the South for nearly a decade (Morris 1984).

In short, although the movement's influence is acknowledged, it is frequently defined as something inevitable or mystical, quite apart from the processes of contemporary politics, and surely beyond the aspirations of the citizens of today. Even in a narrative of influence, the neglect of context and organization in favor of spontaneity or ambiguity in origins, what Taylor (1989) terms a myth of "immaculate conception," undermines the prospects of subsequent mobilization, giving little clear direction to today's organizers. Told by established authorities, narratives of successful protests of the past, ranging from the Boston Tea Party to the March on Washington, have the ironic effect of reinforcing the primacy of institutional politics (Polletta 1998a, b), and editing out the ongoing contentiousness of American politics (Meyer 2007).

Conclusion

By separating the analysis of claimed movement influence from questions of assessing or effecting influence, I've tried to introduce a conceptual problem to studies of social movements, one that merits more attention and substantive research. Starting with the disparity between popular and scholarly evaluations of movement influence, the question is why some movement actors are more likely to get a preferred story of influence to a broader public than others—and how. This concern unites the literature on social movements with a largely separate literature on collective memory and reputation. Hoping to stimulate empirical research, I've identified a number of factors that I argue make it easier for some movement actors to claim credit than for their influence than others. Particularly, campaigns that seek inclusion of a disadvantaged minority, that is, a concentrated benefit offered to identifiable actors, are better positioned to make claims of influence than those that seek collective benefits. Organizations that survive and flourish are far better positioned than those that falter or fade away to get their version of the story out and make it stick. Both of these factors affect the capacity of sponsors to project a narrative of political influence effectively, and aren't inherently surprising: well-established organizations and well-placed individuals have better access to both resources for cultivating and projecting preferred narratives and to mass media that will amplify them.

But placing people in power isn't enough. Identifiable individuals entering politics often claim allegiance with the movements of the past, even emphasizing their own careers as the product of those movements. At the same time, the visible representation of such individuals in positions of power makes it harder to make claims about either ongoing collective disadvantages or the necessity of protest politics as a strategy. Their very presence can undermine claims about disadvantage or exclusion, and focuses the locus of activity exclusively within political institutions rather than outside them as well.

For groups that mobilize on the basis of belief, the prospects of claiming credit are even worse. Individuals identified with an environmental or peace movement, for example, when in power, are likely to qualify that identification. Legislative demands require a willingness to compromise and qualify that bodes badly for social movement politics, which do best with sharp absolutes. Would-be allies outside government will disparage the self-proclaimed environmentalist in congress who supports an acceptable standard of toxic discharge or the declared peace activist who votes for a military budget that includes money for nuclear weapons. Additionally, groups that must mobilize on the basis of belief encounter serious risks in claiming victories, and may be loathe to do so. Such groups cultivate support by emphasizing the most proximate threat and the urgency of the moment, and thus the necessity of action.

The inherent problem for activists is the challenge of *claiming victories gracelessly while continuing to mobilize*. In looking at British labor, Voss (1998) points to a "fortifying myth" as a way to do so. While she uses the concept as a means to cope with defeat, in fact, the construction of a myth explaining the past is important to all sorts of challengers, regardless of their relative success. A fortifying myth extends the historical scope of a story line, allowing activists to recognize past efforts as a foundation for organizing in the present and future. Such a myth identifies a reasonably permanent collective actor, for example, organized labor, drawing a boundary between it and authorities. The clear boundary line encourages all concerned to see each victory or defeat in a social movement episode to be part of a larger story, one whose origins and eventual outcomes extend beyond the boundaries of a single campaign—or even life.

That a fortifying myth is difficult to construct and sustain in the US shouldn't be surprising, given the broader terrain of American political culture, which emphasizes individual, rather than collective stories, and short-term pragmatism rather than long-term struggle. Those who have been most successful in sustaining these myths have been, understandably, religious communities and ethnic minorities. But these stories carry double-edged messages. For religious activists, the long story of standing against war and the preparations for war, for example, is one told to emphasize persistence and moral clarity, not political influence; protest is witness, not politics.[9] In the case of the civil rights movement, both activists and mainstream culture have effectively negotiated a myth which ascribes responsibility for large changes in politics and culture to charismatic personalities, particularly Martin Luther King, undertaking extraordinary risks.

---

9 Daniel Berrigan, arrested numerous times over the past three decades for peace work he considers prophetic, rather than pragmatic, emphasizes his preference for working with other religious people, who are committed to the long haul, and don't need to see immediate impact for their efforts. See Berrigan and Coles 1971.

The dominant narrative is the drama of the exceptional, the dream, rather than an alternative that emphasizes a century of organizing.

Many other challengers in the United States have been far less successful either in claiming credit or creating new fortifying myths. The failure to do so means that every new campaign reinvents itself, *de novo*, identifying an atmosphere of crisis as a vehicle for mobilization. Such efforts can win sporadic victories, and have the fruits of their labor claimed by others. Some participants will leave activism, feeling frustrated by the perceived futility of their work, and new organizations will constantly hold the primary responsibility for new mobilizations. By learning how to find and promote narratives of history and policy change that emphasize the purposive efforts of citizens to make the world better, we improve their prospects of doing so in the future.

Chapter 4
Notorious Support: The America First Committee and the Personalization of Policy

Gary Alan Fine

In pursuit of resources, most social movements attempt to recruit as many supporters as possible. Supporters translate into power, both financially and in providing bodies for collective action. Yet, adherents may have characteristics that can be used by opponents to typify and undercut the messages that the movement intends. Movements are thus faced with what Jasper (2004: 8) speaks of as an "extension dilemma," tied to whether a movement chooses to have open or restricted boundaries. A trade-off exists between size and control over its public face. The reputation of a movement can taint its goals.

How do movements respond when the identity of supporters is used to discredit their moral character? This is a problem for social movements that welcome disreputable participants, but it is also a problem for those that gain such adherents without intent—or against the wishes of the movement. To be sure, "disreputability" is not an objective characteristic, but a claim that those engaging in reputation work make in the hope that relevant audiences find it plausible and consistent with previously accepted beliefs.

I examine how movements are stigmatized and then cope with this stigma through strategies of organizational role distance. With few exceptions (Gamson 1997; Haines 1988; Mansbridge 1986; Snow 1979), social movement scholars have not addressed how the character of movement supporters can become a rhetorical resource to stigmatize a movement, or the strategies that attacked movements use to respond. Yet, reputational politics is a strategic way in which opponents can shape the efficacy of movements (Fine 2001; Turner and Killian 1987: 255–8; Hunt, Benford and Snow 1994: 197–9).[1]

In democratic societies, most movements, excepting those that are tied to identity politics, do not rigorously screen potential members. Even if a movement wished to do so, it often lacks the resources to control its boundaries.

---

1   The role of reputation work in the framing of social movements has been most clearly studied in the way in which deviant religious movements, such as the Hare Krishnas or Unification Church, are framed by their opponents (Bromley and Shupe Hr, 1979: chs 8 and 9; Rochford 1985: ch. 7). These religions, as insiders see matters, come to be defined as cults from the outside.

Perhaps the movement openly or secretly welcomes such supporters. Or, perhaps the movement sees the political background of such members as irrelevant, or perhaps such support is undesired but tight control is not possible. Whatever the motivation, openness leaves a movement vulnerable to charges that it is *the kind* of organization that is characterized by such disreputables (Goffman 1963).[2] The movement's character is besmirched by opponents who point to such individuals as emblematic; and, if the attacks are intense, targets must neutralize the stigma (Hewitt and Stokes 1975). As Turner and Killian (1987: 256; Snow 1979) claim, opponents suggest that the movement is not respectable because of its participants. In the worst case, such character attacks potentially delegitimate a movement, weakening its effectiveness, and, in the extreme, becoming a self-fulfilling prophecy, leading a movement to accept the illegitimate means that opponents suggest have always been present (Turner and Killian 1987: 257). But even if these attacks do not destroy the movement, they may shape it in persuading potential members that they would or would not feel comfortable as part of the group. Further, such discourse transforms debates about policy into debates about character.[3] Reputational politics may be more dramatic, engaging, and entertaining than dry and technical discussions of substance. The concrete form of personal politics trumps the abstract consideration of policy (Martin and Powers 1983).

The challenge of boundary maintenance in creating an organizational reputation is a generic problem for political organizations. The archetypal instance of the problem involves mid-century American "front" movements that were either organized or infiltrated by members of the Communist Party of America (Selznick 1952: 115). The presence of communists allowed opponents to frame such groups, referring to supporters who were not members of the party as "fellow travelers." Given the difficulty of judging internal motivation, ascertaining the legitimacy of these charges is complex, leading to counter-framing of such attacks by antagonists (Hunt, Benford, and Snow 1994: 197) as "witch-hunting" or "red-baiting," assailing the morality of the attackers (Morgan 2003; Powers 1998; Jenkins 1997).

Civil rights organizations were similarly criticized (Pinckney 1968: 82). Communists were active in the movement when few other whites would lend their support. Opponents of the civil rights movement alleged Communist infiltration (or "dominance") to question the movement's goals, claiming that the goals were a smokescreen for subversion. Many of the civil rights

---

2   Several types of members are undesirable for movements: (1) those whose views or affiliations are disreputable in the larger society; (2) those whose goals differ from the movement's primary goal (that is, those that wish to "hijack" the movement for their own ends); and (3) those who wish to use different tactics (militantly aggressive members in more decorous movements) (James Jasper, personal communication, 2004). I emphasize the first of these types.

3   For this reason ministers and other religious figures are so inviting as representatives of social movements.

movement's Northern supporters, sensitive to charges of McCarthyism, did not find such charges persuasive, however; and the attacks may have strengthened the movement as they weakened the power of red-baiting (McAdam 1982: 148). Even after the decline of concern with domestic communism, the presence of "black radicals" was used to question movement intentions (Haines 1988). In turn, opponents of a civil rights agenda were described as "racists," again transforming political disagreement into personal censure. In a similar vein, Mansbridge (1986: 112, 130) demonstrates how the opponents of the Equal Rights Amendment claimed that supporters were lesbians (women who "hate men, marriage and children"), in order to suggest the "true" goals of the amendment.

As in the struggle for civil rights and gender equity, movements often are constituted as coalitions of individuals or organizations (McAdam, Tarrow, and Tilly 2001). While movement coalitions may be internally contentious or even may divide and become rivalrous (Phelan 1997; Ryan 1989; Spelman 1988; Waite 2001), broadening the range of groups has strategic value because it provides spaces for disparate actors. Some groups emphasize reform, while others under the same movement umbrella demand structural changes. The presence of radical groups may legitimate more moderate organizations (Elsbach and Sutton 1992). Radical and moderate groups converge in creating public awareness and recognition, public definition, outside resource support, access to decision makers, and goal attainment.

Haines (1988: 1) speaks of a "radical flank effect," citing Malcolm X, who intimates of his own radicalism: "If white people realize what the alternative is, perhaps they'll be more willing to hear Dr King." Although Malcom X would not phrase it this way, he professed to be a shill for Dr King, asserting that radicals may make moderates seem acceptable. By shifting the boundary of political discourse through their own "character," radicals move moderate proponents of social change toward the political center. This constitutes a "positive radical flank effect." However, a "negative radical flank effect" can occur as well, as deviants can stigmatize a movement as illegitimate.

Radical flanks can be effective in a movement with both moderate and radical organizations. Yet sustaining an organization with both moderate and radical participants is difficult because of internal conflict and the use to which opponents can put the presence of radicals. Reputation work in creating group boundaries determines organizational legitimacy through the values of members (Fuller 2003; Cohen 2000), their identity (Gamson 1995; Taylor and Whittier 1992); and how the organization presents its character (Dutton and Dukerich 1991).

Organizations select membership criteria, either self-consciously or implicitly. In this they face two dilemmas: the "dirty hands dilemma" (Jasper 2004: 13), suggesting that some goals can be achieved only by unsavory methods, and the "universalism dilemma" (Jasper 2006; Mansbridge 1986: 182), raising the desirability of movement selectivity versus openness. The dirty hands dilemma presents the question of ends versus means, suggesting a trade-off between social justice and procedural ethics. The universalism dilemma, likewise reveals a tension between process and outcome. It asks whether movements need be democratic in process or if it is enough that a movement's goals are desirable (Polletta 2002). The battles in the 1940s over excluding "reds" from political organizations—e.g., labor unions (such as the Congress of Industrial Organizations) or political groups (such as Minnesota's Farmer-Labor Party)— reflect these dilemmas. Most ironic was the decision of the American Civil Liberties Union in 1940 to exclude communists from their board of directors to preserve their institutional legitimacy, despite their ideals (Powers 1998: 159). Likewise, as Gamson (1997) describes, the International Lesbian and Gay Association, an umbrella group, expelled the North America Man-Boy Love Association (NAMBLA) from affiliation after a wave of negative publicity. Whether because of affronts to the identity of core members or because of how the presence of controversial actors shapes their public reputation, organizations may establish barriers to participation.[4]

To explore the importance of boundary maintenance on movement reputation, I chose a historical case study, the America First Committee (AFC), the leading isolationist organization during the "Great Debate" of 1940–1941. During this time, Americans debated the proper response to the war in Europe, a war subsequently labeled World War II. Choosing a single case has advantages and limitations. Social movement research historically has depended heavily on the case study methodology (Snow and Trom 2002; Lofland 1996) in which an investigation of a single social movement develops sensitizing concepts and suggestive theories. While there has been debate over the boundaries of a case (see Ragin 1992; Orem, Feagin, and Sjoberg 1991), focusing on a particular social movement permits scholars to explore topics of movement analysis. The case study method provides an opening in which social processes can be examined in rich detail, providing a beginning for subsequent generalizations. To be sure, the benefits in observing particular group strategies may be offset by the absence of comparison that permits addressing the circumstances under which strategies and counter-strategies are employed or are effective. Case studies prove valuable as an impetus for further research, but by their singular focus demand additional research to test the hypotheses that a case study suggests.

In the case of the AFC, opponents used the presence of disreputable members such as "fascists" and "anti-Semites" to smear the organization, a tactic subsequently used in the late 1940s by conservatives against alleged communists (Haynes 1996: 54; Kauffman 1995: 19; Cole 1962: 192). I detail the response by

---

4   These barriers are analytically distinct from barriers that movements that specialize in identity politics place on membership to admit only those (women, gays and lesbians, African Americans) who belong to the group that the organization serves. While both kinds of organizations "exclude" members, the basis of exclusion can be based on a rejection of the stigmatized characteristics of the excluded or on a positive desire for a community based on common identity. Some organizations may choose to exclude members for both reasons and sometimes the justifications flow into each other.

the AFC to attacks on the character of their supporters and how they attempted to police the boundaries of their organization and preserve their reputation. The AFC hoped to be an umbrella organization for all those who believed that the United States should not become involved in the European war, trying to gain support from socialists, liberals and conservatives, business executives, and labor leaders. In this endeavor, they rejected being part of a movement coalition, believing that other non-intervention groups had unacceptable beliefs or disreputable members (Cole 1953). However, the AFC's role as the main movement organization created the presence of an internal radical flank. When such a flank could successfully be tied to central figures in the organization, such as Charles Lindbergh, the movement found attacks difficult to counter.

The presentation of the character of members and supporters is an important tool through which reputational entrepreneurs (Fine 1996) frame the moral stature of movements, thereby creating plausible lines of narrative (Davis 2002) that can overwhelm or marginalize their substantive policy concerns. While movement outcomes are inevitably overdetermined, in certain cases participants are made to represent the public face of the groups to which they belong, a form of organization identity work both from inside and outside (Dutton and Dukerich 1991; Hunt, Benford, and Snow 1994).[5] Identity shaping increases or decreases the likelihood that individuals will choose to join on the grounds that they are or are not "that kind" of person. The protection of movement character is the first stage to having a legitimate voice in public discourse. Organizations become judged as legitimate political actors and then find their views are treated as credible positions by the media (even if those views are attacked). As Turner and Killian (1987: 256) discuss in their analysis of "respectable movements," the proponents of social change gain a voice if they are defined as standing within the boundaries of legitimate political action. Of course, beliefs help define movements, and movements can change over time, but the reputation of leaders provides a central marker as to the character of the group. Thus reputation work is central to social movement analysis.

I describe three reputational strategies by which groups with universalistic membership criteria are attacked through their supporters and stigmatized as a whole. Opponents claim that (1) disreputable members are typical of participants (*deviant generalization*), (2) prominent disreputable supporters characterize the organization (*guilt by association*), and (3) the organization espouses the beliefs of such figures (*ideological uncovering*). These three strategies are not always clear-cut as the line between typicality and prominence is blurred; likewise, the presence of a prominent supporter and organizational support of his or her views can be conflated.

---

5   Movements vary in this, in part as a function of whether a movement selects its own leaders (as SCLC did with Martin Luther King) or whether the choice of leader is made by the media, more likely to choose someone who makes good copy by his or her extremism, as the case in the Vietnam anti-war movement (Gitlin 1980).

If an attacked group accepts the definition of these supporters as disreputable, it may engage in a set of counter-strategies, including denying that disreputables are representative and attempting to exclude them (*border control*), suggesting that opponents have similar reputational problems (*mirrored stigma*), and claiming that they are the victims of sabotage in which the disreputables are tools of their opponents (*subversive rivalry*). Often there is an overlap in strategies, as when denying that disreputables are typical is bolstered by a claim that they are undercover agents. Of course, some groups may embrace these stigmatized supporters, attempting to change the boundaries of who and what is legitimate (for instance, embracing those who advocate violent action or alternative forms of sexuality)—an issue that involves strategies distinct from the case at hand. My aim in explaining these various strategies is not to offer an exhaustive list of the possible strategies on which a movement can rely. Rather, I offer these strategies as representative of the ways in which the alleged character of supporters are tied to, or separated from, movement goals.

I treat claims and counter-claims with a degree of agnosticism. In terms of the creation of reputation, what matters is whether publics accept these claims, whatever their empirical validity. Claims are not randomly made or randomly accepted, however. A politics of plausibility is at work (Fine and Turner 2001), based on the obdurate reality of movement member-ship. As I describe, the standard historical reading (Cole 1953; Doenecke and Wilz 1991) of the America First Committee indicates that pro-Nazis were absent in the leadership of the organization and were a relatively small proportion of the local leadership and membership. With the presence of prominent political, business, and literary luminaries, coupled with an attempt to insure that pro-Nazis were excluded from membership, such a defense of the movement's character is surely correct. But to the extent that particular attacks or defenses could be bolstered by accusatory or exculpatory evidence, they gained in credibility.

Although it is not central to the theory, I accept the historical claims that the AFC had legitimate leadership directing an organization that sincerely believed in the values of non-intervention, rather than serving as a shill for Nazi ideology. Some members held beliefs that could be described as anti-Semitic (such as Charles Lindbergh), but that is different than hoping for a German military victory, advocating concentration camps, or tolerating genocide—beliefs accepted by very few. It is possible to separate the debate over the virtue of American non-intervention from attacks on the ideological character of members.[6]

---

6 Attacks on members can be personal—and separate from movement goals—or ideological: claiming that a member was an adulterer as opposed to claiming that a member is a Nazi sympathizer. When leaders are attacked, either strategy is possible. Delegitimating a leader for any reason (as happened with the Klan in the 1920s) can be sufficient to weaken a movement. However, when classes of members are attacked, typically personal attacks are less plausible.

Some organizations, because of the ambiguous nature of their goals and members who support these goals, are more vulnerable to personal attacks. It was easy—and plausible for some—to believe that those who supported policies that had the effect of bolstering Nazi strategy must have had sympathy with that strategy. Because of the apparent congruency of non-interventionist goals and Nazi goals, it was essential for the AFC to demonstrate the good character of members. To be sure, virtue is historically situated and contested. Some support for Lindbergh and for the AFC likely derived from the implication that an organization named America First pushed not only to stay out of war, but also to enshrine values of traditional American Protestant culture.

I rely on archival materials at the Hoover Presidential Library (HPL) in West Branch, Iowa, the repository of the papers of General Robert E. Wood, the chair of the AFC, and other leaders of the organization, as well as the papers of Wayne Cole, the historian whose work on the movement is considered authoritative. I examined the archives at the Hoover Institute (HI) at Stanford University, where the papers of the AFC are stored. In addition to archival data, I compiled all articles published about the America First Committee by the *New York Times, Washington Post,* and *Chicago Tribune*. The first two papers were interventionist, and the third was a leading voice of non-interventionists. I also read the secondary literature on the AFC, of which the work of Wayne Cole (1953, 1962) and Justus Doenecke (1979, 1990) are the most highly regarded. Many analysts reveal political perspectives, some admiring (Searles 2003, Buchanan 1999; Kauffman 1995) and others critical (Johnson 1944; Berlet and Lyons 2000; Wallace 2003). Several wartime treatises (Sayers and Kahn 1942; Carlson 1943) on the "Nazi underground" (in which the AFC was included) were propaganda designed to discredit Roosevelt's enemies.

The America First Committee

Today the America First Committee is recalled as a right-wing isolationist organization that, because of its unwillingness to confront Nazism, belongs in the dustbin of history. As historian Alan Brinkley (2004: 37) phrased it, the America First Committee was "much maligned in retrospect for its many reactionary arguments, for the anti-Semitism of some of its members, and most of all having taken a position discredited by history." The bombing of Pearl Harbor and what was learned from that attack contributed to this belief. Supporters distanced themselves while critics used the defunct organization to attack those who doubted America's global involvement.

After the Nazi non-aggression pact with the Soviet Union in August 1939, Hitler's invasion of Poland in September 1939, and the fall of France in June 1940, however, the situation was different. While most Americans supported Great Britain, hoped for an Allied victory, and believed that America should strengthen its national defense, there was no unanimity as to how America should support the allies. Most Americans opposed sending troops to Europe (Cole 1953: 52). Roosevelt and his 1940 Republican opponent Wendell Wilkie proclaimed their desire to keep the United States out of this European War, even as the situation became increasingly grim (Doenecke and Wilz 1991: 97). During 1939–1941, the US Congress, at the urging of the Roosevelt administration, altered American neutrality legislation, repealed the arms embargo, and passed a compulsory military service measure. Prior to Pearl Harbor, most interventionists supported "all-out aid short of war" (Cole 1953: 7). The Committee to Defend America by Aiding the Allies was established in May 1940 to promote this view.

Those who opposed American involvement in European struggles became increasingly concerned, feeling warfare was inevitable. Like other citizens, most non-interventionists supported the British (Cole 1953, 1962), but recalled World War I with its killing fields and inadequate peace, producing massive inflation and the rise of totalitarian states on the left and the right. While both Communists and Fascists opposed involvement, most non-interventionists, Democrats and Republicans, held consensual American values.

In the spring of 1940 a group of students at Yale Law School gathered to discuss what might be done to prevent American involvement in the war in Europe. In June 1940, the group, led by R. Douglas Stuart, son of the vice-president of Quaker Oats, decided to form an organization to advocate for a strong defense and non-interventionism. Early members included Gerald Ford and Kingman Brewster Jr (Kauffman 1995). Through meetings with Democratic, Republican, and Progressive politicians (such as Senators Burton Wheeler, Robert Taft, and Robert LaFollette), Stuart was directed to General (ret.) Robert E. Wood, chairman of the board of Sears Roebuck (Cole 1953: 12). In July 1940, Wood sent letters to leading American non-interventionists asking them to serve on the sponsoring committee of the new non-interventionist organization, the Emergency Committee to Defend America First (later shortened to the America First Committee or AFC). The establishment of the America First Committee to counter the CDAAA created the "Battle of the Committees" (Cole 1953: 7).

From its founding in the summer of 1940 until disbanding immediately after the attack on Pearl Harbor the AFC helped to shape the political debate, particularly in the Midwest. There, it had the strong support of the influential *Chicago Tribune*. At the height of its power the AFC had some 850,000 members and 430 local chapters (Cole 1953: 30). Although the AFC is considered in retrospect a conservative organization, some suggest—with exaggeration—that "it began as an optimistic, democratic movement of the left" (Brinkley 2004: 37). Although the organization was not much marked by pacifism and included more conservatives than liberals, the early AFC strove to create a diverse social movement, held together by broad principles of non-intervention and a strong national defense (Searles 2003; Cole 1953; Doenecke 1979: 232; Graham 1941). Many top leaders were businessmen and Republicans, but efforts were made to woo socialists such as Norman Thomas, Democrats such as Joseph Kennedy (whose son Jack was a member), and labor organizers such as John Lewis's daughter Kathryn. Because of publicity over their conservative members, retaining liberals, union members, Democrats, pacifists, Jews, and socialists was difficult (Wallace 2003: 202–3; Cole 1953: 71). Nevertheless, those members were welcomed. The AFC tried to recruit Jewish members and hire Jewish employees to demonstrate that they represented all segments of American life. Lessing Rosenwald, a business executive, and former Congresswoman Florence Kahn were elected to the AFC board, although both later resigned (Wallace 2003: 258; Searles 2003: 49), in part as a result of how the organization had been typified in the media.

Although the principles of the AFC changed slightly over eighteen months, they were succinctly stated in the *Washington Post* in January 1941:

1. The United States must build an impregnable defense for America.

2. No foreign power, or group of powers, can successfully attack a PREPARED America.

3. American democracy can be preserved only by keeping out of the European war.

4. The cash-and-carry[7] provisions of the existing Neutrality Act are essential to American peace and security. (January 5, 1941: B1)

The AFC headquarters were in Chicago, where General Robert Wood ran the organization with the help of R. Douglas Stuart Jr as national director and a small staff. Broad policy for the AFC was made by the board of directors, although Wood and Stuart largely had a free hand in determining these policies. In addition, the organization established a national committee, which it attempted to make as broad as possible, including Henry Ford (until he became too controversial), Charles Lindbergh, former Democrat Congresswoman Florence Kahn, and actress Lillian Gish. To engage the public, AFC headquarters approved a plan to form local chapters. This approach involved citizens in non-interventionist activity, but, given the absence of central control, it also caused many problems. While the national office attempted to maintain oversight through a few field representatives and to set policies through memos and a chapter manual, most local chapters were started by interested citizens, and each selected their own officers and developed their own programs. With 450 local chapters, it was not surprising that some of these officers and programs proved controversial, discrediting the national organization (Cole 1953: 17–34). The structure of the organization led to its vulnerability to attacks.

---

7   The cash-and-carry provision prevented the American government from loaning money to Great Britain to purchase armaments. To obtain weapons, the British had to pay for them.

Despite its activity, the AFC was not effective in preventing congressional passage of the foreign policy proposals of the Roosevelt administration. Still, its presence may have prevented the administration from pushing certain interventionist measures. During 1941 the Roosevelt administration successfully sponsored a series of measures to provide support for the allies including the Lend-Lease Act, extension of the draft, and revisions to the Neutrality Act. Supporters of the American First Committee were thwarted in preventing the passage of this interventionist legislation. Neither could they prevent themselves from being labeled isolationists, despite acceptance of international trade and diplomatic engagement. While there were many reasons for the AFC's legislative failures and for its inability to recruit and keep liberal non-interventionists, one contributing factor was the inability to shake opponents' claims that the organization served as a mouthpiece for the Axis.

The Problem of Boundaries

Despite a movement's preferences in characterizing its members and goals, critics often assert that members and goals are not how they are presented; the critics attempt to strip the movement's forms of identity management. Even if a movement starts with conventional participants and policies, if it has open borders, it can be "hijacked" by those who do not share the legitimate goals or tactics of the group, or so opponents claim.

Such a strategy made sense as an attack on the AFC. Because the AFC demanded the US remain neutral in the European war, it was likely that Americans who desired an Axis victory would support the AFC and for its critics to notice. Hitler and Goebbels praised the America First Committee (Johnson 1944: 165; Wallace 2003: 279), as did the German-American Bund, domestic fascists, anti-Semites, and communists, during the Nazi-Soviet Pact.

The organization diligently attempted to distance itself from disreputable individuals and groups, but such people joined the organization, contributed money, attended rallies, and occasionally led local AFC chapters (Cole 1953). Some supported the organization because they felt that keeping America out of war indirectly benefited causes they supported (such as an Axis victory). Others joined because they felt that the goals of the organizations matched their values (such as anti-Semitism). Still others were fully legitimate members but by their presence shaped the public face of the organization (bitterly anti-FDR Republicans).

As Jenkins (1997: 203) points out, the America First Committee needed to be seen as mainstream to influence political elites. Yet, it was not in the AFC's interest to alienate potential supporters on the right, such as followers of Father Charles Coughlin, the anti-Roosevelt, anti-Semitic radio broadcaster. The AFC had to walk a rhetorical tightrope, striving like many social movements to gather resources and support, while at the same time preserving its moral credibility.

The America First Committee operated with a radical flank that was both internal and external. Externally, other organizations also fought attempts to provide American support to the Allies. These groups ranged from the semi-legitimate No Foreign War Committee, to Father Coughlin's Social Justice movement, to protofascist groups such as the Silver Shirts, the German-American Bund, the Christian Front, and the Mother's Movement (McEnaney 1994). The existence of these groups had both positive and negative effects. Their presence made the AFC seem moderate and patriotic in comparison. Yet any link to these groups was used to suggest the "hidden purpose" behind the America First Committee.

The AFC faced an internal dilemma as well. Without extensive investigation, it could not ensure that disreputable individuals did not gain the veneer of legitimacy (Berlet and Lyons 2000: 147). Both communists (Morgan 2003: 204) and fascists (Wallace 2003: 279) encouraged supporters to join. As Leviero (1953: 364) notes, "the America First Committee was the magnet for all the forces, well-intentioned as well as evil, that swirled so passionately around the keep-out-of-war motive." A trade-off occurs in drawing boundaries, preserving credibility at the cost of resources and an ideology of universalism (Gamson 1997; Jasper 2004).

Reputational Accounts and the Strategy of Attack

When political groups discuss issues of consequence, it is not surprising that debate will be contentious. What is more surprising is that the debate often centers on issues of the moral stature of participants, rather than their policy. This is not to suggest that the substance is ignored, but it may be less important than the question of what kinds of people support the policy, as if the implications of the policy can be read through the identity of its proponents. The roughest debate takes individual actors as moral prototypes; character claims come to stand for movement ideas.[8] If opponents can suggest plausibly that movement actors are illegitimate, this stigma can rub off on their ideas. This is reflected in the attitude change literature that finds that the moral stature of the persuader influences the plausibility of the claims (Cialdini, Petty, and Cacioppo 1981).

---

8   This is dramatically evident in senatorial confirmation hearings in which the character of the nominee often serves as a stand-in for policy disputes. The confirmation of Clarence Thomas serves as the defining case in which his alleged sins were the wedge by which his opponents attempted to deny him a seat on the Supreme Court. Thomas, for his part, also attempted to make the hearing about his character, minimizing his political stance, claiming for instance that he had not really considered the debate on abortion policy.

Such a debate was evident in the case of the America First movement. Venomous smears aimed at the movement originated from established political figures and opposing groups (Fine and McDonnell 2007). Secretary of the Interior Harold Ickes, the Friends of Democracy's Leon Birkhead, artists such as playwright Robert Sherwood, and even President Roosevelt were unstinting as they impugned the patriotism of AFC members. The Roosevelt administration asked the FBI to investigate the America First Committee (see the Hoover Presidential Library file, hereinafter, HPL file) and leaked discrediting information (Haynes 1996: 28–9; MacDonnell 1995: 155; Fried 1999: 196). The charge that the AFC was "un-American" was leveled by leaders of the New York Chapter of the CDAAA (*New York Times*, February 23, 1941). Liberal Congressman Samuel Dickstein requested that the House Un-American Activities Committee inquire into the patriotism of the AFC (*Chicago Tribune*, September 3, 1941). The America First Committee was denied permission to use public venues in Miami, Philadelphia, and Atlanta, and at Brooklyn's Ebbets Field, because of its allegedly subversive character (*New York Times*, May 4, 1941; Jenkins 1997: 202; *Chicago Tribune*, June 14, 1941). As in later red-baiting incidents, individuals aligned with the AFC lost jobs or organizational positions because of their support for the non-interventionist organization[9] (*New York Times*, October 8, 1941; Fine and Shaw 2006).

Ardent interventionists used three strategies, as noted, to discredit the AFC through characterizing its supporters: deviant generalization, guilt by association, and ideological uncovering. In persuading potential non-interventionists not to join the AFC and marginalizing the policy demands of the organization, these strategies constitute "frame disalignment" (see Snow and Benford 1988) that situates the organization outside the bounds of legitimate political discourse. In deviant generalization, the organization's enemies point to disreputable members and claim that these individuals represented only the "tip of the iceberg," the presence of a large and dangerous radical flank. Guilt by association suggests that any linkage of a legitimate leader with a prominent disreputable individual, sometimes outside of the movement, calls that leader's sincerity into question. Finally, opponents engage in ideological uncovering, proclaiming the "true" beliefs of the movement, propounded by

---

9   Most dramatic was the case of actress Lillian Gish, "General Wood was in the office today and related a conversation he had just had with Miss Lillian Gish here in Chicago. Miss Gish stated that since her active association with the America First Committee, she has been 'black-listed' by movie studios in Hollywood and by the legitimate theater. She has been seeking employment in Hollywood during the past several weeks, and her agent has finally notified her that he can now obtain for her a movie contract which will bring her $65,000. This contract, however, has been offered upon the condition that she first resign from the America First Committee and cease all her activities on behalf of the Committee; and upon further condition that in resigning, she refrain from stating this reason for her resignation" (Cole files, "National Committee/ Lillian Gish," HPL).

deceptive supporters. The hidden intent of the group can be discerned from the alleged effects of its proposals, implying that the radical flank is using the movement as a cover for disguised ends. I extend the analysis of accounts (Scott and Lyman 1968) and disclaimers (Hewitt and Stokes 1975) by arguing that accounts interpret policy through character.

Deviant Generalization

Without doubt, the membership of the America First movement included some disreputable individuals. For instance, Mrs John H. Connell wrote to Senator Gerald Nye (Nye File, Box 2, HPL): "I am for the America First Committee 100% .... God Bless America without Jews and Communists."[10] When opponents bring such supporters to the public's attention, it undercuts the movement's character. Following deviance amplification theory (Wilkins 1965), these individuals' presence suggests others are present too, even in the absence of evidence.

Many attempts at generalization were based on claims about the audiences at America First rallies. Opponents routinely argued that the rallies were sponsored by disreputable elements. When the prominent New York Rabbi Stephen Wise warned Senator Nye that a meeting at which he was to speak was sponsored by anti-Semites and fascists, Nye responded, "Not in one of fifty or more speeches this spring on subject of keeping out of war have I failed to receive notice that the meeting was of anti-Semitic origin and sponsorship" (Telegram, May 21, 1941, Nye files, Box 1, HPL).

Accounts of America First meetings by their opponents asserted—and surely exaggerated—the proportion of disreputables in the audience. Interventionist columnists Joseph Alsop and Robert Kintner (*Washington Post*, May 28, 1941: 11) wrote: "Fair-minded persons in every city where [AFC public meetings] have been held have noted with distress the extremely high proportion of men and women with obvious Communist or Bundist affiliations among the honest pacifists and old-fashioned little-America advocates in attendance." The progressive New York newspaper *PM* reported that the meeting included "a liberal sprinkling of Nazis, Fascists, anti-Semites, crackpots and just people. The just people seemed out of place .... Audience reaction would have pleased Joe Goebbels, the Nazi propaganda minister" (Cole 1974: 148). Reports of booing of President Roosevelt, Nazi salutes, and assaults on protesters treated these isolated actions as emblematic. Most extreme was the leftist journalist John Roy Carlson (1943: 239–40), the author of the bestseller *Under Cover*, "the mob

---

10   There are several such letters. One letter suggests that Jews and communists are working together to build a tunnel from Siberia to Alaska in preparation for an armed take-over. This writer suggests that our military needs to stay home to keep order while claiming "I am not advocating the killing of Jews" (Nye File, Box 2, HPL). Some of these letters are surely from individuals with psychiatric illness, but the existence of the letters reveals that the AFC was a magnet for individuals with grievances, real or imagined.

howled 'patriotism' in a screaming crescendo of Nürnberg supernationalism ....
A wide assortment of thugs and sundry hooligans from the goon squads were
scatted throughout the crowd .... 'Who wants war?' the speaker asked, waiting
for a reply. 'The Jews are the war mongers,' the mob yelled back waving flags."
Of a later New York rally, City Council President Newbold Morris claimed
fancifully that at least 60 percent of those in attendance were pro-Nazi (*New
York Times*, May 25, 1941). Articles in major newspapers, tied to journalistic
standards of objectivity, suggested that these elements were minor features of
AFC rallies (Cole 1953: 125–6) and concrete evidence of large numbers of pro-
Nazis was absent. Still such attacks by which deviance is generalized allow those
without independent evidence to treat these claims as plausible assessments of
the character of movement supporters.

Guilt by Association

The frequently encountered belief that one can know others by the company
that they keep is well established both in popular belief and in sociological
analysis (Cloward and Ohlin 1960). A person who hangs out with gang members
is assumed to be one. An individual approved by communists is assumed to
have sympathy with those who cheer. The America First Committee faced this
vexatious problem. At various points, the organization was plagued by praise
from domestic rightists, as well as by unwanted support from Berlin.
    These attacks differ from merely magnifying the number of disreputables
in the membership or in an audience. Alleging that the AFC was supported by
fascist leaders was to imply that respected leaders were crypto-Nazis and that
the AFC was itself a fascist group (Powers 1998: 165; Chatwin 1968: 208).
    Ruth Searles (2003: 33), an AFC employee, suggests that this strategy
represented a conscious effort to "associate America First in the public mind
with organizations of questionable motives." Interventionists smeared the AFC
with the actions of William Dudley Pelley and his Silver Shirts, a profascist
group, modeled explicitly on Hitler's Brown Shirts, and with Joseph McWilliams
and his Christian Mobilizers. Although supporters of Pelley and McWilliams
were excluded (Cole 1953: 119), opponents used these extremists to suggest that
"where there's smoke, there's fire" (Smith 1973; Doenecke 1979: 237).
    The claimed linkage between the America First Committee and the Nazi
regime had even more rhetorical power. Opponents claimed that support from
German sources constituted a "a large part of the funds for supporting the
America First movement" (Cole 1953: 126). *The New Republic* (October 6,
1941: 422), calling for a congressional investigation of the AFC, asserted: "the
thing that is dangerous about America First is that it has become the effective
general staff of all the fascist, semifascist and protofascist elements in America
... it has connection with all the groups that are complaisant about a Hitler
victory or even welcome the prospect of it." When Nazis praised the American

First Committee, their remarks were trumpeted by opponents as exposing the organization (Cole 1953: 108).

The Roosevelt administration and its combative Secretary of the Interior Harold Ickes, led the attempt to link the America First Committee with Nazi leaders. As Doenecke and Wilz (1991: 154) report, "the administration used guilt-by-association tactics, doing all it could to impugn the motives of its opponents. Indeed, it deliberately linked patriotic opposition to Nazism." Ickes announced that "Nazi fellow travelers have their own organizations, probably the most important of which is the America 'next' committee .... The tie-up between the America 'next' committee and professional Fascists and anti-Semites is clear and scandalous" (*Washington Post*, April 14, 1941).

Ideological Uncovering

In impression management, motivations are hard to discern—a misty Goffmanian world of assertions and illusions. As a result, conspiratorial claims about disguised goals or hidden messages are plausible.[11] What is the true intent of apparently benign policy demands by seemingly legitimate figures? Were these isolationists sincere, deceived by the fascists (Sayers and Kahn 1942: 203), or were they concealing their true mission? Even without conscious intent, their ill-advised statements could be recognized as supporting disreputable foes. Claims makers did not have to demonstrate that their opponents truly had secret goals, but could imply that they were either knaves or fools, despite the seemingly justifiable beliefs. As a result, interventionists claimed that the non-interventionists' desire to stand apart from the struggle in Europe aided—intentionally or not—the Nazi cause. In that way, they were able to minimize the other movement goals of preserving the economy and saving American lives.

Such attacks were common, and were distinct from claims that pointed to a large proportion of members as disreputable or that asserted that leading figures had specific disreputable connections; they attempted to uncover the malign effects of plausible rhetoric. Ambassador to Great Britain Joseph Kennedy was called "in effect, the enemy of the American way of life." Democratic Montana Senator Burton Wheeler was labeled "a twentieth-century Benedict Arnold [who] stands now in the same position as quisling" (Chatwin 1968: 127, 213). Alexander Woolcott told his radio audience, "Whether [the isolationists] admit it or not, whether they like it or not, whether indeed that is any part of their purpose, they are working for Hitler. Have you any doubt—any doubt at all—that Hitler would have been glad to pay Lindbergh an immense amount— millions for the work he has done in the past year?" (Chatwin 1968: 210).

---

11   In some cases movements may wish to send different messages to their multiple audiences (King and Fine 2000; Jasper 2004: 10); here I focus on the claims that a hidden message is being sent to a disreputable audience.

Lindbergh proved a particularly inviting target for the opponents of the AFC. He was a figure of tremendous celebrity, both because of his transatlantic flight and the kidnapping of his son. During a visit to Germany in 1938 Lindbergh accepted the Service Cross of the German Eagle from Field Marshal Göring at the US Embassy (Berg 1998: 377–8). This honor—and Lindbergh's refusal to return the medal—was used by his enemies to suggest that he admired the Nazis. Why else would he keep the medal?

Lindbergh's prominence, coupled with his links to Germany and his illstated remarks, made him a focus of interventionist attacks. His enemies suggested that he secretly was aiding the Axis. In April 1941, Secretary of the Interior Harold Ickes attacked Lindbergh as "the No. 1 United States Nazi fellow traveler … every act of his and every word … proves that he wants Germany to win" (*Washington Post*, April 14, 1941: 24). Presidential speechwriter Robert Sherwood spoke of Lindbergh as one of Hitler's bootlickers and claimed that his Nazi flirtation was a "mental aberration" (Wallace 2003: 251). Even President Roosevelt described Lindbergh as a Nazi (Cole 1974: 128).

Lindbergh aided his enemies. At a September 1941 AFC rally in Des Moines, he suggested that "Jewish groups" were—along with the British and the Roosevelt administration—were pushing America to war (Doenecke 1990: 37-38). He also argued that Jews' "greatest danger to this country lies in their large ownership and influence in our motion pictures, our press, our radio, and our government," and speculated—or warned—that if war came, tolerance towards Jews might disappear (Doenecke 1990: 37–8). The speech provoked a firestorm of opposition and an opening for critics of the AFC to suggest that Lindbergh "truly believed" in Nazi ideology, despite his denials in the speech and elsewhere. The *San Francisco Chronicle* declared: "The voice is the voice of Lindbergh, but the words are the words of Hitler." Wendell Wilkie, the GOP candidate in 1940, described the speech as "the most un-American talk made in my time by any person of national reputation" (Cole 1953: 146–7).

Interior Secretary Harold Ickes attacked leaders of the AFC: "Isn't it about time that some of these fellows should wake up to the fact that they are playing Hitler's game; that they are either Hitler's conscious tools or dupes" and that "they are lending aid and comfort to the enemies of democracy—to those who would enslave them and theirs … our Nazi fellow travelers pretend as they may … [they] wish to see Hitler successful and victorious" (*Washington Post*, April 24, 1941).

The most extreme example of this strategy was the pamphlet distributed by the Friends of Democracy, which proclaimed: "The America First Committee: The Nazi Transmission Belt" (1941: 1).[12] The authors allege—somewhat disingenuously—that they "do not question the integrity of the leadership and membership of the America First Committee nor the sincerity of its

---

12   The pamphlet was so extreme that it was disavowed by several members of the Friends of Democracy board, but it still was distributed widely and well-publicized.

program. But we do seriously question the wisdom of the policy makers and the soundness of a policy which has the unqualified approval of Adolf Hitler, Benito Mussolini and their agents in the United States." They wrote: "The America First Committee, whether its members know it or not and whether they like it or not, is a Nazi front!" The pamphlet attempted to uncover the consequences of the seemingly legitimate-sounding beliefs of the AFC, suggesting that honorable leaders were aiding those that they alleged that they opposed. If a group supports profascist policies, the implication is that knowingly or not, it is pro-fascist itself. Since the choice was between being an insincere traitor and a naïve dupe, the non-interventionist was damned either way. In either case, his or her persona was at risk. These claims transformed policy disagreement into a form of reputational rivalry, just as was evident during the Red Scare. Or, in our current context, "patriotic" attacks are made on those who question the strategies and tactics of homeland security.

Preserving Morality through Reputational Defense

To preserve their public stature, groups under attack must publicly defend their own moral credibility. Not only must they fight for their ideas, but for their identity through organizational presentations to external audiences (Mitroff and Kilman 1984). When effective, attacks persuade audiences to doubt a target's legitimacy. Even a defense or denial can further publicize the charges. By causing a target to expend time and resources in responding, other movement actions are precluded. Thus, several movement defensive strategies involve a strong offense, condemning or blaming their opponents, hoping to inflict similar opportunity costs.

Attacked groups attempt to bolster their personal credibility and to prevent frame dis-alignment in the reputational battle. Among their strategies are border control, mirrored stigma, and subversive rivalry, each addressing the personalization of policy. First, movements can actively patrol their boundaries, hoping to blunt criticism by excluding problematic members or at least demonstrating that core members are sincere in distancing themselves from undesirables, excluding their radical flank. Second, they can assert that their opponents have the same problem, finding disreputables among their enemies. Finally, organizations can allege that these moral condemnations involve subversion or dirty tricks by organizational enemies, alleging that their opponents sponsor infiltration of disreputables. An organization diverts attacks to avoid moral culpability (Hewitt and Stokes 1975). Through border control, mirroring the attributed stigma, and counter-attacking against dirty tricks, institutional identity can be preserved.

Border Control

Although most organizations desire to maximize supporters and financial resources, organizations may reject fully open membership (Jasper 2004). Non-exclusive criteria for belonging may not serve an organization well in that the moral character of participants can be used to characterize the message.

The America First Committee sought, sincerely it appears, to exclude undesirables. In a letter to potential organizers, Robert Bliss, Director of Organization, emphasized: "There is no room in our program for Nazis, Fascists, Communists, Bundists, or any persons with leanings that place the interests of a foreign country ahead of those of the United States. We do not countenance anti-Semitism nor anti-administrative activity. We are nonpartisan." (Wood files, Boxes 26 and 25, HPL). The organization asked prominent citizens to provide references for potential leaders of local chapters: "Pertaining to our connection, actual or prospective, with the person named above, we desire information concerning his (or her) standing and integrity" (Wood files, Boxes 26 and 25, HPL). Contributors of over $100 were investigated, and some checks returned, including a check to the Oregon chapter for $20 from the German War Veterans, even though there was no evidence that the group was connected with the Bund (Searles 2003: 41). A check for $1.00 was returned because of comments about the president (Wayne Cole files, "Policy on Undesirables," HPL). Members of the German-American Bund and Father Coughlin's Social Justice movement were informed that they were not wanted (*New York Times*, May 9, 1941; Cole 1953: 135). Henry Ford was dropped from the board of directors because of his earlier anti-Semitic statements; and chapters were warned to avoid such prominent anti-Semites as Gerald L.K. Smith. The AFC asked both the House Un-American Activities Committee and the FBI for help in pruning its files (Searles 2003: 34–5). As the organization became more controversial, R. Douglas Stuart, Jr., the AFC national director, wrote chapter chairs: "It is not unlikely that certain elements which seek to promote racial and religious intolerance may mistakenly conclude that they will now be welcomed in the ranks of America First. Careful as we have been, we must now scrutinize each membership application with redoubled care" (September 23, 1941, Wood files, Box 25, HPL).

Beyond this intensive review of potential members and contributions, the behavior of members was policed. Chapters were told not to cosponsor events with other organizations without approval from national headquarters (memos from Robert L. Bliss, January 21, 1941, Wood files, Box 24, HPL). The visits of vehement AFC members to their congressmen created problems for the organization, and chapters were ordered to exert control: "There are instances wherein a people's lobby in Washington becomes more destructive than constructive .... During the extension of service bill unpleasant incidents arose and we must ask all chapters to exert a more rigid control upon whom they ask to represent them on a trip to Washington" (memo from M.R. Page Hufty, Wood files, Box 25, HPL; see also Mansbridge 1986: 146).

Headquarters were less able to control AFC rallies than chapter meetings or personal lobbying, allowing spectators to think of themselves, and be thought of by others, as part of the movement. At a May 23, 1941 rally American fascist Joseph McWilliams was derided from the stage by New York Chapter Chair John T. Flynn. Despite cries to "throw him out," McWilliams remained (*New York Times*, May 24, 1941: 6). At a Hollywood rally signs reading "Nazis, Fascists and Communists, please keep out" were posted at entrances. In Denver an open letter was printed in the program, "Dear Mr Nazi, Mr Communist, Mr Fascist: We have been falsely accused by 'commercial patriots' of association with your charlatan, demagogic organizations. This is to inform you that no invitation has been extended to any of you to attend this mass rally of patriotic Americans" (Cole files, "Policy on Undesirables," HPL). Activities outside the venue, even if unconnected with the rally, proved embarrassing and were used to characterize supporters: "There is one menace that ... is only apparent when a public meeting is under way. We refer to the practice of other organizations handing out literature to people attending America First rallies .... Tell these people that they are not wanted. Try to get police protection to avoid such an unfavorable impression as that made by some of the objectionable literature" (memo from Robert L. Bliss, February 11, 1941, Wood files, Box 25, HPL).[13]

Some boundaries cannot be so easily controlled, however. Certain organizationally central figures may have reputations that are solidified, which limits boundary work. Distancing is not possible because of how observers, both inside and outside of the movement, view these key figures. In other words, these figures have *sticky reputations*. The reputational association may be so tight that either embracing or distancing these figures undercuts organizational goals.

Lindbergh proved such a figure, particularly after his infamous Des Moines address in September 1941, described above. Lindbergh was simultaneously the greatest asset of the AFC and its greatest vulnerability—a flashpoint for admiration and controversy. Although he had been asked to lead the group, he declined, but addressed rallies. Through his close affiliation in the public mind, the AFC could not disassociate itself from Lindbergh's controversial remarks and persona. He personified the non-interventionist movement (Cole 1953; Wallace 2003).[14]

Because of Lindbergh's link to the AFC, the speech and its reception posed a painful problem. Several prominent supporters, such as the socialist Norman

---

13   Mansbridge (1986: 130–31) describes a similar dilemma for NOW in its demonstrations in support of the ERA. Because of the criticism received for being radical feminists, the organization decided not to permit lesbian and socialist banners at its demonstrations and instituted a dress code.

14   This remains the case today, as evident in Philip Roth's (2004) fictional, but compelling, *The Plot Against America*, describing the manifold destructive effects of the election of "President Lindbergh."

Thomas, refused to speak for the group; and others resigned from the national committee. Leaders of the AFC realized that reputation work was necessary as the organization was tarred as anti-Semitic. Yet, despite the torrent of criticism, Lindbergh was hugely popular and had become the AFC's public face. Most members supported Lindbergh (memo from Kenneth Nordine, n.d., AFC files, Box 1, HI archives). In addition, most of Lindbergh's associates believed, however much they regretted his remarks, that he was not personally anti-Semitic and that the charges were made strategically by their opponents. The national committee met a week after the speech and decided to stand by the flier, denying that either it or Lindbergh was anti-Semitic. Instead, the committee asserted that the interventionists had "injected the race issue" into the political debate.

By being unable to distance themselves from Lindbergh, now more persuasively portrayed as pro-fascist, the organization was placed on the defensive, pushing away otherwise supportive moderates. With such a central figure seen by many as disreputable, the organization could not credibly separate itself from other disreputables. Each reference to Lindbergh reminded the public of the "controversial" character of the organization, from which it never fully recovered. While Pearl Harbor ended the debate, interventionists had won the battle over character.

Through actions and talk, the AFC strived to purge and purify the organization. Yet, given both limits on organizational action and the porosity of movement boundaries in a democratic society, such attempts were imperfect. This returns us to Jasper's universalism dilemma. If all citizens should be given equal access to organizations, how can groups prevent these individuals from being used to characterize an organization by their opponents?

Mirrored Stigma

One way stigma is minimized is by arguing that failures apply to one's opponents as well—the "so are you!" strategy of childhood argumentation. The mirrored stigma strategy implies that the moral charges are justified, but that the target cannot be considered a moral derelict because a full cleansing of disreputables is impossible. While private organizations can and do establish barriers to participation, tight limits on membership are often viewed with suspicion in democratic societies.

Shortly after the shattering of the Nazi-Soviet Pact, Lindbergh, speaking before an AFC rally in San Francisco, twitted interventionists over their newfound allies:

> Two weeks ago, the interventionists were accusing the America First Committee of associating with the subversive influence of Communism. Now, I suppose it is our turn to ask whose meetings the Communists attend. The America First Committee has never accepted Communists or Fascists in its membership .... But the idealists

who have been shouting against the horrors of Nazi Germany are now ready to welcome Soviet Russia as an ally. They are ready to join with a nation whose record of cruelty, bloodshed, and barbarism is without parallel in modern history. (Wood files, Box 26, HPL)

Later the AFC responded pointedly to press coverage that Father Coughlin's book, *Social Justice*, was sold outside a New York rally, and that attendees cheered remarks critical of Great Britain:

On July 17, the Committee to Defend America and Fight for Freedom Inc. held a pro-war rally in the same hall presided over by Wendell L. Wilkie. Outside the meeting communists distributed copies of the Daily Worker, the New Masses and the latest statement of the Communist Party. Inside the hall communists revealed their presence by applauding references to the Soviet Union. Most of the speakers emphasized their hope that the peoples of the dictator countries would be freed, and mentioned specifically Germany, Italy and the conquered territories. But they failed to mention Stalin's people. (AFC Bulletin No. 432, July 22, 1941; Wood files, Box 25, HPL)

When the House Un-American Activities Committee decided to investigate both sides of the interventionist debate, General Wood wrote to Chairman Martin Dies, stating:

Now that the pro-war groups are urging an American alliance with communist Russia, they have the ardent and open support of the communists. I assure you that the America First committee will give its full cooperation to your committee in this investigation .... I trust the pro-war committees will take a similar attitude if, like America First, they have nothing to hide. (*Chicago Tribune*, November 14, 1941: 2)

In a society in which various forms of anti-Semitism were endemic (Novick 1999), few groups were free of its taint. While many rabid anti-Semites admired Hitler, others, more genteel, were interventionists. Gregory Mason, chair of the AFC's Stamford-Greenwich-Norwalk chapter, noted that the New Canaan Country Club was restricted, despite many interventionist members. He proposed a public debate on the topic: "Resolved: That the Committee to Defend American by Aiding the Allies is riddled with Anti-Semitism" (Gerald Nye files, Box 1, HPL). William Leonard, executive chairman of the Brooklyn chapter of the AFC, commented: "The membership and contributor's lists of the Warmongering committees throughout the United States is studded with the names of Klu [sic] Kluxers, Anti-Semites, and Anti-Christians; some of their very important financial support comes from business interests that refuse employment to Jews" (September 21, 1941; Nye files, Box 2, HPL).

To be sure, the fact that the AFC made such defensive claims did not mean that these assertions were accepted by opponents. Hitler's brutal anti-Semitism was qualitatively different from the genteel anti-Semitism of suburban America or even Southern racial violence. Still, the AFC recognized that if the extension dilemma of open membership could be linked to its rivals, it could plausibly claim that these disreputables were simply a cost of operating in a democratic culture.

Subversive Rivalry

A third strategy is to blame opponents for one's troubles. When faced with embarrassment, a movement can suggest that those who have the most to gain are behind the problem: disreputables are present not because of the organization's policy, but as a dirty trick of one's opponents. Agent provocateurs may act out a script written by an organization's enemies.

The New York chapter chair, John T. Flynn, was so incensed by the tactics of the interventionists that he wrote a thirty-eight-page document, "The Smear Offensive," detailing under-cover strategies to create disunity in the non-interventionist movement (Wood files, Box 5, HPL). Senator Nye remarked similarly, "The present effort looking to the breaking up of the united noninterventionist front which has been centered in the America First Committee is so obvious that one day the record will be extremely clear as respects the interventionists in this country for injecting anti-Semitism in this present controversy" (letter to Martin Loewenberg, September 29, 1941, Nye files, Box 2, HPL).

The AFC was concerned about organizational disruption, noting in one memo: "be sure that you know the people who are taking large amounts of your literature—or that they are actually doing good work with the pamphlets. We have found sometimes that it is a trick of those who are not friendly to our point of view to ask for quantities of literature which may or may not be distributed. We have actual evidence that some has been thrown away or destroyed" (bulletin no. 38, January 31, 1941, Wood files, Box 24, HPL).

The greatest concern was the activity of British agents. The British struggled to manipulate American public opinion and foreign policy, and while the effects of a handful of British agents should not be exaggerated, they did attempt to diminish the effectiveness of non-interventionist individuals and groups. Joseph Kennedy, FDR's non-interventionist ambassador to Great Britain, warned General Wood that "the other day in talking to an Englishman ... he told me that their friends in Washington were working very hard to have you give up the job in the America First Committee" (letter to Robert E. Wood, December 11, 1940; Wood files, Box 8, HPL). Ed Webster, New York chapter secretary, wrote to Senator Nye warning that "We have been bothered by certain individuals who have attempted to upset the movement by professing to be with us but then advocating measures that are so extreme that we might be called to account for subversive activities. One person in particular ... has come in to us and attempted to upset some of our members. It is a deliberate attempt, possibly by a British agency, to frame the America First Committee and discredit them" (October 23, 1941, Nye files, Box 1, HPL).

We now know that a top secret unit, British Security Coordination, run by legendary spy-master William Stephenson with Churchill's support and Roosevelt's informal approval, tried to discredit the non-interventionist movement and encourage American public opinion to support aid to Britain (MacDonnell 1995: 95; Wallace 2003: 283). Agents spread disinformation and rumor, manipulated opinion polls, and provided interventionist organizations and journalists with damaging information. Most dramatically, confirming AFC suspicions, the BSC printed false tickets to the America First meeting held at Madison Square Garden on October 30, 1941. The agency hoped to disrupt Charles Lindbergh's talk by placing interventionists in the audience; low attendance at the talk doomed the plan (MacDonnell 1995: 95).

However powerful the actions of agents provocateurs and dirty tricksters might have been *in fact*, the sociological issue is the belief in (and the claims of) subversion. Such public claims—legitimate or not—could excuse the organization for being unable to control or eradicate its radical flank. The targets suggest that they could never eliminate such disreputables as long as their opponents continued their subversive tactics. The troublemakers were not of the movement, but belonged to their opponents, besmirching *their* character.

The Personalization of Policy

The case of the AFC reveals the importance of organizational character and its rhetorical construction in the establishment of public reputation in a policy domain. In a democratic society most mass social movement organizations, unless they explicitly deal with issues of identity politics, are expected to have universalistic membership criteria and be open to all. This is the dilemma of extension (Jasper 2004), and is particularly true of social movements where size can translate into influence. Yet, organizations are known by their members, and in the case of contentious politics, counter-movement groups search for discrediting information that smudges the moral stature of their opponents. Negative reputations can matter in decreasing the appeal of the organization to potential members, increasing the difficulty of acquiring resources, or making problematic the relationship of the organization with gate-keepers and opinion leaders. The feasibility of policy prescriptions is insufficient, their proponents must be credible as well.

While I focus on the presence of anti-Semites and fascists in the non-interventionist movement, the same dilemma occurs elsewhere. The presence of communists in groups such as the American Civil Liberties Union, the CIO, and the NAACP gave opponents rhetorical ammunition to suggest that their claimed purposes hid their real goals. These groups were forced to demonstrate, often by exclusion, that their intent was pure. The problematic relationship of the North American Boy Love Association with gay activist groups reveals a similar problem (Gamson 1997), as does the struggle of VOCAL (Victims of Child Abuse Laws) to deny charges that abusers shape the organization's agenda (Fine 1995).

The depiction of movement supporters' character can reveal a pitched battle among reputational entrepreneurs, attempting to increase or disrupt affiliation. Competing rhetoric is not sufficient, however; the social location of the parties matters as well. Some groups—interventionists, for instance—have a tighter linkage to major media outlets than do their opponents.

Within the struggle, several strategies can shape reputations or contest these claims, linking a movement organization to its radical flank. Attackers can amplify the proportion of disreputables in an organization's membership, exaggerating the radical flank (*deviance generalization*), draw linkages between leaders and those with established negative reputations, connecting the organization to an external radical flank (*guilt by association*), and suggest that outcomes of preferred policy accords with the desires of disreputable groups, creating a hidden radical flank (*ideological uncovering*). In this way, attackers gain the better of the debate, provided that their attacks play into culturally accepted narratives, making the fears seem plausible. Whether or not the attacks are ultimately successful, they place targets on the defensive, stigmatizing them as controversial. This drains resources from the organization's instrumental goals, and limits its reach.

In response, reputational defenders focus on excluding controversial members or erasing their presence, minimizing this radical flank (*border control*); contending that opponents, too, have a radical flank (*mirrored stigma*); and alleging that the organization is falsely discredited by opponents, denying the presence of a radical flank (*subversive rivalry*). Being reactive, they may be less effective as reputational strategies than the original attacks. To the extent that those attacked as extreme are tied to the core of an organization's reputation (as in the case of Lindbergh), adequate distancing may prove impossible.

The political significance of organizational reputation extends beyond this case study. The dilemmas of the America First Committee have parallels in the attempts of other social movements to cope with reputational attacks. A similar strategy was evident in attacks on communist front organizations only a few years later, using controversial members to stand for the entire organization, and subsequently critics used the presence of supporters to attack civil rights, gender rights, anti-war, and anti-immigration movements, as well as citizen militias. This case study points to the need for more research on the conditions under which reputation work is found in social movements.

The extent of personalistic attacks aimed at a social movement is variable, both in their magnitude and amplitude, in their frequency and their effectiveness. The case of the AFC suggests that movements that address issues of national defense, because of their ties to the legitimate existence of the state or to the interests of rival states, may be more likely to provoke personalistic attacks as they lead to a questioning of the hidden motives of those who proclaim policy. A similar case involves groups that pushed for the recognition of the Chinese communists in the postwar era, where respected policy advocates were accused of having secret communist sympathies. We also find personalistic attacks targeted against those who opposed the Vietnam War and in attacks on those who call for a US pullout from Iraq.

A second hypothesis is that "hot" movements that deal with emotional issues and ideologies may produce reputational attacks, as disagreement is transformed into distaste. By questioning the core values of their opponents, activists shift to attacks on the moral character of their rivals. Here one can examine whether personalistic attacks are more evident when the debates are more politically central. Perhaps personalized attacks are selected as a rhetorical strategy when opponents feel that they must not lose the battle. It is a strategy of the desperate.

Further, we might hypothesize about the contrasting effects of a radical flank inside and outside an organization. As pointed out, the AFC was constituted as an umbrella organization, rather than a part of an organizational coalition. Perhaps an organizational coalition protects a movement from reputational attacks. It is difficult to maintain a radical flank and a moderate center within the same organization. The two contest for reputational dominance, at least in the public mind. Within a movement coalition, different groups can effectively serve as radicals and moderates, while not directly stigmatizing each other. Coalitions permit organizational differentiation. When both groups exist in the same organization, the radical flank can be used to typify the organization by opponents. These hypotheses, of course, are only suggested by a single case study. Yet, they point to the fruitfulness of examining how personalistic attacks shape movement credibility and imply strategies for response.

This study raises the question under which conditions are attacks and defenses most effective. Much depends on the stance and interests of the media as gatekeepers for public cognition and collective memory. Perhaps the support for the AFC in the Midwest resulted from characteristics of Midwesterners, their sense of history, or the economic and political interests of the region, but much also depended on the hegemony of the *Chicago Tribune*, a sharp contrast with the stance of the *New York Times*. National and regional media validate arguments and provide evidence for popular judgments. With the fragmenting of elite media through Internet communication a greater diversity of perspectives may be possible. Each citizen can gather alternate claims more easily.

Finally movements often rise—and fall—on the shoulders of celebrities. Being so linked to Charles Lindbergh had benefits and costs. Some movements embrace core figures, active or legendary—Martin Luther King, Malcolm X, Joe Hill, John Brown, Cindy Sheehan—whose public persona characterizes the movement. While movements can benefit from the prominence of these focal figures, if they become discredited, the movement suffers. And, as in the case of Charles Lindbergh, these figures can become ripe targets for opponents.

Social movement theory rightly addresses issues of resources, of ideologies, of networks, and of tactics, but social movements also depend upon reputation. Through the ability to establish a reputation movements and their opponents make *moral character* central to organizational credibility. We feel comfortable judging people, perhaps more so than their ideas. As a result, debates over war and peace become a battleground for reputational politics.

PART III
New Directions in Cultural Analysis

Chapter 5
Speech Act Theory and Protest Discourse: Normative Claims in the Communicative Repertoire of Three Russian Movements

Sveta Klimova

Although conflict is commonly viewed as confirmation of divisions within society, it is also an intensely normative affair. As Ralph H. Turner (1996: 1) observes, the actions of social movements "are invested with a strongly normative sense. Adherents of a social movement are concerned to correct an injustice, not merely a misfortune." Therefore, he recommends, "explaining the normative element and the process by which it develops must play an important part in any comprehensive theory" (ibid.). This chapter is informed by a similar understanding, which is a very different perspective from the one that dominates contemporary social movement research. The latter is shaped by the concepts of mobilization and confrontation. It is widely accepted that social movements set up organizations, recruit participants, craft messages, foster collective solidarities, gain publicity, and mount campaigns in order to confront an opponent. Whichever perspective we take—resource mobilization, political process, political opportunity, dynamics of contention—it is safe to say that most current social movement research is based on the assumption that parties engaged in conflict act instrumentally with respect to their goals and strategically towards each other. The outcome of such interaction depends ultimately on the balance of power within the relationship (see, for example, Tilly 1978; Tarrow 1994; McAdam, McCarthy and Zald 1996; McAdam, Tarrow and Tilly 2001).

The majority of research in the framing perspective also rides on this assumption. For a strategic interaction, protesters and their opponents spend a considerable amount of time talking to each other and to third parties. However, these communicative efforts are recast as attempts by protesters to mobilize useful meanings for instrumental purposes. These are known as frames. In the strategic-instrumental model, communication is conceived as a symbolic struggle where the alternative interpretations sponsored by movements and their opponents compete for the attention of the relevant audiences (see Snow et al. 1986; Snow and Benford 1992; Gamson 1992, 1995; Tarrow 1992;

Johnston 1995, 2006). Frames are tailored to discursive opportunities, or those features of the structural environment that determine the chances of frame to find resonance with the audiences (Koopmans 2004; Ferree 2003). In the final instance, it is the discursive opportunities combined with the framing strategies chosen by movement organizers that determine communicative success. By comparison, the content of communication appears insignificant as long as it "resonates." It is widely acknowledged that the content of frames is normative. Understandings about injustice are mobilized in various strategic contests. However, beyond the frames being useful, context-specific, and skilfully deployed by organizers we know little about the way such normative meanings achieve resonance.

The framing theory does not do justice to communication that constitutes the act of protest. Protest involves expressing concerns and voicing demands and a whole range of other such communicative actions that cannot be reduced to framing, which is essentially an activity of deploying meaning strategically. Take, for example, such a time-honored protest technique as petitioning authorities. It is part of the repertoire of contention, to use Tilly's term (1995). Petitioning is a communicative act insofar as it involves putting together and delivering a document for consideration of the authorities. But protesters may write a petition in order to communicate a demand or to seek protection from higher authorities. The action of demanding is distinct from the action of petitioning. The former is a communicative action insofar as it is accomplished by uttering words, i.e., by conveying a certain meaning. If petitioning is an act of engaging in a specific form of communication, demanding is the act of communicating a specific meaning. One is purely communication; the other is pure meaning. Of the two actions, petitioning is more easily identifiable as action: it has certain physical qualities: the text of the petition, the effort that goes into writing one. The act of demanding, on the other hand, is less visible as action, consisting entirely in the exchange of intelligible meaning.

The lack of "physical" attributes tends to make actions like demands invisible to protest scholars, who in their understanding of collective action rely on the image of struggle. However, language itself confirms the status of demands as action. A demand, for example, is used both as a noun and a verb. In his study of changing patterns of protest, Charles Tilly identified actions by the verbs used in press reports of protest events. Alongside verbs that describe physical actions, such as "assemble," attack," "fight" or "disperse," he lists verbs that describe *communicative* situations, such as "negotiate," "communicate," "deliberate," and "petition," as well as verbs that refer to actions accomplished *through* communication, for example, "decry," "request," "complain" or "demand." Although the distinctions are mine, they trace a gradual change from a more physical to a more communicative type of action, which coincides with the establishment of deliberative parliamentary politics and the rise of social movements. Tilly's focus prevents him from identifying a class of actions that are accomplished purely by conveying meaning. But it is this type of action, which acquires importance in deliberative politics, as Habermas (1984; 1987) argued, referring to it as communicative action.

This chapter offers a way of analyzing such communicative actions using an approach based on the speech act theory. Drawing on my research into three protest movements in Russia, I shall show that protesters perform a whole range of actions when engaging in public communication with their opponents and third parties. More importantly still, these actions can only be performed within a certain kind of relationship, namely, a relationship based on shared (or assumed to be shared) understandings of right and wrong. As I hope to demonstrate, injustice is more than a frame mobilized in strategic contests. Unlike framing scholars, I view protest as primarily a communicative event. Even the most militant of movements, whose preferred mode of relating to the adversary is violent confrontation, feel a need to engage in a public discourse, addressing audiences beyond the circle of their immediate supporters. As for routine forms of protest, such as complaints to authorities, they do not amount to much more than communication. The common denominator in different forms of protest is disagreement communicated. This chapter examines the various ways in which this is achieved. As I show in my analysis, when undertaking communicative actions protesters make normative claims defining the current situation as the negation of what ought to be and the other's expected response as the right course of action.

Speech Act Theory

Oxford philosopher John Austin first observed that in social rituals "the uttering of the sentence is, or is part of, the doing of an action, which ... would not *normally* be described as saying something" (Austin 1962: 5). He proceeds to draw a distinction between words that *do* things, or "performative utterances" (e.g., "We find the defendant guilty," "I promise to pay the bearer on demand," "You are fired"), and words that merely *say* things, or "constative utterances" (e.g., "the share prices have fallen"). The distinction proved short-lived. Having set out to explore the differences between the two types of utterances, he soon came to realize that, insofar as words form part of social situations, all utterances are performatives (1962: 138). In other words, reporting a fact is not unlike delivering a verdict. In both cases, by uttering words in social contexts the speaker seeks to secure social effects. The audiences adjust their actions by selling shares or looking for another employment or in other appropriate ways. Thus, every act of saying (or locution) contains an act of doing (illocution), which aims to achieve a social effect (perlocution). Insofar as it seeks to alter or maintain some aspect of social reality, the issuing of an utterance is a social act.

The social effect is not always guaranteed. A promise may fail to inspire confidence, an explanation can be rejected, a warning ignored, a verdict overturned. When the audiences fail to react in the manner expected of them, the speech act is lacking perlocutionary success. A statement misfires (or to use protest theory language, fails to resonate with the audience) because some of the conditions ensuring felicitous communication are missing (1962: 14–15). For example, sincerity is important in promises, entitlement to speak, in the delivery of verdicts. The felicity conditions, as he calls them, bear some resemblance to protest theory's discursive opportunities. In both cases, communication achieves intended effects when certain vaguely specified conditions are in place, or fails when they are not. Austin (1962: 120) attempts to deal with communicative failure by dissociating illocution from perlocution: while illocutionary acts succeed when social convention has been properly invoked, the same convention does not ensure perlocutionary success. In a similar vein, protest scholars invoke convention (in their case, frames prevalent in cultural contexts) to explain communicative success, while the concept of discursive opportunities takes care of variability of success with the same frames.

Insofar as sentences form part of social situations, the speaker is obliged to follow rules of extralinguistic nature. Perlocution is not a linguistic phenomenon at all: it succeeds or fails due in large part to the understandings the speaker shares with the audiences, which form the background of any communicative act. The lack of communicative success cannot be explained by opening a gap between illocution (the social action performed in the utterance) and perlocution (the effects it secures), which is then filled with discursive opportunities or felicity conditions. When the communicative force implicit in the statement proves impotent to achieve desired social effects, this does not mean that social convention has not been properly invoked, rather that the convention itself is problematic in such cases. Problems surface in disagreement when audiences fail to accept the utterance as right: a perlocutionary failure triggers the problem-solving process, a search for agreement. This is particularly applicable to situations of protest. When words expected to produce social effects fail, this may be because the audience's understanding of required felicity conditions does not match the speaker's. Yet, both act on their understandings of what they and the other agree upon.

The title of Austin's book *How to Do Things with Words* is somewhat misleading. The only things we can accomplish with words are *relations* among individuals. "Performative utterances" suggests unproblematic performance of social conventions. But this is not so in a great majority of cases where successful performance of communicative actions is often hampered by disagreement. As Habermas (1984: 38) argued, in rational communication validity claims are raised, criticized, and rejected or accepted by participants. Successful performance of speech acts depends on the strength of entitlement to the audience's agreement. It is not owing to felicitous conditions or favorable opportunities that communicative actions succeed. Neither concept can explain why such agreement is granted. Nor indeed why the speaker makes the statement in the first place. Only by locating communication within a relationship of shared understandings of right and wrong can we account for the communicative actions undertaken as well as for their effects.

Three Russian Movements

In my research I focus on three social movements in southern Russia. All occurred in the region of Saratov, where I conducted my research in the autumn and winter of 1995–1996. With the country in turbulence throughout the decade there was no shortage of movements to choose from. The three movements selected were by far the most prominent mobilizations in the region at the time, generating a great deal of controversy and attracting large support base. For comparative purposes they also offered a good range of issues to explore: ethnic politics, environmental risks, and economic grievances.

Anti-Autonomists

Special rights and privileges promised by the Empress Catherine the Great attracted large numbers of mostly German-speaking European settlers to the banks of the lower Volga in the second half of the eighteenth century. By 1897 Volga Germans, as they came to be known, formed 6.92 percent of the population in the Saratov region, which made them the largest ethnic minority group ahead of Ukrainians and Mordovians. In October 1918 Lenin signs a decree recognizing the self-proclaimed Autonomous Region of Volga Germans, or the Workers' Commune of Volga Germans,[1] which six years later gained the status of the Autonomous Republic.[2] In August 1941 with the German army advancing on the Eastern front, Volga Germans were accused of collaboration and forcibly deported to Siberia and Kazakhstan, where they lived under surveillance until 1955, when following the death of Stalin they began to regain their civil rights. In 1964 the treason charges were dropped, and ten years later permission to return to places of former residence was finally granted. After several failed campaigns to get the republic back in the 1960s and 1970s, the pro-autonomy movement began to bear fruit during the Perestroika. In 1989 a commission set up by the first competitively elected parliamentary body drafted proposals recommending restoration of the autonomous republic to complete the political rehabilitation of Volga Germans.

Shortly afterwards protests erupted in several rural districts of the former republic where German speakers now constituted less than 5 percent of the population compared with 66 percent according to the 1933 census. Around seven thousand people gathered in the central square of Krasnoarmeisk, former

---

1   *Trudovaya Kommuna Nemcev Povolzhia* (or *TKNP*).
2   *Avtonomnaya Sovetskaya Sotsialisticheskaya Respublika Nemcev Povolzhia* (or *ASSR NP*).

Balzer, on December 6, 1989 to take part in a rally, which was to be the beginning of a six-year long on-and-off campaign against the republic, which saw pickets in the centre of Moscow, roads blocked by protesters during Yeltsin's visit to the area, improvised local referenda with 80 percent turnout, more rallies and petitions organized by a network of district committees bearing names such as Defence, Unity, Fatherland, Russia. With demographic odds stacked against them and more ethnic Germans opting to emigrate to Germany the republican case gradually collapsed, but not without the help of the anti-autonomy movement, which, much to the dismay of the progressive press, took on the pro-autonomy government and won.

Chemical Safety Champions

When in January 1993 Russia among one hundred and fifty-seven states signed the international "Convention on the Prohibition of the Development, Production, Stockpiling and Use of Chemical Weapons and on their Destruction," its chemical arsenal was among the largest in the world at 40,000 metric tonnes of toxic agents stored at nine sites across the country. The Saratov region on the lower Volga hosted two of them. On the right bank of the Volga at the Shikhany army base and the affiliated research institute new chemical agents had been developed, tested, stored, and buried in the regime of military secrecy for a number of years disregarding the risks for the environment and the population of the nearby industrial town of Volsk. Across the river in the town of Gorny another army unit guarded a chemical warehouse where 1,200 tonnes of outdated first-generation chemical agents had been stored in dilapidated containers since 1943. Both towns were to play a major role in the chemical demilitarization programme: in Shikhany the destruction technologies were to be tested while full-scale destruction of chemical agents including those transported from other sites was to be conducted at a newly built facility in Gorny. Once the plans were announced the locals who for years had borne the risks of living in close proximity to chemical weapons were up in arms. With the tight schedule prescribed by the Convention, the absence of environmentally safe disposal technologies, the army in charge of the demilitarization process, and given the history of the government disregard for the safety of the population, the locals had reasons to be concerned.

In Shikhany the protests were led by a research scientist and a former army officer, both members of the Volsk local council, who faced legal prosecution for making public disclosures about the Russian chemical warfare programme. In 1993 they formed the "Union for Chemical Safety" campaigning for a more environmentally sound approach to chemical demilitarization. While one action after another was mounted in Volsk there was little sign of protest activity in Gorny where the locals had to be stirred into action by the Saratov-based environmental group with links to American and worldwide environmental organizations. On September 25, 1994 1,348 local residents signed a petition to the Ministry of Defence and the State Duma following a mass rally in the central square, as part of the international campaign day. A few months later a group of local activists formed the "Social-Ecological Movement of the Town of Gorny," joined by two hundred and forty-three members on its first day. With the government bound by requirements of the international convention to destroy the chemical stock by 2010 the movement could only expect smaller victories such as improving the environmental component of the demilitarization programme. In 2002 the chemical weapons destruction facility was officially unveiled in Gorny.

Deceived Depositors

When in 1995 a number of investment funds suddenly discontinued operations leaving around 425,000 of people in the Saratov region alone without their savings, journalists were quick to draw comparisons with the tale of Pinocchio who is persuaded by his enterprising friends to plant a few gold coins in his possession in the field of miracles located in the land of fools expecting a money tree to grow overnight. Such comparisons were not unjustified: the massive advertising campaign promising large and quick profits was hard to resist at a time when the annual inflation ran at 30–40 percent. This was not the first nor would it be the last time when lifetime savings have been wiped out overnight, this time, however, the blame did not rest entirely with the government. Hundreds of anxious customers began to gather outside their investment funds offices, and soon twenty-three initiative groups formed the Regional Committee for the Protection of Depositors and Investors' Rights. The first national congress of such regional committees was held in Moscow in June 1995. The Committee's activities ranged from registering all those who lost their savings to campaigning for compensation while working in close cooperation with the surviving financial ventures and the regional authorities. In the run-up to the election the government too was responsive to pressure given the scale of the problem. A number of presidential decrees were followed in May 1996 by the parliamentary bill on compensations to deceived depositors and investors.

Data Analysis

For each movement I collected texts generated in various communicative encounters some of which are characteristic of protest, such as meetings, conferences, rallies, pickets, and other public gatherings, while others are more mainstream such as interview opportunities, media appearances and publications. The main audiences of the texts are the authorities, the opponents, movement supporters and the wider public. Although in all the three cases there is a distinct group of actors who can be properly regarded as the opponent—the pro-autonomy movement, the military-industrial complex, and the fraudulent financial companies—the authorities too are included in the category having taken the opponent's side. Of the three movements only anti-autonomists, however, address communication to the opponent as a distinct group. Among the authors of the documents are movement leaders and activists, ordinary members of movement organizations, and supporters among local residents and the general public. The genres of texts include rally resolutions, petitions to authorities, speeches at public gatherings, letters to the press from movement supporters, media interviews with the leaders, press articles authored by leaders and activists, leaflets, posters, booklets and newsletters published by the movements. Table 5.1 sums up the numbers of different categories of documents analyzed.

Some of the documents come from personal archives of movement leaders who kindly made them available to me; others were obtained by searching the periodicals collections in local libraries. Interviews with movement leaders provided additional information about the three protests, but the transcripts were excluded from the sample of documents analyzed since the communicative situation was not typical of protest especially in Russia at the time (indeed some movement leaders had difficulty understanding my role as a researcher).

I analyzed all documents I could obtain for each movement, and am, therefore, fairly confident of the representativeness of my sample—although I cannot guarantee it. A much smaller size of the sample for the third case is to be explained by the fact that the movement had not been long in existence by the time the research was conducted, and partly because it did not generate as much publicity as the other two.

My analytical procedure involves compressing texts into formalized statements representing speech acts. In the process of identification of speech acts certain minor details of the actual sentences can be discarded provided they do not alter the illocutionary point conveyed. Several grammatical sentences can add up to making one illocutionary point, i.e., constitute one such statement. Therefore the original text emerges considerably smaller, as if compressed, from this procedure. Naming the speech act performed in the statement, like any interpretation, relies more on skill, which improves with practice, than on any set of rules. In this respect it is not dissimilar to frame analysis. Often only by encountering the same statement again and again one begins to see the illocutionary point clearly.

My analysis identifies several types of communicative actions, which I call the communicative repertoire of protest. But let us be clear on this label: I am not referring to an arsenal of strategic resources but rather ways of communicating normative disagreement. My analysis reveals a side to protest communication that has been obscured and overshadowed by the explosion of interest in strategic responses to political opportunities, mechanisms of political contention, and—especially regarding the analysis of protest discourse—tactical framing by social movement groups and organizations to maximize resonance of the movement's message. The communicative actions I identify do not fit

Table 5.1 Protest texts by type of document

Classes of documents	Number of documents		
	Anti-autonomy movement	*Chemical safety movement*	*Depositors' rights movement*
By type of audience			
1 Authorities: petitions, rally resolutions, letters	10	9	10
2 Supporters: rally speeches, newsletters, leaflets, brochures	59	36	3
3 Wider public: media interviews, articles, press releases, letters to the press	8	18	3
4 Opponents: speeches, letters, appeals	5	0	0
By author			
1 Participants in rallies, conferences	7	5	1
2 Movement organizations, members	35	41	14
3 Local residents, members of the public	24	9	0
4 Councillors, deputies, politicians	11	4	1
5 Experts (e.g., scientists, academics)	5	4	0
By document genre			
1 Resolutions, decisions, declarations	5	5	1
2 Appeals, petitions, proposals	8	6	4
3 Speeches, talks	31	6	1
4 Brochures, leaflets, posters	5	3	2
5 Letters (to authorities, opponents, press)	6	3	5
6 Articles in the press	6	22	2
7 Articles in movement newsletters	21	12	0
8 Media interviews	0	6	1
Total number analyzed	82	63	16

easily into the mobilization mould: rather than mobilizing symbolic resources the Russian protesters are acting within a moral relationship.

Accusations: Naming the Offence

One of the most common speech acts was a description of an action, usually taking the form, "Someone is doing/has done/is about to do something."[3] But to understand what the speaker is trying to accomplish in this statement, we have to consider the statement in the context of its communicative situation. The context would tell us that the subject of the putative action is the opponent (or the authorities taking the opponent's side), while a closer look at the opponent's actions would reveal that the statement describes a very particular act of rule-breaking. What the speaker is saying effectively is, "The opponent is doing / has done / is about to do something wrong." Now there can be no mistake about the social action being performed in the statement. The opponent is being accused of violating the rules they should have followed.[4] Here are representative quotes from the three movements that demonstrate this.

> The German nationalists from the Revival Society, encouraged and financed by Germany taking advantage of the political and economic instability [in Russia], want to turn several districts of the Saratov region into a German republic on the Volga. So states the programme adopted at their first emergency congress. (From an article by member of the Protection committee in Stepnoye district, published in the committee's newsletter in November 1991)

> The politicians and the military, who take decisions behind our backs signing contracts under the pretext of the Convention [on Chemical Weapons], in effect manipulate our lives in their own parochial interests, violating our rights to life and

---

3   In Searle's taxonomy (1979) it would belong in the class of assertives committing the speaker to the truth of the proposition: "[It is true that] A is doing/has done/is about to do X."

4   It is hard to overestimate the importance of the communicative situation for identifying the illocutionary point conveyed in the statement. Reporting an event may also involve making statements describing others' actions, as in "the delegation has visited the designated site today." Praising, likewise, involves naming the other's actions: 'the local authorities have shown understanding of our problems." But in neither of these cases a wrongdoing is described. Some statements, however, bear a closer resemblance to accusations with regards to naming misconduct, but the latter is less serious and regret rather indignation is expressed in the statement. I have classified such statements as reproaches, or criticisms. For example, the deceived investors in their correspondence with the local authorities reproach (or criticize) the latter for failing to offer greater support to the committee than the latter expect.

health guaranteed by the Constitution. (From a petition to the State Duma from residents of the town of Gorny, September 1994)

The local organs of government, including the administration, courts of law, the procurator's office, the federal intelligence service and the ministry of internal affairs, the department of tax police, tax inspections, other auditing agencies, the anti-monopoly committee and others subsisting on taxpayers' money, do not fulfil their functions of protecting the citizens' rights, are not capable of enforcing order and bringing to justice the swindlers and frauds [who caused the loss of savings]. (From public rally resolution, Saratov, October 1995)

These statements resemble Searle's (1979: viii) example of an indirect request: "Sir, you are standing on my foot." Here too the speaker attempts to secure a change by naming the act of wrongdoing. In movement accusations as in Searle's example, prior agreement on the rules that ought to be observed is presumed, which makes it possible to communicate a normative expectation implicitly simply by naming the actions. Yet a comparison with Searle's example is instructive in terms of the assumptions that the speaker makes in one case and fails to make in the other. The statement about the foot works as a request because the speaker is assuming rightly that the offender is (a) committed to the rules invoked, and (b) not realizing he is breaking the rules. If neither had been the case, the response may well have been, "Is there a problem?" In the case of the misplaced foot, the simple statement works as a directive, while in the case of protest, a similar type of statement only succeeds as an accusation.

Table 5.2   Distribution of speech acts across movements

Speech acts	Anti-autonomy movement	Chemical safety movement	Depositors' rights movement
Accusations	147	190	13
Demands	18	45	15
Proposals	6	18	34
Help pleas	0	2	0
Declarations	3	0	0
Prescriptions[a]	48 (+10)	46 (+11)	8 (+2)
Protestations	34	7	1
Exhortations	2	0	4
Threats	2	1	2
Warnings	18	1	7

a   This includes "ought to protest" statements, whose numbers are given in brackets.

In the case of the three protest movements, numerous accusations have been made against the opponent. I have counted one hundred and ninety for the chemical safety movement and one hundred and forty-seven for anti-autonomists (see Table 5.2).[5] The list of charges is equally extensive ranging from failure to observe the norms of democratic governance by not consulting the public on chemical disarmament to conspiring to prolong the chemical arms race, and from undermining stability of the country in restoring the former republic to a morally reprehensible act of breaking a promise in doing so. However, though normative expectations have been conveyed, the accusations brought against the opponent are not as effective in terms of securing change. When protesters make accusations they expect the other to be unwilling to comply and ready to challenge the charges brought against them. Unfortunately for protesters, the wrongdoing is not clear-cut and indisputable as it is in the case of a wrongly placed foot. This does not stop them making accusations. In fact the uncertainty of the outcome may explain why the charges are so numerous. Whenever there are reasons to doubt the opponent's normative commitments or the rules themselves appear to be ambiguous, the speaker faces a more difficult task of demonstrating that an offence has indeed been committed.

If we look at the actions incriminated to the opponent and authorities, it is more common to find protesters describing consequences and implications of the other's actions rather than just naming the action—as in stepping on someone's foot. Instead of "they are planning to build a destruction facility for chemical weapons in the town," they are more likely to say, "they are putting the lives of our children at risk" or "they disregard the local opinion" or even employ a metaphor as in "they are conducting war against their own people." These statements are naming actions that are more unequivocally wrong in a moral sense compared with taking steps to destroy the stock of chemical weapons, which far from being wrong have the authority of the international community behind them. In the case of chemical weapons, a whole range of accusations, for example, elaborate the risk element of the programme adopted by the government. The help of experts (scientists) is enlisted to argue the case that the existing programme is unsafe. Sometimes the experts, their credentials established, simply state that "there are no safe destruction technologies presently available either in Russia or the USA to eliminate the environmental damage," sometimes they cite scientific evidence to substantiate the risk claim. Some of the accusations aim to expose the hidden dangers that have not been acknowledged by the government or the military, such as the secret dumping of chemical waste over the years. Anti-autonomists too rely on experts (academic historians in this case) to bring historical evidence to make the case for illegality

---

5   In the case of the deceived investors, accusations do not play a comparable role being outnumbered by demands, for example, which does not happen in other cases. Perhaps this is due to the movement not feeling the need to present their case to the public to the same extent that the other two movements do.

and political expediency of the Soviet government's decision to create the republic in the first place, or to uncover cases of violation of the rights of ethnic minorities in the former republic.[6]

While the charges brought against the opponents are serious they are not indisputable. The issues that gave rise to the three protest movements—the safe destruction of chemical weapons, the justice of reinstating the republic of Volga Germans, the hardships caused by massive losses of savings—mark out contentious normative territories where right and wrong are not as firmly fixed perhaps as the case may be with rules of polite conduct but remain as binding as if they were. It is not accidental that most of the rules which allegedly have been breached are invoked by naming the actions. The audiences are expected to recognize the act of wrongdoing. Moreover, most of the texts containing accusations, even those addressed to the opponent are also aimed at the wider public. Thus, petitions to authorities are reprinted in newsletters and local newspapers. The role of the third party in determining the fact of offence is crucial. One could say that it is the public that needs to be convinced in the final instance that someone is standing on someone else's foot and that such an act constitutes an offence against rules of acceptable conduct, for accusations to have their effect.

The act of accusation would be neither possible nor meaningful outside a normative relationship, in which the public plays an important mediating role. By claiming that the opponent has acted wrongly protesters also reaffirm the fact of prior agreement at the very moment when this agreement is being tested. Apart from the normative expectations no other reasons are offered to the opponent to change their course of action. Moreover, while protesters have reasons to doubt the opponent's commitment to rules they so easily disregard, they are not prepared to revise their normative expectations. The debate does

---

6   It is relatively rare to find protesters citing articles of law or the Russian constitution, though it does happen, to establish the fact of offence, as in this statement: "the aforementioned decrees and acts contravene Article 3 of the Constitution of the Russian Federation, which proclaims the people the sole source of sovereignty, Articles 2 and 4 of the Declaration of Human and Citizen Rights of the Russian Federation, as well as Article 74 of the Penal Code, which makes criminal any discrimination direct or indirect on the grounds of ethnicity" (from resolution of the regional conference of the anti-autonomy movement, November 1995). Most of the time, however, the rules protesters appeal to remain implicit in the naming of the opponents' actions. This is hardly surprising: had protesters been able to refer to specific articles of specific laws a legal action would have been more likely than protest. When legal norms do get invoked the references tend to remain general: to rights and principles rather than acts and articles, as in "from the point of view of international law the republic [of Volga Germans] formed in the early 1920s did not have the necessary legal basis," or "the local authorities funded by the taxpayers have failed to protect the constitutional rights of citizens [who lost their savings]." In the case of chemical weapons, the legislation itself is criticized for failing to ensure the safety of the population.

not proceed according to the rational formula envisaged by Habermas (1984, 1987). Instead of suspending problematic normative understandings until both sides can rationally achieve a new understanding, protesters continue to insist that the opponent is doing wrong. As if the normative expectations themselves need defending above anything else, having been threatened by the opponent's misconduct. What seems to be at stake in this debate is not so much the opponent's actions as the normative status of those actions.[7] By raising accusations protesters aim to undermine the opponent's normative position. Accusations represent a form of normative reasoning in the discourse of protest. We might call this reframing with strategic intent. Yet insofar as the pressure brought to bear upon the opponent is achieved by making explicit the act of offence in the eyes of the public, we cannot truly say that one frame has been dislodged by another in the course of a power struggle.

Explicit Expectations: Demands, Proposals and Help Pleas

Accusations communicate an expectation to the opponent without making it explicit. It falls to other statements to articulate the expectation. One such statement is a demand. Of all communicative actions it is perhaps most commonly associated with protest. Like delivering petitions, forming picket lines, and marching in great numbers, demand making belongs to the ritualized core of protest actions. Demands belong in that class of statements in which the illocutionary act is performed by the main verb in the first person, singular or plural: "We demand that you/opponent/authorities do X."[8] For example:

> Considering the current situation, we demand that the plans to create a German sovereignty (*gosudarstvennost*) on the Volga be abandoned by all levels [of government], since we believe the decision to create the national-territorial entity of ethnic Germans in 1918 was forced by political and military pressure from Germany and therefore illegitimate from the point of view of international law. (From resolution of 2nd conference of representatives of workers' collectives of seven districts of the Saratov region and two districts of the Volgograd region, November 1990)

> Expressing solidarity with residents of other regions put in danger by the proximity of sites of the military-chemical complex, and understanding the importance of

---

7   Habermas (1984, 1987) does not allocate any meaningful role to the audience in his model of rational debate. Insofar as the debate has to be inclusive to be considered rational it excludes the very notion of the audience. By contrast, the role of third parties may explain the apparently irrational quality of communication in real-life conflicts with both sides talking past each other from their respective normative positions.

8   Speech act theorists call such statements "explicit performatives" (Searle 2002: 158).

destroying this most barbaric weapon, the chemical weapons, while demanding that ecological safety measures be strictly observed, the meeting decides the following: to demand a ban on all work on the destruction of chemical weapons until legislation is passed to regulate all aspects of the problem, with obligatory discussion of draft bills in all concerned regions. (From decision by residents of the towns of Volsk and Shikhany taken at a public rally on the problems of the destruction of chemical weapons, September 1995).

We, participants in the rally, on behalf of all the deceived depositors in Saratov and region, demand that at the federal level, the President, B.N. Yeltsin, and the head of government, V.S. Chernomyrdin, admit responsibility for the financial and legal chaos (*bespredel*) in the country and take urgent measures (before the general elections) to resolve the crisis involving the deceived depositors and investors. (From rally resolution, Saratov, October 1995)

Insofar as the point is to get someone to do something, demands are directives like commands and requests. Like other directives, demands communicate an entitlement the opponent is supposed to recognize without the speaker having to make it explicit. In the majority of cases the right is asserted implicitly, but occasionally protesters make it explicit by adding justification as in this example: "We demand that a referendum be held on the destruction of chemical weapons in the district; local residents are entitled to choose the their own and their children's future."[9] The speaker raises a validity claim rather than merely using linguistic resources in a strategic fashion. We demand what we believe is due to us or rather what is overdue. An employee requests a pay rise, but the union demands it. We ask for favors but demand what is our right. Demand presupposes shared understandings of right and wrong but suggests also a corrective effort. The other is asked to honor the obligation they have neglected. One can detect a hint of frustration mixed with rightful indignation at the opponent's failure to follow the right course of action in the act of demanding.

Demands are predominantly found in texts addressed to the authorities, such as petitions (*obrashchenie*) and resolutions of public meetings (*rezolutsia, reshenie*). Thus, of eighteen demand statements in the anti-autonomists' discourse fifteen (83 percent) occur in these two kinds of documents. The figures for the chemical safety champions and deceived investors are respectively: forty-two out of forty-five (93 percent), and thirteen out of fifteen (87 percent). By contrast, texts addressed to the opponents as a distinct group—found only in the case of the anti-autonomy movement—do not contain a single demand. Instead, protesters formulate their expectations in the form of appeals to the opponents' good will urging them to make the right choice. As in the following statement: "We appeal to the good sense of your people, that you realistically

---

9 This statement concludes a petition to the Russian President and the head of Volsk Town Administration signed by sixty-three medical professionals.

evaluate the situation around the German republic on the Volga, that you do not succumb to propaganda by the extremists' (from an appeal to Soviet Germans, November 1990). A rightful expectation, it seems, can take many forms. Facing the opposition directly protesters do not find themselves entitled to demand as they do when they speak to the authorities of all levels. Perhaps the absence of demands suggests that protesters recognize the opponent's right to pursue their cause by similar means. Perhaps demands are only appropriate in communication with the government claiming to represent the people, someone we can call to account.[10] We demand of actors who have failed in their duty towards us.

Demands draw their authority from collective decision making by members of the public. The collective voice issuing demand in the overwhelming majority of cases is neither an existing collectivity (e.g., local residents) nor a movement organization. Instead, most demands are made by what can be called emergent protest collectivities such as public rallies, conference of workers' collectives, meetings of local residents, which seem to authorize the demands: 78 percent (fourteen out of eighteen) for anti-autonomists, 91 percent (forty-one out of forty-five) for chemical safety champions, and 87 percent (thirteen out of fifteen) for deceived depositors. The self-identified subject addressing demands to the opponent is "we, participants in the rally/conference/meeting (*meeting/ konferentsia/sobranie*)." In this sense, a public gathering can be seen as a means of collective decision making, its climax being the passing of the resolution and/ or petition, which are read out and voted for before being sent to the designated authorities. Sometimes protesters actually say this: "The meeting takes a decision to demand." Endorsed by participants in a public gathering, demands express the collective will of the relevant public vested with authority in its own right. The ritual of decision making makes this will manifest and, through collective authorization, increases the weight of the demands.

Proposals

As Table 5.2 shows, deceived depositors prefer to formulate their expectations to the authorities as proposals. Like demands, proposals convey the illocutionary point in the main verb: "We propose that you/opponent/authorities do X." For example, "The Committee puts forward a proposal to the aforementioned organizations to draw up and carry out a joint economic program on mutually beneficial terms to find solution to the crisis of insolvency involving lost deposits."[11] Unlike demands, proposals do not imply an obligation to act.

---

10   Before 1989 when the first competitive elections were held in the Soviet Union, demands in the discourse of opposition were as unthinkable as the institution of political opposition itself.

11   From an appeal to heads of state and commercial banks and the Economics Committee of the Regional Administration by the deceived investors movement, October 1995.

Rather, the speaker appeals to the opponent's interests, though rarely explicitly as in the above example. As with the moral basis of demands and accusations, the consequences of right versus wrong actions usually remain implicit. Also, whereas demands may antagonize the opponent by suggesting a wrongdoing to be corrected, proposals articulate what the opponent can do to resolve the conflict, and are thereby less oppositional. It is as if proposals are intended to show the other how to achieve what ought to happen. While demands remain firmly in the normative domain of entitlement, proposals enter the realm of what is possible and practical.

A true proposal presupposes a unity, however fragile, of interests. Insofar as the actions expected of the opponent entail benefits for both sides, proposals are essentially offers of cooperation. Of the three movements, the aggrieved bank customers take the most explicitly cooperative stance: not only had they put forward an economic program envisaging specific measures involving tax incentives, asset transfers and government-issued bonds to resolve the crisis, they also had drawn up an equally detail draft of a bill, "On the Protection of Rights of Depositors." Theirs is also protest that found the most positive response among the authorities with the president issuing a number of decrees promising to tighten financial controls and investigate possibilities of compensating the losses. In the case of the anti-autonomy movement cooperation takes the form of compromise. One can find several mentions in the movement's discourse that protesters are prepared to concede a national-cultural autonomy (*kulturno-natsionalnaya avtonomia*) for Volga Germans, as well as for other ethnic groups, as an alternative to the republic,[12] but this suggestion was eventually abandoned. In the first case, cooperation takes the form of offering the opponent a helping hand, while in the other protesters make a concession without being too persistent.

Many proposals, however, are not clearly differentiated from demands. The chemical safety protesters especially seem to be in two minds about the kind of pressure they are exercising. The content of proposals and demands is nearly identical in their case: fourteen out of eighteen (78 per cent) replicate demands almost to a letter. Likewise, the anti-autonomy movement demands and proposes that the government abandon plans to restore the republic, finding it appropriate to add to the proposal, "in order to stabilize interethnic relations in the region," which can be read as an incentive spelling out mutual benefits of the prescribed course of action. The incentive, however, follows a normative justification, "considering that re-establishing the republic contravenes international and Russian law," which can also be found accompanying a

---

12   Without granting political sovereignty to an ethnic group residing on a specific territory, the cultural autonomy recognizes their right to preserve and promote ethnic identity as a set of linguistic, religious and other cultural practices. With all autonomous formations territory-based, cultural autonomy had no precedent in the Soviet constitutional history.

demand with the same content (quoted earlier). There is no mentioning of benefits at all in proposals put forward by the chemical safety movement, where normative justification prevails. But one can observe a slight change of tone and phrasing with proposals appearing more neutral and dispassionate compared with demands. Thus, a proposal to repeal a government decision to classify all information pertaining to previous work on chemical and biological weapons describes the decision as "contravening the Constitution and other laws of the Russian Federation," whereas the demand condemns it as "justifying genocide against the people of this country."[13] The sole difference between proposals and demands in those cases when they seem to be interchangeable is in the voice of the speaker. While most of the demands are made by public gatherings larger than the movement, all proposals are submitted either by the movement organization or its leaders. On its own the movement does not feel entitled to speak with an authoritative voice. This may also explain the less belligerent tone of proposals compared with demands.

Help Pleas

A help plea is an expression of collective distress. The emphasis is firmly on the grievances endured not so much by the speaker as by those on whose behalf they appeal. Instead of asserting rights or invoking benefits, protesters describe an acute need. The collective voice here is desperate rather than assertive. The speakers cast themselves in the role of victims of injustice rather than a collective actor undertaking to put it right (as in demands, and to a lesser extent, proposals) A fairly detailed account of suffering experienced by the victim usually precedes a cry for help, as in the following example:

> Today, when all mothers in Russia mourn their sons who died in Chechnya we are losing our children in time of peace because of a terrible weapon that slowly kills everything alive. We, women and mothers of the town of Gorny, are deeply concerned by the situation in our town, which is situated within the zone of storage of chemical weapons. They call us "the town of the doomed." And this is true. In 1989 on an experimental facility to test technologies of disposing of lewisite by chlorination 7 tonnes of the toxic agent have been destroyed in just two months. We did not have to wait long for the results. Many local residents suffer from skin lesions and abscesses, which do not heal and are not diagnosed by doctors. ... Nine out of ten children in the town suffer from diseases of respiratory, digestive or nervous systems. The results of research on children's health conducted in 1994 confirm this. ... What awaits our children and us? Certainly slow and painful death. We do not want to die! But even elementary health care is beyond our reach. The local medical centre is lacking specialist doctors. ... Travelling to Saratov is too expensive ... as many of

---

13   Accusations like these are often woven into demands and even proposals as justifications. But since they perform a secondary role I did not count these instances among accusations proper.

local residents, especially men, are either out of work or do not get paid for months on end. ... We find ourselves in a state of confusion and despair! Who will help us, residents on the town of Gorny, to stop this madness? Even in the Second World War chemical weapons were not used to fight the enemy. Now these weapons are aimed against the people of this country and the future of its children. We, residents of the town of Gorny, have become the first hostages and victims of this deadly weapon. (From petition to the President of Russia, 1995)

What protesters are effectively saying is, "We are in a desperate situation suffering greatly and undeservedly, help us." I have quoted so extensively from this petition to show how a help plea achieves its perlocutionary effect. One grievance after another is described building up towards a climax. The audience to whom the expectation is addressed is invited to empathize with the plight of the local people, especially children. In the second petition the focus too is on children's health, and though in both cases this can be explained by the identity of the speaker (mothers, medical staff of the children's hospital), it is also true that suffering is perceived to be greater when it is undeserved. Whereas in the case of demands and proposals the opponent's reasons to meet the expectation were normative commitments to honor or benefits to consider, here the opponent is stirred into action by the sight of suffering and compassion. To convince the audience of their suffering the speaker has to engage the audience's emotions. Though wrong has undoubtedly been committed, the measure of wrong is the degree of suffering rather than the extent of deviation from the rules. The emphasis shifts from the perpetrator to the victim.

The fact of offence is downplayed in help pleas. There is no villain in this tale of suffering apart from an impersonal chemical weapon causing ill health and even taking people hostage. The only offender is a relatively minor villain: in a solitary accusation inserted in the petition, the local administration is blamed for being unconcerned with the plight of the town residents. This seems to be general pattern: minor figures of authority appear as main villains in help pleas. The major villains typically named in demands and accusations are often recast in the noble role of the savior of the locals. The role would be familiar to anyone with at least some knowledge of Russian political history with its deeply ingrained tradition of paternalism. Over centuries of the autocratic rule it was not unusual for the as-yet-to-develop public to speak from the position of helplessness and despondency when addressing the highest authorities. Nor was it unusual for authors of countless petitions to attribute blame to minor agents while investing all their hope and faith in the power and benevolence of the Tsar. What is unusual is to find the President of the post-communist semi-democratic Russia filling the role cut for the absolute but benevolent monarch.[14]

---

14 Admittedly, only in two petitions protesters seek help from the president in a way that is more typical of subjects appealing for protection of the Tsar. The authors of the other petitions I analyzed, who happen to be either protest gatherings or movement organizations, prefer to accuse and demand rather than plead for help. All the more

Concluding the discussion, demands, proposals and help pleas represent three modes of addressing an expectation to the opponent. The latter is asked to honor their obligations in the case of demands, consider possible advantages in the case of proposals, and administer justice by helping the aggrieved in the case of help pleas. All three communicative actions require a normative relationship. Even in proposals, which appeal to the other's interests, the normative element remains strong, as evident from justifications that accompany them, and from the overlap in the content of proposals and demands. Demands and help pleas both appeal to the other's normative commitments, but whereas demands assert rights invoking rules that have been violated, help pleas arouse compassion for the suffering endured by the victim. Demands require a strong sense of agency characteristic of the public in a democratic polity. Help pleas displaying a very weak sense of agency belong within a paternalist political tradition with one side dependent upon the other for protection. The sense of entitlement is stronger in demands and weaker in help pleas, with proposals occupying the middle position. These three communicative actions are also associated with different speakers: demands being issued by protest gatherings, proposals by protest organizations and help pleas by members of the public in their everyday roles. The correlation between the form of entitlement and the identity of the speaker seems to suggest that normative considerations rather than strategic rationale determine communicative choice. Only within a normative relationship is the choice of action restricted by who the speaker is, whereas in a strategic interaction it depends entirely on resources available to the actor.

Perfomatives: Declarations, Protestations, Prescriptions

A well-known protest tactic such as direct action has its communicative counterpart in declarations. These are statements that neither assert a wrongdoing

---

striking therefore to find such a close resemblance between contemporary petitions written in the mid-1990s in a formally democratic Russia and a famous 1905 petition addressed to Nicholas II, which sparked the first Russian revolution. This petition starts with a harrowing account of misery endured by the workers and residents of St Petersburg —"we have become beggars; we are oppressed and burdened by labour beyond our strength; we are humiliated; we are regarded, not as human beings, but as slaves who must endure their bitter fate in silence" and so forth—continuing with an explicit cry for help: "do not deny Thy people help; lead them out of the depths of injustice, poverty, and ignorance." Here too we find minor figures of authority taking blame for the suffering of the working classes: "we have been enslaved, with the help and cooperation of Thy officials." Perhaps the only marked difference between the earlier and present-day petition is the absence in the latter of any signs of submission characteristic of the former, when even reproaches pledge loyalty: "Sire! Is this in accordance with God's laws, by the grace of which Thou reignest?" Quoted from the translation appearing in Harcave (1965: 285–9).

by the opponent nor communicate a normative expectation. Instead, normative facts are brought into existence by the speaker uttering appropriate words effecting relevant contexts, as in, "I hereby declare you husband and wife" (Searle 1979: 17). These and other utterances common in social rituals are the original performatives of the speech act theory. In the statement below, members of the anti-autonomy movement declare something to be the case with comparable results. The declaration itself begins in the last four lines and is preceded by an elaborate justification that adds legitimacy to the undertaking:

> Considering that the agreement signed by Russia and Germany and a series of other government decisions on phased reconstruction of the German republic build up social tension to the point of explosion; realizing that the government assurances about taking into account the public opinion are worthless since no concrete measures have been proposed to secure the rights of the resident population; seeing how thoroughly and persistently the preparatory work is conducted to restore the republic; implementing the norms of international and Russian law, the conference of the regional association "Fatherland" decrees (*postanovlyaet*): the districts on the Volga forcibly and unlawfully separated from the Saratov *guberniya* between 1918 and 1924 and returned to the Saratov *oblast* in 1941, now inhabited by the 500,000 strong multi-ethnic population are an inseparable part of the Saratov *oblast* and of the Russian Federation. (From a movement conference resolution, November 1995)

Yet it seems that declarations are relatively scarce in social movements' communicative repertoire (see Table 5.2). This may be true for two reasons: First, unlike demands or accusations, they lose their perlocutionary force through repetition. To make reality, one declaration should suffice provided the felicity conditions are in place. If not, repetition would not make the declaration more effective. Among the felicity conditions the status of the speaker is of major importance. This brings us to the second reason. One has to be vested with proper authority to create social facts of binding quality by merely declaring them existing. While local elected officials may possess such authority, the same cannot be said of movement members attending a conference (as in the above quote) or a rally. This may explain a string of justifications preceding the declaration, which serve to compensate for the lack of authority. But despite their efforts, the declaration in the quote remains problematic: the desired perlocutionary effect—to seal the status of the disputed districts—has not been created. Similar declarations by elected officials are more effective, which is why protesters often refer to such decisions in their own statements. To state that the elected representatives have declared that there will be no republic in the district amounts to saying, not just that the council is against the republic, but that in being against it they are expressing the will of the local population and doing so in the strongest possible terms while exercising their legitimate powers. A similar effect is achieved when protesters quote the results of the local referenda. In such cases, the illocutionary point changes. When it is not the council or a referendum stating "we declare" but those who elected them or passed the referendum, the speaker is neither making facts nor simply stating them, rather they are expressing a disagreement, in effect, making a protestation.

Protestations

Saying no, stating that you are against something, that one disagrees, disapproves, opposes, does not support, or is angered by it amounts to saying "we protest." The action performed in such statements is the action of protest itself. To avoid confusion with the regular meaning of the word, I would call the communicative act of protest *protestation*. Quoting referenda results and local councils' declarations of opposition fall in this category. But there are also other statements that communicate disagreement without commanding quite the same degree of legitimacy. As in this example taken from an article published in the regional environmental newspaper by a movement activist: "While welcoming efforts by companies to develop technologies of chemical waste disposal, we protest against turning the town of Shikhany into the dumping ground for Russian chemical waste, where under the slogan 'waste into profits' poisonous substances are being brought by trainloads from across the country without approval by the Ministry for Nature." The largest number of protest statements, thirty-four, was found in the anti-autonomy movement (which is not surprising given their highly oppositional stance), with seven cases in the chemical safety protest and 1 in the deceived depositors movement. That the last two movements could not sum up their disagreement as effectively may be due to their more positive stance reflected in their appellations: for the safe destruction of chemical weapons, or for the protection of rights of depositors and investors.

Prescriptions

In situations of disagreement it is not uncommon for one or the other or the third party to prescribe what the others are to do. Participants in the Russian movements attempt to influence the opponents and the public by insisting that they do something as a matter of obligation. The speaker attempts to commit the audiences to a certain course of action by asserting it is the right course by virtue of what the speaker and their audiences know about right and wrong. The propositional content of these statements can be summed up as follows: "you/we ought to do X/what is right." "Ought" in this formula is a shorthand for different expressions of obligation common in the Russian language such as "must" (*dolzhen*), "can" (*mozhet*) , "it is necessary that" (*neobkhodimo*), etc. Normative commitments are being explicitly invoked rather than conveyed implicitly as in other speech acts. Ought-statements, or prescriptions, to designate them by the illocutionary act performed, constitute the next most numerous category of speech acts after accusations, with a single exception of the deceived depositors movement where they are outnumbered both by demands and proposals: forty-eight, forty-six and eight instances respectively have been identified across the three cases.[15] Some of them are reproduced below:

Today we are lacking basic necessities like soap and washing powder, sugar and sweets, clothes and footwear, and we are wasting time discussing the ethnic question. Before we solve the spurious ethnic question by forcibly installing the autonomy the long-suffering people of the Saratov region must be given an opportunity to feed and clothe themselves. (From a speech made at a public rally, December 1989)

The main criteria in all decision-making on destruction of chemical weapons must be the safety and health of the population. ... The disposal technology must be selected with participation and approval by the public, and must not entail emission of toxic, highly toxic and long-lasting waste into the atmosphere, water and soil. (From declaration of the 1st International Meeting of Non-Governmental Organizations on Chemical Weapons in Saratov, October 1995)

In order to compensate lost deposits to clients of financial companies, savings and commercial banks, as well as outstanding certificates and bonds for the 1992–93 harvest, and repay those defrauded by privatization vouchers, it is necessary to create the legal base, i.e., pass laws on protection of the rights of investors and compensations of deposits, so that every citizens can be secure knowing that in the nearest future such laws would be passed. (From a newspaper article by movement leader, 1995).

Perhaps more than any other speech act discussed so far prescriptions demonstrate that social movements, whatever their alleged motives, are about setting things right. It would be fairly pointless to address a statement containing "ought" to someone outside the reach of assumed normative agreement, like for example an enemy in combat or an opponent who pursue their interests paying lip service to normative commitments. Ought-statements would not work within a strategic framework. For a prescription to succeed the audiences and the speaker must subscribe to same notions of right and wrong, or at least assume that they do. On the other hand, a blatant failure to do what is prescribed as the right course of action might not necessarily reveal the presence of strategic intent or underlying interest, as scholars like to suppose. It might also indicate that what is right is neither engraved on stone tablets nor written out in ample volumes of the legal code, rather in most cases participants in a normative relationship have to rely on fairly basic and preliminary understanding of what it is that they decide to agree on. When protesters are saying "it ought to be"

---

15   These do not include "we ought to protest" addressed to potential supporters, which both encourage and exonerate protest by making it a normative choice. The numbers can be found in brackets in Table 5.2.

they are making a normative judgement, pointing out a discrepancy between reality and normative expectation. The normative truth of "it ought to be" is not demonstrable in many cases. It is not possible to trace their assertions to a rulebook to determine whether or not they assert correctly. They rely on their assessment of right and wrong as it appears to them as citizens or as local residents affected by the problem. Their judgement may be wrong. It may be right. But we would not know it until the disagreement is resolved to mutual satisfaction, which rarely is the case.

Instrumental Reasoning: Exhortations, Warnings and Threats

With the possible exception of some proposals, the speech acts discussed so far belong in the domain of normative reasoning. When protesters accuse, demand, plead, declare, protest or prescribe, they act in response to what they believe to be a failure to honor commitments or adhere to shared understandings of right and wrong. However, influencing the actions of policy makers often requires a different kind of persuasion, in which the speakers extol the benefits or warn of the hidden perils of pursuing a certain course of action. Whether the benefits or costs are shared by both sides in the debate or the focus is on what the other stands to gain or lose, the speaker engages the interests of the audiences in order to influence their actions.[16] I call statements that describe the benefits that would follow if the opponent were to adopt a certain line of action *exhortations*. Their propositional content can be summed up as follows: "If you do [as we urge you to], you will [reap benefits]," even though in all but one case among the movements I studied the "if" remains implicit. Exhortations are relatively rare: only two instances found in the anti-autonomists case and four in the deceived depositors discourse.

When they occur, exhortations seem to play a supporting role in movement discourse in that they usually accompany and compliment other communicative acts. Consider, for example, the following statement: "By doing so you will help alleviate tension in ethnic relations in the area of the proposed republic, further the development of the perestroika processes, promote the rule of law, and increase prosperity of the Soviet people." This exhortation, which concludes a petition to the Supreme Soviet from participants in a public rally held in the town of Stepnoye in January 1990, appears to be describing the benefits of the action participants encourage the other to take. The action, named in the previous statement, contains the demand to authorities: "Listen to the voice of reason, the voice of the public—do not split Russia into medieval principalities! Do not let another injustice befall the peoples who call the Volga region their

---

16   The two forms of reasoning mirror two rationalities identified by Weber (1968) the difference being that when making value-rational or purpose-rational choices the actor reasons with oneself trying to determine what is the right thing to do.

home!" The action already has a normative meaning of preventing an injustice, but the exhortation that follows urges the authorities to consider the benefits that pursuing the normatively right course would bring. The emphasis merely shifts towards the instrumental argument without affecting the normative reasoning that dominates the rest of the petition. In the deceived depositor movement, exhortations accompanied and reinforced proposals. However, in both movements, the list of benefits looks short and unimpressive compared with the extensive range of charges levied against opponents, as if benefits have been added as an afterthought without much conviction or as if the benefits are indeed too slim to get the opponent interested. The fairly limited range of benefits further supports the proposition that instrumental arguments merely supplement normative reasoning.

Warnings

More common than exhortations but closely related to them are warnings. Rather than advocate the benefits, the speaker alerts the audience to the costs of pursuing certain lines of action. Protesters appear to be warning the opponent of the consequences, harmful for their interests, they have failed to consider. The propositional content is similar to that of exhortations: "If you carry on doing what you do, you will inflicts costs upon yourself." The following is an example of a warning employing instrumental reasoning: "It is worth noting that the current situation is unpredictable and can have serious consequences for the region's economy leading to a further drop in living standards of the least protected groups of the population and aggravating relations between the population and the authorities."[17] The deceived depositors, from whose petition this statement is taken, frequently invoke political repercussions for the authorities of the crisis if it stays unresolved. All seven warnings found in the discourse of this protest mention growing discontent among "citizens-depositors-voters," which the movement barely keeps under control, alluding to the possibility of further social unrest affecting the results of the imminent elections. The chemical safety movement finds the least use for instrumental reasoning with just one incidence of warnings and no exhortations, . On the other hand, protesters against the Volga-German republic resort to warnings as often as they articulate demands. Of eighteen cases of warnings in their discourse thirteen predict ethnic tension leading to a large-scale conflict citing examples of such outbreaks in other parts of the former Soviet Union following its collapse, and the distress they caused.

Whether or not the ethnic conflict will occur on the Volga is a matter of probability at the time when the warning is made. A prediction may turn out to be untrue. The fact of offence, on the other hand, belongs in the present;

---

17   Appears in a petition to the regional government from the Committee for the Protection of Rights of Depositors and Investors, July 1995.

its truth is easier to establish by referring to normative commitments. As harmful as the consequences attributed to actions may be, for as long as they remain uncertain they do not have the same persuasive power as the normative argument. Instrumental reasoning works best in those spheres of life where probabilities are calculable, for example in the production or distribution process where previous experience, technological knowledge or tenets of economic science apply, allowing for accurate predictions of the outcomes of routine processes. In all other cases the element of uncertainty may be too great to depend upon predictions regarding the future development of events. Unable to weigh the goals against the likely consequences of his actions a Weberian purpose-rational actor may well be forced to rely on value-rationality to help him choose the right thing to do. For protesters too, demonstrating that a wrong has been committed presents itself as a more robust reasoning strategy than using instrumental argument persuading the opponent of the costs and benefits, which may or may not materialize.

It is worth noting the difference in the uses of instrumental argument by the three movements. The anti-autonomy movement, the most oppositional of the three, opts for warnings. Compared with exhortations their warnings are well substantiated by evidence to make them more convincing. Indeed, with precedents of ethnic conflicts elsewhere they do have a reasonably strong case. Their historical expertise also allows them to argue that ethnic Germans putting themselves in a vulnerable position by relying too much on support of the German state. The deceived depositors movement, the least confrontational of the three, favors proposals, which outline in considerable detail what needs to be done to achieve mutual advantage. By contrast, the benefits and costs articulated in exhortations and warnings are too vague and general to be convincing. Finally, the chemical safety movement makes no use of instrumental reasoning, but it cannot avoid having to convince the authorities of the risks of pursuing a certain policy as part of the normative argument, drawing on scientific evidence to demonstrate that the authorities are exposing the environment and the population to considerable danger, i.e., committing an offence.

Threats

There is a better way to engage the opponent's interests than speculating about future costs or benefits whose probability is undetermined. One can exhort or deter by promising sanctions or offering incentives. This type of persuasion relies less on reasoning than on mobilization of resources. We are dealing with strategic interaction pure and simple where the amount and deployment of resources determine the outcome. The reasoning element is confined to making the audience believe that the promised sanctions or rewards are realistic, and that their interests will be affected. When either of these conditions is missing, threats and inducements are unlikely to be effective.

Whether it is to do with the lack of specific resources on their part or with the general understanding that offences should not be rewarded, the Russian protesters never make use of inducements but do resort to threats a few times: twice the deceived depositors and anti-autonomy movements and on one occasion the chemical safety protesters. The propositional structure of a threat is similar to exhortations and warnings: "if you do not do X (as we urge you to), you will suffer sanctions," although "if" in this case is always explicit. Consider the following examples:

> We say to the government of the USSR: if the opinion of the population of these regions is not taken into account, we will be forced to resort to the last measure, political strike. (From petition of the first inter-regional conference of representatives of workers' collectives, February 1990)

> In case our demands are not satisfied, residents of the towns of Volsk and Shikhany reserve the right to defend themselves by other means. (From resolution of a public rally in Shikhany, December 1993)

> If these demands are not met by 7 November 1995, [we shall] launch a political campaign to boycott the local and parliamentary elections. (From resolution of the public rally in Saratov, October 1995)

The ability to cause disruption or withdraw support is the main resource the three movements can count on to put extra pressure on the opponent. The threatened sanctions include civil disobedience and political strike (the anti-autonomy movement), mass protest actions and boycott of elections (deceived depositors) and vaguely phrased "other means of self-defense" (chemical safety protest). The character of the sanctions suggests that protesters do not threaten lightly, promising no more than they can deliver. The deceived depositors movement is capable of organizing the "masses of deceived depositors," as they like to refer to them, with whom they maintain regular contact in their advisory capacity. Moreover, boycott as a method of withdrawing cooperation in the least disruptive way is also in line with their overall cooperative approach to the problem. By contrast, the anti-autonomy movement with its all or nothing attitude has proven itself capable of disruptive methods of protest, such as picketing and roadblocks, to make their threats realistic. Only the chemical safety movement utters the single threat without much conviction, used as they are to conventional forms of protest.

But however big or small a threat, the use of sanctions by protesters makes sense only within the framework of normative argument. In all the cases when threats are made the sanctions are conditional on the acceptance of demands, which themselves carry a normative meaning of rightful expectation. Moreover, in three out of five instances protesters claim the right to impose sanctions. Further resistance is justified with reference to the prior agreement the opponent would fail to honor by not meeting their expectations. Insofar as such agreement is presumed the sanctions are used, not merely as a means of pressure, but with a normative significance of punishment. Even attempting to exercise force protesters cannot help acting within a normative framework empowered by prior agreement. These threats have little in common with the so-called argument from force, where the truth of a proposition is backed up by resources mobilized to make the other accept it as true. The force being exercised in these cases is normative force similar to that underpinning juries verdicts. Like other forms of instrumental persuasion (namely, exhortations and warnings) threats are woven into the normative argument, which dominates the discourse of the three Russian movements. In proportional terms, too, instrumental arguments relying on the persuasive power of costs and benefits, whether imposed as sanctions or self-inflicted, play peripheral role in the three protests.

Conclusion

To analyze the normative dimension of protest I have employed an approach based on the speech act theory, which treats communication as action in its own right. Unlike much research focusing on social movement messages, this approach is free of strategic bias. In the framing perspective, for example, communication between protesters and their opponents resembles a contest, in which symbolic resources are mobilized to construct representations of reality with a view to dislodging a competing representation (e.g., Snow and Byrd 2007). An approach based on speech act theory moves away from this representational approach to meaning and focuses on the pragmatic function of communication, revealing a whole range of social actions accomplished by communicative means, as I have demonstrated in this chapter. These communicative acts usually fall below the radar of the framing theory and are hard to describe as mobilizations of resources, or strategic framing efforts as such.

Looking at the communicative actions performed by participants in the three Russian movements, it is hard not to conclude that protesters act on their understandings of right and wrong, which they also assume to be the opponent's understandings. The analysis of speech acts suggests that protesters are trying to right a wrong acting within a normative relationship. It might be tempting to dismiss it at once as just a strategy, but to do so one needs better proof than simply an assumption that such communication unfolds within relations of power and contention. If these protests had been strictly strategic interactions, then the opponent's failure to act as expected would not have provoked the moral outrage and accusations embodied in their texts. A rational actor would simply adjust their strategy accordingly. But if actors consider it rational to accuse and demand, protest and prescribe we are dealing with a normative relationship where disagreement is a problem to be resolved. The evidence suggests that protesters attach normative meaning to the opponent's failure to act as expected. It is purely a matter of supposition to argue that in doing so they engage in strategic framing.

There is only one possibility to explain protesters' reliance on normative meanings without having recourse to the strategic-instrumental thesis, and that is to place protest within a normative relationship. Suspending a judgement about it being a product of power and resource distribution, we can examine how the origin, trajectory and outcome of conflicts involving social movements are influenced by shared, or assumed to be shared, notions of right and wrong. Normative relations impose their own constraints and grant their own unique form of power. It seems to me that the normative dimension has been unjustly neglected in the analysis of protest events, which is all the more surprising given how often a moral position informs the analyses of protests of various kinds. When it comes to explanation, strategic properties and instrumental uses of frames are given more weight than the normative meanings communicated by social movements. However, reintroducing the normative dimension into protest studies may require rethinking of how we approach norms. A relationship based on shared understandings of right and wrong need not be equated with unproblematic reproduction of agreement nor exposed as a work of power.

Chapter 6

Frames, Framing, and Keying: Biographical Perspectives on Social Movement Participation[1]

Ingrid Miethe

Social movements are not only temporary social phenomena; they also change significantly as they develop. Some movement actors that today maintain a central position will occupy secondary roles tomorrow. Issues that today form a movement's focal point are later forgotten, and movements may suddenly take on a direction that seems at odds with previous positions.

Based on empirical research on a Women for Peace group in the GDR, this chapter will provide some answers to the question of what causes these kinds of unexpected changes in movement trajectory. Women for Peace groups, founded in 1982, were the first major mobilization of women to attain public visibility. These groups formed in response to a government plan to include women in compulsory military service (cf. Miethe 1999b, 2000). The petition against the new draft law is said to have been signed by some 200 women (Kukurtz 1995), an extremely high number by East German standards. The regime backed down and left intact a network of women's peace groups under the umbrella of the Protestant church. The women's peace groups considered themselves primarily as pacifist groups with a critical stance toward the regime, and only incidentally as women's groups. The women used the official channels of protest—writing petitions to state agencies—and more importantly made use of critical church publicity, such as politically motivated worship services, prayers of supplication, grassroots church councils (*Kirche von Unten*), and vigils. A small proportion of these groups consisted of women active in the church, and dealt with Christian topics such as feminist theology. The vast majority of the groups included Christian women and women active in the church, but considered the church mainly as an umbrella. (see Miethe 1999a, 2000; Miethe and Ulrich-Hampele 2001).

The existence of such groups was a condition for the development of social movements in the fall of 1989. The evolution of these citizens' movements represented a new level of opposition to the East German regime. The New

---

1   The chapter has greatly benefited from comments and suggestions from Myra Marx Ferree, Silke Roth, Virginia Penrose, and Hank Johnston. They bear no responsibility for the present version.

Forum, initiated in September 1989 was the first step out of the dissident ghetto. The foundation of the New Forum kicked off the feverish creation of similar political groups and platforms, including Democracy Now (*Demokratie Jetzt*) and Democratic Awakening (*Demokratischer Aufbruch*). These groups consciously stepped outside the semi-public space of the church and very rapidly grew into a publicly visible mass movement. Afterward, however, they disappeared from the public spotlight as quickly as they had entered it. The former dissidents split apart in all political directions, even in diametrically opposed ones, after 1989.

The Women for Peace groups, as both a women's movement organization and a peace movement organization, was theoretically a *bridging organization* (Roth 1997, 2002) in which women gathered under the umbrella of two collective action frames. One was determined by the political activity of working for peace, the other provided opportunities for women to meet about gender issues. With respect to the question posed at the outset of this chapter, there are two turning points in the histories of these two frames. The first began in the mid-1980s and led to a change in membership. In those years it became apparent that not everyone connected with both the peace and female-gender frames anymore. Some members unsuccessfully attempted to stress feminist issues as the movement's focus, which is why many younger women with feminism as their main concern left to form their own feminist group. Those feminist groups came to understand themselves as the "independent women's groups of the GDR" whilst the Women for Peace movement withdrew more and more from the network meetings and drifted away from the "women's movement organizations" into the opposition movement-scene. The "Women for Peace" therefore co-initiated the independent women's movement of the GDR, but distanced themselves from it later on (cf. Kenawi 1995; Miethe and Hampele 2001).

The second turning point came form the political changes associated with the dismantling of the GDR. During this time of rapid change, Women for Peace amalgamated with the various mixed-gender civil movements in the GDR, especially the New Forum and the New Democracy. By joining the political opposition, the Women for Peace dissolved as a women's movement organization. After the events of 1989, many participants, instead of pursuing women's issues, continued their political activities by joining the new social or political groups formed after re-unification or withdrew completely from the political stage. This was a choice that, quite markedly, was made many women who had formerly been central figures in the movement.

How can such developments be explained? Why do actors withdraw from social movements that they co-founded and dominated for so long? The research into social movements does not provide many answers to date. As I will show, a closer inspection of the biographies of the central actors in such movements helps to explain this phenomenon. The framing concepts offer a good theoretical basis for any explanatory construct since they are a means to depict mental constructs as well as subjective meanings. Frame literature, however, cannot provide answers to all the aspects of the questions raised above since it has developed in a direction that is only partly helpful. What we find today in the frame literature is a focus on frame alignment as strategic behaviors of SMO (social movement organization) leaders. This chapter argues that in order to comprehend the dynamic processes and development of a social movement it is helpful to investigate frame alignment processes the way Goffman originally intended, which is significant at the level of membership, not marketing. By introducing his concept of "keying" Goffman offers the possibility to relate the biographical disposition of single actors in a movement—reconstructed through empirical biographical research—to the social movement itself. On the following pages I will first outline my theoretical concept which draws from Goffman's theory, and then transfer the theory to the empirical research example, a biographical study on the members of a "Women for Peace"-group in the GDR.

Framing concepts have gained widespread acceptance in recent years in social movement research. Although these concepts are theoretically derived from Goffman's (1974) classic concept of framing, to which Snow et al. (1986: 464) explicitly refers in his well-known article, what is most often applied in social movement literature is not Goffman's own concept, but Snow's use of it. Yet a reflection on Goffman's original concept of framing can contribute a great deal to an understanding of the dynamics of social movements and the actors participating in them. This is because Goffman's original concept—also enables us to reconstruct *how* and *why* certain frames emerge—and what their function is for the participants.

The well-known article by Snow et al. (1986), "Frame Alignment Processes, Micromobilization, and Movement Participation," was a milestone in linking together social psychological and structural/organizational perspectives, and in pointing out the importance of interpretative factors in understanding social movements. Snow built on Goffman's classic concept to define frames as mental and cognitive orientations which determine the perception and interpretation of events. The meaning of certain events or structures is not presumed to be given or known, but is to be reconstructed. Collective action frames arise out of shared interpretations of the same situation based on shared past experience or common cultural backgrounds. The ideas raised in the 1986 article were developed further in the years to follow by Snow himself, on the one hand (e.g. Snow and Anderson 1987; Snow and Benford 1988, 1992; Snow and Oliver 1995), and were adapted by other movement researchers on the other (e.g., Gerhards and Rucht 1992; Jaspers 1997; Johnston 1995; Noonan 1995; Oliver and Johnston 2005; Ryan 1991; Steinberg 1998; Swart 1995). This concept has also been repeatedly criticized. Critics have pointed to the concentration on recruiting strategies (Jaspers 1997), the danger of conflating frames with ideologies (Oliver and Johnston 2005), the insufficient modification of the theory for non-democratic or totalitarian societies (Noonan 1995), and the gendered structuring of the framing concepts, through language for example (Ferree and Merrill 2004). Benford's detailed and comprehensive "Insider's Critique" (1997) highlights problems such as the neglect of systematic empirical studies, the descriptive bias, reification, monolithic tendencies and the static tendency to focus on frames as "things" rather than on the dynamic processes from which they arise. It is not my purpose in this chapter to summarize those contributions here.[2] Rather, I would like to concentrate on the critique concerning the tendency to consider frames as static. I will argue that a renewed consideration of Goffman's concept can help to develop a more interactive and dynamic perspective.

In recent years, an increasing amount of work has been done to connect framing with other concepts in movement research, such as resource mobilization perspective (Snow and Benford 1992), political process (Snow and Benford 1988; McAdam, McCarthy and Zald 1996) or political sociology (Gerhards and Rucht 1992). This led to increasing compatibility between framing concepts and other concepts in movement research, and consequently many movement researchers today draw on a combination of different concepts, including framing (e.g., Kamenitsa 1998; McAdam, McCarthy and Zald 1996; Ferree and Roth 1998). But this development also led to declining interest in questions of how and why frames emerge, and how the processes of frame formation can be empirically recorded. Instead, a perspective on movement participation has taken root in which frames are seen as static descriptions of a given condition, in spite of the argument by Snow et al. (1986: 466) against this. This development has been the subject of intense criticism by the proponents of the framing perspective (e.g., Benford 1997; Oliver and Johnston 2005; Johnston and Oliver 2005). Analysis, according to Benford's critique (1997: 415), concentrates on the description of the frame, and neglects the process of *framing*, i.e., the process which produces the given frame. Frames are thus often conceived as fixed entities which move away from emerging processes (cf. Oliver and Johnston 2005: 188).

Oliver and Johnston (2005: 188) see two reasons for this development: "First, the concept of frame resonance (Snow et al. 1986) gave individual cognitive schemata an organizational dimension by making their generation a strategic task of the SMO, namely to link the movement's frame to existing beliefs and values. ... While strategic framing is a process, the emphasis is on the content. ... The second source of fixity in framing theory is the growing use of the master frame concept." The concept of master frames (Snow and Benford 1992), which deals with cycles of protest on a generalized level, further reinforces the static tendency because it is "linked to cycles of protest, and works at the most general level of analysis" (Oliver and Johnston 2005: 188–9).

This static point of view, as Snow and Benford pointed out as early as 1988, can be countered by making a distinction between *frames* and the process of *framing* (Snow and Benford 1988: 198). Whereas frames are relatively static

---

2   For an overview of recent developments compare Noakes and Johnston 2005.

state descriptions, framing describes the process by which these frames are constructed. Both frames and the framing process are rooted in the collective level: individual actors are not the objects of analysis. Yet collective action frames can have very different meanings for the actors involved. In order to reach conclusions concerning people's individual and collective action, not only the individual frames and principles of framing need to be described, but also the meaning of these constructs for the individual. This is the point where social movement research should go beyond the concepts described by Snow to uncover the principles of frame construction and their meaning for the specific actors. When the framing concepts have been extended in this dimension, it becomes possible to address questions as to why actors join a social movement, and then withdraw from it again under changed conditions. Such questions are usually left up to social psychology or addressed by concepts on collective identity (e.g., Andrews 1991; Gamson 1995). However, as I will show, the framing concepts themselves also have the potential to address such issues.

The theoretical foundation for this direction is already at hand, namely in Goffman's frame analysis itself. In the following discussion of Goffman's concept of frame analysis, I concentrate primarily on the points that have not been dealt with by proponents of the framing perspective and link these neglected points with the existing reception of the framing concepts in social movement research at three levels of analysis. The empirical basis I use here is a biographical study of a women's peace group in East Germany (Miethe 1999a).

Goffman's Original Concepts and Social Movements

Although the proponents of the framing perspective (Snow et al. 1986; Snow and Benford 1988; Benford 1997) refer explicitly to Goffman time and again, their reception of Goffman, compared with the original concepts, is abridged at certain points. These gaps are due to the fact that the frame alignment process as conceived by Goffman was taken up to the group level when it was applied to social movement research. Yet the concept of individual frame formation, which Goffman described as the keying process—was not applied. The adoption of Goffman's concept of keying—so my argument here—makes it possible not only to describe collective action frames and the process of framing, as the proponents of the framing perspective have done, but also to describe the individual frame alignment processes that underlie, produce and change the collective action frame and can help to develop a more dynamic, interactive understanding of frame alignment processes.

Goffman (1974: 10f) follows Bateson in assuming "that definitions of a situation are built up in accordance with principles of organization which govern events—at least social ones—and our subjective involvement in them." These principles are what Goffman refers to as "frame."

Frames allow people to make sense of events that would otherwise be meaningless. Situations are interpreted with reference to a "primary framework." As Goffman put it:

> I say primary because application of such a framework or perspective is seen by those who apply it as not depending on or harking back to some prior 'original' interpretations; indeed a primary framework is one that is seen as rendering what would otherwise be a meaningless aspect of the scene into something that is meaningful. (1974: 21)

According to Goffman, several primary frameworks are available for understanding events in any society, and together these frameworks form a major part of the culture of a social group (27). The individual "is likely to be unaware of such organized features as the framework has and unable to describe the framework with any completeness if asked, yet these handicaps are not bar to his easily and fully applying it" (31).

Existing primary frameworks are subject to many kinds of changes: new experiences need to be integrated; earlier notions prove untenable; disappointments or mistakes cast doubt upon the framework; "misframing" necessitates reframing (302). In such situations, primary frameworks need to be transformed in a process Goffman calls "keying." This is the process by which a given activity, one already meaningful in terms of some primary framework, is transformed into something patterned on this activity but seen by the participants to be something else" (43–4).

This transformation can be repeated: the number of successive keying processes is unlimited. It becomes increasingly difficult for the analyst to distinguish between the primary framework, its transformation, and the transformation of the transformation. Goffman suggests that each successive transformation can be seen as adding a layer or lamination to the activity. This process can be considered from both sides:

> One is the innermost layering, wherein dramatic activity can be at play to engross the participant. The other is the outermost lamination, the rim of the frame, as it were, which tells us just what sort of status in the real world the activity has, whatever the complexity of the inner laminations. (82)

Goffman does not specify what exactly the primary framework is. He solves this problem only in a relatively pragmatic way by stipulating that the primary framework is the earliest one we can find. Thus, in the empirical analysis we can never be sure of having identified the truly original framework, but use the term primary framework to refer to the deepest layer we are able to reconstruct.

Goffman goes on to recommend designating a frame by its rim or outermost layer. This outer rim is only identical with the core in the case of an activity that is defined entirely within a primary framework. Much more frequently, the description of the outermost layer will elucidate only the end result of the keying processes. Very different keying processes can yield a very similar rim, however; and conversely, different rims may arise from similar keying processes. Applied to social movement research, this means that people with very different motivations can temporarily join together in the same social movement, while on the other hand people with similar motivations can find themselves in widely varying social movements, sometimes even opposed to one another.

Although several actors may be in agreement on the rim of the frame—which in social movement research may represent shared issues, agendas, attitudes or cognitive interpretations—their frames are not necessarily based on the same keying processes or on similar primary frameworks.

If human beings were isolated entities, these findings would be of no consequence. But because people are always social beings who perceive and interact with one another, "ambiguities," "errors," and "frame conflicts" ensue. For what motivates people to action is their perception of what is going on and what needs to be done, regardless of whether or not the outward frame corresponds to the underlying primary framework (345). In other words, I react to behavior based on what I perceive as the other's outer rim. Even several actors joining together in a social movement do so based on a mutual attribution of the others' frame *rims*—not the underlying primary frames or keying processes.

It has often been pointed out in social movement research that social movements are not static, but change over time (e.g., Snow and Oliver 1995; Kamenitsa 1998; Snow and Benford 1992; Benford 1993a; Whittier 1995; Roth 1997, 2002; Flam 1998). As situations change for participants, new keying processes are necessary, which stand in relation to the individual primary framework and hence can lead to a completely different outer frame. The temporal dimension reveals the different keying processes underlying the frame rim. Studies of the changes in an SMO over time therefore have the best chance of discovering not only the frame rims, but also the underlying keying. The reframing that takes place as an SMO changes may make sense in relation to the individual actor acting in accordance with her own primary frame, and yet not necessarily correspond to the expectations of another participant who is not aware of the underlying primary frame or keying.

Let us imagine an actor in an imaginary SMO that has formed under a collective action frame. Over the course of time, this individual actor may change, or the SMO itself, that is, majority of the group, may change. Such changes may be externally driven—by events, or processes of social change for example—or self-produced, as by stages of personal development. If just one individual actor changes, the members of the group may suddenly perceive that individual as changed, and no longer compatible with the collective frame. If the majority of the group changes while the individual actor does not undergo the same process, the actor perceives the group as different, and considers that his prior commitment to the group was based on a misconception. The earlier collective action frame seems to have been an illusion, and it becomes obvious that the group only superficially or temporarily shared a frame, which the actor is no longer willing or able to support under the changed conditions. The actor may also see his membership in the group as the result of a self-delusion. He discovers that he "misframed" events, and his thoughts and actions were based on misconceptions. In this situation, another group—possibly even one that was previously considered an opponent—may prove to be closer to the individual's primary frame. According to Goffman, "individuals exhibit considerable resistance to changing their framework or frameworks" (28). In other words, people tend to tolerate certain deviations from the norm as long as "effective cover is maintained" (347). At some point, however, either an individual or a group of actors can no longer keep up appearances, and a "frame break" occurs: the collective action frames must be renegotiated.

Both the SMO and the actor concerned have can deal with the changed situation in a number of ways. Goffman points out the option of "flooding out" from the frame (350). Applied to social movement research, this means that the actor leaves the group which has become foreign to him. Equally central for the dynamics of groups, however, is another possibility which Goffman does not emphasize: namely the mechanism of banishment from the frame, in which the actor, who is perceived as foreign to the group, is constrained to leave it. This occurs especially when the group is not willing to revise the existing collective action frames.

A third possibility in addition to these mechanisms of withdrawal and rejection is that the changes that have taken place lead to a collective or individual reframing. According to Goffman, every social situation is transformable to the extent that new keying processes occur—processes that can be actively encouraged. Goffman identifies two kinds of new keying processes. One possibility is what he calls "upkeying" (359), in which a new layer is added to the existing frame. In terms of social movement research, this can refer to the addition of new issues or strategies to the collective action frame. The other possibility is of course "downkeying" (366), i.e., the removal of a layer from the existing frame. In social movement research, this may mean that the group or the individual abandons certain issues or strategies. In either case, such keying processes can lead to a new fit between individual and collective frames, so that the actors can remain in the group.

Snow et al. pointed in their 1986 article to the mechanisms of "frame extension" and "frame transformation." The authors were referring mainly to SMOs' strategies of gaining new adherents through extension or transformation of existing issues or strategies. Social movements are not only interested in recruiting new members, however, but also keeping their existing members bound to the SMO. For this reason it makes sense to examine the processes described by Snow et al.—which correspond to "upkeying" in Goffman's terms—on this level of interaction within the group. In order to keep a member in the SMO, the group can transform the collective action frame or integrate new issues, so that existing members are willing and able to stay in the group—in spite of the biographical reframing processes they have undergone.

Up to now I have concentrated on describing the interaction between the actor and the group. This focus follows from my initial question as to why people join social movements for a time and then leave them again under new circumstances, and from the corresponding choice of the empirical setting described here. The chosen focus should not obscure the fact that, from Goffman's point of view, it makes no sense to distinguish between micro, meso and macro perspectives. Rather, all three spheres are seen to be in constant interaction. Interaction between state or society and social movements, or among different social movements, is also based in principle on the same keying processes, and is subject to the same errors and illusions, and can therefore be analyzed using the same theoretical tools. Not only individual actors, but even "the hardest reality is subject to systematic alteration, provides only that a keying of some kind can occur" (493). An empirical development on this level would exceed the scope of this article, however, and require an expanded research setting.

Theoretical and Methodological Consequences

I suggest that Goffman's original concepts have important consequences for research on social movement participation and, more generally, how we can think more comprehensively about framing processes. They imply that a description of the rim alone—corresponding, in the current usage of frame analysis, to the description of a collective action frame—does not tell us about the ideological evolution of a social movement group, and especially as it pertains to cognitive changes among individual members. Every event and every change within the group can lead to new framing on the part of the participants. Depending on the primary frameworks and the underlying keying processes, this reframing can produce very different and even opposing frames in the same movement. I suggest that the frequently observed phenomenon of actors in a social movement—often the movement's very initiators—suddenly leaving for reasons invisible to the researcher is often linked to such keying processes. Also, changes in social movements due to the succession of new generations (Whittier 1995; Roth 2000, 2002) can be traced to and has consequences for keying processes.

Although describing a frame's rim probably the most common strategy in social movement research, is not sufficient to answer these questions of why people join and later leave a social movement. Moreover, identifying only a frame's rim is a research strategy that fails to capture processes of change. In contrast, tracing the deeper constructive mechanisms that produce the outer frames—a process that takes place over time—imparts a dynamic dimension to the analysis, one which must consider individual, group, organizational, and structural-political levels in the analysis. The researcher's interpretation of the frame's rim is deepened (on an individual level) and broadened (on a structural level) by the discovery of its primary framework and the keying processes that have shaped it. This is especially important for a better understanding certain types of changes in social movement groups, such as internal conflicts, goal shifts, schisms, factionalism, and group growth or demise. If this process is not included in the analysis, the researcher misses an important source of dynamism in the production and evolution of the collective action frames.

Therefore I suggest that a comprehensive approach to research in social movement framing must include three levels of analysis. The first is well known: the description of the collective action frames, or more accurately frame rims, used by the groups or SMO at any point in time. This is an exercise in describing the content of a frame, a common strategy in social movement research that often takes for granted the dynamism that lies behind the frames. Johnston's (2005) schematic representations of various frame "snapshots" are examples of the focus on content rather than process. Second, a detailed description of the framing process is a central compliment to the first, and introduces a dynamic element. This level focuses on *how* those snapshots are formed through ongoing collective work, negotiation, reworking, and renegotiation of ideas about what is taking place and what must be done at the group level. Steinberg's (1998, 1999) dialogic analysis of meaning and captures the ongoing collective and creative processes of framing at the collective level—processes intended by Snow et al's original theorizing but often lost as other researchers applied their ideas. Finally, there is the *keying* level, or the analysis of *why* these frames were formed and what their function is for the actors. Studying the keying process peels away layers of meaning—Goffman uses the term laminations—to push the researcher's understanding back to more fundamental levels of participant motivation. Whereas the first two levels have been discussed and applied widely in social movement research, the third, while harking back to Goffman's original concept, has been routinely disregarded.

While snapshots of collective *frames* and descriptions of collective *framing* processes are situated on the level of the group or the interaction of different groups, the *keying* analysis—as I will apply it—deals with the level of the individual actors, their interaction with the group, and their biographical experience of larger social processes. This is why the reconstruction of primary frameworks and keying is not merely a matter of psychology and social psychology—too micro a focus to be relevant to social movement research. As I will show with reference to the Women for Peace group, the keying process is always in part a reflection of large scale social processes, political contention, broad historical changes in society; and because these factors shape the lives of individual actors, these actors come to movements with shared histories, or in Goffman's terms, shared primary frameworks, which are then the raw materials for group interaction and the creation of new meanings through keying. For example, domestic violence is a social problem, which, among other things is linked with a history of patriarchy. As a socio-historical problem experienced individually, it can motivate initial participation in women's groups, where, subsequently, keying processes may politicize and reshape initial interpretations (primary frameworks) of what the individual member sees as possible and necessary.

A focus on keying also has methodological consequences. First, as Goffman makes clear, people's self-understandings will typically show limited correspondence to their primary frameworks. This means that primary frameworks and subsequent laminations cannot be analyzed only with a respondent's own statements. They will tend to reflect only the outer rim of the frame and usually will not reveal keying processes without intensive probing and analysis. It is not enough to discern the cognitive elements, as the form of discourse analysis does (cf. Johnston 1995: 221; 2005: 238; Mayring 2000), because these won't capture emotional and deeper motivational factors that are not always accessible to conscious reflection. A methodology of keying processes must provide analytical instruments that can identify and distinguish between primary frameworks and their transformations, and reconstruct the keying processes by which frames are generated. This is a method that must be able to reveal changes that occur over time.

There is a huge literature on biographical research, which cannot be described here but which offers ways to address these empirical requirements.[3] While there exist very different forms of biographical research, common to most of them is that they study, not only the moment of life currently under focus, but also how it is embedded in the actor's life history—that is, how momentary positions come about and how they change. Thus, both subjective meanings and changes over time can be observed through the analysis of actors' biographies. An empirically oriented analysis of biographies also makes it possible to identify different layers of interpretation of a social situation.[4] Different layers may be analyzed depending on the methods of gathering and evaluating data and shed insight into how an individual is "keyed" into a social movement group. The deepest layer that empirical analysis can uncover will be, for practical purposes, the primary framework. The depth to which an investigation of keying must penetrate depends on our objectives. Hermeneutic methods of analysis, which take the latent meaning of the subjects' statements into account (cf. e.g., Oevermann 1979; Ricoeur 1981), can bring to light deeper "layers" than analytical methods that concentrate on cognitive information or self-interpretations.

---

3 For a survey, see e.g., Bertaux (1981); Chamberlayne, Bornat, and Wengraf (2000); Denzin, Lincoln (1994). See also the controversy between Bertaux and Fischer-Rosenthal and Rosenthal.

4 This is not intended as an evaluation of various analytical methods, but merely to distinguish the present analysis from other methods—some of which also go by the name of biographical research—which use biographies simply to illustrate findings obtained by other means, and thus uncritically follow the subjects' own self-interpretations.

The importance of biographical concepts for the study of social movements has recently become evident in a growing number of investigations that work with very different methodological approaches (Polletta 2006; Klatch 1999; della Porta 1992; Flam 1998; Jaspers 1997; McAdam 1989; Moore 1996; Roth 2000, 2002; Whittier 1995). The empirical example that follows is a biographical study based on hermeneutic case reconstructions. A group discussion with six members of the same Women for Peace group was also recorded. By depicting the results of this group discussion, the collective action frames of the group, or to use Goffman's terminology: its frame rim, are delineated first. Following this delineation I shall present the results of the biographic interviews which give visibility to the keying processes on which the collective framing process is based.

Frame Rims in the East German Women's Peace Movement

In this section I present what might be called standard frame analysis, a detailed description of the three dominant frame rims that were identified in the group discussion. This analysis does not capture dynamic elements of the group's interpretative work by which these frame rims were created and sustained, but describes only the frame's content at the point when the group discussion was convened. Although the group discussion took place only in retrospect (in 1996), it offers a better insight to into the group's frame rim than for example the written documents I received. As the women themselves stated, during the dictatorship there were limitations on what issues could be named. Therefore, only selected group activities were put down in writing and even those written sources must be read with a critical attitude.

The women themselves organized the group discussion, and invited long-term members who had participated until the group's dissolution. In other words, the participants in the group discussion were women who had significantly contributed to the group's collective action frame over a long period. Women who had left the group earlier on or who had only briefly been associated with it were interviewed individually. This constellation of the group discussion also permits the assumption that the discussion reflects the collective action frames that remained significant until the group's dissolution.

The group discussion took three hours and was videotaped and later transcribed. It developed independently and without specific directions, that is, the interviewer did not intervene in the discussion process. In the conversation the group members reviewed the aspects that were important to them during the existence of the Women for Peace and the meaning they placed in their collective activities.

The group discussion was analyzed using the method of documentary interpretation described by Ralph Bohnsack (1993, 1997). This method of evaluating a group discussion focuses not on the particularities of specific individuals, but on the collective elements. In other words, the method is aimed explicitly at the group level with the purpose of identifying collective action frames. The process of framing itself—that is, the way in which the collective action frame is produced—can be identified in the interpretation of the group's interaction. Analysis of the group discussion identified two central frames: an anti-dictatorship frame and a confronting-fear frame.

The Anti-Dictatorship Frame

In my analysis of the group discussion, it was clear that participants shared an understanding of the East German regime as a "dictatorship," the key element in the first collective frame. The women drew a connection between the GDR and the preceding dictatorial regime under the Nazi party, understanding both regimes as dictatorships. Structural parallels between the two regimes were seen, for example, in the issues of weapons deployment in the GDR, military education in schools and kindergartens, the lack of freedom of speech, and mendacious propaganda. These women contested the East German regime's claim to be the better, peace-loving Germany in their political activity by pointing to the country's increasing militarization. The collective action frame that emerges as a key statement in the group discussion is that the women became politically active so that "my children won't be able to say one day, 'you stood by and let it happen, just as they did in the Third Reich'." That is to say, political activity in the GDR is part of an intergenerational controversy that originates in the conflict with the Nazi dictatorship.

The women had apparently made and discussed this connection between the Nazi and Communist dictatorships in their group before 1989. From the group's extant documents (cf. Bildungswerk 1990), however, it appears that this theme was never used publicly. In its publications, the women's peace movement joined in the official East German discourse of peace and antifascism. The mechanism at work here has been described by Noonan (1995: 87) with reference to Chile: SMOs in non-democratic societies use "the same discourse and frame as the state" because it is "the safest mobilization strategy." In the group discussion, as women looked back on their written petitions, they were angry about their "submissive tone," although they said that it was protective mechanism that they used intentionally at that time.

The Confronting Fear Frame

The women's peace movement, like the peace movement in general, has nonviolence as one of its core principles. Yet, as one might expect from Goffman's analysis, close inspection of the group discussion reveals that nonviolence has very different levels of meaning. The second dominant frame was a shared recognition that joining together with other women was the best way to deal with the fear of violence, which otherwise, each woman would have to bear alone. In the words of one participant, "That's also a reason for our whole group experience. We have to admit that together we were better able to tolerate stand and to experience the subjective fear that each of us had."

Analysis of the group discussion revealed that on the collective level this frame refers to the fear of state repression. Pre-1989 movement documents also mention other topics, such as fear of nuclear weapons deployment, fear of death in nuclear war and fear for the children's future (cf. Bildungswerk 1990). A commitment to peace as an individual and as a woman is held up to the state's violence and despotism, and alternative strategies for action are identified and practiced, such as passive resistance and training in nonviolent action. Through membership in the group, the women were no longer alone with their fear, but were able to discuss it with one another, and make arrangements for child care in case of arrest, for example.

Because the atmosphere of the group discussion was comfortable and the discussion was allowed to develop independently, some of the topics that came up were very personal. For this reason, the discussion not only depicts the frame rims of the movement, as is the case with published documents, but it also at times depicts topics of deep personal interest to the women, topics that they would most certainly not have published movement reports. Because I also collected biographical data for participants, it was possible to access layers of meaning that lie beneath the group's rim, the various laminations upon each member's primary frameworks that they brought into their original participation, and reconstruct the keying process for these two collective frames. In comparing analyses of the separate interviews with the group discussion, we find themes being layered upon participant's primary frameworks that were often different from the two collective frames, and in which the frame rims were only visible in a modified form.

Biographical Perspectives: The Keying Process

In order to demonstrate the importance of keying, I will draw on narrative biographical interviews that I conducted between 1994 to 1998.[5] The women who were interviewed all had (1) participated in the founding phase of the Women for Peace group; (2) continuously participated in the group's activities; and (3) remained active until the group's dissolution in 1989. The interview group thus comprised sixteen women. They were born between 1941 and 1968. The interviews were conducted as open narrative interviews. Each interview began with the following opening question:

> Please tell me your family story and your personal life story. I am interested in your whole life. Anything that occurs to you. You have as much time as you like to tell

---

5   For more details and the different phases of data collection and analysis see Miethe 2002.

it. I won't interrupt you with questions now. I'll just make some notes on the things that I may like to ask you more about later.

The structure of these open narrative interviews was oriented after Rosenthal (1993, 2003). As the above quote indicates, interviewees were allowed to tell their stories in their own way, structuring the narration as they themselves see fit. At the end of the main narration came a "question and answer period," in which they were asked to elaborate topics that they had referred to. Last of all, the interviewer asked questions about topics that the biographer had not addressed. The interviews took between three and six hours. They were taped and later transcribed without omissions.

The transcribed interviews are analyzed by hermeneutic case reconstruction (Rosenthal 1993, 2004). This method is especially well suited to demonstrate the theoretical issues discussed in the previous section since it attempts to identify the "layers" underlying the self-interpretations—the subsequent rims of the frame—through the reconstruction of the latent meaning. The central steps of analysis are:

1   Analysis of biographical data (life history): This step works by analyzing the data that is largely free of interpretation by the biographer (e.g., birth, number of siblings, educational data, chance of place of residence, membership in parties or social movements) in the temporal sequence of the events in the life course. Data are taken from the interview as well as from other sources. Central question of this step of analysis is: What has a respondent experienced during his/her life?

2   Analysis of life story (structure of self-presentation; reconstruction of the life story, narrated life): The general goal of this step is to find out which mechanisms control selection and organization and the temporal and thematic linkage of text segments. Basis for the analysis is the transcribed interview.

3   Contrastive comparison of life history and life story: This step aims to find possible explanations for the difference between the two levels described before, i.e., between past and present perspective. In other words, contrasting helps find the rules for the difference between the narrated and the experienced.

4   Development of types and contrastive comparison of several cases: The biographical case reconstruction leads finally, to the development of types. For this step the generalization of individual cases on the basis of contrastive comparison of several cases is required. The aim is a theoretical rather than numerical generalization (Glaser and Strauss 1967).

This analysis goes beyond the level of self-interpretation or finding patterns of orientation to reconstruct deep structures which guide the person's actions, and which may or may not be identical with, and in some cases may be diametrically opposed to, the subject's self-interpretations. This is not the place to depict in detail the rather complex method of analysis, a full description of which is found in Meithe (1999a). Suffice it to say that the following discussion does not address the level of single biographies but rather compares biographical typologies derived from intense analysis of transcripts. Two biographical types were identified in the group.

The "Dealing with National Socialism" Type[6]

The first type is in many ways an East German parallel to the Western "1968" generation (Miethe 1999). For this type, political debate is centered around the treatment of the family's history during the Nazi period. Representatives of this type primarily include women born during the war and post-war years, and their political activity is linked to the dynamics of family history and intergenerational conflicts. They have strong ties to their family of origin, and vicariously undertake the resistance that their parents failed to muster against the Nazi regime and the East German state. As mentioned earlier, the central motive behind these women's political activity is, "so that someday my children don't ask me the questions I asked my parents." It becomes apparent, however, that in reality these women never did take their parents to task for their passivity, and their own political activity is a means of dealing with the conflict between themselves and their parents' generation that was involved in the Nazi period.

To give one example of this biographical constellation, Ms A, born in 1945, attributed her early activity in a Women for Peace group to her upbringing in a Christian family, and to her grandfather's history of resistance.

> Well, that [my political activity in the group] has to do with my biography; an important factor, more than likely, is my upbringing in an Protestant Christian family; my father was a pastor. And going back still further, I have a grandfather who belonged to the Confessional Church,[7] was imprisoned under the Nazi Reich, was in N.N. [name of the camp], with N.N. [a prominent

---

6   For a detailed presentation of one of the cases on which this type is based, see Miethe 2002.

7   Although the Nazis at first took little notice of the church, the party leaders decided in 1932 to found their own organization of "German Christians" (Deutsche Christen, DC). In 1933 most of the clergy and laity followed, but the polarities within the movement that became apparent in autumn of 1933 soon led to a split, followed by a struggle over orientation within the church. In spring of 1934, the Confessing Church (Bekennende Kirche, BK) was formed at the Synod of Barmen in opposition to the DC (Kupisch 1966: 93). The main points on which the BK diverged from Nazi policy were the extension of racial laws into church affairs and state interference in the church beyond supervisory functions. The grandfather was among the founders of the BK, and was arrested in 1941 after his public confession and interned in a concentration camp.

member of the Confessional Church] in those days and was a founder of the Confessional Church, and I think that was important for my life.

In this way she constructs a tradition of resistance motivated by Christian values that extends from her grandfather, through her father, a pastor, to her. The tradition that unites the family is one of struggle against atheistic, totalitarian systems. Both Nazi Germany and Communist East Germany were seen as such systems. As a consequence, the woman describes her collective political activity as, "It made sense right from the cradle, from my roots."

A very different biographical situation was that of Ms B, born in 1943. Here parents did not belong to the resistance against the Nazi regime, but quite the contrary, were active supporters. Thus, she did not link her political activity to a family history of resistance against totalitarian, atheistic systems like Ms A. For her, participation in the Women for Peace group was in reaction to Nationalist-Socialist family. She states:

> And part of it [my activities in the group] was that my parents were Nazis, you see my mother was a party member, like the model German Lisl, right? And my father, he was an officer, and surely not harmless. My son has letters he wrote to Himmler, letters from him to Himmler, hm, right, hm, I simply thought all the time: stop it, I didn't want my children to question me like I questioned my parents, that was part of the reason, one of the reasons why I didn't want to join the regime, I didn't want to be one who has to ask why I kept still why I do such things to myself, that was one of the important things.

Even though Ms B's family history was very different from Ms A's, both were connected in their biographies—and therefore joined under one type—because their Women for Peace activities originated from family histories regarding the Nazi regime and because the GDR was seen as a authoritarian and repressive political system.

Due to its parallels with Nazi Germany, the GDR regime was of great symbolic importance to the women of this type. With the fall of the GDR after 1989, these actors lost the central point of reference for their political activity. The GDR had been woven into their biographical self-construction, and could not be easily exchanged. Accordingly, the political opening and subsequent dissolution of the GDR was a rupture, and most of the women corresponding to this type withdrew from political activity after 1989. Ms A describes her disillusionment in the years following 1989:

> And I couldn't continue with the same enthusiasm follong the political change because simply so much was new to me and didn't seem right anymore, you see, I mean it wasn't about being politically active successfully, we never were successful ((I'm sure you were), quite the opposite we were active and created problems for ourselves and today we could be active, and perhaps with success in some points,

but I'm confused, you see, I mean I don't even know the enemy, right, I don't know where the trenches are anymore.

This is where the first type differs most strongly from the second reconstructed type, one which is more closely liked with women's issues—"dealing with domestic violence."

The "Dealing with Domestic Violence" Type[8]

The communist regime was only of secondary importance for individuals of a second type, which I have designated as "Dealing with Domestic Violence." This type was not limited to a certain age group or social milieu. The analysis shows that their political activity represents a way of coming to terms with experiences of violence in the family. A women's peace group that has nonviolence as one of its core principles is a protected space for growth compared with the domestic violence these women have experienced. Activity in the group allowed them to experience themselves as active, capable, and powerful. The group's solidarity reduced the women's personal feelings of powerlessness, isolation, and despair.

Ms C serves to exemplify this constellation. For many years she lived together with a husband who abused her to such an extent that she eventually attempted suicide. Her political activity was situated fully within the context of this domestic violence: the more difficult the family situation was, the more she directed herself outward politically. "I became more and more militant and self-destructive." The beginning of the activity in the group was fully embedded in the context of a difficult family situation, one that was such a burden to her that she thought about suicide again.

> And then I, very often I must say, I thought about suicide again. That was, I was often very sad. And then when I said, from time to time, "Karl, we have to talk about everything, I can't go on living like this, this can't go on," then it was, "Whatever's wrong with you, I want to watch television now, I'm tired." So, well, and in this situation, into this, yeah, maybe that was the beginning, in this situation I heard about the draft law for women. And I thought now you can do something.

The group attachment that she experienced through her activities in the women's group enabled her to review her own difficult family situation. The group supported her finally to leave her marriage. She stayed with the group until 1989.

Since people who experience violence cannot easily tell their story, the facts are often referred to indirectly so that it remains difficult to choose suitable

---

8   For a more detailed analysis of an individual case on which this type is based, see Miethe 2000.

citations from the interview. Often the true relevance of these experiences of violence for participation in the women's group comes to light only when differentiating the interview material in a careful analysis of the order of topics addressed and the links construed by the order. For example, Ms D, found in Women for Peace family attachments her own family never offered. Her natural mother neglected her when she was a child and Ms D spent many years in a children's home. After returning to her natural family she experienced massive sexual abuse and physical violence by her stepfather. As a young adult during a difficult personal crisis she began attending the women's group, which came to replace the mother. In her own words, "They always were a bunch of mothers to me." The political opening and subsequent dissolution of the GDR was only of minor biographical importance for this type, since their political activity before that point was not dependent on the specific regime. "I came from one patriarchal system into the next. Where's the difference?" asks a woman of this type regarding the change from the GDR system to the reunited Germany. Accordingly, the representatives of this type continued or increased their political activity after 1989. As a rule they are today active in mixed-gender contexts. They are partly members of the Green Party, are sometimes political representatives in city or federal state political bodies, or they joined new social movements, often those concerned with human rights.

What's Going on Here According to Goffman?

What is the relevance of these biographic reconstructions with respect to Goffman's concept that we introduced earlier. How can the framing perspective grow by adding the biographic focus to its methods? What exactly does the biographic focus capture that is new?

When comparing the analyses of the single interviews with the group discussion we recognize what Goffman would term different laminations of a frame. The topmost lamination that at the same time describes the group's frame rim may be called the "anti-dictatorship-frame." This is the collective aspect that all group members interviewed confirmed: to oppose a dictatorship by joining the women's group. This is also the very concrete level of their political activity. However, the biographic analysis as well as the analysis of the development of the group as a whole shows that this frame is far from being supported by all participants to the same degree at all times.

We can thus detect differences in certain laminations when comparing the individual biographic processes (through typologies) with the collective process at the level of the collective frame. The focal biographic issue of the type "Dealing with National Socialism" is nearly identical with the issue at group level. This is to say the collective political activity is to a large part identical with the primary framework of the individual women of this type. It comes as no surprise that it was precisely these women played a vital part in the history and development of the group and formed the active core group. Even though other frames may be found in the group, too, this is the dominating frame.

The type "Dealing with Domestic Violence" is a different matter. Even though this type too addresses the issue of reduction of fear by collective activity, the fear on a group level is reduced to the fear of state-sanctioned repression and the protective measures to be taken. The fear of violence that many of the women encountered and which formed the basis of their political activity of these women did not enter the collective frame. The collective frames addressed in the group discussion thus only partially form the primary framework of the group. The representatives have to perform an up-keying process, to use Goffman's term, meaning their own primary frame (domestic violence) has to be extended by the issues of state violence and dealing with national socialism.

While the representatives of the first type form the "core group"—all central founding women are of this type—the representatives of the second type fluctuate more. The latter more frequently left the group if they found other groups that are more relevant to their own primary framework, for example the feminist groups that were newly forming in the mid-1980s. Their slogan, "your private life is a matter of politics," addressed the issues of the second type of women much more closely and with it their primary frameworks. Consequently, when the issues of the Women for Peace group moved too far from these women's primary framework, leaving the group to look for new activities that better represented their primary frameworks was one possibility. In an in-depth analysis, it emerged that only those women for whom family history during Nazi times was also a central biographical issue stayed with the Women for Peace group. The dominant group frame was close enough to their own primary frame.

The importance of keying became most obvious when confronted with the question of continuing political activity in the years after 1989. The answers to this question show that the frame of fighting a dictatorship formed merely the "rim" which was more or less important to the women depending on their individual biographic disposition. The type, "Dealing with National Socialism," saw their political activity come to an end when the GDR ended. Goffman calls this process the "down-keying," meaning that a level that had once been relevant no longer exists. In those cases the level was very close to the primary frame and the cessation of the level concerns the women to such an extent that they are unable to transform the collective frame, rather they leave it. It is a different case with the "Dealing with Domestic Violence" type. Although these women share the impression that the GDR is a dictatorship, this stance is not their primary framework and their political activity can very easily be transformed to other issues. *Collective* activity is most central to the women of this type, since such activity enables them to find ways of dealing with their experience of fear and violence. The *issues* of the activity are however quite easily exchangeable, so that these women looked for new collective contexts after 1989.

Conclusion

Why is it a good idea to include keying processes in the analysis of social movements? The comparison shows that the reconstructed collective action frames have different meanings for different types of actors. Representatives of the different types acted differently depending on the meaning of the frame—that is, depending on the underlying keying processes. The differences became manifest with the changes of 1989 when the dicatatorship dissolved. Whereas the collapse of the GDR was of minimal importance for representatives of the second type as far as the reasons for their political activity were concerned, for actors of the first type the same event marked the climax and the end of their political activity. Although in the group discussion there is a common sense of a need for further political action in the period after 1989, no collective action frame emerged on the group level and the group dissolved.

While outside observers were very surprised to see that East Germany's former dissidents acted very differently after the passing of the GDR in 1989 and drifted apart even into opposing political camps, this is not so surprising the differences that might be operative in their biographical typologies. Generalizing from my analysis, the social changes after 1989 brought to light the different keying that lay beneath the collective action frames of GDR activists. We saw that the women acted differently according to their different primary frameworks, as described in the typology. Although all the women equally welcomed the advent of parliamentary democracy, and—as the collective orientation schema in the group discussion shows—understood Germany after unification as an "open society," their decision with regard to political activity was very different, ranging from withdrawal from all political activity to increased activity, according to their respective biographical types and underlying keying. It is suggestive that these processes were operative for other activists too.

Expanding the repertoire of framing concepts to include the keying process described by Goffman can thus contribute to a more interactive and dynamic understanding of social movements. The keying concept offers a view of movement participation that is less static than the approach criticized in recent years by the very advocates of the framing perspective. It allows us to describe not only the operative frames and framing processes, but also the biographical processes that produce the given frame. This means that social movements can be not only described statically, in a sort of snapshot, but conclusions can also be drawn about their development and the reasons why they evolve along one path rather than another. Developments that can be described also include the fluctuation of participants in a social movement. In this way the question why people join a protest movement, for example, and later leave it, can be answered in much more detail. According to the approach presented here, this question must be addressed not just by studying the group's collective action frames, but most importantly by reconstructing the meaning of these frames for the actors themselves. In other words, the concept presented here proposes to identify *what* (the frames), *how* (the framing process), and *why* (the keying process). The step backward to Goffman becomes a step forward for our understanding of social movements. Biography, the group history, and the interaction of the individual experiential backgrounds should therefore be included in the investigation, even if my primary focus is on the group.

Chapter 7
Figurative Speech and Cognition: Metaphoric Analysis of a Shipyard Union Dispute

Gabriel Ignatow

Rather than treating grievances and political opportunities as objective, given, and exogenous to organized movement groups, cultural analysts of social movements have recently focused on cognitive and linguistic processes by which factors relevant to collective behavior are themselves interpreted collectively. Theoretical and empirical studies within this tradition have investigated an array of issues including cognition, ideology, and identity (e.g., Johnston and Klandermans 1995; Kubal 1998; Polletta 1998; Tarrow 1992; Jasper 1997). Much recent work, including papers by Fine (1995), Billig (1995, 1992, 1991), Johnston (1995, 2002, 2005), MacLean (1998), and Steinberg (1998, 1999, 2000), has begun to focus explicitly on the role of language within social movements and other political processes. Fine, for example, examined narrative framing on the part of VOCAL ("Victims of Child Abuse Laws"), a social movement founded in response to a series of well-publicized cases involving parents wrongly charged with abusing their children (Fine 1995: 138). Steinberg (2000; 1999), in a more elaborate series of studies of the rhetoric of organized cotton spinners and weavers in early nineteenth-century England, has developed a "dialogic" approach to social movement culture inspired by the early twentieth-century literary theorists Bakhtin and Volosinov , and by the writings of a number of "rhetorical" social psychologists, including Billig (1995, 1992, 1991). McLean (1998), taking an alternative theoretical tack, has investigated the political culture of Renaissance Italy through both quantitative and qualitative content analyses of patronage-seeking letters. His results show the discourse evident in the letters to be irreducible to the social positions of the writers. Instead, the writers were found to develop "frames of meaning" by assembling cues available from their cultural backgrounds, in order to build relationships and improve their social standings and careers. As with the work of Fine and Steinberg, McLean treats political culture as an analytically autonomous factor, irreducible to social and political structures, analyzable via content analysis, and having demonstrable sociopolitical consequences.

While cultural analysts generally view culture—approximately, the "symbolic-expressive" aspect of human social behavior (Wuthnow 1984)—as both irreducible to economic and political factors and relevant to collective action, there is a lack of consensus on several key theoretical points, including (1) the apt unit of cultural analysis, (2) the intersubjective coherence of culture, and (3) the degree to which public rhetoric reflects grassroots ideologies and symbolic-linguistic practice.

Units of Cultural Analysis

To the present, cultural sociology continues to be characterized by varying views about the most fundamental units of culture—a debate that subsumes the definition of culture itself (cf. Alexander 1990; Wuthnow et al. 1984; Wuthnow and Witten 1988). The social movement literature is similarly encompasses different views on how best to conceptualize and operationalize culture. In particular, one debate centers on a split between emphasizing, on the one hand, cognition and the human psyche, and on the other, language and discourse.

The predominant tradition in the study of interpretive practices of social movements, "frame analysis" (Snow et al. 1986; Benford and Snow 2000; Snow 2004) has followed Goffman in conceptualizing frames largely in terms of individual cognition. Frames are interpretive schemas that enable individuals "to locate, perceive, identify, and label" occurrences within their life space and their world at large (Goffman 1974). Collective action frames in particular perform this interpretive function by simplifying and condensing aspects of an otherwise unpredictable world, in ways that are "intended to mobilize potential adherents and constituents, to garner bystander support, and to demobilize antagonists" (Benford 1993b: 197; cf. also Eyerman and Jamison 1991).

Contemporary students of social movements have argued that by largely ignoring a wide body of literature in the analysis of language, frame analysis has bypassed a critical path by which culture informs action. In particular, by emphasizing cognition over discourse, frame analysis has (1) retained an overly instrumentalist and individualistic theoretical outlook (Donati 1992; Polletta 1999), (2) elided the collective, i.e., cultural, nature of interpretation (Polletta 1997), (3) remained characterized by conceptual ambiguities (Zald 1996), and (4) failed to evolve rigorous methods for analyzing, rather than describing, interpretive frames (Benford 1997; Johnston 1995: 68). In an extended critique, Steinberg (1998) has taken frame analysis to task for failing to problematize the role of discourse in interpretive processes, and for consequently inadequately defining the relationship between frames and ideology, and between cognitive processes and macro social phenomena. With Billig, who has argued that "anticognitivism" (1995: 68) is an appropriate starting point for the linguistic analysis of social movements, Steinberg has made the most pointed argument for the replacement of cognition with discourse in cultural approaches to collective behavior.

The Coherence of Movement Culture

Cultural sociology has in many respects inherited cultural anthropology's tense ambivalence toward construing cultures as coherent, unified systems of meaning (Sewell 1999; Smelser 1992). Where cultural anthropologists of the 1960s and 1970s tended to represent cultures as neatly integrated wholes that were consensual, mostly resistant to change, and clearly bounded, in the 1980s and 1990s, increasing attention was paid to acts of local resistance to dominant cultures, to change over time, to the weak boundaries between cultures, and to the complexity and "loose integration" of modem culture.

Within the study of social movements, both sides of the coherence issue are well represented. Fine (1995, 1982, 1979), for example, has made perhaps the clearest and most consistent case for viewing social movement cultures as highly coherent and bounded. He has introduced the term "idioculture" in order to denote the uniqueness of the internal cultures created, over time, within social movement organizations. Within such intensely interacting groups, members are, through discourse, "cohesively linked" (1995: 129) to one another. While not necessarily homogenous, social movement cultures are nonetheless bounded, distinguishing insiders and outsiders, and "constitutive" in the sense of creating, rather than resulting from, meaning, interaction, and social structure.

Conversely, Steinberg (1999, 1998) has consistently argued that social movement cultures are characterized by a fragmentation of meaning, idiosyncratic subjective experience, and individual acts of resistance. By these lights, discourse is not constitutive of the group, nor does it serve to link members into a community, but is instead "fraught with underlying ambiguities and contradictions" (853). Mirroring the turn within cultural anthropology of the past several decades, Steinberg posits that group culture is not consensual or taken for granted, but is instead structured through a "conflict-riven process of meaning" (854)—one that reflects, rather than creates, social structures.

Public Rhetoric and the Grass Roots

Benford (1997) has argued that the empirical literature on social movement framing suffers from a pervasive "elite bias" due largely to the methods most frequently employed by researchers, which generally include interviewing movement leaders and key activists, or analyzing media accounts or movement-generated or related documents (Benford 1997: 421). Benford argues that this tendency has led investigators to elide "non-elite framings" and the construction of "folk ideologies" (422). Further, intramovement disputes or "frame contests" (Ryan 1991) are very rarely the subjects of research, yet they are a ubiquitous feature of the internal politics of movements (Benford 1993a). Thus while elite rhetoric is surely more easily procured than is group discourse, this methodological convenience has come at a cost, and we currently have no analytic means for understanding the degree of consistency between a movement's public statements and its grassroots discourse.

Language and Cognition

Johnston (1995, 2002, 2005) has sought to inform debates within cultural analysis through investigation of the complex *interaction* of cognition and language (1995: 220). This seems eminently sensible, given the extraordinary development of cognitive science as an independent discipline, the influence of the "cognitive revolution" across the humanities and social sciences, and innumerable experimental demonstrations of the existence and pertinence of mental imagery (e.g., Shepard and Cooper 1982), and of the influence of cognitive schemas on language (Holland and Quinn 1987; Lakoff and Johnson 1999; Fernandez 1991).

The basic idea guiding Johnston's brand of "micro-discourse analysis" is that, through close attention to language, "the analyst can reconstruct a schema that systematically shows the relationships between concepts and experience represented in speech" (Johnston 1995: 220). The method devised by Johnston to accomplish this is too elaborate to cover here in detail. It involves line-by-line analysis of transcribed interviews with social movement participants, whose utterances are characterized in terms of their pragmatic intent, the social role they convey, and other interpretive categories.

While Johnston claims that the methods he has evolved are "only rough" and await further development, his are the only methods yet developed that even attempt to systematically reveal the cognitive frameworks linking language and thought within collective behavior. Yet in terms of the theoretical disagreements addressed in this paper, Johnston's method of interpreting the interview responses of movement participants is deficient on several fronts. First, the approach is overly individualistic both in theory and method. His professed aim is to aggregate, based on the linguistic practice of a single individual, to the level of group discourse. Surely movement participants, when questioned in a formal interview, will behave, speak, and presumably think differently than participants engaged in intragroup discourse. And we currently have no way of knowing, with any precision, how the behavior of individuals engaged in collective action differs from that of solitary persons.

Second, despite his claims, Johnston's content analytic methods are ultimately more social-psychological than cognitive-linguistic. For Johnston, the analysis of "schemata" incorporates a variety of phenomena, including "the speech situation," "social roles," "pragmatic intent," and "tone, pitch, cadence, [and] melodic cues," all of which are standard concerns of sociolinguists, but are not cognitive per se. These phenomena are quite distinct from cognitive schemata, mental imagery, or any of the standard grist of cognitive science and cognitive linguistics. In the hopes of extending Johnston's theoretical and methodological program, it is to this latter area of inquiry—the quickly developing field of cognitive linguistics—that I now turn to lay out my approach to the role of culture in social movements. I refer to the approach as metaphoric analysis because it involves focusing on the occurrence of figurative speech in movement discourses, and role of figurative speech in structuring social movement discourses.

New Directions in the Study of Language and Cognition

Given the turn to language and cognition within philosophy, literary theory, and the human sciences, it is perhaps surprising that sociology—in particular cultural analysis—has not been much influenced by the emerging cross-disciplinary study of what has come to be known as *cognitive linguistics* (e.g., Lakoff 1987; Lakoff and Johnson 1980; Gibbs 1994; Fauconnier and Sweetser 1996). Diverse research traditions have arrived at the view that language is, at base, a carrier of figurative signs and symbols—a view traceable to the founders of the field of semiotics, including Peirce (1991) and de Saussure (1972 [1909]; cf. Giddens 1987: 196). Linguists, cognitive scientists, and anthropologists have begun to investigate the intimate interrelationships of language and cognitive faculties such as mental imagery and cognitive schemata. While the sociological study of collective behavior has mostly remained aloof from these efforts, the emerging approach is mirrored in recent sociological views of the *evolution* of cognition and language. Jonathan Turner (1996: 14), for example, has proposed that since vision is the dominant sense modality, and since the pre-wiring for language developed among hominids (early humans) with enhanced control and integration of sense modalities under vision, cognition is probably visually based. Further, spoken and written language are, evolutionarily, added on to more primal visual bases of cognition; and thus the most basic units of communication are gestalts (or "folk models": cognitive and visual configurations; see Holland and Quinn 1987) rather than information sequences.

Goldberg similarly argues that even the simplest sentences encode, as their central senses, types of nonverbal events that are basic to human experience (1998: 203–20). Event types are seen as special cases of "conceptual archetypes" (Langacker 1991)—recurrent, sharply differentiated aspects of everyday human experience. These experientially based models are seized upon in language as the prototypical values of basic concepts. Taken together, these views have several implications for the study of cognition and language, and suggest that language may be basically figurative in nature. That is, human language does not operate, as computer languages do, in terms of information sequences and syntactic rules. Rather, written and spoken language depends on semantics, on conceptual archetypes based on subjective bodily experiences (such as up-down, in-out, straight-curved, hot-cold etc.). Moreover, the set of conceptual archetypes is finite (Goldberg 1998: 205). The entire set of archetypes can be thought of as marking, on a cognitive-linguistic level, the structure and limits of the "repertoire" (Tilly 1995) or "toolkit" (Swidler 1986) that constitutes, in prominent sociological conceptions, culture.

Conceiving of cognition as encoding basic experiences by way of mental models has had major implications for both theory and empirical linguistic research. The study of figurative thought and the way it may be manifested linguistically in metaphor and other tropes, has gained prominence (Fernandez 1991). Experimental research by cognitive scientists and psychologists supports the view that figurative language is not only ubiquitous, but plays a significant role in shaping "problem setting" (Schön 1979), decision making, and behavior. For example, Read and his colleagues found that metaphor use in political communications increased both participants' recall of passages and speeches, and linking of written passages and orators (Read, Cesa, Jones, and Collins 1990). In a subsequent study, the experimenters found that metaphor use influenced participants' attitudes toward the subject of a written passage (in this case, seat belt legislation). Johnson and Taylor found that positively and negatively valenced metaphors embedded in newspaper articles affected participants' ratings of both the issues and persons mentioned in the articles (Johnson and Taylor 1981). Similarly, Bosman found that metaphorical descriptions of a political party systematically influenced participants. All this suggests that figures of speech such as metaphor, metonymy, synecdoche, simile, and so on, all matter when we pay attention to how people talk. Insofar as movement participants endeavor to be liked by potential recruits and by one another, have their ideas remembered, and alter the political attitudes of others, the images and experiences embedded in language should affect mobilization.

Data

The data are from one of the most notable episodes in modern British labor history: the 1971 "work-in" by the unions of the Upper Clyde Shipyards in Scotland. The Upper Clyde Shipyards was a consortium of four shipyards—the Govan, Linthouse, Stenhouse, and Clydebank yards—allocated along the Upper Clyde River in the north of Scotland. During the summer of 1971, the union was threatened by several government plans to divide the four shipyards, to sell off one or more yards, and to close down others. In July, the 8,000 workers of the Upper Clyde took possession of the shipyards and, despite the mandate of the Tory government, continued to work. What came to be known as the UCS "work-in" was the largest of the 190 workplace occupations that occurred in Britain between 1971 and 1975 (Woolfson 1976).

Ultimately, the union was successful in staving off attempts to close any of the shipyards. In October of 1972, a new contract preserving the four yards intact was signed by the union and the government. The contract was considered a major victory for the union, both in the popular press and by the union members themselves (BBC 1972; Hay 1972), as the Tory government was pressured into a wide reversal of its industrial relations policy for the region, and was forced to pay for a massive reflotation of the loans financing the UCS. Further, the work-in helped catalyze subsequent workplace unrest, including demonstrations by dock workers in Pentonville, and anti-unemployment strikes by miners (Woolfson 1976).

During the summer of 1971, the conservative regional minister Nicholas Ridley argued in a series of letters to his fellow ministers that the shipyards of the Upper Clyde should be divided and sold to private industry at low prices. For Ridley, whose family had owned the biggest shipyard on the Tyne River, labor agitation at the UCS threatened to encourage wage increases in other shipyards in the region. Unbeknownst to Ridley or the government, UCS union members had attained a copy of the now infamous "Ridley report," and waited until the second week of September to publish it. By then the government, led by Ridley himself, had closed the Upper Clyde Shipyards. The report, published in the local and national press, summed up Ridley's earlier discussions with other shipbuilders on the Clyde, and spelled out his findings regarding the financial viability of the four yards. In his view, the yards on the Upper Clyde were a "cancer" whose militancy was forcing up wages elsewhere. The profits of the remaining private yards were suffering as a consequence. So, concluded Ridley, the government should "put in a government 'butcher' to cut up the UCS and sell (cheaply) to the Lower Clyde." The report, and particularly the term "butcher," were seized on by the union leadership, as will be seen below.

The ideal data set for exploring a social movement organization's internal discursive culture would be detailed transcripts of a group's discussions over time. Such data would allow for an investigation of unfiltered popular language, though the data would preferably cover a lengthy period, rather than only brief encounters. Luckily, just this kind of data set was constructed by Charles Woolfson in the 1970s (see Foster and Woolfson, 1986). Woolfson, who was a social science doctoral student at the University of Glasgow at the time, recorded meetings of the shop stewards of the Upper Clyde Shipyards in Scotland during their 1971 "work-in," which turned out to be one of the most notable episodes in modern British labor history. Woolfson later transcribed the recordings. These transcripts were analyzed by Woolfson and later by Collins (1996, 1999). The transcripts are exceptional in their level of detail, their completeness, and the length of time they cover. The transcripts are of exceptional quality, in that they are rich in nuances of local pronunciation,[1] and appear to comprehensively record every statement made in the meeting. The full set of transcripts comprises three volumes covering a span of just over a year, and includes meetings of the shop stewards only, mass meetings of the shop

---

1   The transcripts record the stewards' speech in excruciating detail. What may appear to be errors in transcription in the portions quoted below are in fact verbatim and correct.

stewards and the rank and file, and several press conferences and interviews with the union's leaders. Transcripts of one of the stewards' meetings, in August 1971, are used in this chapter.

The meeting examined here is a relatively early one, and revolves around the British government plan, articulated in the "Ridley Report," to close down some or all of the four yards. Faced with this new threat, the debate in the meeting primarily concerned tactics to thwart the government plan. The stewards, including their chairman James Airlie, Jimmy Reid, Sammy Barr, Jim McCrindle, Willie Robertson, Alex Bill, and a number of others, are divided among themselves over whether or not to encourage Archibald Kelly, a capitalist entrepreneur, to make a bid to the government for the four yards. The upside of the possible bid is that it would demonstrate to the government and the public that the yards are commercially viable as one unit. This might pressure the government to retain all four yards. However, the potential buyer has a reputation for buying shipyards and selling them off for scrap. So the downside is that if we were to make a bid for the four yards, it might somehow go through, and the union could face the complete loss of all of their four shipyards. Importantly, the transcripts show the stewards to have been divided over whether or not to encourage the bid. James Airlie, Alex Bill, Sammy Barr, and Willie Robertson supported the bid, while a clearly definable contingent opposed it. Each faction was faced with the task of winning over their fellow stewards.

Two aspects of this particular dispute require mention. First, the faction in favor of negotiation with Archibald Kelly (the potential buyer) led by the chairman James Airlie, won. Second, initial analyses indicate that the stewards in favor of negotiation spoke slightly more than did the opposing faction. Out of a total of 1,023 lines spoken, stewards favoring negotiation accounted for 537 lines from the transcripts (52 percent). The opposition faction accounted for the remaining 486 (48 percent).

The full set of transcripts also contains several press conferences and interviews with union leaders. The press conference examined here was held September 23, 1971, and was the first following the August 12 stewards' meeting. It was held by James Airlie and Jimmy Reid—both of whom were present at the stewards' meeting. In it they discuss the union's strategy and position with regard to negotiations with the government. As an example of the type of public discourse often examined in research on social movement framing, the transcribed press conference provides, in combination with the transcripts of the stewards' meeting, an opportunity to compare grass roots and public linguistic practice.

Methods

The content analytic methods developed in this chapter are substantially new. Their purpose is to provide rigor in extracting figurative language from the transcripts so that the cultural analysis of collective action might be more empirically grounded. In introducing these methods—which I label metaphoric analysis—an epistemological note is called for. Believing, with Walter Lippmann, that for the individual, political reality is the intersection of "the world outside and the pictures in our heads" (1925), these methods are aimed to get at both that which is signified (external reality, the world outside) and signifying symbols (clues to subjective meaning). Philosophers of language and cognitive linguists have come up with numerous terms roughly synonymous with signified and signifier (e.g., de Saussure 1972; Peirce 1991). Here I employ the standard vocabulary of contemporary cognitive linguistics: the term "topic" denotes an externally real phenomenon, and "vehicle," the metaphor, metonym, etc., conveying the meaning of the topic. Folk models are thus figurative models—vehicles—of real sociopolitical factors relevant to the collective.

Content analysis of the transcripts was performed by the author. Coding involved exhaustive analysis of every sentence of every shop steward who spoke at the meeting. References to any of *three topics* were extracted and coded. Based on several strands of contemporary social theory, these topics were chosen for their presumed relevance to the union members and for their codability. These include *social actions*, the *general situation*, and instances of *reflexive language*.

Social Actions

Gamson's (1992) work on political language suggests that for social movements to gain adherents, the *actions* of individuals and social groups must be interpreted in such a way as to spur contention. In particular, Gamson argues, potential movement participants are more likely to mobilize if they adopt an "injustice frame" by which the actions of an outgroup are presented as morally unacceptable. The crystallization of an injustice frame "requires a consciousness of motivated human actors who carry some of the onus for bringing about harm and suffering" (29). Based on peer-group interviews of members of working-class Boston communities, Gamson found evidence for the existence and effects of injustice frames. First, he argued for a strong overall relationship between injustice frames in media discourse and popular discourse, on issues ranging from affirmative action to nuclear power (58). Second, participants in the peer group conversations who adopted an injustice frame were also more likely to adopt an "adversarial frame" specifying "a clearly defined them" who are perpetrators of unjust social actions (112). Third, the adoption of an injustice frame was strongly associated with support for remedial collective action. Thus this theoretical approach, and the empirical evidence for the effects of the framing of social actions, suggests that members of disputing factions in the shipyard stewards' meeting will use differing forms of language to talk about the actions planned and executed by relevant social actors. For example, they will frame the actions of the British government as adversarial, unjust, and immoral, or else as rational and morally within bounds.

The Problem Setting

While particular representations of social groups and actions may be necessary for mobilization, they are arguably insufficient without a more general guiding image of the situation facing a group. Schon (1979) has labeled this process "problem setting," and argues that much of the interpretive work shaping social decision making occurs at this initial stage of issue framing or interpreting the situation. The idea is that social problems are not given: they are constructed by human beings in their initial attempts at making sense of complex and troubling situations. The initial assessment of a situation determines both the kinds of purposes and values people seek to realize, and the directions in which they seek solutions. For Schon, the interpretation of social issues often takes the form of stories or scripts built around core generative metaphors: "Each story conveys a very different view of reality and represents a special way of seeing. From a situation that is vague, ambiguous, and indeterminate ... each story selects and names, "different features and relations which become the 'things' of the story ... [which] proceeds via generative metaphor" (146). This view—that mental frames built around core metaphors structure patterns of social interpretation—suggests that within the stewards' meeting, members of disputing factions are likely to use different figures of speech to talk about the general situation facing the union.

Reflexivity

Benford and Hunt (1994) argue that processes of "counterframing" and "reframing" are endemic to social movements. Here, movement participants question frames with which they disagree, and offer alternatives. In a similar vein, much research on social movement framing has tended to emphasize the conscious and instrumental manipulation of interpretive frames. By this perspective, frames are "deliberately chosen worldviews, which can be embraced or suspended depending on leaders' perceptions of strategic imperatives" (Polletta 1997). Clearly, the issue of whether participants in social movements question cultural models or else enact them in a taken-for-granted manner speaks to the question of the intersubjective coherence of such models. As such, it has been a source of debate and a catalyst for research. For example Steinberg (2000; 1999), in his studies of the rhetoric of organized cotton spinners and weavers in early nineteenth-century England, has shown how the workers came to configure available ideological frames to suit their own purposes. Steinberg argues that the labor leaders were well aware that they were transforming oppressive ideological material (in this case the dominant British theories of political economy espoused by factory owners) into the stuff of solidarity and political contention. This argument yields at least one correlate for a linguistic view of framing: that interlocutors are aware of (or capable of reflection on) the frames employed by themselves and others. The formal term for linguistic reflexivity is *metalanguage* (in this case, perhaps more accurately *metapragmatics*: cf. Silverstein 1993). Thus, if counterframing has a metalinguistic aspect, and actors regularly reflect on, manipulate, and challenge linguistic frames, then members of disputing factions in the stewards' debate would be expected to question the validity of each other's linguistic frames.

Coding Scheme

Based on the arguments above, the topics coded for in the content analysis include the *social actions* (i.e., tactics) planned or executed by each side, and the *problem setting* facing the union. Both metaphorical and non-metaphorical "vehicles" were coded. Also, instances of linguistic reflexivity were noted.

References to each of the three topics were coded in terms of a respective set of categories. For *social actions*, referring, for example, to the strategy of using a possible bid for the four yards by the capitalist Kelly as leverage against the government, or to government plans for the future of the shipyards, references were coded as either metaphoric (e.g., "butcher this industry") or non-metaphoric (e.g., "it's a political exercise"). For the *general situation* facing the union, references were coded as metaphoric (e.g., "the other hurdles we'll have to cross") or non-metaphoric (e.g., "long-term best interests of the workers"). Also, several statements concerning the union's situation were coded as *reflexive statements* because they directly contradicted metaphoric assertions made by others.

Results

The results of the content analysis are presented in three tables. Table 7.1 presents all mentions of *social actions*, Table 7.2 all mentions of the *problem setting* facing the union, including several reflexive statements (more on these later), and Table 7.3 a comparison of public and grassroots rhetoric. These tables reveal a set of dramatic differences in the rhetoric of the opposing factions within the stewards' meeting.

Opposing Folk Models: Pressure and Violence

The content analysis indicated that two linguistic signifiers recurred through the course of the stewards' meeting: a "pressure" metaphor representing the social actions of the union itself, and a set of metaphors of a violent fight representing the union's general situation—in particular, the relationship between the union and the government. These metaphors were parts of the group's ordinary discourse, as they are for many groups engaged in collective action. They are everyday metaphors that, because of the figurative nature of thought and language (Lakoff and Johnson 1980), structure larger systems of meaning. These metaphors were employed in distinct ways by two factions within the stewards' meeting.

Pressure   The pro-negotiation faction employed a very limited set of metaphors to depict the union's planned tactic to thwart government attempts to break up the yards (coded as a *social action*: see Table 7.1). This language revolved around a central "pressure" metaphor (cf. Kempton 1987; Gentner and Gentner 1983 for explications of similar models). From almost the start of the meeting, the chairman refers to the plan to pressure the government into negotiations.

> there is also a political problem there, surely, the solution, if they want a way out, and I think *the pressure's building up,* and they're looking for a way out. (UCS transcripts: 3; all italics are mine)

The metaphor was repeated several times through the course of the meeting (see Table 7.3).

> We feel it might no' be the Kelly formulation but it's the first start to it and *it'll place this government under considerable pressure.* (UCS transcripts: 5; all italics are mine)

> I think here that if you're gonnie reject any plan that will *put the pressure on this government,* it would be a mistake. (UCS transcripts: 12)

> It's important politically and *the pressure now goes on the government* and that's where we want to keep it. That's the tactic as we see it. (UCS transcripts: 15)

A second trope that is closely related to the pressure metaphor involved imagery of "smoking out" the government into the open. By soliciting a bid from the capitalist Kelly, the union would place the government in a politically awkward position, such that the government's degree of commitment to the workers' livelihood would be made public. This metaphor was repeated time and again.

It smokes this government out if we can get a bid for all four units because one of the points that Eden was making, that no one yet was interested in eh bidding for the four units intact a) *that would smoke them out* and b) its important in oor opinion that to get a solution to this the government is in a dilemma. (UCS transcripts: 3)

I don't think they'll go for Kelly, I don't think he's got the eh eh the acumen or the ability to operate such a complex, that's a personal point of view but *it smokes the government out*, it's the first time anybody's publicly said that they'll bid for the four units, but more important is *the pressure can now go on* from the the movement in order that the capital is made available for the reorganisation. (UCS transcripts: 5)

It puts the government in a ludicrous position and as Jimmy Airlie says, *it'll smoke them out ... in the open* and I think we can use this for political propaganda. (UCS transcripts: 14)

Noo, we've nae love for Kelly nor anyone else, that's the idea of the exercise, *to smoke this government oot*. (UCS transcripts: 14)

As the stewards' debate primarily concerned the wisdom of negotiating with Kelly, the hegemony of the pressure metaphor for this tactic is of great relevance. James Airlie and his fellow stewards who favored negotiation with Kelly framed their proposed social action by way of two closely related metaphors based on "pressure" imagery (of "pressuring" the government and "smoking them out" into the open). Attempts by the opposition to rework this frame were limited, and the opposition presented no alternative interpretation—perhaps because "pressure" metaphors were part of the stewards ordinary discourse, and thus taken for granted. However, while the pressure frame was ubiquitous, this trope for the union leadership's planned tactic is more fully understood in the context of the abundance of violent conflict metaphors used by the faction of stewards opposed to the plan.

Fighting the [good] fight   Where the stewards in favor of negotiation rarely mentioned the government, the opposing faction continually rendered the government as an adversary, employing a rich set of interlinked metaphors to describe the government and its actions vis-à-vis the union. A statement by one of the stewards is indicative of much of the language used by the opposition side:

Right from the very start when the government announced their plan to *axe the UCS,* we mounted a campaign .... Alright, we've got the public sympathy, we're getting money in, getting letters but the Government are still gonnie go ahead wither *their bloody plan to axe the rest of us*. (UCS transcripts: 25)

Table 7.1   Mentions of social actors

	Faction favoring negotiation	Opposing faction
Metaphoric statements	"Smokes this government out" "Smokes the government out" "To smoke this government out" "It'll smoke them out in the open" "Place the government under considerable pressure" "Put the pressure on" (2) "The pressure now goes on to the government" "The pressure's on the government, and really on" "Put the ball back into the government's court" (2) "Keep our fingers on the pulse" "Puts the government in a ludicrous position"	"The government's off the hook"
Non-metaphoric statements	"It's a political exercise" "The exercise"	None
Reflexive statements	None	"Pressure going on the government" "Get the pressure off the government"

Note: numbers in parentheses refer to the number of occurrences of each quotation in
    the transcripts.

A great deal of the opposition rhetoric revolved around the metaphor *of fighting*
the government. The conciliatory language of the pro-negotiation side is absent
here. Instead, union-government relations are framed as an endless struggle:

> Now I'm no' naive enough to think that at the end of the day ... there'll be nae
> redundancies. I realize there would be. But at the same time, *the fight here,* the thing
> that's kept us together is the fact that we've decided that not one of these sections
> will close down. (UCS transcripts: 10)

> I think myself it's a terrible mistake to listen to Kelly because Kelly's ideas divide to
> me, are nae to us, no' in *the fight that we've put up,* that I don't, the *fight that we've
> put up* is quite simple. (UCS transcripts: 10)

> You're no *fighting the Government*, you're only *fightin' private enterprise.* The
> government's aff the hook. He's given this job getting them off the hook. (UCS
> transcripts: 15)

Jimmy, mainly because *we're in a fight against the government* and they're attempting to do away with the Upper, with the shipbuilding in the Upper Reaches .... (UCS transcripts: 18)

It disnae matter what plan you're doing, or what development of the plan, if it in any way attacks the livelihood of our fellow workers then *we'll fight it and fight it again*. (UCS transcripts: 26)

Thus, fighting imagery was common in the discourse of members of the faction opposing negotiation. It captures their assessment of the problem, namely, that confrontation with the government and private capital was the real issue, and the stewards' goal should be to defend the union brotherhood.[2] This, of course, was not the position of the stewards in favor of negotiation (see Table 7.3), who used imagery more appropriate to talks—i.e., pressure metaphors.

Taken-for-granted Categories

Questions of the reflexivity of social movement culture speak to issues of cultural coherence. If movement participants are continually reevaluating and openly questioning each other's tropes and other rhetorical practices, then conceiving of culture as internally coherent and intersubjectively homogenous is troublesome. Instead, a more postmodern view of culture as fragmented and wide open to idiosyncratic subjective interpretation would be warranted. Thus reflexivity is central to theoretical debate within the cultural analysis of social movements (e.g., Johnston 1995, 2002, 2005; Johnston and Klandermans 1995; Steinberg 1998) and within cultural sociology generally (Sewell 1999; Wuthnow et al. 1984).

In the case of the shipyard stewards' August 12 meeting, there is essentially no evidence of linguistic reflexivity. Union members on the opposing sides never questioned each other's linguistic practices as such. Rather, in several instances, stewards altered their interlocutor's metaphor to suit their own purposes—while retaining its basic structure. This pattern is exemplified in the following quotation—an attempt by a steward opposing negotiation with Archibald Kelly to rework the "pressure" frame to his own ends:

Mr. Chairman, this wan, you're talking about pressure going on the Government. I would disagree with you on this one, for the simple reason. Plessey's is the glaring example to *get the pressure off the government*. So they gave it to private enterprise.

---

2   It is interesting to note the co-occurrence of emotive metaphors (of fighting and violence) with discussion of social solidarity. The question of how this Durkheimian finding of "effervescent" symbols reinforcing social bonding is socially constituted may be a worthwhile topic of future research (e.g., Ignatow 2007).

Table 7.2   Statements of the general situation facing the union

	Faction favoring negotiation	Opposing faction
Metaphoric statements	"Get off the ground with the government" "Face up to the facts o' life" "The industry would need to be dismantled and butchered" "They would butcher this industry whole communities tomorrow if they made a profit. But that would only be if we were lying back letting them" "The other hurdles we'll have to cross" "That's part of the game" "The only way you don't face that is to lock yourself away don't leave the hoose" "Arriving partly at a stalemate" "We know where we're going" "It's got to be butchered" "We're cutting you up"	"At the end of the day" (2) "The fight here" "The fight that we've put up" (2) "We should keep the fight we've got" "We've got the government on the run" "You're no fighting the government, you're only fighting private enterprise" "We're in a fight against private enterprise" "Cut up the UCS once he gets it" "Axe the UCS" "Their bloody plan to axe the rest of us"
Non-metaphoric statements	"Redevelopment of Clydesbank" "Re-organization" (7) "Could mean an expansion" "Best interests of the industry long term" "Long-term best interests of the workers" Long-term best interests of this industry" (3) "Keep this industry intact" "Save all the jobs" "This new redevelopment" "Long-term policy" (2) "Redevelopment"	None
Reflexive statements	"The fight is about one thing" "Well I don't agree that anybody's getting sold down the river" "Nobody's going down the river"	None

Note: numbers in parentheses refer to the number of occurrences of each quotation in the transcripts.

Kelly takes o'er. Six months later he turns roon and says, I'm shuttin' this yin and ahm shuttin' that yin. (UCS transcripts: 15)

The steward never questions whether "pressure" metaphors are a reasonable to frame the issue being debated. Instead, he adopts the metaphor (seemingly unreflexively) while turning it towards his own end: in this case, to oppose the tactic under consideration. One of the stewards favoring negotiation, Alex Bill, reworked the opposition's fighting the fight image in a similar manner:

Well look, I'm quite amazed at the shop stewards here, because what is all this fighting about. *The fight is about one thing,* that the government have said to the UCS, you're not on for any more money, we're cutting you up, you're not viable .... So our first commitment is to put up the necessary finance to retain the yards in the Upper Clyde. You're no *fighting the government,* you're only *fightin' private enterprise.* The government's off the hook. He's given this job getting them off the hook. (UCS transcripts: 30)

Thus, in the case of both "pressure" and "fighting" metaphors, the images are taken-for-granted and sufficiently malleable to express multiple ideas. As linguistic vehicles, they are adopted wholesale, seemingly unreflexively, by the participants in the dispute, adding credence to the notion that culture—in the context of this particular collective action—is collective, coherent, and to a degree, thematic.

Elite and Grassroots Framing

Two of the union stewards, James Airlie and Jimmy Reid, held a press conference a month after the August meeting. In it they expounded on their bargaining position with respect to the government, their unwillingness to even consider breaking up the four yards, and their opposition to every plan proposed by the government thus far.

Comparing the transcripts of this press conference to those of the stewards' meeting allows for examination of the relationship between grass roots and public discourse, which may in turn address Benford's (1997) argument that examining the public rhetoric of social movements provides little insight into processes occurring at the grass roots.

The results of the comparison were striking and, frankly, unexpected. In large measure, the stewards holding the press conference (James Airlie and Jimmy Reid) engaged in the same linguistic practices as in the closed meeting. The dominant tropes at the meeting—pressure and fighting metaphors—emerged again. For example, in his initial remarks, Reid employed the familiar violent conflict metaphors (of "butchery" and "fighting") to depict the government's plans and the union's situation:

Now if anyone examines it, it's precisely Davies' proposals in the House of Commons umpteen weeks ago. *It's the butchery of the industry* .... Our reaction's been consistent, this is the proposal *we've been fighting against the outset.* And I want to make this perfectly clear. It's the decision and position of the workforce in the UCS that they would have no truck with *this butchery of our industry.*

Responding to a reporter's question on union tactics, Airlie likewise employed the familiar "pressure" metaphor

We are saying that we are, our position remains clear, that we are not leaving these yards, they'll not, no contraction, not a job down the road and we will put the pressure on the government from the broad movement.

The transcription of the press conference is relatively short, containing only 106 lines of text. Reading the transcripts, it is hard to imagine that the entire transcribed portion of the press conference lasted more than 10 minutes. Yet in this brief period, both of the dominant folk models found in the stewards' meeting were strongly in evidence (see Table 7.3). They were easily available resources—cognitively because of they were figurative images, and linguistically because of their common usage in the grassroots meetings. It is especially suggestive methodologically that mechanisms that impart elite-grassroots continuity are cognitive and linguistic.

Table 7.3   The public and grassroots framing

	Grassroots metaphors Stewards' meeting, August 12, 1971 (1023 lines of transcribed text)	Public metaphors Press conference with J. Airlie and J. Reid, September 23, 1971 (106 lines)
Violence	"Butchery" of this industry (1) "Butcher" this industry (1) "They would butcher the industry" (1) "It's got to be butchered" (1) "We're cutting you up" (1) "The fight is about one thing" (1)	"Butchery" of this industry (2) "Butcher" this industry (1) "Fighting" the government" (1)
Pressure	"Pressure" the government (5) "Smokes out" the government (4)	"Put the pressure on the government" (1)

Note: numbers in parentheses refer to the number of occurrences of each quotation in the transcripts.

While generalizations based on a single case are unwarranted, the unexpectedly high degree of overlap between public and grassroots discourse—overlap brought to the fore by a metaphoric-analytic focus—speaks to debates within social movements scholarship. Currently, the literature is split between work on framing that tends to emphasize framing contexts, relations between movements, and relations with external constituencies (such as the general public or potential recruits), and work on movement culture that examines processes occurring within movements themselves. There has been little discussion regarding interaction between the two: between intragroup discourse and public rhetoric and symbolism. The lack of research on the interaction between these two phenomena might suggest that little actual interaction exists. And yet, the public rhetoric of the shipyard stewards mirrored their private discourse. Perhaps they were simply too naive to hone their rhetoric for a larger audience. While superficially plausible, this explanation is awkward, given the extraordinary strategic and organizational skills displayed by the stewards during the course of the work-in. As a preliminary explanation, I suggest that two factors are at work here: the presence, of *two* men at the press conference, and the fact that both men were themselves present at the stewards' meeting. These explanatory factors are discussed more fully below.

Implications for Theory and Research

The strategy of metaphoric analysis was developed to bring some greater degree of rigor to the formal analysis of social movement culture than has previously been the case. While it is a methodology elides many processes relevant to framing, including especially numerous social psychological factors (particularly as compared with Johnston's method), it also has several important advantages. It encourages examination of the everyday interpretive frames used by movement participants, rather than those of movement leaders, the media, or individuals who are otherwise unusually eloquent, educated, or charismatic. It takes culture absolutely seriously, while leaving room for a kind of microagency—in the cognitive-linguistc sense of focusing on an individual's ability to modify and transform preexisting frames to suit his own purposes. It takes steps to resolve questions of whether culture, in the context of collective action, should be treated as an individual-level cognitive phenomenon, or else in terms of communal discourse. To be precise, the method of content analysis developed for this project is designed to illuminate cognitive frameworks linking the external world, ideas, and language. These frameworks cannot be observed directly. Instead, their presence and structure must be inferred from investigations of observable, overarching patterns of language use within a social group or organization. Thus the method of extracting metaphors, metonyms, and other linguistic "vehicles" from transcriptions of interactional discourse allows for the examination of overarching patterns of language use that remain obscure with more individualistic methods. Metaphoric analysis, in a sense, is a method that bridges Johnston's cognitive focus and the indeterminancy of Billig's rhetorical focus. It brings a new focus to the study of cultural processes of collective action, and holds the potential to empirically inform questions about the location and coherence of social movement culture, and the degree to which movement leaders' rhetoric reflects grassroots ideologies and language.

Units of Culture

In placing both cognition and discourse at the conceptual center of an analysis of the culture of a collective action, I have taken up a research direction pioneered by Johnston (1995, 2002, 2005). However, as noted above, extensive research suggests that the interaction of cognition and language informs culture most clearly and forcibly via figurative language has been shown to be ubiquitous in everyday life, not merely a rhetorical device but a fundamental process. The relevance of this perspective for cultural analysis is that the discursive trope—the metaphoric or metonymic model of a given external topic—becomes a viable unit of systematic analysis. While collective cognitive-linguistics processes of representing complex, abstract topics in terms of simple, familiar models have been well documented and theorized (e.g., Durkheim 1933, 1965 [1915]; Moscovici 1961; Wagner, Elejabarrieta, and Lahnsteiner 1995), these processes have not previously been examined in the context of collective action. In the shipyard stewards' discourse, two such folk models were predominant: pressure and violence models. These models, or frames—at once cognitive and linguistic, subjectively real and collectively diffused—are discrete, investigable units of analysis for cultural approaches to collective action.

Collective Coherence

A key contribution of this study is to show that when cognitive models embedded in language are treated as units of metaphoric analysis, we can more rigorously address questions of the collective coherence of culture. For example, if individuals participating in collective action were found to employ idiosyncratic, unshared tropes, then it would be difficult to conceive of culture as intersubjectively coherent. However, for the Upper Clyde shipyard stewards, exactly the opposite phenomenon was found. Folk models of pressure and violence were indeed collective, voiced by numerous stewards in more than one setting at different times. However, the group's culture was not homogenous. Instead, it was divided along factional lines. The faction, i.e., small numbers of like-minded individuals within an organized group—rather than the individual, movement group, organization, or society—may well be the fundamental locus of political culture. Fleck (1979 [1935]) has outlined a similar view. His argument is that collective culture (in his words a *thought collective*) is the product of, at minimum, a dyad:

A thought collective exists wherever two or more people are actually exchanging thoughts .... [A] stimulating conversation between two persons soon creates a condition in which each utters thoughts he would not have been able to produce either by himself or in different company. A special mood which would not otherwise affect either partner in the conversation buy most always returns whenever these persons meet again. Prolonged duration of this state produces, from common understanding and mutual misunderstanding, a thought structure that belongs to neither of them alone but nevertheless is not at all without meaning. (44)

The shipyard stewards' discourse reflects the view of Fleck and others (e.g., Fine 1995, 1985, 1979) that small groups produce cultures irreducible to the sum of individuals' ideas and personalities. The total lack of reflexive language on the part of the stewards lends further support to the view that the group's culture is largely taken for granted. And the similarities between their grass roots and public discourse shows that this culture can manifest itself across domains, which in turn suggests that it is indeed coherent.

Elites and the Grass Roots

Why did the shipyard stewards talk the same way in their press conference, in front of a room full of reporters, as they had weeks earlier among their fellow union members? The history and success of the UCS work-in, and the transcripts of the stewards' meetings, each suggest that the stewards were highly adept and self-aware as manipulators of the media and as movement organizers and strategists. In all likelihood, they enacted the group's "pressure" and "butchery" models simply because they were available, and perhaps because they seemed effective. Without further studies of social movements examining both groups' public and grassroots discourse, we will have no means of understanding cultural or social processes occurring between the two domains, but the close analysis of transcripts like these, using methodologies informed by advances in cognitive and linguistic research, is the place to begin. In the case of the UCS shipyard stewards, however, the high degree of isomorphism between public and grassroots linguistic practice suggests that two factors may be at work. First, following Fleck's (1979) ideas about the determining force of dyadic communication, the fact that the press conference was held by two stewards, rather than only one, may have played a role. If culture is manifested and transmitted socially, then perhaps the dyad is, as Fleck suggested, the minimum social unit in which political culture, in the sense of taken-for-granted interpretive models having political consequences, is created and innervated. The second, and more straightforward, potentially relevant factor is that both James Airlie and Jimmy Reid were *present* at the group meetings. They were fully engaged in the factional debates occurring among the shipyard stewards, including especially the August 12 meeting examined in this chapter, and that these models were invoked by them easily because of their "figurativeness" is central to memory retrieval.

These two factors are perhaps more relevant methodologically than theoretically. Since most research on social movement framing has examined the rhetoric of movement leaders rather than that of grassroots participants, then in determining or judging the degree to which a leader's rhetoric reflects the group ideology, researchers would do well to keep in mind that the group culture is more readily transmitted by sub-groups of two or more than by lone individuals, and ascertain whether group spokespersons were present at and engaged in group meetings.

Conclusion

We may never be able to put culture into a regression equation to sort out its independent effects on the development and outcomes of collective action. So long as human groups create and transmit meaningful symbols, culture will be omnipresent, and hence difficult to quantify in an absolute manner. However, the content, coherence, and form of culture continue to be topics of lively debate both within social science generally and in the cultural analysis of social movements. The results of the present study support a particular view of culture—one among several currently debated alternatives. The culture of the Upper Clyde Shipyard stewards was not so much a sum of individual interpretations, of cobbled-together subjective meanings, as it was collective, coherent, and largely taken for granted. The divisions evident within the group were factional, not individual. The stewards' collective culture—their idioculture—can be seen as a web of meanings structured by cognitive-linguistic models based on familiar and systematically related binary oppositions (which may help their cognitive availability), such as high versus low, forward versus backward, us versus them, and pressure and release (see especially Table 7.2). This array of tropes is characterized by, at minimum, a "thin coherence" (Sewell 1999) whereby otherwise arbitrary signs and symbols are made meaningful via their grounding in embodied experience and their web of positively and negatively charged interrelations. The relevance of this conception of culture to collective action is perhaps best captured by Weber, who conceived of the social influence of ideas in his famous metaphor of a railway "switchman." Here the social forces that influence collective action only do so insofar as they are interpreted, collectively, in terms of meaningful symbols and binary oppositions that, like switchmen, "determine the tracks along which action has been pushed" (1946: 280). Emotive, interrelated symbols—not brute social and economic forces—channel thought and direct groups toward, or away from, action.

PART IV
Strategy, Innovation, and Cultural Performance

Chapter 8
Making the New Polis: The Practice of Deliberative Democracy in Social Forums[1]

Donatella della Porta

The global justice movement (GJM) became visible through counter-summits that, as in Seattle in 1999 and in Genoa in 2001, contested the official summits of international governmental organizations, especially the G8, World Bank and IMF, WTO, and the EU. However, perhaps the movement's most significant cultural innovation has been social forums, set up as spaces of engagement and exchange among activists. Although the first large-scale social forum, the World Social Forums (WSF), was in part organized as an alternative summit—scheduled to coincide with the World Economic Forum (WEF) in Davos, Switzerland—it was conceived as an independent space for encounters among civil society organizations and citizens. Generally, social forums emphasize creating networks of diversity, multiple discourses and identities, and face-to-face engagement that parallel some versions of postmodern models of cultural practice. Social forums are guided by the high valuation of one overarching ideology, diverse in its many facets and practice, that of deliberative or participatory democracy.

Since the very beginning, the WSF showed a large mobilization capacity. The first meeting, held in Porto Alegre in January 2001, was attended by about 20,000 participants from over 100 countries, among them thousands of delegates of NGOs and social movement organizations. Its main aim was the discussion of "another possible globalisation" (Schoenleitner 2003). Since then, the subsequent WSFs in Porto Alegre (2002 and 2003), Mumbai (2004), and again in Porto Alegre (2005), had exponential increases in the number of attendees, as well as the number and organizational efforts of participating groups. The

1   This chapter is a revised and updated version of an article published in *Mobilization*, vol. 10, no. 1, 2005. The research reported here has been conducted as part of a project on discursive democracy, sponsored by the Italian Ministry of the University and the project on Democracy in Europe and the Mobilization of Society (Demos), financed by the European Commission. Elena Del Giorgio ran the focus groups, with the help of Fiammetta Benati. Iain L. Fraser has translated a previous draft. Sarah Tarrow helped with a careful copy editing. I am grateful to Hank Johnston and Sidney Tarrow for comments on a previous version.

WSF also gained large media attention. According to the organizers, the WSF in 2002 attracted 3,000 journalists (from 467 newspapers and 304 radio or TV stations), a figure which doubled to more than 6,800 in 2005 (Rucht 2005: 294–5). As Dieter Rucht observes,

> During its relatively short existence, the WSF has become an institution in its own right and can be seen as a kind of huge showcase for a large number of issues, groups, and claims. … Within the short period of their existence, WSFs have become a trademark that has begun to overshadow its competitor, the World Economic Forum, in respect to public attention. It is also a structure that, according to its slogan 'Another world is possible', raises many hopes, energises many participants, links large numbers of issues and groups, and—last but not least—contributes to the creation of an overarching identity and community as expressed in the vision of a meeting place for the global civil society. (2005: 291)

Since 2001, social forums also developed at transregional, national and local levels. Panamazonean Social Forums were held in Brazil and Venezuela in 2004; African Social Forums in Mali and Ethiopia, Asian Social Forums in India (Sommier 2005: 21). Among them, the European Social Forum (ESF) played an important role in the elaboration of activists' attitudes towards the European Union, as well as the formation of a European identity. The first ESF took place in Florence on November 6–9, 2002. Notwithstanding the tensions before the meeting,[2] the ESF in Florence was a success: not only was there not a single act of violence, but participation went beyond the most optimistic expectations. Sixty thousand participants—more than three times the expected number—attended the 30 plenary conferences, 160 seminars, and 180 workshops organized at the Fortezza da Basso; even more participated in the 75 cultural events in various parts of the city. About one million participated in the march that closed the forum. More than 20,000 delegates of 426 associations arrived from 105 countries—among others, 24 buses from Barcelona; a special train from France and another one from Austria; and a special ship from Greece. Up to 400 interpreters worked without pay in order to ensure simultaneous translations.

The second ESF, held in Paris in 2003, involved up to 60,000 individual participants and 1,800 groups, among which 70 unions, in 270 seminars, 260 working groups and 55 plenary sessions (with about 1,500 participants in each); 3000 worked as volunteers, 1000 as interpreters. According to the organizers, 150 000 people participated in the final march. The third ESF, in London in 2004, involved about 25,000 participants and 2,500 speakers in 150 seminars, 220 working groups and 30 plenary sessions, as well as up to 100 000 participants at the final march. The fourth one in Athens in 2006 included 278 seminars

---

2   With centre-right politicians, but also many opinion leaders expressing a strong fear of violence in a city considered particularly fragile because of its artistic value (to the point of suggesting limitations to the right of demonstration in the "città d'arte").

and workshops, and 104 cultural activities listed in the official program; there were 35,000 registered participants and up to 80,000 participated in the final march.[3]

The format of the social forum epitomizes the nature of protest events as arenas for encounters—an element that was however present also in many previous forms of protest, such as factory occupations, but in the social forum process is openly thematized. Not by chance, the ESF is represented in the press as "an exchange of concrete experiences" (*La Stampa*, 10 November 2003), "an agora" (a gathering place—*Liberazione*, 14 November 2003), "a kermesse" (a fair—*Europa* 3 November 2003), a "tour-de-force of debates, seminars and demonstrations by the new global" (*L'Espresso*, 13 November 2003), "a sort of university, where you learn, discuss and exchange ideas" (*La Repubblica*, 17 October 2004), "a supranational public space, a real popular university, but especially the place where to build European nets" (in *Liberazione*, 12 October 2004). The spokesperson of the Genoa Social Forum (that organized the anti-G8 protest in 2001), Vittorio Agnoletto, writes of the ESF as a "nonplace": "it is not an academic conference, even though there are professors. It is not a party international, even though there are party militants and party leaders among the delegates. It is not a federation of NGOs and unions, although they have been the main material organizers of the meetings. The utopian dimension of the forum is in the active and pragmatic testimony that another globalization is possible" (*Il Manifesto*, 12 November 2003).

The common basic feature of a social forum is in fact the conception of an *open* and *inclusive* public space. Participation is open to all civil society groups, with the exception of those advocating racist ideas and those using terrorist means, as well as political parties as such. The charter of the WSF defines it as an "open meeting place." Its functioning, with hundreds of workshops and dozens of conferences (with invited experts), testifies to the importance given (at least in principle) to knowledge. In fact, the WSF has been defined as "a market place for (sometime competing) causes and an 'ideas fair' for exchanging information, ideas and experiences horizontally" (Schoenleitner 2003: 140). In the words of one of its organizers, the WSFs promote exchanges in order "to think more broadly and to construct together a more ample perspective" (ibid., 141). References to "academic seminars" are also present in the activists' comments to single meetings published online (see e.g., http://www.lokabass. com/ scriba/eventi.php?id_eve=12, accessed 20/12/2006). Writing on the ESF in Paris, the sociologists Agrikoliansky and Cardon stressed its pluralistic nature:

Even if it rearticulates traditional formats of mobilisations, the form of the "forum" has properties that are innovative enough to consider it as a new entry in the

---

3   Data on participation are from the entry European social forum in Wikipedia (http://en.wikipedia.org/wiki/ European _social_forum, accessed December 24, 2006).

repertoire of collective action .... An event like the ESF in Paris does not indeed resemble anything already clearly identified. It is not really a conference, even if we find a program, debates and paper-givers. It is not a congress, even if there are tribunes, militants and *mots d'ordre*. It is not just a demonstration, even if there are marches, occupations and demonstrations in the street. It is neither a political festival, even if we find stands, leaflets and recreational activities. The social forums concentrate in a unit of time and space such a large diversity of forms of commitment that exhaustive participation in all of them is impossible. (2005: 47)

What unifies these different activities is the aim of providing a meeting space for the loosely coupled, huge number of groups that form the archipelagos of the GJM. Its aims include enlarging the number of individuals and groups involved but also laying the ground for a broader mutual understanding. Far from aiming at eliminating differences, the open debates should help to increase awareness of each other's concerns and beliefs. The purpose of networking-through-debating was in fact openly stated already at the first ESF in Florence, where the Declaration of the European Social Movements states:

We have come together to strengthen and enlarge our alliances because the construction of another Europe and another world is now urgent. We seek to create a world of equality, social rights and respect for diversity, a world in which education, fair jobs, healthcare and housing are rights for all, with the right to consume safe food products produced by farmers and peasants, a world without poverty, without sexism and oppression of women, without racism, and without homophobia. A world that puts people before profits. A world without war. We have come together to discuss alternatives but we must continue to enlarge our networks and to plan the campaigns and struggles that together can make this different future possible. Great movements and struggles have begun across Europe: the European social movements are representing a new and concrete possibility to build up another Europe for another world.

In this sense, the social forums can be considered as settings created for the experimental practice of an oppositional culture focused on the ideal of deliberative democracy. Although deliberative democracy has become a fashionable term in the area of political theory that examines the evolution of democracy, its ideological and normative aspects initially discouraged empirical research. In this chapter I present the results of an ongoing empirical study about how the ideal of participatory or deliberative democracy is put into practice in various social forums. Social forums, as places of encounters and exchange of ideas, often become settings where different performances of the participatory ideal are experimented with and modified in practice. I will present our findings about the general organizational contours and the ongoing reflexivity about decision-making processes. Creating open assemblies in which overlapping networks can come into contact to enrich the discourse is a basic social forum goal. These are settings that allow numerous identities to engage, with the idea that, not only increased understanding among diverse groups can emerge, but cultural innovation too. There is a strong normative bias against "hegemonies" and "monolithic identities." The network structure of social forums, their diversity, and their emphasis on cultural practice and engagement, nicely exemplifies current models of complex cultural performance.

Although there is variation in the ways that deliberative democracy is performed in different social forums, as an initial step, it is possible to identify its basic characteristics can be identified. *Mutatis mutandis*, the core ideology includes:

1   *Preference (trans)formation.* "a process through which initial preferences are transformed in order to take into account the points of view of the others" (Miller 1993: 75). In fact, "deliberative democracy requires the transformation of preferences in interaction" (Dryzek 2000: 79). In this sense, deliberative democracy differs from conceptions of democracy as an aggregation of (exogenously generated) preferences.

2   *Orientation to the public good.* In this model of democracy, "the political debate is organized around alternative conceptions of the public good"; above all, it "draws identities and citizens' interests in ways that contribute to public building of public good" (Cohen 1989: 18–19). Democratic self-restraints should prevent people from pursuing self-interest (Miller 2003: 195). A deliberative setting facilitates the search for a common end or good (Elster 1998).

3   *Rational argument.* Deliberative democracy is based on reason: people are convinced by the force of the better argument. In particular, deliberation is based on horizontal flows of communication, multiple contributors to discussion, wide opportunities for interactivity, confrontation on the basis of rational argumentation, attitude to reciprocal listening (Habermas 1981; 1996). In this sense, deliberative democracy is discursive.

4   *Consensus.* Decisions are reached by convincing others of one's own argument. Decisions must therefore be approved by all participants—in contrast with majority-rule democracy, where decisions are legitimated by votes. In this sense, deliberative democracy is consensual.

5   *Equality.* It "requires some forms of apparent equality among citizens" (Cohen 1989: 18); in fact, deliberation takes place among free and equal citizens (as "free deliberation among equals" [ibid.: 20]). At least, "all citizens must be empowered to develop those capacities that give them effective access to the public sphere," and "once in public, they must be given sufficient respect and recognition so as to be able to influence decisions that affect them in a favourable direction" (Bohman 1997: 523–4). Deliberation must exclude power deriving from coercion, but also avoid an unequal weighting of the participants as representatives of organizations of different size or influence.

6   *Inclusiveness.* All citizens with a stake in the decisions to be taken must be included in the process and able to express their opinions. This requires

the deliberative process to take place under conditions of plurality of values, where people have different perspectives but face common problems. Deliberation (or even communication) is based upon the belief that, while not giving up my perspective now, I might learn if I listen to the other (Young 1996). In this sense, deliberative democracy is linked to the concept of associational democracy.

7   *Transparency*. In Joshua Cohen's definition, a deliberative democracy is "an association whose affairs are governed by the public deliberation of its members" (1989: 17). Public deliberation can "replace the language of interest with the language of reason" (Elster 1998: 111).

In social movement studies, these characteristics often have found their way into discussions about organizational forms of movements, often returning to the traditional cleavage between those who praise organizations as effective instruments of mobilization (Gamson 1990; McCarthy and Zald 1987) and those who fear an iron law of bureaucratization (Piven and Cloward 1979). Although researchers have focused on different forms and trends of organizational structures and developments (for instance, Kriesi 1996; Rucht 1996; della Porta 2003) and typical network forms of movements (Gerlach and Hine 1970; Diani 1995; see della Porta and Diani 1999, chs 5 and 6 for a review), an instrumental vision has tended to prevail. As Clemens and Minkoff (2003: 156) have recently noted, with the development of a resource mobilization perspective, "Attention to organization appeared antithetical to analysis of culture and interaction. As organizations were understood instrumentally, the cultural content of organizing and the meanings signaled by organizational forms were marginalized as topic for inquiry."

Moreover, empirical research often emphasizes the limits of direct forms of democracy, in particular the "tyranny of the majority," how small groups exclude newcomers, and the risks of "hidden" leadership (among others, Freeman 1974; Breines 1989). The debate on deliberative democracy could open fruitful perspectives, first, by recognizing the role of values and norms in the choice of organizational models. Moreover, empirical research on contemporary movements could help to highlight the learning capacity of social movements—in particular their capacity to invent solutions to the difficulties of implementing principles of direct democracy and participation repeatedly identified by scholars and activists. In what follows, I attempt to develop these ideas based on the early results of an ongoing research project on deliberative democracy in the global justice movement, with a focus upon the functioning of social forums.

The Research

The strategic performance of internal democracy is particularly relevant for a multifaceted, heterogeneous movement such as the global justice movement (della Porta 2007), which has defined itself a "movement of movements") that incorporates many social, generational, and ideological groups as well as movement organizations from different countries. As early studies on this subject are showing, this movement has a more pluralistic identity, weakly connected organizational structure, and multiform action repertoire than previous movements (Andretta et al. 2002, 2003; della Porta and Mosca 2003). Moreover, global justice activists develop "tolerant" identities as opposed to the "totalitarian," or at least organizational, identities of the past (della Porta 2004). Although the research project contemplates a cross-national comparison of Italy, France, Germany, Spain, Switzerland, and the UK, I refer here in particular to the Italian social forums.

Our research began with a pilot study focusing òn on social forums in Tuscany. We combined different methods to assess the advantages and disadvantages of each: (a) discourse analysis of documents; (b) participant observation; (c) survey; (d) in-depth interviews with informants; and (e) focus groups. For the *discourse analysis*, I reviewed the websites of the four editions of the European Social Forums as well as local social forums active mainly in Italy and other umbrella organizations involved in the social forum process. The sites contain information about the statutes of the organizations, organizational ideology and structure, formal decision making, division of labor, etc. Regarding *participant observation*, we attended the general assemblies and other open meetings of six Social Forums in Tuscany (Florence, Prato, Arezzo, Lucca, Livorno, Pisa and Massa)—combined with *in depth interviews* with activists. Additionally, within the Demos project, representatives of local social forums were interviewed in Italy, France, Germany, Spain, Switzerland and the UK. Although we considered our interviewees mainly as informants, we chose an interactive technique to stimulate their active participation (Holstein and Gubrium 2002). The interviews confirmed the high degree of self-reflexivity present in the movement (Melucci 1989): internal democracy emerged as an important topic of discussion. Interviewees reflected upon past experiences, showing important learning processes, but no solution yet seemed satisfactory to address the main organizational dilemmas (participation and efficacy, equality and specialization, etc.). We also conducted *survey research* during the European Social Forum in Florence in November 2004,[4] which gave a measure of the

---

4   We had used survey in a research on the anti-G8 protest in Genoa (Andretta, della Porta, Mosca and Reiter 2002 and 2003). A brief introduction stating the aims of the research was included in each questionnaire, and the interviewee was asked to fill in closed or semi-closed questions. The survey has the advantage of systematically collecting information from a large sample. In particular, we were able to collect data about the socio-demographic characteristics, trust in institutions, and previous participation experiences of the activists—that is, variables that affect decision-making processes and the development of deliberative processes. For reasons well-known, however, surveys have limitations in the analysis of concrete organizational praxis and organizational values (Dryzek 2004). Besides the difficulty of assessing the effect of the

commitment and varied backgrounds of political and social participation. And finally for more in-depth knowledge of activists' values and meanings, we turned to *focus groups*, where the self-reflexive capacity of the activists seemed better stimulated. Following Blee and Taylor (2002: 107), a moderator facilitated the discussion by presenting the main focus of the research, and then stimulates debate, trying to involve all the participants and cover the main topics.[5] The focus group is "an ideal strategy to explore social construction processes" (Johnston 2002: 83)—especially useful to collect information about subgroups of the population and on issues of interest to them.[6] These methodologies allowed us to focus on the culture of deliberative democracy in social forums, namely the understanding of democracy and the values that support that understanding.

Focus groups allowed us to analyze the ways in which the organizational ideology of the global justice movement acquires meaning and normative strength, as well as how these norms and understanding were collectively constructed and shared. We decided to work with six groups, constructed with the aim of representing the main submatrices of the movement—different ideological positions, but also "unorganized" members (that is, those who did not belong to specific associations)—and also different degrees of commitments (excluding, however, the leaders). Each of the six groups (with an average of eight participants) was heterogeneous in terms of gender, but homogeneous by political generation. They were composed as follows: (1) teenagers (high school students; 17 to 20 years old); (2) the new generation, in their 20s, 21 to 27 years old; (3) the "lost generation" of the 1990s, socialized in a period of low protest, 28 to 35 years old; (4) the 1977 generation (in Italy, particularly radical years; 36 to 43 years old); (5) the 1968 generation, 44 to 59 years old; and (6) the postwar

---

interviewee's attempts to provide "socially desirable answers or rationalization," surveys tend to produce superficial or very standardized responses: "feelings and emotions, people's uncertainties, doubts, and fears, all the inconsistencies and the complexities of social interactions and belief systems are matters that are not easily rapped with survey questionnaires" (Klandermans and Smith 2002: 27).

5   Developed by Lazarsfeld in the Bureau of Applied Research of Columbia University in the 1940s, from the 1950s to the 1990s, focus groups were mainly used in applied research (especially for commercial or electoral purposes). Often triangulated with surveys (for the formulation of questions or interpretation of responses, in a form of member validation), they have recently re-emerged.

6   In social movements, two large research projects have used group interviews (both of them in the 1980s): one was led by Alain Touraine on the student, antinuclear, regionalist, women and labor movements in France (see Touraine 1981); another was led by Alberto Melucci on the ecological, women's, and youth movements in Milan, Italy. In both cases, the attention focused on the meaning-making processes in the movements. Touraine aimed at an in-depth analysis of the "I (dentity)-O(pposition)-T(otality), that is the fundamental self-understanding of the movement, or the highest meaning of its action. Melucci's research, "utilizing an experimental qualitative method, was designed to investigate the process of forming a collective actor" (1989, 236), with particular attention to the qualitative and affective dimension of individual experience.

(and still active) generation, 60 and older. In what follows, verbatim quotes from these focus groups will be cited by numbers 1 to 6, referring to the specific groups, the letter to the activists, and the page number to the transcripts (60 years and older).[7] We chose this methodological strategy because our survey had confirmed the forum's multigenerational makeup and we wanted to check for specificities in the conception of democracy of the different generations. We also wanted to analyze how learning processes and path dependencies interacted in each political generation. Second, we thought that age homogeneity would ease intragroup communication. In the (relatively) small movement environment, it was not possible to include only people unknown to each other; however, we tried to mix, as much as possible, members with different organizational locations and therefore loose relationships.

The researcher-facilitator opened each group opened with the question, "What is the movement/what does the movement represent for you?" and thereafter introduced various stimuli for discussion. The debates then covered, in different order, such topics as the organizational profiles of the movement, its network structure, the role of larger associations and political parties, the role of individuals and their "subjectivity," the strategic choices, the common values, and the understanding of politics and democracy—with particular attention to the mechanisms, advantages, and problems of internal practices of democracy. The topics to be covered and stimuli to be used were specified by the investigators with the help of a psychologist, an expert in the use of focus groups in the private sector and for political parties. The psychologist was also present in some of the meetings and read and commented on the transcription of the sessions. All of the sessions were taped and transcribed. Transcriptions were then analyzed, mainly by indexing the main themes that came out of the groups. Though a process of reading and re-reading, index codes were assigned to parts of the texts. Main themes were selected, and excerpts from each focus group were listed together.

Our experience indicates that, beyond stimulating the participants to develop their reflection upon the sense and functioning of the movement, focus groups also provided a sort of experimental setting for the investigation of internal processes of deliberation—performances common in social forums. Although the activists did not "decide" in proper terms, they did interact with each other, communicating on central issues. The climate of the discussion was always relaxed, and potential conflicts were addressed with irony and good humor. Also, the focus group, with its use of mediators and facilitators and horizontal

---

7   In what follows, quotes from focus group refer to the internal report "I figli dei fori," edited by Elena Del Giorgio. The numbers (1 to 6 refer to the specific focus groups); the letter to the activists. Quotes from interviews with activists of local Social Forums refer to internal research reports on the Livorno Social Forum Lucca Social Forum, Massa Social Forum, Arezzo Social Forum, Prato Social Forum, and Pisa Social Forum, all edited by Elena Del Giorgio.

communication, mirrors the actual functioning of the movement's groups (for more details on methodological aspects, see della Porta et al. 2004).

Between Nodes and Networks: Opportunities and Challenges

Social movements have a network structure whereby cultural meanings are performed and experimented with. With a low level of institutionalization, formal associations coexist with small, informally structured groups; coordination is weak; recognized leadership is often lacking; organizational boundaries are flexible; and membership rarely involves holding a membership card. Social movements have been described as typified by a segmented organizational structure, with groups continually arising, mobilizing, and declining; *polycephalous*, with a plural leadership structure; and *networked*, with groups and individuals connected through multiple links (Gerlach 1976). These general features appear in even clearer form in the globalization mobilizations. In internal practices, the challenge of building a transversal and supranational identity brought about a search for an organizational structure that emphasizes several deliberative characteristics: in particular, inclusiveness (versus exclusiveness), reticularity (versus hierarchy), direct participation (versus delegation), consensus (versus voting), etc.

Network Structure and Inclusiveness

> The Turin Social Forum wants to be an open place in which also the individuals, as well as the organized actors, can meet and work together; a space in which internal differences are accepted and given positive value, and not considered as an instrument to be used in order to acquire lager visibility and impose working contents and methods; a space in which there should be no place for hegemonic attempts and instead the search for a sufficient degree of maturation and consensus as guiding principles for each initiative. We will experiment with an organizational path that favors participation, research of consensus and achieving largely shared decisions. (Document 9, Proposal of organizational structure of the TSF)

Most local social forums, as the Turin Social Forum quoted above, made reference in their constitution to the Charter of Principles of Porto Alegre and the "work agreement" of the Genoa social forum. They usually present themselves as open, public arenas for permanent discussion, collaboration, and cross-fertilization, not as organizations. Empirical research on institutional arenas usually measure organizational inclusiveness in terms of the capacity of all those present in a given representative body to have their opinion expressed and heard. Inclusive policy making has often been evaluated on the basis of the involvement of representatives of different organized interests (i.e., business and labor). Social movements, as networks of people who affirm common values and perform similar identities are by definition selective. Their degree of social and/or ideological homogeneity might vary, however, together with their emphasis on equality or diversity.

The open and inclusive structure typical of many social movements (particularly the women's and peace movements) appears in globalization movements with heightened reticularity. The global justice movement is in fact formed of networks of networks that reach beyond single issues and single countries; many of its organizations are themselves transnational nets of hundreds of groups; and the preferred form of action—the campaign—is oriented to involve groups with heterogeneous specific concerns and ideological leanings. International counter-summits and campaigns, but also local-level protests, are normally organized by structures coordinating hundreds if not thousands of groups. More and more, various types of civil-society organizations are evolving from a hierarchical structure toward a network-based model (Clark 2003: 2). Moreover, "a recent phenomena has been collaboration between organizations in different sectors" (ibid.: 23)—including consumers' associations (Mowjee 2003a: 41), transnational unions (Muro and Themundo 2003: 57), and groups advocating increased access to HIV/AIDS drugs (Mowjee 2003b: 75). The protest against the WTO meeting in Seattle was called for by over 1500 groups, as compared with the 133 that organized a similar protest in Berlin in 1988 (Clark and Themundo 2003: 116). The mobilization against the G8 in Genoa was largely coordinated by the Genoa Social Forum (GSF), which brought together some eight hundred groups of extremely varied sizes and origins. Jubilee 2000, demanding the remission of unpayable debt for the poorest countries, was a platform of hundreds of organizations, coordinated mainly via the internet (Grenier 2003). The social forums allow "the huge diversity of civil society actors comprising the movement to come together, while imposing minimal commitment and common standards" (Schoenleitner 2003: 129).

Our surveys indicate that activists in anti-globalization mobilizations are rooted in a very dense network of associations, ranging from Catholics to ecologists, from social volunteers to trade unionists, from human-rights supporters to feminists, often with multiple memberships in associations of various types. While 97.6 percent of demonstrators interviewed at the protest against the G8 in Genoa in July 2001 stated they were or had been members of at least one association, 80.9 percent said at least two, 61 percent at least three, 38.1 percent at least four, 22.8 percent at least five, and 12.6 percent six or more (Andretta, della Porta, Mosca, and Reiter 2002: 184). A survey of the activists at the European Social Forum held in Florence in November 2001 confirms the density of multiple and plural associational membership (Andretta, della Porta, Mosca and Reiter 2003), as well as overlapping participation in groups as different as religious communities and self-managed youth centers, unions and environmental associations, student groups and charities (della Porta et al. 2004).

The mobilization of these associational networks is achieved by a particularly flexible multicentered organizational structure. In comparison with past movements, the global justice "movement of movements" highlights the presence of weak links between groups with differing organizational models. Mobilizing heterogeneous groups in fact requires a network structure that respects their specific features by bringing them into contact. Statutes stress inclusiveness, *inter alia* via the role assigned to a general assembly. The main organizations forming the global justice movement in Italy—such as Attac, Rete Lilliput (Lilliput Network) and the Disobedients—are in turn networks of various associations and individuals. Rete Lilliput emerged in the late 1990s from the "Tavolo Intercampagne" (Intercampaign Table), a coordinating committee of associations that, since the 1980s, organized protest campaigns, especially on global justice and solidarity. The programmatic document of the "Tavolo Intercampagne," entitled "Launching the Net," stated, "We are not thinking of a national structure that would suffocate the multiplicity and diversity under a single name. On the contrary, we want to start a process of communication from below, a networking, a federative path towards a common project" (quoted in Veltri 2003: 6). The organization is in fact structured around local nodes, with varying composition and a high degree of autonomy from the center. Traditionally, the anarchists stressed the plurality of (anarchist) groups converging in federation and platform (Chiantera-Stutte 2003: 144–5). Statutes of the Italian local social forums state that the movement is composed of "a kaleidoscope of colors and experiences" (Catania Social Forum in Piazza and Barbagallo 2003: 6).

Interviews with activists show a pride in the "plurality of the movement." As an interviewee of the Sicilian Social Forum points out, "it is important and necessary to defend and enhance the multiple beliefs and ideological, political, cultural, and religious positions." (in Piazza and Barbagallo 2003: 22). Focus groups confirm that the activists value inclusiveness as part of the movement's identity, revealing how this belief is constructed in the interactions between members of different groups. The movement's strength is located in its capacity to network associations and individuals. According to one activist, the movement manages to bring together

> many situations ... that in previous years, especially the last ten, did not come together enough, only came together around big issues and for very short periods, and always with a highly emotional impetus; while instead this is, I feel, the first experience I have had in such a live way of contacting and networking, where being in contact and in a network is one of the most important factors .... This is the positive thing ... the value of the social forums. (4G: 89)[8]

---

8   Participants in focus groups remain anonymous. We cite their verbatim statements using a number and a letter: the numbers 1 to 6 refer to the specific focus groups that draw on activists from the different social forums (see note 4) and the letter to the individual activist-participant.

The network is defined as more than a sum of the groups, for it is in the network in which the activist "gets to know people, forms relationships, becomes a community" (4A: 92). It aims at facilitating relations by building a network of individuals and associations. As one activist observes, "A word [that] I feel is key to a different way of doing politics is the concept of relations ... the ability to create and amplify relationships counts more than the ability to send them down from above" (in Del Giorgio 2002: 252).

Horizontality and the Role of Individuals

On the basis of the positive experiences with non-hierarchical common work we want to put into practice the idea of a political network. The Social Forum improves coordination and tries to support the initiatives of the single groups, to spread their content and to develop the practical action through a culture of reciprocal respect that would allow for communication and learning. (Leitlinien der Zusammenarbeit im Social Forum Berlin, Fassung vom 19 September 2003)

As with the Social Forum Berlin, many local social forums stress horizontality as a fundamental value. The emphasis on horizontality that in general characterized new social movements is even stronger in the global justice movement. The first Intercontinental Meeting of Peoples Against Neo-Liberalism organized by the Zapatistas in August 1996 saw the formation of People's Global Action, a flexible coalition of hundreds of groups from the South and the North brought into contact through a website. Subcomandante Marcos, spokesman of the Chiapas rebels, stressed that "this intercontinental resistance network will be the means through which the various resistance movements can help each other. This intercontinental resistance network *is not an organizational structure, has no head or leaders, no supreme command or hierarchy*" (in Routledge 2003: 337).

Though direct democracy is a cultural pattern inherited from past movements, in actual fact global-justice groups attempt to address the mistakes of the past. The main institution of the social forums is the regularly held assembly, but there are adjustments aimed at avoiding flaws of past organizational forms (or "assemblyism"). Several strategies are used to eliminate the influence of powerful (although semi-hidden) leaders whose authority may come from a large organizational base or strong rhetorical skills. The organizational statutes of the new global associations and social forums limit the delegation of power in various ways. The rotating of chairs at meetings prevents leadership from becoming consolidated. Leaders are very often replaced by spokespersons to inhibit centralization. Their public mandate is generally limited in time and confined to a thematic field. In the Italian Rete Lilliput, as well as in Attac and the Disobedients, local groups nominate speakers (usually with a limited mandate) to represent them at national assemblies. The anarchist federations as well as the Black Blocs often work via a "committee of spokes"

(Chiantera-Stutte 2003: 148 and 160). The forums frequently single out "spokes" with competencies restricted to a thematic area.

Even "spokes," however, are criticized in the name of horizontality. According to written documents, Rete Lilliput "refuses the personalization and professionalization of political commitment and does not want to be identified by the large public with one or more persons" (in Veltri 2003: 13). Moreover, the role of spokes (or a "technical committee" in the case of Rete Lilliput) tends to be limited to logistical issues and urgent decisions. Among the Disobedients, spokes are not formally appointed to national assemblies and their role is mainly "technical" (Becucci 2003: 79). In the *Bilanci di Giustizia* (Balance of Justice) network, composed of local groups demanding fair trade, the speaker's position rotates among all group members (Rosi 2003: 102). Only some of the local social forums have appointed speakers, and these are often rotating positions (Fruci 2003: 176). In the Lucca Social Forum in Tuscany, "there's a rotating coordinator for every assembly, who takes minutes and receives material for drawing up an agenda for the next one, at which the new coordinator is appointed and it starts all over again" (Lucca Social Forum: 4–5). In Massa and Livorno, the choice of spokespersons emerges "from time to time according to what's got to be done," rewarding competence and involvement in the movement" (Livorno Social Forum: 6).

Frequent *consultations* are usually considered necessary in order to avoid hierarchy and delegation. The internet is used to express members' opinions through listservs and telematic referendums (on Rete Lilliput, see Veltri 2003: 16). The Genoa Social Forum had a committee of spokes, but also a general assembly that met every three weeks during the preparation of the anti-G8 protest (Fruci 2003: 170). According to Becucci (2003: 89) the national assembly of the Disobedients meets every three months and, following the principles developed by the Zapatistas, the council members (including speakers of the various local groups, parties, and unions) return to their bases in order to report and discuss any important decision (ibid.: 90). In Attac, there are frequent calls for more participation, with an emphasis upon frequent consultations and demands for limiting the role of the national committee to routine implementation of the decisions taken in general assemblies (Finelli 2003).

Activists especially note the concrete difficulties in implementing the horizontal model. Though "we all know we have to find new ways of doing politics ... nobody ultimately gets what these forms might be" (Massa Social Forum: 7). Many activists remain critical of the practical functioning of the assembly. Interviewees point to the fact that "sometimes decisions are taken by those who remain at the assembly until late" (activist of the Catania Social Forum, quoted in Piazza and Barbagallo 2003: 7), and "not everyone can get up to speak since a small group of people (a politico-bureaucratic caste) tend to centralize the decisional mechanisms" (Catania Social Forum, in Piazza and Barbagallo 2003: 8). The representativeness of the assembly is regarded as doubtful. According to one activist:

Thank God this is not a movement of big meetings, since at big meetings it's hard for anything to be decided seriously ... who is to be represented, who's there besides, but what about who's not? Why aren't they? The participation summing up on Porto Alegre taught us a few things about this, I mean, what assemblies are really representative. (3C: 66)

If commitment by individuals is high in stages of heavy mobilization, "once mobilization ebbs and there's a calm period all the problems associated with internal organization return" (Livorno Social Forum: 11). Indeed, the very associational density presents obstacles to building a deliberative atmosphere. As one participant in the focus groups notes,

The biggest problem ... is still how to combine different, historically established practice ... a fluid thing like the movement with organized areas .... It's not hard for me to get along with A, in no way, it's harder to relate to structure as such, which at a certain point has its position, has to maintain it, and the practice of contamination and consensus can break down and lead to the things you were talking about, namely that this movement has in fact never set up representation to date, and I don't think its even able to do so today. (3E: 65)

One much-felt risk is the *manipulation* by the best organized—what activists call "putting a hat on." One activist observes:

Among the flaws I can see is the tendency to hegemony by some groups ... which I feel would mean destruction ... since ultimately as long as it's varied, it's a movement, but once it's the expression of a voice, calling it a movement, well. (1D: 11)

Another related problem is "the media protagonism of some people that make a move only to get into the papers" (1D: 11). As one Florentine social forum activist says,

I call it the showcase mechanism, the fact that everybody needs to defend their identity, only to go and repeat things that have already been said, announce things everybody knows, repeat the content of leaflets being distributed, bits of communication that are just to show they exist, and all that burdens the discussion a lot ... instead of a discussion with intersecting opinions. (4G: 96)

As empirical research has demonstrated, the assembly format can be controlled by "leaders and petty leaders, men and women, who turn up at the forums and try to hegemonize, little games and that" (2G: 44). At some forums, "this attempt to 'put a hat on' to lead us in one direction or another" (5D: 131) is noted and feared. The limits of "horizontality" are in fact linked to previous organizational repertoires. As an activist of the Catania Social Forum explains in an interview, the capacity to develop inclusive and horizontal communication "depends upon the culture of the organization you belong to. The culture should stress welcoming and opening towards others" (in Piazza and Barbagallo 2003: 6–7).

The organizational values that the activists stress, however, are participation and respect for differences. Linked with participation, the respect for *subjectivity* is in fact perceived as a new and positive aspect of the movement. The activists define their individual participation as fundamental, building a conception of militancy that values individual subjectivities. In contrast with the totalizing model of militancy in past movements in which members were subject to group discipline, individual experiences and capacities are valued. The emphasis on the individual instead of the organization respects the subjects instead of "annihilating them" in the community. As one Italian activists say, "if subjectivity dies then the whole movement dies a bit, or else it ends up like everything else, like the parties. For me, politics also means building a society in which subjectivities can coexist, can be rich .... Subjectivity is me with what I have to say, it is what I propose" (in Del Giorgio 2002).

Reopening the Public Sphere

In the words of a speaker for the Venice Social Forum, the forum's aim is "to spread direct participation and citizenship to defend common goods from private economic aggression and to re-establish priority of politics on economics" (Interview with a speaker for the Venice Social Forum). Direct participation involves making and defending claims in a public setting, which, according to direct-democracy proponents, is a way citizens can defend the "public good." It is held that the open voicing on positions has a positive effect on the quality of the discourse, as it pushes individuals to reason in terms of public good. Empirical research on institutional politics has tended to emphasize transparency in terms of the formal part of the decision-making process—for instance, the public meeting of parliaments. As for social movements, general assemblies have been the traditional spaces for public debate, although less visible forms of decision making have prevailed, especially in periods of repression. The principle of openness to the public has been particularly emphasized in the global justice movement, where assemblies are usually open not only to members, but also to outsiders (see, for instance, the statute of Rete Lilliput that stresses the importance of leaving space to the individual creativity and emphasizes diversity as a positive value inside and outside the organization). The main decisions should be taken in open and visible assemblies. In fact, the construction of "convergence spaces" "that facilitate the forging of an associational politics that constitutes a diverse, contested coalition of place-specific social movements" has been noted (Routledge 2003: 345). For the global justice movement, the "forum" quality of some arenas is particularly relevant—that is, the presence of places where, according to Lichterman (1999: 104), "critically collective discussion about members' interests and collective identities" develops. Lichterman continues, "The forum shrinks if members come to assume that their collective interests and identity are obvious and need not to be discussed, or if they talk only to strategize." In reality, it seems that the global justice movement falls short of its participatory goals.

Activists complain that some leaders hold meetings outside the assemblies. Others mention that the very creation of solidarity internally reduces openness to the outside. One activist states,

> After a bit, at the full assembly, with all the discussion of everything and everyone, some people couldn't stand it any more. Those who stayed on were in a sense of one mind, and the new ones that came along, I've seen this even recently, didn't find things easy. (Arezzo Social Forum: 7)

And according to another activist,

> The Florence-wide assemblies are really dreadful, with really useless discussions because the decisions are then taken by the three that turned up and then arranged to meet the next day and put them on the list at 2:00 in the morning, saying tomorrow at 3:00 we'll meet at the Casa del Popolo ... so as to screw them all. (1E: 30)

Discursive skills are indeed unequally distributed, favoring a few better-organized members over the vast number of individuals and more informal participants who are less organized. As one activist from a group of "critical consumers" states,

> There was this magnificent charter according to which political and deciding power lies with the assembly that meets every fortnight and is the sole body that can vote and make decisions. And is run dreadfully according to me .... *It's so boring* .... *It's always the same ones that talk*, with twenty years of political experience behind them, and ultimately the language is exclusive, and if you try to bring up some innovative aspiration you're of course expelled. (4A:96)

Decisions are made not just informally but also in a more elite fashion:

> In fact this movement, as well as having these broad participatory moments, also has much more restricted sessions, in which agendas, proposals and political documents are drawn up. Objectively, these sessions involve representatives of organizations who are not always the epitome of novelty, even in terms of their practices .... For instance, the assembly of social forums that closed the European Forum .... While there was the assembly and all the networks brought their agendas up, for all the 360 things that were said, it was then a restricted group, not elected by anyone, that actually pulled the threads together. (3C: 66)

Notwithstanding these difficulties, the movement reopens a public sphere that had been shut off in earlier decades. The dimension of an open space is in fact stressed in the organizational statutes of many groups. The coordination of the European Social Forum presents its goal as constructing "a wider public space in which the networks, associations, movements, social forums, the different social actors, can debate with each other and intertwine their contents, practices, and campaigns. A space that belongs to all" (Fruci 2003: 187). The local social forums in Italy define themselves as open, public arenas for permanent discussion; a forum is, in this interpretation, "a tribune for the local civil society" (Fruci 2003: 174).

Reasoning or Passion?

> We are a group of participants to local social forums all over Europe, who are starting networking between local social forums in Europe. The purpose of the network is to get to know each other, learn from each other, build up memories, exchange experiences on operating practices and processes, and on activities taking place in local social forums. (https://wiki.sheffieldsocialforum.org.uk/ LSFDec2004#EU_ LSF_statement; accessed 22 June 2007)

This public statement, issued from the Third European Social Forum in London, was made at the end of the meeting of the Local Social Forum Network in Europe. The words testify to the relevance of both the symbolic construction of knowledge (to "learn" and "build up memories") and its accumulation (to "exchange experiences"). According to deliberative-democracy theory, the aim of the discourse in public assemblies is to use the strength of one's argument rather than one's passion as a means to define and reach consensus about the public good. Much research on the institutional implementation of deliberative principles refers to the quality of discourse. But where and to what extent can "reason" be utilized by social movements for whom emotional appeals and visions of future utopias are important motivations? If we conceive of reason as synonymous with rationality or lack of passion, social movements are far from the best sites for developing high-quality, reasoned communication; in fact, the role of emotions is not only recognized, but welcomed as necessary for collective mobilization (Jasper 1997). Our research stresses continual efforts to create an open arena of debate, with tolerance for different ideas and a high degree of respect for knowledge and specific competences.

The global justice movement lays particular stock in internal communication. The functioning of the World Social Forum (WSF and the various regional social forums, with their hundreds of workshops and dozens of conferences with invited experts, testifies to the importance given (at least in principle) to knowledge. In the words of one of its organizers, Guenther Schoenlietner defines the WSF as "a market place for (sometimes competing) causes and an 'ideas fair' for exchanging information, ideas, and experiences horizontally"

(Schoenleitner 2003: 140). He states that the WSF promotes exchanges in order "to think more broadly and to construct together a more ample perspective" (141). Investigating recent movements, Francesca Polletta stresses the use of deliberative discussion by activists:

> They expected each other to provide legitimate reasons for preferring one option to another. They strove to recognize the merits of each other's reasons for favoring a particular option ... the goal was not unanimity, so much as discourse. But it was a particular kind of discourse, governed by norms of openness and mutual respect. (Polletta 2002: 7)

In the focus groups, a quest for dispassionate, open confrontation emerged. For all the activists' fears of manipulation and bureaucratization, they identified a shared hope for a flexible, multilayer organizational structure that could create arenas for confrontation among different associations and subjectivities, by which these would not just act in common but also transform each other reciprocally, building new identities, values, and communities.

> The desire for change is so widespread that it overcomes the organizations. The organizations can't manage to sustain it .... There's this great spread of mailing lists, initiatives, leafleting. There's no one site or body that brings them all together. There's a very broad offer, in which the individuals can orient themselves without having to select exclusively, this is a movement open to all. (4A:92)

Furthermore, specific expertise is particularly valued, as reflected by the frequent establishment of "thematic working groups" in the organizational statutes. They exist (at least on paper) in Rete Lilliput, as well as in most local social forums. Knowledge is not presented in an elitist fashion as the skills of the few but as the rich subjectivity of the many. According to the statues of the fair trading cooperative in Florence, "All have a personal richness to share with the others" (Rosi 2003: 116). Many social forums are structured in thematic groups with independent empowerment for developing protest events and campaigns. An emerging trend is that spokes are becoming carriers of substantive knowledge (i.e., relating to the environment, immigration, social policy, urban planning, gender issues, information, civil rights) and interactional-relational competencies (i.e., mediation, conflict resolution, dialogue, and hearings). Working groups that employ "mutual listening" as well as knowledge accumulation are regarded as increasingly important:

> Working groups are very important from my point of view, giving the capacity to grow together, in the search for and also production of content in the working groups ... so much so that by now in the Florence Social Forum alone there are some ten groups, and they're getting along wonderfully. They are getting along that

way because they are attached to some sort of knowledge, to a content, to some substance, and they go on to produce initiatives. (5D: 131)

Substantive competencies are valued in terms of specific contributions to the construction of knowledge. In the words of one participant in the focus group,

> That's what ought to come forth, and this has to be the line to bring out those who are working inside with *specialist knowledge* greater than mine and make them disclose it to me ... for by putting everybody's skills together, everyone looking for an alternative system, we can say I'm not against but I'm for, and that's a verbal gap that is not easy. (2G: 45)

Consensus and Divergence

According to a statement issued by the Turin Social Forum regarding its organizational structure, it "will experiment with an organizational path that favors participation, research of consensus and achieving largely shared decisions." This is a form of decision making in which people try to convince each other of their own arguments, rather than taking a vote or negotiating a give-and-take settlement. The consensus method should enable all to express their opinions, learn from others, and reach decisions that are easier to implement because they are shared. Although consensual and participatory democracy has been emphasized in previous movements (Mainsbridge 1985; Breines 1989; Lichterman 1996), the challenge for the global justice movement is to combine the expressive advantages of deliberation with pragmatically efficient decision making. In fact, "Today, direct action activists embrace consensus but not the deliberative styles that they associate with 'new age' or 'Californian' protest—self-oriented ... and unconcerned with practical politics" (Polletta 2002: 4). The voting procedure generally follows wide debates oriented toward consensus building, and is limited to final documents proposed at the local assembly, national forum, or global forum. Stressing respect for differing opinions, the social forums are meant to be a particular locus for the exchange of ideas where—on the basis of argumentation open to everyone's contribution—consensus is reached around values built up together. There is also emphasis—much more than in past movements—on the importance of reaching consensual decisions and on tolerance and openness towards differing experiences (Epstein 2000).

While the consensus method was initially proposed by the student movement and later taken up with more conviction by the feminist movement, it nonetheless proved hard to run, tending to slow decision making to the point of obstructing action. Many global justice groups revived the consensus model but created new, more or less formalized rules to help overcome the impediments deriving from continuing differences of opinion or manipulation of the process by a few. As a sociologist who has studied the evolution of participatory democracy practices in American movements notes,

> A sixties activist would be surprised by the procedural machinery that today accompanies the democratic deciding process. There are formal roles—timekeepers, facilitators, observers of feelings—and a sophisticated range of gestures. Raising moving fingers as if playing a piano indicates support for a point; making a triangle in the air with forefinger and thumb of both hands indicates concern with respect for rules of the deliberative process; a raised fist indicates an intention to veto the decision. (Polletta 2002: 190–91)[9]

For instance, the Direct Action Network, which coordinated the 1999 Seattle blockade on the WTO delegates, developed a complex formalization of the consensus-oriented decision process. Within small affinity groups, two "facilitators" (a position that rotated inside the group) were charged with leading the debate and encouraging participation by all. When it seemed a consensus was close, the facilitators summarized the proposal emerging from the debate and invited participants to express their positions, which may have ranged from veto to support and through a range of intermediate choices like nonsupport, reservations, and abstention.[10]

The role of consensus is stressed in the statutes of many new organizations of the global justice movement. On March 2003, the national assembly of the Genoa Social Forum embraced the consensual method as "a way to work on what unites us and continue to discuss about what divides us ... so that everyone can feel that the decisions taken are their own, although with different degrees of satisfaction" (quoted in Fruci 2003: 189). Attention to consensus building, with requirements ranging from unanimity to semi-unanimity votes (with the possibility also to express dissent without blocking a decision supported by a large majority) characterized groups as apparently different as the French Agir contre le Chomage (AC!) (Mouchard 2003: 65) and the Italian grassroots union Cobas (della Porta 2003). Rete Lilliput defines the "method of consensus" as a process in which, if a proposal does not receive a total consensus of all participants, there is further discussion in order to find a compromise with those who disagree; if disagreement persists and involves a numerically large minority, the project is not approved (Veltri 2003: 14). In the organizational statutes of Attac France, article 10.7 refers to the "search for a consensual decision" (in Finelli 2003: 35). Attac Italy, less centralized than its French counterpart, stresses the need for frequent consultations—on the model of the Zapatistas'

---

9 The global justice activists distinguish themselves from what they criticize as the "California style," favoring feelings over action, and seek to combine consensus and decision, with a certain pragmatism that sometimes even goes as far as accepting the principle of qualified majority—often two thirds (Polletta 2002: 190–91).

10 Facilitators were used for instance in the participatory process of writing a Charter for the Fair Trade consortium in Italy (Rosi 2003: 127).

"walking and questioning" (Finelli 2003: 46). All Sicilian Social Forums state that decisions have to be taken by "massima condivisione" (maximal level of sharing) (Piazza and Barbagallo 2003). The Disobedients emphasize their search for "unanimity" in decision making (Becucci 2003: 90).

Interviews with informants confirm the value of consensus building. They often stated that the clash of different positions during discussions is supposed to help reach better solutions. As an activist of the Lucca Social Forum explained, after "extensive, highly charged" initial debates on the organizational formula,

> We reached a sort of synthesis. Organizationally, it is supposed to work like this: The assembly takes decisions and is sovereign, but hardly ever votes. It seeks to reach a synthesis equilibrium, a decision that is maximally shared by all, with practically no decisions taken with a noose round your neck—so that an event is organized but nobody comes, so the people don't simply just say yes .... That's the reason why there are hardly any votes. If there is a vote, heads are counted, individuals, again, to emphasize the value of the assembly, and the associations are not counted. (Lucca Social Forum: 4)

Our research shows acceptance of a limited consensus in which multiple identities are emphasized, as opposed a single organizational identity. According to one activist from Bologna,

> [I believe that] one of the great steps forward is that you can say one day I'll go and keep the Tobin Tax stand, another I'll go with the Lilliput network, or I'll put on the white overalls. The strength of this movement is the very fact you can do things and join things, make your contribution even if you have no faith-like swallowing of everything, you can join, one time, twenty percent or thirty percent. (del Giorgio 2002: 234)

Building a common organization thus does not rule out other memberships. Indeed, multiple organizational memberships are seen as an enrichment, enabling the building of a common identity. As one activist explains, there is participation "as long as I can manage to find myself."

> For instance, my collective ... we joined the social forum right from the beginning, and kept it up, and what keeps us there is also collaboration at the tables that might even have interested us rather more, since a university collective like ours often chooses to be ... "in parallel" is too crude ... but "transversal" to the forum. Certainly, there are interpretations, confrontations, identities that also lead you to create a group .... Therefore, either we try an internal battle within the forum itself, by encouraging group divisions, and ultimately you are going to block the work of a whole series of people or comrades, or else the fact of saying *I participate as long as I can manage to find myself* ... maybe choose to have more external participation, to go along to give a contribution on individual questions, and it's there that the

various collaborations arise among groups about pieces of knowledge, training and all the rest. (2D: 46)

Transforming Preferences or Negotiating?

The practices of consensus seeking strengthen bonds, trust, communication and understanding. On the other hand, decision making based on voting creates power blocks, power games, and hegemonic strategies, excluded and included, hierarchies, thus reproducing the same kind of social relations we are opposing. This productivist mentality is the same as our managers and our bosses, all so focused on "results", forgetting the life process that goes into producing those results, hiding the voices excluded for the sake of results, and so excluding different results that would be possible if those voices were included. We have a chance to redefine for ourselves what democracy is, and make it a living example for others. (https://wiki.sheffieldsocialforum. org.uk/LSFDec2004#EU_LSF_statement; accessed 22 June 2007)

Social forums, as the London Social Forum quoted here, define themselves as arenas for discussion oriented towards mutual understanding through the inclusion of different "voices" instead than negotiation among representatives of (more or less powerful) groups. In the global justice movement, the awareness of the movement's pluralistic composition is intertwined with an appeal for the construction of a common discourse. Yet there are instances when the ideal of open engagement is not realized in practice. For example, there is a phenomenon labeled "intergroups" that is highly stigmatized. In the words of one respondent, these are "federations of organizations that sometimes reach agreement but then compete when they can ... because those organizations are in competition and cannot accept one of them following after the other and so forth" (5E: 132). Intergroups are condemned as an expressions of "bossiness" by the better organized over the "individuals" (see also Fruci 2003: 172). In the logic of intergroups, "what is represented are genuine organizations, associations, with a name .... There's delegation, there's representation" (4G: 108). Among intergroups, there is coordination of interests and negotiation, whereby "the envoys of the various parties trying to get out of it what they can," according to another respondent (4A: 108). This is seen as undemocratic because it excludes the less organized. The same respondent continues:

I've been at some assemblies and some meetings in Rome, and according to me it's a real disaster there, I even felt they were mocking me in a way ... anything but consensus method. Who decides is a small group of people that speak a language all of their own. (4A: 108)

The focus groups confirm that, notwithstanding the already mentioned problems in implementing a deliberative model of internal democracy, there is a perceived capacity to *transform initial identities*, developing the feeling of belonging to a community. An activist recalls:

> I got caught up in the wave of enthusiasm too, and got involved in forty-five different activities .... According to me, the individual is activated specifically by curiosity, from having heard something said, by all these colorful demonstrations, by the desire to be there .... You get there .... You also see yourself being offered nice things, and maybe you'll join and go in a direction your way of feeling takes you. *You won't stand aside to check out everything. Probably you'll come into the network, get to know some people, form relationships, become a community* ... of whatever type ... and then maybe gradually you'll become aware of all the entities, and leave some to join others .... There's a lot more room for such things. (4A: 92)

Relations of mutual trust frequently develop during common initiatives, such as campaigns and counter-summits. In joint actions—especially when the scale is smaller, such as small working groups—the capacity is seen for building common values, for "fluidifying," In the words of one activist. The various organizational solutions adopted are thus often defined in pragmatic fashion as experimentations, efforts to get as close as possible to the participatory model that results in real communication and understanding:

> I, personally, in the contamination and in participation in the movement, have come back to believe in certain things and have come to realize that ... it's one thing to arrive at a democratic situation more or less in assemblies where, de facto, more or less preconstituted positions clash, and then there's a vote and a majority and a minority. That's quite different from building a participatory pathway, in mutual respect, where the various positions *fluidify* and the various areas, even the organized ones ...for in the forum there are areas and organizations ... including mine ... that are really organized, yet there's a *new willingness to really fluidify* ... ultimately there's not that trauma that there is in the long run in those organizations that work with the old system instead. (3C: 66, emphasis added)

Interaction around concrete objectives helps, in the activists' view, to build an ever more solid common base. Different subjects join to "get it together" around concrete objectives and build a gradually broader common path. In the following exchange during one of the focus groups, activists of the Florence Social Forum stress how acting together produces identity, as common initiatives—even if initially based upon only few common concerns—increase mutual understanding in a (slow but) important process of reciprocal exchanges.

> 4E: A Forum brings together absolutely different entities, but at least on the big issues they manage to come together .... That's its richness ... the capacity to bring together differing entities that can at least talk about the big issues.

> 4C: That is, I believe that even only a year ago, for instance, it would have been impossible to communicate with each other the way we are doing now .... all that much. I repeat, it's fine that way, since if the confrontation had been a year ago according to me the social forum would immediately have split. It wouldn't have stood up and maybe today the times would be ripe, perhaps ...

4F: Yes, I too think this method worked. I don't know whether over time, there you are ... but for now it's maybe the method that has enabled so many different entities to stay together ...the method you were talking about, of going ahead only on some things, emphasizing the points of convergence, and going forward ... without tackling any maybe too thorny points, no? But likely in time the thing ... but so far the experience is very positive in that sense .... For me, given we're talking about the 1980s ... I don't remember anything of this sort .... There's always been communication difficulties among different universes .... This type of capacity for synthesis had never existed, and that's very positive, even if it's based on the premise of not tackling some thorny points that sooner or later will come along. (4C; 4E; 4F, 89–90)

To conclude, at least from the normative viewpoint, there is trust in a deliberative democracy where individuals (rather than associations) bring their contributions to the *debate*, working toward the emergence of the common good. The deliberative element emerges particularly in the acknowledged higher capacity for dialogue:

The forum has something evangelical, that is, something new, something we were waiting for, something there was a need of .... How is it new? It's new particularly in the way of arguing, the way of confronting each other, in its caution, its different mode of approach, avoiding oppositions. It's bringing together components that are very far from each other and very different, that see each other a different way today. (6G: 144)

Democracy in Movements: Some Conclusions

Our study has identified several characteristics: (1) internal differences are the driving force in the search for forms of participation that respect individual subjectivity and avoid exclusive commitments and vertical control; (2) consensus rules are privileged vis-à-vis majority rules; (3) direct participation is emphasized over representative mechanisms; and (4) leaders are considered as "speakers" or "facilitators." The specific structure of the movement, involving many well-developed organizations, makes the principle of equality among participants difficult to implement, although the delegation of power is limited. Consensual methods are implemented with varying degrees of commitment and success. The social forums open arenas for confrontation, yet decisions are often still taken informally in small groups. The search for the "better argument" is expressed in particular in the development of a specific knowledge. Although intermittently and with more success in some stages of mobilization than others, the movement nonetheless seems to have succeeded in the delicate task of building collective identities that can be presented as plural and tolerant.

The problems that emerged in the functioning of previous movements have not been entirely resolved. Experimentation is underway, with varying success, to seek more democratic models of internal organization. The organizational model chosen adopts instruments from the past and attempts to adapt them to a current situation. While the assembly remains one of the principal arenas of internal democracy, there is nonetheless a search for new rules (facilitators, limitation of delegation, search for consensus) to limit the traditional problems of direct democracy. The "movement of movements" has the peculiarity of building itself upon a dense and rich network of movement organizations, often the product of previous protest cycles. It builds upon the experiences of organizational institutionalization, but also upon reflexive criticism of it. These networks of networks provide important resources but also pose challenges to maintaining open public spaces without discouraging individual participation. In terms of building internal public spheres, the challenge is to maintain a deliberative as opposed to a strategic form of communication. But innovation is especially visible in a value system that stresses diversity rather than homogeneity, subjectivity rather than organizational obedience, transparency—even at the cost of effectiveness, open confrontations oriented to consensus building over decisions; and ideological "contamination" rather than ideological puritanism.

These values could be simply inherited from the outside. The evolution from hierarchical centralization to a network structure involves not only the movement organizations but also firms and public administrations, given the effectiveness of networks in reducing coordination costs and facilitating transmission to the center of information collected on the periphery (Anheier and Themundo 2002). Deliberative democracy is a suggested solution for decision making in different arenas—and movements can reflect changes in organizational ideology developed in other circles and for other purposes.

It seems, however, that if movements have adopted some ideas from their environment, they have adapted them to suit their values and objectives. The organizational elements we have highlighted are indeed subject to adjustment to a number of challenges that the movement has to face, given the available resources.

In the first place, the challenge of post-Fordist society causes a weakening of traditional identities, with fragmentation particularly marked in the social basis of the workers' movement. The deregulation of the economic market, with the spread of nontraditional jobs, has helped to fragment the social reference point for protest. Even the social movements of the libertarian Left have seen a tendency to specialize around single issues. At the same time, however, there has been a structuring of more or less formal organizations and groups linked to various movements emerging in the 1970s and 1980s, but also to the "old Left." Under these conditions, the movement faces the challenge to keep different, heterogeneous groups together by developing tolerant identities. In a reticular, flexible structure, the forums represent arenas open to horizontal communication and relying on respect for differing opinions.

Second, one element of postmodernity is a spreading of a culture that emphasizes the role of the individual. Processes of "individualization" have in fact been seen as obstacles to the development of collective action, taking away the strong identifications of the past. On the other hand, as some scholars of social movements (especially Melucci 1989) have already indicated contemporary societies offer multiple resources for building complex identities. In some circumstances, collective action has been observed even within cultures marked by personalism, i.e., "ways of speaking or acting which highlight a unique personal self. Personalism supposes that individuality has inherent value, apart from one's material and social achievement, no matter what connections to a specific community or institutions the individual maintains" (Lichterman 1996: 86). The challenge for contemporary movements is, then, to develop a model of internal democracy able to bring all the subjectivities together by valuing the role of individuals rather than sacrifice for the collective.

Finally, neoliberalism, by shedding light on markets' unwillingness to self-regulate and governments' incapacity to intervene, has delegitimized representative democracy. Globalization as the liberalization of movements of goods and capital has spread an image of the growing inability of national governments to intervene in major economic and social problems (starting with unemployment), with particular deterioration in policies for reducing inequality. International organizations seem, for their part, to be oriented towards investment in a policy of favoring free trade, with a growing democratic deficit in public decisions. While these circumstances tend to reduce citizens' trust and interest in democratic participation, the new cycle of protest, by contrast, is witness to a growing demand for politics—albeit of a new, unexpected type—from the new generations in particular. In this sense, the challenge for the movement is to build an organizational model that can enable broad participation in joint campaigns, combining social engagement and political effectiveness.

Even if many local social forums disappeared after some years of mobilization, the existence of a European network that is still active and contributes to the ESF organizational process testifies to the capacity of this type of arena to survive over time. Additionally, even when local social forums collapsed, they helped promoting the mobilizations that followed by both facilitating relations of mutual trust between activists of different groups and by spreading horizontal and consensual decision making as a way to construct new networks. Especially, the experiences within the social forums pushed activists and organizations to bridge their specific concerns with more general and global ones as well as a a conception that emphasizes "horizontality" as bottom-up, non-hierarchical networking of individuals and groups with different backgrounds (della Porta and Mosca 2008). Although many of the social forums had a relatively short life, they had however long-lasting effects on the organizations that took part in them.

Chapter 9

Movement Strategizing as Developmental Learning: Perspectives from Cultural-Historical Activity Theory

John Krinsky and Colin Barker

New York City, 2000. For the past four years, activists from Community Voices Heard (CVH), a group devoted to encouraging organization among the city's poor, have been campaigning against city hall's "workfare" system. Their immediate goals have changed over time. At first, highlighting the program's poor compensation and working conditions, they hoped to inflame public opinion against the program as a whole. In late 1997, the state legislature denied workfare workers "employee" status, turning campaigners to agitation for a "transitional community jobs" program as a better model than workfare for both getting welfare recipients into work, and providing community benefits (Krinsky 2008). Coalitions won victories, but they turned out to be paper only. At state level, they won legislation but with no follow-up money or appropriate regulations. On the municipal level, they got the City Council to consider transitional jobs legislation, but faced strong opposition from the mayor.

Frustrated at these setbacks, CVH turned to a new organizing tactic. Sympathetic academics helped design a survey that their members could administer to other workfare workers. The aim was both to spread the word about CVH's organizing, and to find out how much money the city was saving by paying workfare workers welfare benefits instead of regular salaries. Perhaps, they thought, we can organize a large demonstration, presenting symbolic invoices to city hall, and demanding payment of the difference.

As we pick up the story, CVH has found a sympathetic academic (the first author) to analyze the survey's findings. His report, just in, confirms what campaigners have been arguing for a long time. Workfare workers are indeed doing work once done by regular, unionized, municipal employees, but without the pay, benefits or rights enjoyed by these regular workers (Wernick, Krinsky and Getsos 2000). CVH campaigners can now offer clear and well-calculated figures to support their case. Yet they are uncertain of the way forward.

Meanwhile, after four years' work, a team of advocacy lawyers has just lost a major case that also dealt with workfare workers' working in regular workers' jobs. Defeat has left them, too, wondering where next to go.

Two of CVH's leading activists, together with the researcher, sit down for a meeting with one of the lawyers. They review the survey results. The lawyer responds to the discussion by passing over a page from the state's welfare law. It expressly forbids workfare workers from doing a significant portion of the work in regular workers' job titles. Surely, suggests the lawyer, you should use your survey to focus a public campaign for immediate *abolition* of the present workfare system? The scope of that proposed demand initially rocks the CVH organizers back on their heels, for it is more radical in scope than anything they had been voicing publicly. They agree, nonetheless, to put the question directly to their members: should we run a campaign for wholesale workfare abolition? In the event, the members readily agree, and the CVH activists set to work on building alliances across the city around this new and more radical demand.

What's Going On?

For anyone interested in movement strategizing, this story has elements of the familiar. Frustrated in their previous efforts, campaigners set out to try something different, in this case more radical. What's involved in this strategic shift?

First, there are some preconditions. Previous work with the lawyer had developed sufficient *trust* between them to allow the CVH organizers to seek his advice on an open-ended basis. In turn, that relationship gave the CVH organizers a modicum of what Marshall Ganz (Ganz 2000, 2004) has called *strategic capacity*, by affording them access to a perspective beyond what they had themselves generated. Thus, they could combine *salient knowledge* of workfare-generated inequality, derived from CVH's membership, with what Ganz calls "heuristic processes" or new models of action and perspectives on their own struggles, gained through alliances with others. With these new perspectives, they could recontextualize their knowledge of their members' lives and demands and start to strategize anew. Additionally, the presence of an academically credentialed researcher provided some extra weight of respectability to the public presentation of their research findings, whose "objectivity" imparted greater seriousness to the abolition claim

Second, the shift of direction has some characteristic features. Everyone at the meeting was motivated to oppose workfare and to draw on each other's expertise. The act of combining the "means" at the disposal of those around the table led to a *dramatic* recasting of the organizers' strategic goal. Though CVH had long argued that workfare should be abolished, they had always regarded abolition as a long-term goal, beyond anything that could provide the programmatic basis of an immediate campaign. That the organizers expressed surprise initially—and that everyone shared something of a sense of elation after the meeting—suggests that the *emotional* and *cognitive* aspects of the strategizing at the meeting are difficult to pull apart. Both the activists and the lawyer alike belonged to groups in whom recent activities had induced both a sense of partial defeat and a sensed need for something new if campaigning was to continue. Everyone in the meeting was thus inclined to be open to new suggestions, at least as a basis for rethinking current strategies.

The new idea needed testing. Polling CVH's membership about a possible new strategic direction was necessary, not just as an act of legitimation—as participatory decision making is a central feature of CVH's practice—but also to enhance the activists' own confidence.

To carry our story forward, once CVH's members ratified the new strategic line, there was an obvious next question: where should they look for allies for a new campaign to abolish workfare? Here, new opportunities were unfolding. The main municipal workers union, District Council 37 (DC 37) was a clear candidate for an alliance. For one thing, its members were being directly hurt by the spread of workfare. For another, the union enjoyed both the institutional access and the legal standing to act against the displacement entailed by workfare. Matters of timing were also significant. The union was currently undergoing a massive reorganization following a corruption scandal that had recently chased most of its most powerful leaders from the union (and some into prison). One aspect of that scandal was that, five years before, despite rank-and-file opposition, the union leaders had rigged the vote to ratify a five-year contract, whose side-agreements had helped enable workfare's dramatic expansion. The same corrupt union leaders had allied themselves with the mayor, for whom workfare was a pet program. Perhaps, then, DC 37's new administrators might promote public opposition to workfare, as a way of symbolizing change at the union (Greenhouse 1999)?

How, though, could the new union leadership be pushed to join a campaign for workfare's *abolition*? How might the CVH activists use their survey report to maximum effect? They tried, unsuccessfully, to get the *New York Times* to run a story on the survey report. When that failed, they gave the "scoop" to the main civil service newspaper. Because, at that time, university student mobilization against sweatshop-made goods was growing and attracting sympathetic attention from labor unions, the researcher and the organizers agreed to include the term "Public Sector Sweatshop" in the article's title. Connecting workfare to the sweatshop issue might both gain general labour support, and, if nothing else, "shame" the municipal union leaders into more intensive action against workfare.

Thinking about Strategizing

All of this suggests, firstly, the *developmental* nature of strategizing: one strategic decision entails a chain of other decisions, aimed at and involving a variety of social relations. Each strategic move entails changes in these relations, remaking the social bases of each subsequent new strategic decision.

It also suggests, secondly, that strategizing cannot be understood if we limit our view to *individuals* making decisions. Rather, as Ganz (2000, 2004) suggests, strategizing is a *distributed process*, occurring in *systems* rather than in single minds, or in the "black box of individual cognition" (Johnston 1995: 218). Even could we pry open the "black box" of individual minds, we could not discover how and why the parties to the meeting—and the union leaders after them—arrived collectively at the view that they could and should oppose workfare more strongly than before.

Instead, strategizing is deeply relational. First, it involves the activity of many actors pursuing various goals. Some goals are consistent with the goals of others, but some are not. Second, it involves actors in *projective* or *prospective* (i.e., future-oriented) attempts to coordinate the activity of others who may partially share their goals, but who also have a set of their own concerns. CVH, DC 37, the lawyers, and the academic all shared a common antipathy toward workfare, but in varying degrees, and for a wide variety of reasons. Also, they operated in overlapping but not identical institutional environments. For example, while CVH operated as a participatory democratic pressure group, DC 37 was a top-down, highly bureaucratized union of 125,000 city employees with 56 separate locals and as many collective bargaining agreements. Third, strategizing involves attempts to overcome blockages to this coordination thrown up by habit and others' attachment to particular means or to conflicting goals (such as the *Times* reporter's lack of interest in the story or the union leaders' interest—until the scandal—in minimizing conflict with the mayor). Fourth, success in coordinating action depends on actors' willingness to align their wills, achievable only through mutual dialogues. In these, relations of trust or mistrust, the cognitive-emotional stances each takes toward what other participants say, and each actor's "reading" or "scenting" of the situation as it develops, all play important parts.

Timing too is an important part of this calibration of the positions that potential allies or adversaries may take. For example, DC 37 would not have proved as promising an ally for an abolition position two years earlier. Also relevant is the way that temporal horizons are set for particular goals. Turning the "abolition" demand into a proximate rather than a long-term goal gave it a new meaning, and affected its power to attract allies—once the lawyer had aligned it to the idea that workfare was actually illegal in terms of current state law.

Standpoints on Strategizing

In this chapter, we attempt to stitch together these various elements of strategizing. This is both a critical and a constructive enterprise. Throughout, we urge a perspective on strategizing that diverges from the dominant microfoundational approach. Social scientists looking at strategy most often use the tools of rational choice theory or game theory, which are bound to rationalist and individualist accounts of cognition and subjectivity. Moreover, they—like much of the symbolic interactionist literature with which they otherwise share little—focus on the choices of a single actor (whether an individual or group), and thereby fail to see the ways in which the entire "arena" of strategy is reshaped due to the ongoing, dramatic, mutually conditioned choices of others (Jasper 2006). In other words, in the process of strategizing, the "game" itself may not remain constant. Even Jasper, who criticizes rationalist approaches to strategy as too narrow, seeks microfoundations in the dilemmas that arise in interactive settings. Conversely, in the most interesting versions of game theory, action *among* settings is understood as shaping action within them (Tsebelis 1999), and even the assumption of a unitary actor is questioned (Hug 1999). Yet game theory has not proven to be very adaptable to empirical research on complex, multiple-actor, interactions (Petersen 1994: 501) and still requires a raft of disciplining assumptions and mathematical prowess beyond that available to many social scientists and certainly beyond the ken of most activists! Though space forbids our confronting game theory's viewpoints directly (Munck 2001), the theory construction we pursue should lead decisively away from them. In this chapter, we attempt to go *beyond* the immediate settings of strategic dilemmas, not to say that they are unimportant, but to understand the ways in which larger structural limitations on action shape actors' strategizing.

In elaborating our perspective on strategizing, therefore, we draw on theories of developmental learning that are, we think, consonant with work on cultural dynamics in the social movements field (Steinberg 1999) and with some recent sociological discussions on culture and cognition (DiMaggio 1997). The theory of learning to which we particularly refer here—cultural-historical activity theory, or CHAT—is better known in departments of education, psychology, and even management than it is in sociology or politics. Social movement scholars' relative unawareness of CHAT is a little surprising, given CHAT's strong affinities with those dialogic and pragmatic styles of thinking about culture which have gained increasing centrality in their field. As a theory of learning, we suggest, CHAT can help scholars better specify the processes involved in movement strategizing. CHAT theory suggests looking at *strategy* as involving and arising from a culturally suffused, emotionally laden process of developmental, distributed learning, and considering *strategizing* as future- and goal-oriented activity within and among systems of joint activity. Understanding strategizing as a developmental learning process opens the possibility of better accounts of strategic shifts and turning points, as subjects discover not only new ways of acting, new alliances and divisions of labour within them, but also new goals and motives for action.

Strategy and Learning as "Activity" and Dialogue

A standard formulation, such as that advanced by Ganz, treats strategy as the means by which "you get what you need to get what you want." Ganz also suggests that strategizing is "a way of orienting *current* action toward future goals" (Ganz 2000: 1011). When we talk about movement wants or needs we imply some kind of *unity of purpose*. But the question then arises, how does this unity develop, or, how do the various parties to strategic decision making *interpret* this purpose?

In our example, the organizers, the researcher, and the lawyer were all united in their hostility in general terms toward workfare, but in tactical-temporal terms their views were not aligned. CVH's organizers had not, till the meeting, where the lawyer urged them to recontextualise their research findings, seen workfare *abolition* as a goal to be directly campaigned for. Until then, "abolition" had not been an *immediate demand*. The act of aligning their interpretations converted the group at the meeting *into* a strategizing subject in its own right. The "completion," so to speak, of the formation of this subject lay in its activity toward an object, and its dialogue about it.

Marc Steinberg (1998, 1999, 2002) and others (Barker 2006; Barker and Lavalette 2002; Collins 1999; Krinsky 2007; Mische and Pattison 2000) have worked with the idea of "dialogue" in the context of social movements, drawing on the writings of Mikhail Bakhtin (1986) and Valentin Vološinov (1986). There are several key ideas running through a "dialogic" view of cultural dynamics, including *utterance, genre, multivocality,* and *dialogue.*

Human communication consists, not of the grammarians' words or sentences, but of "utterances," as brief as a sigh or a smile or as long as a novel. The utterance is the building block of dialogue, an act in a social relationship that expects and demands a response, and an act that is at once cognitive and emotional in content. In this view, an utterance is an event in a relationship.

The concept of genre refers to the idea that speech develops characteristic forms, fitted to particular settings and social relationships. Like "repertoires" in social movement studies, genres bear the imprint of the spatio-temporal contexts in which they congeal. Just as grain seizures featured as part of a popular protest repertoire in a Europe with localized markets conjoined with abject poverty and actual surpluses, but fail to "fit" contemporary European politics, so too speech genres are an important "index of society." Familiarity with genres enables speakers to "play" with them, recombine their elements, import usages associated with other genres, etc., and thus contribute to the "multivocality" of speech. Thus, as familiarity with religious processions and festivals provided popular politics with a form of collective action out of which contemporary marches and rallies grew, "official genres" may be parodied, developed critically, subverted, turned to other purposes.

Multivocality suggests that a given "utterance" may always be interpreted in various ways. Its interpretation in dialogue is a function of the expectations and genre conventions that interlocutors bring to it. These expectations include the "emotional-volitional" tone of both utterances and others' responses. Thus, where interlocutors trust each other (as in our example above, or in Ganz's account of the Farm Worker leaders' development of strategic capacity), the process of strategizing according to common goals may be advanced. Where trust frays, as in the well-documented example of SNCC after 1964 (Carson 1995; Payne 1995; Polletta 2005; Robnett 1997), strategizing may be severely stymied. Where there is complete mistrust, even the well-intentioned may have their motives called into question (Barker 2006). In any case, the dialogic interaction is a *drama* of sorts, however improvisational, in which subjects *actively* interpret each other's utterances, and through them each other's intentions.

Though these ideas have mainly been pitched against theories of "framing"— in which "frames" or "ideological packages" of diagnoses, prognoses, and motivational symbols are "sent and received" by activists and potential recruits, bystanders, and authorities without their meanings changing—they have clear relevance to discussions of strategy in social movements, as well.

Cultural-Historical Activity Theory

CHAT's roots lie in the work of Lev Vygotsky (1978, 1986) who treated human beings' consciousness as a historically emergent product of their active relationship with material nature and with culture. Vygotsky distinguished humans from the rest of the animal kingdom by their systematic use of tools and signs as "mediating instruments" to control their environment and to develop social organization. Humans pass on to later generations a whole elaborated set of material and ideational instruments that they use to transform the world around them and whose use and development also continuously transforms the character of the species that creates and deploys them. Humans are also inherently social beings, whose development as individuals is intimately dependent on the patterns of cooperation they create among themselves in the context of their own species' larger historical development. Their culture is itself a historical achievement. Its emerging forms must be assimilated by each successive generation to be further used and developed. Yet its inheritors are not mere passive receptors but creative users, just as the culture they receive and transmit is itself an always-changing phenomenon.

Of all the "tools" developed by humankind, perhaps the most significant is speech, whose elaboration alters and enables simultaneously the structure of individual consciousness, the forms of sociality, and the development and transmission of technical achievements. Human consciousness, in this account, is anything but static, but is, rather, engaged in a constant process of learning—that specific process of adaptation by which humans develop. And significantly, it is inherently social, for the very means it uses—above all speech—are drawn from society.

Learning in CHAT studies is more than a simple "internalizing" and "assimilating" of existing cultural practices and ideas. It is a creative activity, involving mastering elements of existing culture so as to both participate in and further develop that culture. To assimilate a culture, itself a historical product, involves learning the use and meaning of that culture's varied artifacts: its words, tools, instruments, operations, ideas, institutions, objects, rules. Learning is a process simultaneously of assimilation and self-development, in which progressive mastery is achieved through interactive communication with other members, achieved through a historically developed system of *signs*, and above all (but not only) *words*. The origins of the higher, specifically human forms of intra-psychic activity thus lie in external, social activity. Children's development involves a whole series of collaborative journeys with competent adults or peers who play a vital cooperative role in helping them to master new tasks. Consciousness in all its aspects is not simply something that occurs only through quas-inatural individual psychological development, but is built up, mediated by individuals' active social relations with others. So also with social movement strategizing: the idea of cooperative, social learning extends to learning by adults whose lives, in a sense, involve constant "strategic" work.

CHAT was elaborated by Vygotsky's collaborator, A.N. Leontiev (1978, 1981), who emphasized the social nature of goal-directedness. In a "primeval hunt," for example, some participants actually drive animals away from themselves by acting as "beaters." Given their goal of eating meat, their actions only make sense when we realize that they are driving the animals towards other participants who stand ready with spears. The hunters are engaged in a *collective activity* through which they coordinate their varied actions. The group's *motive* involves a co-alignment of a variety of individual goals. On this basis, Leontiev proposes a distinction between (individual) "action" and (group) "activity." To make sense of human actions, we need to locate them within the larger activities of which they are part. Activities are *realized* through goal-directed actions, and exist only in the form of chains of such actions (Leontiev 1981), meaning that, in shared activities, we are constantly engaged in assessing our own parts, and "strategizing" our relations to them, in temporal progression.

These ideas have been further systematized by the Finnish theorist, Yrjö Engeström. If Vygotsky's basic idea is of *action* as a three-way relation between subject, mediating instrument, and object, consideration of *activity* requires attention to additional, social factors, producing a multiple relation that includes such matters as group "rules," "division of labor," and "community." Engeström has offered a diagrammatic representation that has achieved considerable prominence in CHAT studies (Figure 9.1).

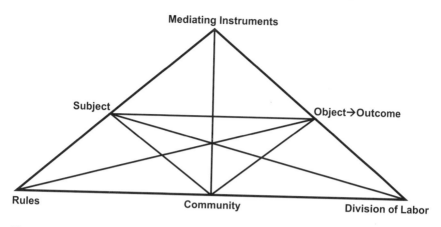

Figure 9.1   Engeström's activity system

Source: Engeström 1987.

Rules refer to habits and repertoires as well as formal rules, and they are sustained in communities through divisions of labor (and are sustained by these divisions of labor). "Community" denotes a collectivity larger than the subject, in which the subject is part of the division of labor, and in which the subject shares some motivation with others in the community. The "community node" is a critical meeting point *among* activity systems, as it represents the collection of a range of subjects with partially overlapping objects. Thus, in the workfare opponents' meeting at the beginning of this chapter, the organizers were part of the lawyer's community and part of the researcher's community, and vice-versa. Only in the course of their meeting did they constitute a *new* subject, whose community included newspaper reporters and labor unions. The introduction of the idea of *collective subjects* pursuing *shared objects* represents an important advance beyond individualist theories of consciousness and cognition.

Expansive Learning and Contradictions

One problem strategic actors may face is that existing cultural materials may provide no easily available answers to a learning problem, forcing subjects to develop their own creative responses. Engeström calls this "expansive learning." He offers a recursive model of cyclical learning driven by contradictions, which can be represented by a spiral diagram (Figure 9.2).

The starting point in box 1 sees participants individually and collectively experiencing a "primary contradiction," expressed as a "need state" (i.e., an only partially articulated idea of a new need) arising from doubts and disagreements about current practices, social relations or received wisdom. The stresses of the situation provoke some kind of initial explanation of the problem and at least

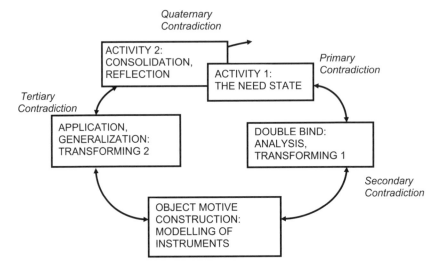

Figure 9.2   Cycle of expansive learning

Source: Engeström 1987.

hints of possible ways forward. In our New York example, when CVH was initially confronted with its own survey results, the organizers were not certain what they could do with them, even though they confirmed their own strong impressions. They were experiencing a kind of programmatic deadlock, a quite common experience in movement development. Such a deadlock can be broken if imaginative experimentation with other possible ways of conducting the activity leads participants to produce potential models of alternatives, whose implications then which need evaluation and testing.

Secondary contradictions can emerge between or among elements of an activity system as these possible alternative solutions are contemplated. Any proposed solution risks upsetting existing procedures or relations. In our workfare example, the idea of a campaign for workfare abolition, as it emerged in the course of the meeting, clashed with the internal rules and division of labor in CVH, necessitating a poll of the membership before the organizers could commit to proceeding.

Tertiary contradictions are discontinuities between established modes of activity and ones that are better adapted towards new ends, which in a sense are " more advanced" in that they already involve significant learning. Engeström suggests that more advanced activity will often be resisted by those attached to established ways of doing things. They will resist testing out new modes of activity, including new ways of dividing labor, interpreting objects, new tools, expanding or contracting communities, and developing new rules that such testing entails. The potential tensions thus generated require a high level of trust, to keep a collective subject from disintegrating. In the workfare example, the strong norms of organizers' accountability to members required them to discuss the new possibilities with members (who turned out to welcome the new activity!).

Finally, quaternary contradictions emerge among "neighboring" activity systems. Activity systems relate to each other in different ways, impinging on and intervening in each other. They can, for example, be "nested," with individuals or subgroups of actors defining one activity system that itself acts in the context of a more aggregated actor, as with, say, an opposition group inside a labor union, or a radical faction within a social movement organization. Also, different actors with different motives may be oriented on the same object. To the degree that one activity system reorients itself via some form of "expansive learning," it will have consequential effects on other "neighboring" activity systems, potentially setting off a chain of further contradictions. In our New York example, CVH's decision to engage in active campaigning for workfare abolition had effects on city hall, on parallel organizing groups, on local labor unions and so on, partly reshaping the whole field of interactions. To recognize this is to break out of the all-too-often partial analyses of movements that Jasper rightly criticizes, where other actors are relegated to "context" and particular movement actors are elevated to the role of the only agents around. The case also indicates the inherent complexity of strategizing, since decisions are liable to have the developmental consequences already noted, and to demand attention to other, parallel and simultaneous problems at the same time.

Although contradictions offer opportunities for expansive learning, not all opportunities are seized effectively. Where contradictions in activity systems are not resolved, any cycle will turn out to be non-expansive, leaving participants with unresolved problems. Blockages may occur at any point in the cycle, and there are no guarantees that, even where "new learning" occurs, it will turn out to be appropriate. As Engeström remarks, activities at each point in the cycle are conducted under conditions of "uncertainty and intensive search," often involving significant stresses and fractures in social relations. Finally, in a nod towards dialogic theories, Engeström notes that activity systems are "multivoiced" and that one feature of an expansive cycle is "a reorchestration of these voices."

Strategy, Structure, Totality

The idea that activity systems may be nested and that expansive learning involves the "reorchestration" of voices in and among activity systems raises a larger issue for the study of strategy, namely, that an adequate study of strategizing cannot be limited to the immediate interactive environment of a given subject. Instead, adequately theorizing strategy and strategizing requires a sense of *structures*, or more enduring patterns of behavior at a range of scales that act as "rules and resources" for action, but also, crucially, as a *target* for strategy as well.

Structures, therefore, like activity systems, are not static and monolithic. They are changeable and internally complex and contradictory. Moreover, if viewed from the dialectical tradition from which CHAT is developing as a perspective on human development, strategy and strategic learning have to be seen as part of, and directed to, a *totality* of relations, rather than as the singular, mostly rational choices of interacting individuals within a rule-bound setting. In this section, we will explain why, and suggest the advantages for studying strategy that viewing strategizing in this way provides.

Let us be clear about our general point: First, in contrast to those who seek "microfoundations" for social action (including strategizing), in our view, there is no specific "level" of activity that ought to be privileged for the study of strategy. We assume that there are wholes or structures that have real effects both as arenas and as targets of action, as "rules and resources" and as objects of activity. Strategizing can neither be brought down to the level of individual consciousness, nor even the interactive "moment" of dyadic or triadic relations. This is not to say, however that social position is sufficient to explain strategy, nor to suppose that the regularities of social stratification, or some other "structural" factor, automatically produce "rules of engagement" with the consensus and regularity supposed by game theory. Second, "structures" are not just "out there" entities, but are discovered, made and remade by those who are subjected to them. How this discovery, making, reconstructing and remediating is achieved is a function, among other things, of just the kinds of factors that Ganz identified as lying behind "strategic capacity," namely, exposure, in relations of relative lack of mistrust, to additional varieties of sources of stimulus, information, and the like.

In real-world settings, anyone strategizing successfully has to recognize that there are "levels" of structure, which vary in terms of the immediacy of their effects on us and in their susceptibility to proximate action. The totality of these structures is, in that sense, multi-leveled, and effective strategizing must handle this complexity. Jasper and game theorists talk about different sizes of "arenas" in which strategizing occurs, but there is another point, namely, that larger "arenas" are not just environments *for* action but also "targets" with degrees of susceptibility to collective action. For example, the Giuliani administration at city hall was part of CVH's "environment" of action. It had obvious and significant effects on the situations in which CVH acted. It was a target for activists, but in different ways or at different levels. The immediate sense in which it was a target was that activists hoped that, if the appropriate form of action could be found, the Giuliani administration could be persuaded to shift its policy on workfare. But it was a more general "target" for quite a few of the activists in that it was also a representative of "neoliberalism" and much else besides. As such, it was a more general environment-and-target for action. Indeed, getting involved in anti-workfare activism was, for organizers and rank-and-file members, alike, usually only one of several ways that they could imagine mobilizing against the governing arrangements in New York

City. Getting a sense of what is possible to alter with available, potentially mobilizable resources and what is more apparently immutable, and thus seeming to be "structural," is part of the strategizing task. The definition and communication of this sense is an activity that must also be constructed of and through historically available artifacts and idioms.

On this basis, we can then move to a further clarification, which is the recognition that everyone's *standpoint* means they can only gain a "partial" view of the whole. It is one thing to know you need a picture of the whole to make sense of the parts, but another to gain a completely adequate one. Building pictures of the totality is something we have to do repeatedly and experimentally. Sometimes a piece of experience can make us redraw our picture to a larger or smaller extent. That is what happened in the meeting with the lawyer. The totality took on new shape: Abolition discourse, which had seemed "out of reach" for practical purposes took on a new "immediacy," as did the sense of who might compose the new "we" that might issue the new challenge (i.e., the newly chastened, partially reformed union might now be available as a conditional part of "a new we"). The "developmental" quality of strategizing therefore involves the dramatic "reorganization" or "reconceptualization" of categories, and thus, the internal representation of new connections made among parts of a much larger picture.

In order to strategize, then, it is necessary to possess some kind of rudimentary "map of the situation," some account of the world which puts the various bits of information accessible to us into some kind of meaningful relation to each other. Such maps are themselves more or less unstable, being open to redrawing in the light of new experiences, new arguments, new insights derived from joint activity with others.

The idea that "structures" both *constrain* and *enable* activity is a basic aspect of dialectical social thought. What needs to be added, is the idea of *immanence*, which refers to the potential an existing activity or an existing group has to transform itself though active interaction with the world, and is another key idea in dialectical thought. To think of structures in this way means that the relative weight of the apparently contradictory possibilities of constraint and enabling should be understood as being in an unstable balance. What at time *t* appears to be a monolithic bloc of constraints can, at time *t+1*, take on a different aspect, as a negotiable space for collective intervention, for joint activity. Equally, from one time period to another, what had previously looked like openings and possibilities can take on the grim appearance of gray, imprisoning walls. The shapes of hope and confidence, the patterns of aspiration and cynicism, fluctuate along with commitments to particular activity paths and particular organizational formats. Every contextualization of activity carries an affectual freight, inspiring or disabling particular forms of joint activity. A *re*contextualization, like that achieved in the lawyer's office in our story, can impart and involve a particularly strong affective charge.

Finally, the idea of totality and structures as key elements in a theory of strategizing insists that in the process of making sense of their situations, subjects totalize, and in so doing, begin to see themselves not as simple entities, but instead, as multifaceted participants in the inherently complex web of multiple memberships and in numerous and sometimes contradictory activity systems. These multiple memberships exert often-contradictory pressures on them, resulting in the kinds of dilemmas that Jasper investigates. They also provide them with various specific tools that they may bring to bear in the course of the joint activities of strategizing, thus imparting to subjects the very possibility of resourcefulness on which Ganz's "strategic capacity" relies.

Reckoning in Space and Time

If, as we argue, strategizing is a developmental learning process, then the strategizing subject's ability to *sustain* development becomes crucial. This is easy when winning is the result, but victories and defeats do not always produce straightforward results, nor do they always present themselves clearly. Rather, they are events or changes in the relations around the victor or the vanquished that must be *reckoned* as victories or defeats in terms of a goal or set of goals. Moreover, we can't discuss "successes" and "failures" in strategizing without specifying what the parameters of these judgments were. At any particular moment, it is possible to win on one level and lose on another. In the successful anti-workfare case, while the re-orchestration of voices into a New York chorus for abolition did help reduce workfare's credibility at the local level, it could not prevent the city's advocates of workfare from gaining a foothold in national policy circles and from selling their local "successes" to congress.

When success is not so clear, actors need what Voss (1996: 252–4) has called a "sustaining narrative" so that, whatever the outcome of this battle, they have reasons to believe that they can return to *win* other battles, and eventually the whole war. Sustaining narratives are one part of a more general task of strategizing in movements, namely, that of actors finding what we might call appropriate "spatio-temporal perspectives" on their own relations with each other and with their goals. Often, movement actors are urged to rethink their own problems and actions, almost to distance themselves from them and draw new connections between them and other potential times, places or institutional settings. When successful, this transposition of ideas and feelings from one genre or repertoire to another helps accomplish the "recontextualization of local knowledge" that Ganz sees as a key to strategic capacity. Activists may find that language or other tools used in one setting, when used in a new context, are invested with new spatial, temporal, and institutional parameters, even if they continue to bear some of their older meanings (Bakhtin 1984 [1929]; Billig et al. 1988; Middleton and Edwards 1990; Steinberg 1998).

In our original example, the "Abolish Workfare" claim had adorned CVH placards for years, alongside a claim that workfare was akin to slavery. It was part of what might be understood as a genre of demonstrating against workfare, appropriate to loud demonstrations on the street, but not to "serious" policy claims in City Council or the courts. It had become little more than a rhetorical flourish against a background of increasingly fatalistic resignation to the idea that workfare was becoming a permanent feature of social policy. In CVH's revised campaign, however, "Abolish Workfare" took on new life and temporal urgency as a claim to be made, as often as possible, with a new set of allies, in the media, and increasingly in "serious" policy settings.

Strategy and Leadership

If strategy is a learning process born of prospective activity within, across, and upon social relations, the question about who strategizes—especially in movements—arises quickly. Just as Gramsci understood that everyone is an intellectual, but not everyone performs the *function* of an intellectual, so in movements not everyone performs the function of a strategizing leader (Gramsci 1971). One aspect of leadership is to give direction to others in ways that fit the circumstances of the setting, of the specific time and place. At the same time, however, to lead in strategizing from the CHAT perspective involves a particular intellectual activity: namely, that of prospectively modelling ways of coordinating activity aimed at a specific end among different settings and situations. This role requires the "strategic capacity" of which Ganz speaks, precisely because it highlights a fluctuating but real distribution of learning and a division of labor within movements. The line is between those whom Gramsci termed "organic" intellectuals, that is, those whose previous reflexive experiences of movements have encouraged them to think generally and comparatively about movement problems, to "think aloud" about these matters, and those whose intellectual contribution at the moment of strategizing consists chiefly in offering assent, doubt, or refusal. This, clearly, is a function of a division of labor, not just in "society" at large, but also within organizations. Hence, in our example, the organizers, graduate student, and legal advocate were thinking aloud about strategy, with the CVH members called on to give assent or refusal for a new rhetorical strategy with respect to workfare. At the same time, however, a leadership core of members worked with the organizers and the graduate student to craft the ways in which the new message would be rolled out at a press conference at the report's release. In a rehearsal meeting the night before the press conference, the members reacted to the graduate student's presentation by telling him, in no uncertain terms, to speak plainly and not in an "academese" to which they could not relate, and worked with him on new language for his presentation.

Nevertheless, the strategizing function does require a focusing of energetic attention (and even a learned capacity to sit through "meetings") that does not attract everyone. One role of organizers is to identify those among the rank-and-file who might be convinced to become grassroots leaders. In CVH, as in other groups, organizers do this by monitoring their own interactions and talking with welfare recipients, public housing residents, and workfare workers, and noting who among them is particularly excited about talking with the organizers and who already is trying to understand their personal problems politically. Then, a whole lot of convincing and courtship sets in to get these potential leaders to commit needed time to the organization. Finally,

> they train WEP workers to run meetings, lead actions, give testimony about the impact of WEP and engage in discussions with elected officials, labor leaders, and the press. Training takes place at organizing committee meetings, in Saturday sessions, in one-on-one meetings in people's homes, and right before actions. Trainings include a combination of readings about political ideology, discussions, presentations, and role plays covering the potential scenarios leaders can expect to face in action. (Minieri and Getsos 2007: 81)

In short, organizers work hard to attract people to whom authority and strategic input can be distributed within the organization.

Conclusion

CHAT seems to offer us some resources for thinking about strategizing in movements, especially because it unambiguously focuses on people trying to solve problems in conditions where there are multiple uncertainties, and because its account of human actors treats them as simultaneously socially (inter-) dependent and creative in their activities. The human figures who populate the CHAT world take in and transform the cultural resources ('tools and signs') developed by their own and previous generations, making and remaking their world. CHAT offers ways of seriously exploring their acting and thinking, with due attention to their emotional (and aesthetic) qualities, and to the complexity of their intellectual constructions. It deserves to be better known in the social and political sciences.

The view of strategizing we have attempted to argue for here owes much—more than we could indicate in a single essay—to previous work in the social movements field, notably that of Marshall Ganz and James Jasper. But we also combine their quite distinct contributions with a dialogic perspective on culture in movements most associated with Marc Steinberg's work. This accounts both for our interest in CHAT as an underlying theory of cognition and development, and for what we think there are some distinctive emphases here. Strategizing is a developmental process, drawing its participants into chains of consequences that involve them both in revisiting and recapitulating old ideas (and re-discovering old problems) and in entering social terra incognita. Without some clarity about future-oriented goals and motives, it loses its coherence, threatening the breakdown of the strategizing entity. And that strategizing entity is, certainly in the case of movements, a collective body, however loosely or tightly integrated. It is not helpful to think of strategizing as something that only *individuals* do. Rather one question, necessarily presenting itself to any movement facing the need to rethink what it is doing and where it wants to go, is *how* its participants are to engage in the necessary dialogical exploration of their dilemmas and find a shared way forward.

Strategizing, being a reflexive process that implicates the identity, the social relations, and the purposes of those engaged in it, is necessarily a learning process. It is a practical process of discovery involving those who undertake it in questions about the character of the social and other obstacles to the pursuit of their ends, but also about themselves and their own capacities and weaknesses. Strategizing—as distinct from mere fantasizing—involves seeking to reshape and coordinate social relations with some actors who may share goals with you, others whose goals may partly overlap and partly contradict your own, and yet others whose active hostility to everything you seek must be anticipated. All of these can be expected to be active in their own right, seeking to reshape you as you seek to remake them and the world that contains you both.

Last, strategizing implicates multiple levels of social reality, from the most immediate and local to the global, and grasping this is a necessity both for those who strategize and also for those who seek to theorize the activity. The problem is neither to deduce strategies from some general theory, thereby effacing the particularities of persons, places and situations in the name of general slogans or principles, nor to attempt to develop everything from the immediate, local and "micro" level. In theorizing strategy, as in practicing it, the real problem is to keep all the balls in the air at once.

PART V
Resistant Cultures

Chapter 10
Strategic Islam and the Transformational Grammar of Chechen Nationalism

Hank Johnston

All cultures have internal resistance, but not all internal resistances give rise to opposition movements and insurgencies. Ann Norton points out (2004: 67) that oppositions within a culture create networks of meaning that, by their very existence, provide contrapuntal definitions of the larger institutional and political networks of state and society. Certainly, this is a process that is broadened and intensified when there is an ethnonational culture within a dominant culture. At times, the intensity of the we-them distinctions, layered with other meanings, becomes so great that it contributes to violent opposition. This is what happened in Chechnya in the 1990s, when the region went from the euphoria of apparent independence, to war, and then to defeat and devastation. Of course, it was not a rebellion just of meanings and symbols. There were key shifts in the structure of the state as the Soviet Union disintegrated, and opening political opportunities in its peripheral regions, but because the Chechen rebellion was richly enmeshed in the various symbolisms of its traditional culture, and especially its historical relation to Islam, this far-off region is a good laboratory for analyzing the role of culture, its relation to structural shifts, and the creative application of agency and strategic innovation.

Chechnya is a region located in Caucasian mountains and foothills along the southern boarder of Russia. During the time of the USSR, it was an autonomous republic (the Chechen-Ingush Autonomous Republic) within the huge Soviet Federated Socialist Republic. While many former Soviet Socialist Republics (SSRs), such as the Baltic states of Estonia, Latvia, and Lithuania, and the neighboring transcaucasian states of Georgia, Azerbaijan, and Armenia, claimed their independence after 1991, Chechnya was the only ethnic region in larger Russian Republic (an ASR—Autonomous Soviet Socialist Republic) to push tenaciously for independence. In August 1991, Chechens declared sovereignty, which invoked a Russian military response three months later. One thousand paratroopers were airlifted to the region, but immediately surrounded by Chechen militias as they landed. An initial stand-off led to a cease-fire, and Russian troops returned amidst great hope and celebration among Chechens, who believed this to be the beginning of a long-hoped-for statehood independent from Russia.

For three years, the region enjoyed de facto sovereignty, until September 1994 when Russian troops invaded again, this time in much greater numbers and with the full resources of a modern army. Chechen militias, many under the banner of Islamic jihad, again fought the Russians to a stalemate, and in March 1996 a treaty was signed, withdrawing Russian troops and heralding three years of virtual independence for the region. Yet from Moscow's perspective, the need to administer the huge Russian landmass with dozens of ethnonatonal regions, complicated by a weak government and disintegrating state institutions, made this a politically intolerable solution. Vladimir Putin was elected a year later with the promise to bring Chechnya back by forcing it to its knees. Russian troops invaded again in 1999 and crushed the rebellion, destroying cities and leveling villages. Today, a handful of Chechen rebels continue to attack Russian soldiers, but generally, a battered Chechnya is now again part of Russia.

This chapter will explore the issues of creative agency, structural opportunities, and the cultural toolbox available to nationalist militants in Chechnya, with the goal of illuminating cultural innovation in a context where structural opportunities were quite fluid. Although there is a long history of Islam in the region, it was not preordained that Chechen nationalism would fight for its independence, nor assume an Islamic jihadist flavor. I will develop the concept of how the basic grammar of a cultural text can be transformed according to changing resource availability and political contexts to help explain the movement's trajectory.

Although Chechnya may seem a distant and obscure case for analysts accustomed to movements of modernity in North America and Western Europe, as a way to approach the cultural analysis of social movements, there is much to be said for this isolated corner of the world where traditional cultural stock was reworked strategically in the context of a disintegrating Russian state and institutional conflict in the newly formed Chechen state. Although seventy-years of Soviet rule brought a modicum of modernization, the Chechen cultural matrix bore the heavy imprint of past traditions, especially in the highlands, which were brought to bear as the movement developed. Chechnya was a transitional culture, where traces of *Gemeinschaft* (village, clan, and tribe) and ritual provided cultural tools that intersected with contexts of modern state politics. A social movement that grows in such a setting is a good place to examine how and why culture gets strategically applied.

Ethnonational Oppositions

In principle, there are several reasons for the inherent oppositional nature of culture. It is partly because defining something as meaningful implicitly invokes its difference with something else, often leading to binary distinctions: good-evil, civilized-uncivilized peaceful-violent. It is partly because adherence to cultural templates is never complete and therefore always at variance in some ways with behaviors that appear as hegemonic and which have more power behind them. It is also because the way people think about themselves is almost never as completely integrated members of a cultural community. Any cultural community is a gathering of outsiders—in varying degrees. This gives rise to the diversity of national cultures that is taken for granted by analysts of advanced liberal democracies. In countries characterized by ethnic-national regions, diversity and opposition are also caused by patterns of incomplete state building whereby differences in language, religion, and collective identity tend to cluster geographically. These cultures-within-cultures exhibit the same inherent forces of difference and conflict as national ones. Although in less developed regions these forces may be mitigated by the strong social pressures of traditionally defined collective networks and identities, they are still there.

In Chechnya, this clustering was played out in ways that led to a strong nationalist movement. Yet, as cultural theorists tell us, Chechen ethnonational culture was not homogenous but rather characterized by different identities, different degrees of integration, and the participation of marginals and outsiders who came to embrace new meanings of the Chechen nation. This complexity is graphically represented in Figure 10.1, where the network nodes represent persons coming together in different settings where the unique aspects of Chechen culture are socially enacted: in village councils, in clan gatherings, in Sufi Islam worship, in coffee shop meetings of friends, in councils of neighborhood associations, collective farms, and even the Communist Party. In this model, the ethnonational culture of the region is represented as a multiplicity of meetings and gatherings where the uniquely Chechen nature of social life there was enacted, affirmed, and changed. Note that some participants in these

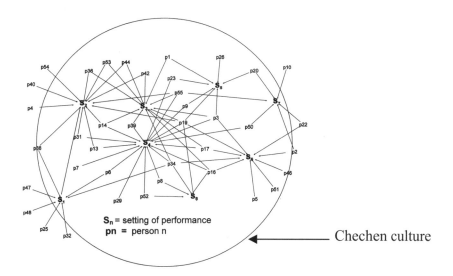

Figure 10.1   A hypothetical and simplified subcultural matrix

performances lie outside the cultural matrix, the more assimilated citizens of Grozny and low-level Chechen apparatchiks, for example. Note too that some performances are closer to the core of the culture than other. For the sake of graphic presentation the actual network qualities of the matrix are simplified greatly—but the basic idea is nevertheless captured: culture as based in a complex web of collective performances in which individuals occupying various social positions bring their own contributions to the table, affirming the past and creating the future.

Recasting Chechen culture in these terms raises the question of cultural patterns and content: What exactly is Chechen culture? How can the analyst speak of it in a way that captures both its traditions that constrain action and it tools available for innovation and strategic thinking? The analytical approach that I will follow in this chapter is to pursue the Chechen cultural text, that is, the basic patterns by which the various performances may be linked. There is good evidence that social action can be broadly understood as text performed by social actors (Alexander and Mast 2006: 15). Research in a variety of settings has shown an interconnectedness and consistency in social action and how the connective tissue of symbolic action is a widely shared, background cultural text. Regarding social movements and protest campaigns this means that the actions, artifacts, and shared understandings of members, while variable, are nevertheless interconnected and symbolically linked and read by each other. But specifically how does a cultural text link them? How is a text read? Why use the term, *text*, at all? Why not simply refer to broadly shared and interrelated of a movement's symbols and leave it at that?

Culture as Text

There are several different answers to these questions, ranging—superficially— from the linguistic and literary roots of cultural analysis to academic fashion, to more profound answers embedded in human action and consciousness. Norton (2004: 22–3) observes, "reading culture as a text is ... what each of us does every day in order to live in the world." We are active participants in the production of this symbolic language, as are those who read it. Empirically, culture's textual quality refers to how people's actions—their everyday behaviors, what they wear, what they say, how they say it—are thoroughly symbolic, both performed by actors and "read" or interpreted by audiences. Commonly, when an employee wears and tie and jacket or a Chechen his traditional *papaha* hat and sheepskin coat, they are making symbolic statements. In these cases, the symbolism is related to self-identity, but the reading by others is thoroughly culturally embedded and culturally confirmed. It may be countered that not everyone who wears traditional garb is projecting the same self-image or even intending to do so, and that, those who read it will also have variable interpretations. But the attributions made by others do not randomly occur, but are patterned according to shared background understandings (Ricoeur 1979: 73–4), which make wearing the traditional dress of a Chechen mountaineer a cultural fact embedded in the interaction rather than purely a psychological expression of self-image. Thus, the intentional use of the symbol is only part of the cultural equation, the interpreters being the other part, as are the actions that their interpretations then may engender. As Wittgenstein (1953) observes regarding spoken words, we are all players in this language game from which we can't escape. The same holds true for the symbolic language of everyday, popular culture. We are born into it and grow into becoming active participants in sustaining and changing it.

These symbols, it is argued, occur in a web of interconnected meaning. Yet it makes sense that if the concept of a cultural text is more than a useful metaphor, this web does not occur randomly but is be structured somehow, and that plotting this structure lies within the realm of social science. Written and spoken texts are not random assemblages of symbols, but are structured according to grammatical rules. This suggests that there may be some kind of rule-governed pattern—a grammar—that specifies how cultural texts are put together or used, a plausible hypothesis given that language lies at the foundation of all human groups and their actions. Language is not only that the medium of culture, but is also how our self-concepts are organized—in great part by thinking about them and speaking about them—to ourselves and to others. Language makes cultural transmission possible and lies at the heart of being human, just as does culture. Regarding social movements and protest, collective actions are plotted linguistically, ideologies articulated, frames negotiated and strategized. Reading these activities as text raises the possibility that they have an underlying structure that can inform the analyst's analysis of events.

At a very general level, that there is a pattern to cultural concepts is not a new idea. The opposition of binary concepts—hot and cold, raw and cooked, sacred and profane—guided Levi-Strauss's structuralism, but these fundamental structural patterns are static and do not comprise a grammar. Grammars, in contrast, are not only fixed structures that can be structurally analyzed by function and position once given textural form, but also are possibilities of expressing meaning yet to be realized. They specify ways that symbols—part of shared culture—can be put together in novel ways to produce new meanings. This is central to the analysis of protest movements because all protest movements are about criticizing existing structures and proposing new possibilities.

It is axiomatic in the study of human speech, in both sentence production and connected discourse that the assemblage of text is not a random process, but rather occurs in patterned ways that, at fundamental levels, are found across all human languages. Regarding sentences, Chomsky's transformational grammar revolutionized linguistics by showing how deep grammatical structures guide the formation of ideas in sentential form. Probably because the human brain imposes limits to what is an acceptable human language is, there are only so many ways that sentences can be formed—a finite number of ways to express an idea. These principles also hold when we look at the more general level of connected discourse. The analysis of narratives shows that, here too, there are fundamental story grammars that impose structure to the performance of verbal accounts. Again—probably structured by cognitive processes— here are only so many ways that a narrative can occur (Labov 1972; Barthes 1977; Ricoeur 1981; Abbott 1995: Polletta 2005). Then, moving to an even more general analytical level, the level of interaction, the structure may be harder to see, but, as Goffman has shown, certain principles seem to be functioning to shape how interaction occurs—a grammar that guides interaction, although he does not use the term.

Concerning social movements, it is plausible that group, organizational, and institutional performances are guided by fundamental grammars that are played out differently according to varying contextual elements of the event. These deep transformational grammars operate among actors in given contexts, and evince flexibility in how they are acted out as the contexts change, but nevertheless provide guiding principles for action. They function much like the deep structure of linguistic grammars, which guide how one a speaker verbalizes ideas according to basic structures, yet inherent in these structures is a degree flexibility in how the components of the sentence are put together to produce meanings. This flexibility is responsive to the factors such as the speech situation, attributes of the intended audience, and normative guidelines, as well as the agency of the speaker. The notion of a transformational grammar for a protest campaign means that the campaign can only be structured in certain ways because of the "grammatical" constraints on how the symbols can be put together, given the issues, history, and context of the movement. Nevertheless, there is ample room for agentic and contextual factors to shape the movement's development. Its cultural text has a deep structure that, like sentences and narratives, can be transformed in patterned ways according to historical, institutional, and/or situational contexts where other influences such as power and available resources, external threats, and so on come into play, activating some "grammatical" transformations and limiting others. This, then, is the task at hand regarding Chechen mobilization: identifying the transformational grammar of Chechen ethnonational culture and tracing how it was variably applied in the changing political contexts during the 1990s. It's a question, as we will see, that focuses especially on how Islam was used during this period.

Related to the notion of a grammar of protest actions, Roberto Franzosi has proposed analyzing protest events by their "story grammars" (1999, 2004). His idea is based on the fact that all action, at its most fundamental level, follows a simple grammatical structure comprised of <subject> <action> <object> and a variety of modifiers attached to each these three components. The modifiers would be type, number, structure, or character for the <subject> and the <object>, and time, space, or type for the <action>. Graphically, we can depict this with a drawing based upon the well-known trees of generative grammar analysis, as in Figure 10.2. Franzosi conducted content analysis of newspaper accounts of collective action in Italy and coded them according to an elementary three-branched structure, which he called a "semantic triplet." He proposes a method of coding protest events based on the subject-verb-object triplets, thereby keeping the coding close to "the inherent properties of the text itself" (Franzosi 1999: 133). Moreover, the basic grammar is based in the matrix of relevant relations, "where subjects related to their actions, actors and actions to their modifiers, and subjects and objects (both social actors) related on one another via their actions" (ibid.).

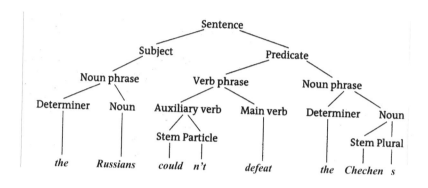

Figure 10.2   Hypothetical generative grammar tree: "The Russians couldn't defeat the Chechens"

Franzosi's method is an innovative way to analyze newspaper data to capture the basic structures of action, with the goal of moving "from words to numbers," as he says. Although among his destinations are regression models and factor analyses, it is a method that also is thoroughly cultural in the sense that actions he plots are the creation of a movement's culture, and specification of the relevant patterns of actions and acts is a way to trace the bare outline of the movement's deep grammar, its fundamental orienting principles that circumscribe innovation and strategy. Moreover, the very notion of a basic story grammar of protest is a way to approach the cultural text; and his basic logic of analysis, based as it is on, frequency—a notion not often found in cultural analysis—is a way to capture the dominant patterns of action whereby a protest culture is created. His semantic triplets present one way that a movement's challenge can be thought of textually.

There are parallels between the idea of a transformational grammar of action and Bourdieu's notion of *habitus*, a general system of individual predispositions, acquired through lived experience, that give a "feel for the game" of social life a second-nature quality. Like a basic grammar, *habitus* is not determining of social action in the strong sense, but rather an enabling factor upon which the actor draws to operate in daily life. Bourdieu also speaks of class *habitus* as the products of shared history and social conditions. These are internalized shared dispositions that make individual dispositions "structural variants" of broad social processes— the "present past" (Bourdieu 1990: 58). The transformational grammar of Chechen nationalism guides strategic action in a way that parallels these formulations of *habitus*, namely shared history giving rise to shared predispositions that are available for application in social action. In the Chechen case, the grammatical representation of these group predispositions takes the form the semantic triplet <Chechen nation> <jihad> <Russians>, that is, shared definitions of the Chechen people waging Islamic-based holy way against Russians, who are defined in binary opposition as non-Chechen, non-believing infidels, and oppressors of the Chechen people.

This is the deep structure of the grammar, but because people are integrated into Chechen society differently, its surface-level application by groups and individuals will vary according to contextual factors. It will introduce modifiers and additions to subjects and predicates, giving the basic text creative applications taken from other parts of their lives and identities. This is a source of creativity and agency that derives, first, from the ability of cultural actors to bring perspectives from the outside, and second, to assert an individuality that is neither oversocialized nor completely subordinated to shared cultural frameworks. We see this when activists combine the raw materials of different grammars, oppositional and hegemonic, in creative ways (Noonan 1995; Steinberg 1999; Johnston 2005). Superficial modifiers of the dominant text may be applied to the basic grammar of the oppositional text, a tactic I saw many times in repressive regimes. In the Soviet Union, it was called "double mindedness" by my informants, but in practice it was "double talk" (Johnston 2005). Sometimes these strategies demonstrate a creativity reminiscent of Scott's analysis (1990) of peasant and slave resistance to their overlords, resistance that is unobtrusive yet innovative in how it exists within the system of domination. In the Chechen case, the other domains of action that are brought to the grammar are traditional village life, Soviet economy and civil organization, Sufi Islamic practice, and male networks of kinship and honor. These are sources of grammatical transformations, so to speak, that have given the Chechen national movement its unique trajectory.

The "Present Past" in Chechen National Consciousness

Early movement groups during the period of perestroika were located in Groznyi, the capital city. The players were second-tier Chechens, reform party members and members of the state apparat, who saw opportunities in the reformist atmosphere for their own advancement as well as for promoting ethnonational interests. The main spark Chechnya's rebellion was the attempted coup of communist hardliners against Gorbachev in August 1991. Just a year earlier, the All-National Congress of Chechen People was formed by village assemblies throughout Chechnya, which elected almost a thousand delegates as the general assembly to replace the republic's Soviet parliament. With the changing political situation, the congress demanded that all official bodies of the Russian state in the republic resign. The congress called upon religious and clan leaders to mobilize mass support. From all over the region, thousands of people poured into Groznyi to seize power from the communists. On August 22, a huge demonstration gathered at Lenin Square to tear down Lenin's statue and raise the Chechen flag. Huge rallies continued for several days until it became clear that the putsch had failed.

All this replicates patterns of mobilization found elsewhere in several Soviet republics, but in Chechnya the euphoria of the mass gatherings continued for months afterwards. The central square became the focus of an unfolding drama of symbols and assertions of a nationhood long-repressed, first after the attempted coup and then, several months later, on November 8, 1991, when ill-planned invasion force of Russian paratroopers was sent packing home on busses. The celebrations that erupted after this event were unprecedented. Men with full beards from mountain villages gathered in Groznyi, dressed in traditional *papaha* hats and exotic garb of the mountaineers: sheepskin coats and high boots, some with silver knives in their thick belts. They arrived in busses, often with banners proclaiming where they had come from, loudly chanting and singing. Some danced the *zikr*, which according to Derluguian (2005) was never before done publicly in the city. This is a ecstatic, ritualistic circle dance of Sufi brotherhood. Its performance is perhaps a measure of the overlap between Islam and ethnic consciousness and augured things to come. Flatbed trucks were brought into the center of town, from which speakers could address milling crowns with bullhorns. From the rallies, cries of "We are Chechens," "This is our country!" rang out, led by the speakers or spontaneously from among the audiences. A carnival-like atmosphere presided. Observers note that mothers walked with children, groups of men gathered everywhere to discuss and debate. At times music and dancing occurred. Children were dressed in national colors and carried Chechen flags. Later, similar images are described by observers after the second withdraw of Russian troops in 1997 (Derluguian 2005: 40).

The Depth of the Oppositional Subculture

The Chechen nation as an imagined community was formed slowly over the past two hundred years, and congealed during the past fifty years of Soviet rule. As recent as 1985, two Soviet scholars observed that a national identity in the Soviet sense of a "modern Chechen nation is still extremely weak, and probably nonexistent." On the other hand, there was a diffuse xenophobic collective identity based on a "holy-war tradition and an undisguised hatred of the Russians" that guided how many Chechens though about Russia (Bennigsen and Winbush 1985b: 189). The rapidly changing political context since 1991, plus the example of other Soviet nations claiming national independence, solidified and mobilized Chechen national consciousness.

Prior to the nineteenth century, there was at best a vague regionally based identity of being Caucasian that embraced common cultural traditions and Muslim *Umma* shared with the Ingush, Daghestanis, Ossetians, and other peoples in the area (Wixman 1980). Chechens lived in numerous tribal "free communities" (*tukhum*) that were fully independent of each other and of outside control. In the late seventeenth century Russia began to settle the region, thus beginning the struggle for land with the Chechens. Over the next one hundred and fifty years, a pattern of Russian settlement, Chechen insurgency, and military response characterized Chechen-Russian relations. Four key events can be identified prior to the October Revolution that define the Chechen national myth.

First, Russian settlement in the late eighteenth century pushed Chechens out of fertile lowland regions in the north into the less productive foothills and mountainous regions. A struggle against Russian settlement began under the leadership of sheikh Mansur, a chief of Naqshbandiya Sufi order. Mansur visited towns and villages in Chechnya calling for a purified Islam that replaced traditional customs with Islamic *sharia'*. He called for a *gazavat*, or holy war, first against corrupt Muslims, and then against the infidel Russians. Between 1784 and 1791 Mansur's force grew to 12,000, and he led numerous attacks on Russian forts and settlements, with some spectacular successes. There were also several devastating defeats, and by 1786 Chechens cooled toward the costly war. Mansur was captured in 1791 and died in Russian prison.

Second, between 1816 and 1827, a ruthless campaign against the Chechens was carried out by General Alexsei Yarmolov. This period represents the first stage of the Caucasus War (which lasted in various degrees of intensity from 1817 until 1864), and during which the Muslim peoples of the Caucasus waged a holy struggle inspired by Sufi brotherhoods against Russia. After Mansur's defeat, Chechens continued to raid Russian settlements. Yarmolov was sent by Alexander I to subdue the Chechens and forcibly incorporate them for once and for all into the Russian Empire. Yarmolov's approach was to eliminate resistance by destroying region's economic base. He burned crops, slaughtered herds, sacked villages, massacred women and children, took them as slaves, and engaged in the deportation of Chechens from northern lowland regions. The strategy was to secure the more easily defensible plains for Russian and Cossack settlers. By driving Chechens into less accessible and socially more primitive areas where traditional tribes and clans were stronger, and were economic existence was more precarious, this policy reinforced traditional structures and intensified the resistance (Dunlop 1998: 16).

Third, several uprisings occurred between 1824 and 1864 which imparted to the Chechen cause a distinctly Islamic orientation under the leadership of different imams (three of whom were Daghestanis not Chechens). Until that time, Chechens were nominally Islamic and were often condemned by Muslim religious leaders as corrupting Islam with animistic and traditional customs. The first was Beibulat's rebellion, which was a short-lived uprising organized around Naqshbandiya sect of Sufism in 1825. Second, there were a number of successful raids against Russian outposts led by imam Kazi Mullah in 1831–1832. At the height of his power he commanded 6,000 foot soldiers and 2,000 cavalry. Third, and most significant, there were several uprisings led by imam Shamil' between 1836 and 1856. Shamil' was also from the Naqshbandiya brotherhood and "transformed the half-pagan mountaineers into strict Orthodox Muslims and introduced Islam into the animist areas of upper Chechnya" (Bennigsen and Wimbush 1985b: 19). In 1840 Shamil' united all the mountain tribes against the Russians, and it required the whole strength of the Russian empire to defeat his forces. In 1856, the Caucasus was occupied by 200,000 Russian troops. Shamil's defeat led to the deportation of 100,000 Chechens to Turkey.

Fourth, after the defeat of Shamil's Naqshbandiya uprising, a new Sufi brotherhood, the Qadiriya, spread rapidly throughout Chechnya. In 1877 a major rebellion in Chechnya was led by Qadiri adepts with the support of the Naqshbandi brotherhood. The revolt was crushed by Russian forces, marking the last uprising until the February Revolution of 1917. Henceforth the Sufi brotherhoods proselytized their strict form of Islam among the mountaineers. "During this period of 1877–1917 ... it may safely be said that virtually the entire population of Chechnya and Ingushetiya belonged to either the Naqshbandi or Qadiri brotherhoods" (Dunlop 1998: 32).

The Communists in Chechnya

The tumultuous years of 1917 and 1918 created an opportunity for Chechnya to break free of Russian domination. With Russia in turmoil, religious leaders in Chechnya and Daghestan gathered to create a regional theocratic state based on the *sharia'*, name an imam to lead it and wage a holy war to expel the Russians. A combined Caucasian force of 10,000 led by Sheikh Uzun Haji fought the White army and in March, 1920, had liberated the mountainous regions of Chechnya, Daghestan, Ossetiya, and Kabarda. The North Caucasus Emirate, as it was called, was created and placed under the nominal rule of the Ottoman sultan. Meanwhile the Red army, which had been giving limited support to the Chechens in their struggle against the Whites, moved in to claim the region for Marxism-Leninism. The Red army was at first naively welcomed, but the antireligious policies of the Bolsheviks and their campaigns against local customs quickly alienated the Chechens. In August 1920 a rebellion against the Reds broke out, which lasted about a year.

The draconian policies of Stalin toward the Chechens between 1920 and the outbreak of World War II can be summed up by a string of broken promises backed up by military repression. Several more uprisings in the name of Islam occurred during this period. So too did efforts to collectivize Chechen agriculture, russify the cities by relocation and immigration, antireligious campaigns, occupation by the Red army to disarm the populace, and the razing of obstreperous villages. This ongoing assault by Soviet authorities, coupled with Soviet policy of using nationality as the basis of administrative control, helped consolidate a Chechen national identity. By the late 1930s, Soviet policies shape a national Chechen consciousness that overlapped with traditional structures of clan, tribe, and religious brotherhood (Ormrod 1997: 98).

The defining event of this national consciousness was the genocide against the Chechens in 1944. Stalin justified the mass deportation of all Chechens (and Ingush, Balkars, and Karachai) from their homelands to Russian Central Asian republics, mostly Kazakh and Kirgiz SSR, by their purported support of Nazi Germany during World War II, although, in reality, Chechen collaboration was not widespread. The deportation of Chechens began on February 23, 1944, when people were summoned under the auspices of celebrating the Red Army's anniversary. The men were immediately arrested, and women told to pack belongings for the next day's journey. Between February 24 and 28 almost 500,000 persons were loaded into freight cars and shipped to Central Asia. Several thousand people avoided arrest but were hunted down and killed by the NKVD troops. Conditions on arrival were grossly inadequate to support so many people. Deportees were assigned exhausting physical labor in agriculture, canal and railway construction and timber industries. It is estimated that 144,704 of the deportees died in the four years that followed (or 23.7 percent).

Stalin died in 1953 and as early as 1954 some Chechens and Ingush began to return illegally to their homelands. In the next two years, Chechens and Ingush began to disappear from Central Asia in large numbers. In July 1956, as part of Khrushchev's liberalization, deportees were "freed," but requested to slowly return to their home territories over the next four years. However, by 1958, about 200,000 had returned to their homes, double the intended number (Dunlop 1998: 77). Many returnees found their ancestral homes occupied, or found their ancestral villages had been completely destroyed. Others were denied employment. Aware of their history of resistance, authorities showed them little sympathy. As their sense of deprivation grew during the Brezhnev years, so too did their national consciousness. The hardships of deportation were fresh in historical memory. Everyone had lost family members. Moreover, local industry, the Communist Party, and government administration formed a classic scenario of internal colonialism. Top posts were in the vast majority held by Russians, forcing many Chechens into the shadow economy. Thus, while the Chechens remained quiescent during the Brezhnev years, their opposition to the Russians was compounded by economic and social injustice. These sentiments were embodied in traditional social structure, which overlapped with the final piece of the puzzle in Chechnya's national resistance—Sufi *tariqa* (or the path leading to God).

Islam in Chechnya

Soviet ethnographers unanimously characterized the Chechens as the "most religious of all Soviet Muslims" (Bennigsen and Wimbush 1985a: 186). Sufi brotherhoods became the basis of the Chechen community during its Central Asian exile. After the mass deportation, Soviet authorities sought to destroy Islam in the Chechen-Ingush territory by closing all mosques and medreses (religious schools). It was a policy, however, that had the opposite effect when, upon return from exile, religious Chechens could only turn to informal and secret brotherhoods that were outside the state's control. Strong family ties insured that Islamic practice was passed to new generations. Under the Soviets since 1980 several new mosques were opened in an attempt to mitigate the influence of the Sufi *tariqa*, but the role of the Sufi brotherhoods remained strong. "Parallel Islam" was a term used by Soviet scholars to describe Sufi brotherhoods.

There were two Sufi brotherhoods that comprise the majority of Chechen Islamic practice. First, the Naqshbandi, was brought to Chechnya by Imam Mansur in the late eighteenth century. It preached a purified Islam that condemned alcohol and tobacco use and certain semipagan rituals such as cult of the dead, vendetta, and elements of Chechen customary law (*adat*). The defeat of Mansur mitigated the influence of the brotherhood, but fifty years later, Sheikh Shamil' reintroduced Naqshbandi to Chechnya, and under the banner of *sharia'* and *gazavat* (holy war) led an uprising against the Russians. Second, the Qadiri *tariqa*, a Baghdad order founded by Abd al-Qadir al-Ghiliani in the twelfth century, was brought to Chechnya in the late 1800s after Shamil's defeat. It was a more mystical cult that preached detachment from worldly affairs and practiced a loud *zikr* (meaning remembrance, as in remembrance of God) with dances, music and song, which were forbidden by both the Czarist government and by the Naqshbandi *tariqa*. Most of the fighters in the 1877 uprising against the Russians were Qadiri, as were the leaders of revolts in 1942 against the Soviets. There are two Qadiri sects, Batal Haji and Vis Hafi brotherhoods, whose membership increased significantly during the Central Asian exile. Both Naqshbandi and Qadiri brotherhoods have long histories of war and resistance against the Russians and Soviets, not only in the Caucasus but also among Central Asian Muslims.

> The adept (*murid*) is accepted into the brotherhood after a ritual of initiation and remains under the control of his master (*murshid*). Throughout his life, even if he is only a lay brother, he must follow a complicated and compulsory spiritual programme. In this programme permanent prayers, invocations, and litanies—loud or silent *zikr*—accompanied by peculiar breathing and physical movements, play an important part and prepare the adept for a state of intense mental concentration. The *tariqa* represent perfectly structured hierarchical organizations, endowed with an iron discipline which is certainly stronger than that of the communist party. (Bennigsen and Wimbush 1985a: 21)

Sufi organization goes a long way in explaining the breadth of the subculture, which in many ways is suggestive of pre-Solidarity Polish Catholicism. Like Poland, the Chechen subculture was sustained by regular religious practice and by special events that brought larger numbers of people together. The Soviets were unable to suppress pilgrimages to holy places, such as the tomb of Uzun Haji, who was leader of the war against the White Army in 1918–1919. Other tombs belonged to leaders of Shamil's rebellion, and to Chechens executed for counterrevolutionary activities by the communists. In a sense they were all treated as Chechen "patron saints" much like the black Madonna enshrined at the Jasna Gora monastery in Poland, and similarly a site of annual pilgrimages. A common feature of resistance in both regions was that these pilgrimage became charged with political meanings (Henze 1995: 25)

During the height of the Brezhnev years, a Soviet sociologist estimated that 53 percent of all ethnic Chechens were believers and 22 percent declared themselves atheists. Also, "half of all Muslim believers in the Chechen-Ingush ASSR are members of a Sufi *tariqa*" (Pirovarov 1975, quoted in Bennigsen and Wimbush 1985a: 188–9). In 1993, after the national movement had peaked, one estimate held that 70 percent practiced Islam, which included the majority of young people, not just elders. According to one observer, this was primarily a result of the clan-based nature of Sufism (Lehmann 1995). In 1991, when we begin our study of Chechnya's Islamic strategy, a plausible estimate is that about half of Chechen households practiced Islam, but that about half of these did so through clan and family-based reasons, and that concentrations would not be in the cities of the northern plains but rather in the rural, mountainous regions.

Drawing on Bennigsen and Wimbush (1985a: 188), there are summary points relevant to the role of Islam on the eve of Chechen national mobilization. First, there was "a complete symbiosis of the very decentralized Sufi organization and the clanic structure. Sufi groups of 30–50 members often comprise all the members of an extended family. Second, there was a blending of loyalties to clanic groups, religious brotherhoods, and Chechen nation. Third, Sufi brotherhoods were both clandestine and militantly anti-Russian, providing ready-made recruitment networks for the national movement and the potential for a strong Islamic influence. Even under the Soviets, Sufi *tariqa* had resources at their disposal—controlled by extended families and clans rather than state and party.

Thus we have the basic contours of Chechen oppositional grammar: a national identity forged in state-imposed hardship, antipathy against the Russians and a tradition of armed resistance against them, which often was waged in the name of holy war or jihad, and finally a parallel matrix of Islamic practice organized along the lines of Sufi brotherhoods. These elements occurred along with other "modifiers" of the cultural text, such as egalitarianism and honor, clan and tribal relations, a Caucasian brand of male machismo, plus the less distinctive elements such as the patterns of Soviet life and party, state, and economic administration. Together, they comprise, not a seamless fabric woven of common themes, but rather a diverse and sometimes conflict-riven text that shares a common medium, much as a text shares as language as the medium of symbolism.

The Strategic Use of Islam

In the remainder of this chapter we will focus on the process of Islamization in the Chechen national movement and how the semantic triplet of <Chechen people> <holy war> <Russians> was creatively applied according to changing political situation and changing players. These changes forced Chechen leaders and activists to reconsider assumptions, but it was a process that occurred within parameters established by the basic cultural text. For example, no one could have anticipated the influx of Middle-Eastern money, but the choices it enabled were shaped by the taken-for-granted quality of the deep text. To capture this process, it is necessary it take snapshots of the grammatical transformations at different points in the development of the movement when the political structure changes significantly. I have chosen three episodes that capture the liminal moments of the movement: the initial declaration of sovereignty in 1991, intensifying political competition in the newly independent state in 1992, and the 1994 invasion.

From Secularism to Public Islam: Summer 1991

It is not widely known is that area specialists did not see the Islamization of the Chechen movement as necessary. In its early stages, Chechen nationalism was mostly carried by the urban intelligentsia in Groznyi and focused on issues common to other Soviet regions during *perestroika* and *glasnost*: democracy, environmentalism, ethnic folklore and traditions, and bringing to light the history of Soviet repression. Islamization did not gain strength until after independence was declared in 1991, and even then was not a major element in the movement until competition between different factions intensified and the question of who's more Islamic entered political discourse.[1]

The secular origins of the movement are strongly linked with demographic patterns associated with modernization and Sovietization. Oil was discovered in Chechnya in the late nineteenth century. Under the Soviets Groznyi became an industrial city, populated mostly by Russians. Soviet policies to modernize the region brought some Chechens into cities and towns as part of a program to create an industrial proletariat. Infrastructural development linked with oil

---

1 The 1991 Chechen state was not an Islamic one based on the *sharia'*. The new constitution was quite liberal, guaranteeing religious freedom for all—a measure that the political use of Islam had not yet progressed very far.

exploitation and planned industrialization brought the towns and cities of the lowland regions into the twentieth century, Soviet style. The mass deportation of 1944 meant that many Chechens, upon their return in 1957, could not go back to the status quo ante, and had to start over in the Soviet economy, many as industrial workers but some—especially the young generation during the Khrushchev years—with low and middle-level administrative jobs in the party and state, most of which were also urban-based. By the last Soviet census in 1989, Chechens made up 42 percent of the urban population, compared with 9 percent in 1959. Modernization under the Soviets created a new stratum of Chechens—educated, urban, and with economic and status interests in state and party apparatus.[2]

Still, these urban Chechens mostly encountered a glass ceiling in the state, party, and oil industry. When political space for challenging regional Russian dominance opened in the late 1980s, their protest repertoires initially looked a lot like those of titular minorities throughout the Soviet Union (Johnston, 2005, 2006: 196–210; also see Derluguian 2005: 178–85). Early contention took the form of secular groups: the Kavakaz Circle (an intellectual group), the Popular Front of Chechnya and Ingushetia, Union for the Assistance of Perestroika, the Green Party, and a group called *Bart* (Harmony). As in the early stages of other regional movements, members were comparatively moderate, intellectuals, and many were from the reformist wing of the party (Lieven 1998: 57). Their immediate political and economic interests resided in an autonomous Chechnya with greater freedoms, but not independence from the Soviet Union. *Bart* was a younger group, more radical than the Popular Front, and highly critical of the conservative party establishment. *Bart* was eventually was renamed the Vainakh Party (a term that embraces both Chechens and Ingush). As some early-riser groups pushed more forcefully for reform, a more radical discourse seemed naturally to bring with it references to Islam. The reason was, in part, because the Chechen nation was linked with jihad as part of the semantic triplet, but this was amplified by factors extraneous to the grammar In Afganistan, Islamic fighters were successfully combating Russian forces in the name of jihad, and, although Shiite-led, the Iranian revolution was a model of revolution against the West, as was the deep text of the Palestinian struggle. The Vainakh Party became a center of nationalist radicalism, for whom a fundamental demand was "the separation of atheism from the state, i.e., the cessation of anti-Muslim religious persecution, and ... the reestablishment of traditional national institutions in the republic such as the Mekjk Kkhel or Council of Elders" (Dunlop 1998: 90). The linking of Islam and traditional governing structures reflects the integrity

---

2   Since the late 1920s, an adjunct to Sovietization was anti-religious campaigns that sought to diminish the influence of Islam. Secularism and atheism, real or professed, were criteria for state and party employment. These moderns maintained clan ties and links to ancestral villages, but it goes without saying that they were not bearded Sufi adepts.

of the deep cultural text at work here, but note the moderation of the demands. There was no mention of instituting *sharia'*.

Nor is it surprising that intensification of Islamic demands, especially calls for holy war, grew in conjunction with the Russian threat, especially in the collective response to the attempted coup of communist hardliners against Gorbachev in August 1991. To repulse the coup d'etat, nationalist leaders called on Chechens to "create underground organizations and armed formations," a Chechen tradition of resistance, as we have seen. The National Congress, an unofficial governing body created to replace the republic's Supreme Soviet, called upon religious and clan leaders to mobilize mass support. It created "battle detachments and strike groups which took control all military bases and communication centers ... throughout the republic" (Dunlop 1998: 101). From all over the region, thousands of people poured into Groznyi to depose the communists from power. On August 22, a huge demonstration took place at Lenin Square, which was—not surprisingly—renamed Sheikh Mansur Square, leader of Chechnya's first jihad against the Russians in the eighteenth-century. A huge portrait of him was displayed there.

Thus, the earliest players were those who had made investments in party and state administration and the audience was Moscow. This is not to say that urban Chechens did not know the basic cultural text, but it is certain that for party members and intellectuals, it was less immediate in their daily lives. But the basic text surfaced to guide public discourse when faced with an external threat from the Russians. It is highly plausible that, at this stage, Islam was introduced to public discourse as a readily available tool through its link in the grammar of contention.

At this juncture, the general secular focus was a strategic decision—a framing decision—shaped by the unique political opportunity structure of *glasnost-perestroika* period. Paradoxically, religion played less of role at this stage in Chechnya than in some other nationalist movements in the USSR: Lithuania, Western Ukraine, Georgia, and Armenia, for example. The reason for this is probably the diffuse structure of Sufi Islam, its attenuated links with public life, and the concomitant weakness of official, state-controlled Islam when compared with official religious organizations in these other republics, which were Christian, not Islamic. Although subject to the same antireligious campaigns and restrictions, the centralized church organizations of other republics—as weak and compromised as they were—could provide resources, organization, and cover in the early stages of the nationalist movements not available to underground Sufism in Chechnya. In varying degrees, early-riser groups in these republics' nationalist movements took advantage of these—Lithuania the most (Johnston 1993).

The early movement's secular quality was not because its members' cultural grammars were weak or absent. To the contrary, the grandparents and parents of this generation had been deported and returned, suffering great hardships, which were surely told and retold in family gatherings. It is safe to say that nearly all players at this juncture were touched by personal loss and death during the deportation (1944–1957). Moreover, clan ties remained strong despite urbanization and Sovietization. Lowland clans integrated into the Soviet system to their benefit (which was resented by the highlanders). Clan identity was part of a person's self-identity. If someone occupied an influential position in Groznyi or town centers, clan obligations meant that they helped others navigate the Soviet system. The surface grammar of the movement's contentious text occurred in the vocabulary of democracy, folklore, ecology, and commemorating the past occurred here, as it did in almost all other titular republics, because of the constraints of Soviet civil participation. The claims and focus of early-riser groups, being strongly affected by immediate structure of political opportunities, are shaped less by the basic grammar of the oppositional text and more by strategic calculations of what is possible. Moreover, it is plausible that the absence of linkages with the basic grammar limited the scope and popularity of these early-riser groups.

Yet because the participants in these first groups shared with all Chechens the deep cultural text, and because movement organizations need popular support to survive, it was only a matter of time until Islam appeared—not *jihad* (yet) but rather Islam as an identifying characteristic of the Chechen nation, the subject of the semantic triplet. This occurred through the linkage of Chechen traditions with Islam. When clan organizations, village councils—traditions that were stronger in the highlands—were invoked as part of the reconstruction of "true" Chechen culture and society, Sufi Islam entered by association. As elders of village councils and representatives of local committees first gathered in Groznyi to form the National Chechen Congress in 1990, they came from all over the region, bringing village mullahs and Sufi *zikrs* with them. Dudayev gave a passionate speech in June 1990. He referred to "constant state of war" that Chechens experienced with Russia and affirmed that "Islam was the binding force of the Caucasian peoples." Beslan Gantamirov, head of the Islamic Path Party, was elected mayor of Groznyi. Now the oppositional script links two aspects of the deep culture: the Russian enemy and Islam.

The Chechen Republic: 1992

The instability of new Chechen state spurred intense political competition for which Islam's availability in the cultural text made it a politically powerful symbol. A major source of state instability was its lack of control over the means of violence during the revolutionary months of late summer and fall 1991. During mass mobilization against the aborted coup in August 1991, Chechen prisons were emptied and convicts given arms to join the defense forces. Groznyi's mayor organized and armed Islamic militiamen to defend the city (Henze 1995: 30). Several other militias were formed at this time. Two months later, in response to Yeltsin's decision to send interior ministry troops to seize airports and quell citizen mobilization, weapons were again distributed to citizens and defense detachments. Yeltsin's ill-planned operation occurred in reaction to the election of Djokar Dudayev as president of Chechnya and his declaration of Chechen sovereignty. The repulsion of Russian force by Dudayev's National Guard and the armistice he signed recognizing Chechnya's "special status" made him a hero as the leader who won de facto independence for the region (in November 1991). By this time, arms were openly traded in the markets, many coming from departing Russian soldiers. As the Russian economy deteriorated and young Chechen men could no longer find work in other parts of Russia, they became available for recruitment in armed gangs and militias, which were headed by seekers of personal power, often with allegiances to clan networks rather than the state.

While Dudayev enjoyed widespread popular support at first, his political base was highly unstable. Fissures formed according to different views of the republic's future relations with Moscow and the form the new state system was to take—parliamentary versus presidential. The National Congress, now the legislative body of the republic, was originally formed by village assemblies throughout Chechnya and modeled on traditional structures of *tukhum* (clan confederations) and *teip* (clans). Factions quickly formed in the Congress along clan lines, often in pursuit of economic interests and business opportunities as the economy destabilized and Soviet-era controls were abolished (German 2003: 79). Criticisms of corruption, economic mismanagement, illegal political maneuvering quickly surfaced. There was conflict between the lowland clans that were more politically connected with the old regime and those from the mountains who saw independence as a means of increasing their status. Dudayev himself recognized the political importance of the clans—he was originally a compromise candidate from a minor clan—and sought alliances to shore up his own power base. Leading clans came to oppose Dudayev when they saw he was attempting to limit their influence. Some opposed Dudayev personally, especially as he became more authoritarian in the face of rising opposition.[3]

The result was the opening of unbridled political competition, the backdrop to the strategic use of Islam by both Dudayev and by his opponents. Dudayev, a Soviet air force general and member of the Communist Party who made his career outside of Chechnya (and married a Russian), was not an observant Muslim and came to power with only a vague idea of the pervasiveness of the Sufi networks in the country.[4] Yet his actions indicate that that he fully understood the symbolic power of Islam, for example, he wanted to be sworn into office

---

3 The politics of this period 1992–1992 are labyrinthine, to say the least. Here I present only the general patterns. There are several detailed treatments, among them Dunlop (1998), and German (2003). See also Smith (2001: 122–43) and Gall and de Waal (1998: 91–123).

4 A tale is told of him at a public meeting encouraging Muslims to pray three times a day, and being awkwardly corrected by a mullah. "Uh, Honored President, it's five times a day." Dudayev replied, "Well, the more the merrier."

on a Quran.[5] He often laid claim to the legacy of Chechnya's past religious and political liberators, Shamil and Mansur. And he was well award of the political importance of Islam and Sufi organizations to his conservative power base in the southern mountainous regions, building mosques and medreses to cultivate their support. According to one observer, "Dudayev actively attempted to turn Chechen Islam into an instrument for the manipulation of mass awareness" (Dunlop 1998: 148). He armed his own militias and Islamic regiments. Under his regime, an Islamic University was begun in Groznyi. Later, in 1994, he declared Chechnya an Islamic state based on *sharia'* when the Russian invasion seemed evident.[6] During this period, there is competition among parties and leaders over who is a better Chechen and a stronger leader of the new republic, which is how Islamic elaborations enter political discourse, not through jihad, but as an elaboration of Chechen national identity. Islam is a readily available resource to political players and pulled into public discourse by strategic decisions taken to increase popular support. This is not a religious revival, it's a revival of political competition in the republic. Remembering that these elements are tools, not determining causes, they enter the matrix of cultural performances and are applied transformationally and contextually. The element of the basic grammar is that there are a limited number of ways that popular support can be attracted, constrained by the basic semantic triplet, but not determined by it. We are reminded of Marx's dictum that people make their own history, but not any way they choose. Here, the basic grammar limits and guides possible transformations.

The various elaborations of the grammar—Islam's relation to the state, the role of *ulema* (Islamic scholars), which strongman is more pious, who wears Shamil's mantle, among others—are its superficial transformations according to contextual factors. They provide the basic material for strategic competition among various political factions. Under different circumstances it is plausible that the basic grammar might be played out differently, say, if there was a rapid, draconian consolidation of power by Dudayev, or if, in contrast to Sufi organization, Islam was highly centralized, as in Shia' ecclesiastical organization in Iran. In the period after the declaration of independence and prior to Russia's 1994 invasion, the institutional weakness of the state and Dudayev's lack of authority and loose Sufi organization led to a highly strategic and fluid use of Islam.

---

5   This was a significant for many Chechens, but showed Dudayev's theological ignorance. Clerics saw it as a questionable desecration of the Quran.

6   Given space limitations this review must gloss many details of this period's political maneuvering, but it captures the basic trend. With Dudayev's decreasing popularity, he attempted to draw support by exploiting traditional forms of social organization and Islam, both of which he had little knowledge upon returning to Chechnya (German 2003: 78). His political competitors used the same tactics

Radical Islam: 1994–1995

During this period, Islamization of the Chechen national movement moved forward rapidly, but not straightforwardly. When Russia invaded in winter 1994–1995, Islamization became less strategic and political in the direct sense it was used in the previous period. In the face of external threat Islam became the unifying force of Chechen fighters. Now an elaboration of jihad, it transcended factional politics, much as it did when first invoked in 1991 during Yeltsin's ill-planned invasion. But in another sense, political Islam soon took on a face that was foreign to Chechnya, that of global jihad. While mobilization for war typically lies outside the bounds of social movement studies, we can continue to trace the trajectory of deep culture during this period insofar as events follow an important theoretical category, namely the introduction of resources into the mobilization equation. Also, that this David-and-Goliath war eventually ended in a stalemate (an armistice was signed in August 1996) attests to the mobilizing power of the complete triplet. Not only could actors draw upon Islamic jihad but also draw upon elaborations of what it meant to be a Chechen (warrior complex and male honor) and what it did not mean (a dishonorable Russian conscript without ties to the land).

Under war conditions, role of Islam as a unifying symbol for preservation of the state was amplified, as is quite typical of other religions and other states during wartime. Related to this is the use of Islam as a means to insure discipline and sacrifice among a rag-tag force, which it accomplished very successfully. The war was waged from the Chechen side by the national army and by several private militias led by warlords who varied in their allegiance to Dudayev and the central command. Most had their own political ambitions and gained in power as they captured Russian weapons and received outside resources from Middle-Eastern global-jihad groups. Among the most powerful warlords were Shamil Basaev, a jihadist who is still fighting today; Salman Raduev, who organized several anti-Russian terrorist actions and developed strong jihadist ties; Movsar Baraev, who led Moscow theater hostage taking in 2002; Movladi Ugudov, one of the earliest converts to radical Islam; and Zelimkhan Yanbardiev—vice president under Dudayev who became jihadist (for a fuller account of warlords see Wilhelmsen: 2005). I will not discuss the war in depth, except to note that it lasted two years and by all accounts seemed to be headed to a Russian victory by mid-1995. Then, on June 14, 1995 Shamil Basaev took 1000 people hostage in a hospital in Budennovsk, in Russian territory. There were also several terrorist explosions in Moscow attributed to the Chechens, and losses among Russian soldiers were heavy. Facing elections, Yeltsin pressed for peace and an agreement was reached March 30, 1996. The question of independence was put off for five years.

The shift to radical jihadist Islam is clear from the brief description of the major warlords. At least in their public stances, these men often used the rhetoric of the Islam and holy war against the infidels, although some observers have noted that in private not all were not paragons of Islamic virtue (perhaps a measure of Islam's strategic use). The first traces of the jihadist shift appeared in the early 1990s as Middle Eastern money began to flow into Chechnya to build mosques and schools. At this time foreign mullahs appeared in Chechnya, as missionaries and to help establish Islamic courts. This was a stricter Salafi or Wahabbist Islam from the Middle East.[7] It has been observed that many Chechens were accustomed to a more flexible interpretation of their faith, one that allowed for their cultural traditions embodied in *adat*, and acceptance was constrained at first, but the Chechen *ulema* (council of Islamic elders) welcomed the resources and worked with Dudayev to facilitate their influence.

By 1994 Muslim fighters began arriving from other countries, according to Dudayev, "Declaring themselves to be soldiers of Allah." Many of these fighters were veterans of Afghanistan who joined transnational brigades (of mostly Afghan fighters, but also Arabs and North Africans), which had been formed to defend Muslim communities in Algeria and Bosnia. Notable is Ibn al-Khattab, who brought about 300 fighters in his International Islamic Brigade, and aligned with Shamil Basaev. His support came from the Al Haramain foundation, which is under Muslim Brotherhood. By the end of the war, foreign fighters were allowed to stay, and Khattab was named a brigadier general in the Chechen army.

For militia leaders, a key motivation behind the adoption of radical Islam and alliances with foreign Islamists was that they provided significant resources to wage battle against the Russians. The alliance between Basayev and Khattab brought big money, international contacts, training skills and recruits to his militia. Raduev, another warlord, boasted that he received money from several different Arab countries and also received jihadi fighters in his Kadi-Yurt camp. Movsar Baraev, who carried out the Moscow theater operation and beheading of four telecom workers, received $600,000 from Khattab. Udugov received Saudi money and Saudi financing for his presidential campaign in 1997 (after Dudayev's assassination by the Russians).

After the war, more Wahabbi missionaries arrived in Chechnya. Payments of $1,000–1,500 and $50–100 per month were paid to new converts The Ursus Martan region became a stronghold of Wahabbism. *Sharia'* courts were established in many villages, and Wahabbis were given positions of judges. These Wahabbis were supported and protected by various warlords during peacetime—protection that they needed because, as foreigners, their support

---

7   Wahabbism is similar to Salifi Islam, but not synonymous. Wahabbism originated in the Arabian peninsula in the eighteenth century as the ideology of the Arab struggle against the Ottoman empire. Wahabbites see it as the path of pure Islam," strict, internally logical, offering an alternative social order. Their goal was to proselytize their form of Islam, taking advantage of a society characterized by disintegration, corruption, criminality, and inequality. Wahabbites also condemned vestiges of pre-Islamic worship, as had Mansur and Shamil long ago. These remained common in Chechnya—*adat* merged with Sufism.

among Chechens was far from unanimous. Aslan Maskhadov, the new president of the republic, tried to expel foreign fighters, but the warlords protected them. When he sought to improve relations with Moscow, they condemned him as not being Islamic enough. The prewar fissures along the lines of clans and militias grew deeper after the war's end because of the presence of radical Islamists and the playing of the radical Islamist card in political infighting among the dispersed centers of power.

The radical Islamist goal was the creation of a Northern Caucasian Islamic state, which Maskhadov opposed. Militia fighters were sent to train in Pakistan toward the end of the war, and during peacetime it was estimated that 1600-2500 fighters were trained in these camps, not just Chechens but also Dagestanis and mujahedeen from former Soviet republics of Central Asia. Khattab created the Peacekeeping Brigade, a militia that included Middle Easterners and North Africans. In 1999, Kattab and Basayev invaded neighboring Dagestan in an attempt to create an Islamic Republic there. It was reported that they received $25 million from abroad to fund this operation, which was authorized by a *fatwa* (a legal opinion) of a Saudi sheikh. This invasion, which was repelled, was the precipitant of the second war with Russia later that year. One Russian analyst, Aleksei Malashenko, estimated that between $10 and 200 million was sent to Chechnya from foreign Islamic groups. Another observer notes that the radical media and websites in Arab and North African countries portrayed the Chechen conflict as their own. As of this writing, the *New York Times* reports that one of the Indian doctors who was involved Glasgow airport car bomb plot was deeply affected by the persecution of Chechens.

Although Chechens had a fully developed notion of jihad (or *gazavat* in their tongue) as part of their cultural text, it is clear that money and resources carried considerable weight during the first war and the peace that followed. As one area scholar put it, "Thus, money can buy ideas" (Wilhelmsen 2005: 40). While warlords benefited by raising the Islamic flag, international Islamists attempted to use the Chechen war as part of global jihad. In terms of the strategic use of radical Islam, it seems that both sides strategically used the other.

During this period, the grammar of Chechen contention encountered a different, foreign text of contention that was backed by considerable material resources. Because this was a time of war and because military victories are won by armaments, materiel, and resources, not ideas, what occurred in Chechnya may be less generalizable to movements mobilizing during peacetime. Still, the idea that resources trump grammar in some contexts is an hypothesis that deserves empirical testing. As during the previous period, the political context during the war continued to be highly factionalized, with competing militias vying for resources. This may have intensified the strategic acceptance of Wahabbist Islam strongly supported by material resources. In times of intense political contention, resources trump deep culture in terms of influences on a movement's cultural-ideological configuration.

Conclusion

I have shown how Islam was variably used according to changing political situations in Chechnya, and that its application and elaboration can profitably been seen as transformations of a fundamental cultural text. This text brought Islam into political events via the definition of the Chechen nation as subject, the verb jihad—to wage a holy war—against the Russians, the object. These three elements formed a semantic triplet of contention that was the basis of further grammatical transformations according to political opportunities and constraints. Just as surface manifestations of meaning in speech reflect transformations of underlying grammatical structures, what the speaker intends to say, and the constraints of the speech situation, so too did the strategic application of Islam reflect transformations based on deep cultural factors (the structure of the basic triplet), the agency of social actors (their political goals), and contextual understanding of what is appropriate and possible (the political opportunities).

The basic text remained sublinear during Soviet times. It came to the surface rapidly when faced with the threat of Russian invasion, when calls for jihad were first heard. Yet during the period of intense political contention among clans and militias, Islam came to political discourse via modifiers of the subject, the Chechen nation, not jihad, which carried connotations of struggle against infidels. The conflict in this case was among fellow Chechens, not the Russians, making jihad an inappropriate basis of contention. Yet, when war broke out in 1994-1995, jihad was again invoked, as the deep grammar would predict, as unifying focus for a rag-tag force of warlords and militias. Also, at this time, contextual influences of political opportunity introduced the modifiers of global and trans-Islamic to the verb of contention, jihad. This was a powerful transformation, rallying Chechens to resist this Russian invasion, yet with it came foreign fighters and Middle-Eastern resources. The modification of jihad, which in the deep grammar was associated with the Chechen nation, now stressed the global Muslim brotherhood. The introduction of foreign fighters and resources challenged the unity that was prescribed under the basic semantic triplet.

This transformational grammar model brings together two strands of contemporary cultural theory. One perspective is represented by the linguistic turn that focuses on narratives, stories, text, and discourse. A basic finding of the linguistic focus is that there are only so many forms that a narrative or a text can take and be successful in its pragmatic communicative goals. Another finding is that the larger discourses of a group or community shape and constrain the words and behaviors of social actors. The second strand is the performative approach to culture, represented by a long tradition of cultural research from pragmatic analyses of speech performance (Hymes 1964; Austin 1962) to Goffman's rituals of self-presentation (1956). Swidler's toolbox metaphor (1986) also stresses cultural performance in that signs, symbols, stories, and scripted behaviors are taken from shared cultural stock and used to navigate daily experience. In social movement research, a focus on strategic framing emphasizes the performative aspects of how organizational texts are produced, whereby leaders and activists draw on their own cultural toolboxes to craft persuasive and resonant messages. A transformational-grammar approach integrates these two perspectives by showing how a dominant discourse—the deep grammar of contention—broadly constrains and shapes action, and yet how it is also flexible, in this case according to changing political context, to produce surface-level transformations of the basic theme.

In the context of contentious politics, relevant texts are invoked, applied, and modified as actors pragmatically seek to accomplish goals. While the Chechen case provides some empirical grounding for the operation of deep grammatical text, it also more generally offers insights into movement development insofar as it captures relationships that are missed by the framing perspective, namely, the variable availability of culture along a continuum of strategic choice and cultural constraint. The transformational grammar of a deep cultural text is a concept that is useful in helping the analyst think about when cultural elements are present but not strategically invoked. Although framing processes are important in contemporary social movements, the contribution of this approach lies towards the constraining end of the continuum and how its juxtaposition with strategic usages brings to the foreground how important political context is in the usage of culture.

Chapter 11
Scenes and Social Movements

Darcy K. Leach and Sebastian Haunss

Charles Perry, in his history of San Francisco's Haight-Asbury district, describes a network of places, shops, newspapers, groups, events, and people that together constituted a kind of hothouse within which the hippie counterculture took root and flourished. In Perry's words,

> A whole world now revolved around the Haight-Ashbury .... By September 1966 newcomers were showing up in the Haight almost daily. Neighborhood windows had blossomed with all sorts of decorations: curtains made of blankets or Indian print fabrics from the Psych Shop, wind chimes, little glass sculptures, or god's-eyes .... [It] was the center of the Northern California psychedelic community. *The Oracle* was the world's only psychedelic newspaper, the Diggers were the only psychedelic political movement, and the Haight had more hippie business concerns than anyplace else. A new batch had just opened, including Annex 13 Books and a store selling bead stringers' supplies .... (Perry 2005)

This is the kind of social and spatial infrastructure that one often sees around more culturally oriented social movements. We call places like Haight-Ashbury a scene. In this chapter we elaborate a working definition of a scene, drawing distinctions between it and other free-space concepts. We then offer several propositions about the roles that scenes may play in social movements, and close with a few words about the future utility of the scenes concept.

Offe (1985) noted over two decades ago that social movements increasingly operate in a realm between the public and private spheres. They seek to "politicize the institutions of civil society ... and thereby to *reconstitute* a civil society that is no longer dependent upon ever more regulation, control, and intervention." They do this "through practices that belong to an intermediate sphere between 'private' pursuits and concerns, on the one side, and institutional, state-sanctioned modes of politics, on the other" (Offe 1985: 820, emphasis in original). Social movement researchers have long been aware of the social formations that make up this intermediate sphere, variously labeling them "free spaces" (Evans and Boyte 1992; Couto 1993; Polletta 1999b; Groch 2001; Futrell and Simi 2004; Johnston 2005), "submerged networks" (Melucci 1989; Mueller 1994), "oppositional subcultures" (Johnston 1991), "social movement communities" (Buechler 1990; Taylor and Whittier 1992, 1995; Taylor and Rupp 1993), "abeyance structures" (Taylor 1989; Taylor and Rupp 1993), "cultural laboratories" (Mueller 1994), "cultural havens" (Hirsch 1990; Fantasia and

Hirsch 1995) "safe spaces" (Gamson 1996; Hill-Collins 2000), "cultures of solidarity" (Fantasia 1988), and "movement halfway houses" (Morris 1986; Rupp and Taylor 1987). By whatever name, scholars have emphasized them as places where oppositional frames and collective identities are constructed. But even as the importance of these spaces has not been overlooked, we still know surprisingly little about their inner dynamics, the circumstances under which they arise, or their effect on social movement development.

In her review of this literature Polletta proposes a typology of three different kinds of free spaces: transmovement, indigenous, and prefigurative spaces. Transmovement spaces may be formal organizations or loose activist networks that serve a large population of activists in one or more movements by offering trainings and other resources to spur mobilization. The Highlander Folk School and the National Women's Party are examples of transmovement spaces. Such networks are characterized by extensive social ties, in which "activists are linked across a wide geographic area, have contacts in a variety of organizations and are often veterans of past movements" (Polletta 1999b: 9). An *indigenous* space, her second type, is one that is "indigenous to a community and initially is not formally oppositional" (Polletta 1999b: 10). These are more isolated networks marked by dense social ties, and are not created by the movement but come to be used by it, such as Southern black churches in the civil rights movement. Lastly, prefigurative spaces are the explicitly oppositional spaces created by movements to enact their countercultural lifestyle in an attempt to prefigure their desired world. Though it depends on their ideology, these spaces are often characterized by symmetrical interactional ties based on egalitarian power relations. As we will show, scenes share all of the traits of prefigurative spaces, but they can also *contain* transmovement spaces and isolated networks of dense ties.

A weakness of many definitions of free spaces is that they tend to focus on their function rather than on identifiable characteristics. To give a few examples, free spaces have been defined as "physical space in which to communicate and share perceptions of [a group's] experiences" (Groch 2001: 65), or "small-scale settings ... where [activists] can nurture oppositional movement identities" (Futrell and Simi 2004: 16). For Polletta they are settings that "generate the cultural challenge that precedes or accompanies political mobilization" (1999b: 1), and Johnston (2005: 110) sees them as places "where intimate association foments collective identity, shared grievances, oppositional frames, and tactical innovation" Such functional definitions tend to breed tautological reasoning, stretching the idea of free spaces to the point where it includes any and all locations that contribute to mobilization. As a result, at least four important differences in the way free spaces are characterized have been obscured.

First, there are significant differences in terms of their *structure and scope*. Some scholars speak explicitly of these spaces as networks (Melucci 1989; Taylor and Whittier 1992, 1995; Taylor and Rupp 1993; Groch 2001; Futrell and Simi 2004), and others discuss only single spaces or leave the question of their number and relation to one another unexamined (Morris 1984; Rupp and

Taylor 1987; Taylor 1989; Evans and Boyte 1992; Couto 1993; Hill-Collins 2000). Some researchers focus on groups and organizations (Morris 1986; Rupp and Taylor 1987; Evans and Boyte 1992; Groch 2001). Others extend the concept to include traditional institutions of socialization, such as schools, families, friendships, parties, and the media (including cyberspace) (Fantasia and Hirsch 1995; Hill-Collins 2000; Futrell and Simi 2004). Some include periodic or one-time gatherings and events (Taylor and Whittier 1995; Futrell and Simi 2004) where others do not. Patricia Hill Collins (2000) includes the black women's blues tradition and the voices of black women writers as "safe spaces" that help to empower black women. Johnston (2005) goes even further, categorizing oppositional speech situations and "event seizures" that occur under oppressive authoritarian regimes (for example, episodes of chanting, singing, and intense cheering at soccer games) as temporary free spaces. Clearly, more refined distinctions among these various types are necessary if we are to better understand their effect on social movements.

Second, there are differences in how free spaces are presumed to be organized. Are they democratically or hierarchically structured? Evans and Boyte (1992) emphasize internal democracy as a necessary attribute of free spaces but others either see them as undemocratically organized or do not specify their governing structure (Rupp and Taylor 1987; Taylor 1989; Couto 1993; Groch 2001; Futrell and Simi 2004). Still others *imply* that free spaces must be democratic by choosing cases that are committed to participatory democracy (Melucci 1989; Taylor and Whittier 1992, 1995; Taylor and Rupp 1993), but without theorizing how their internal structure may affect mobilization.

Third, there are differing views regarding free spaces' role in cultivating the skills and values of citizenship in a representative democratic polity. Research on voluntary associations suggests that this depends not only on the degree to which the spaces themselves are democratically organized, but also on the kind of democratic structure (e.g., representative, direct, collectivist; see Fung 2003). While only a few scholars explicitly discuss this dimension (Morris 1986; Evans and Boyte 1992; Couto 1993), it seems clear that undemocratic or simply oligarchic free spaces (Rupp and Taylor 1987; Taylor 1989; Futrell and Simi 2004) would not cultivate democratic citizenship skills. Other research suggests that spaces organized in a more radically egalitarian manner (Melucci 1989; Taylor and Whittier 1992, 1995; Taylor and Rupp 1993) also may not foster the skills needed in a *representative* democracy because they reject the principle of representation in favor of non-hierarchical, consensus-based self-governance.

Fourth, there are differing views regarding whether free spaces are created by the movements or existed beforehand as mainstream organizations that catalyze mobilization. This is important because spaces already embedded in mainstream society will tend to afford a narrower range of latitude in the ways movements may use the spaces. Also, if we focus on these indigenous spaces, we are also likely to privilege their role as proto-movement organizations and their importance in the early stages of mobilization, whereas appropriated countercultural spaces are likely to be more important in the later phases of the movement, functioning primarily to create and preserve movement culture.

These four distinctions suggest that different kinds of social and cultural spaces are likely to affect movements' development, recruitment, and longevity, as well as their relations with other movements and with bystander publics, in different ways. In order to understand precisely the role of scenes in social movements, then, we need to more clearly distinguish them from the more commonly recognized free-space concepts.

Scenes

A good starting place is to identify the main dimensions on which scenes differ from free spaces as they are commonly understood in the literature. Based on our review, there are four common assumptions underlying discussions of free space. First, they are seen as places where group members are able to interact beyond the reach of oppressor group—affording a degree of autonomy and agency to participants.[1] Second, they are treated as necessarily political and linked to social movements.[2] Third, free spaces are almost always portrayed as having positive effects on social movements, functioning to facilitate rather than hinder mobilization.[3] Fourth, they are frequently presumed to be attached only to politically liberal or left-leaning movements.[4] Of these four characteristics, the first is the only one that is usually made explicit and is probably true of all free spaces. The others are commonly assumed, but not always empirically warranted.

Other than the assumption of autonomy, none of these characteristics is necessarily true of scenes. Scenes are not necessarily political, and when they are political, their orientation is not necessarily left-leaning. Scenes are not necessarily attached to social movements, and even when they are, a scene

---

1   Ironically, the "free spaces" described by (Evans and Boyte 1992), who first coined the term, are the least free for oppressed groups, because they are characterized as necessarily public and open to all – as pluralistic spaces in which people learn to articulate their interests (by debating those with other interests) and develop the civic skills necessary for participation in a representative democracy. This definition would seem to exclude separatist spaces where members of dominant groups are unwelcome, as well as spaces used by countercultural groups who reject representative democracy.

2   Exceptions here are Couto (1993) and Polletta (1999b), who both allow that some free spaces develop prior to and independently of social movement mobilization, and may in that sense be pre-political. But it is still taken for granted that they will eventually *become* political, and their functions for non-political subcultures are not theorized.

3   Again, Polletta is the exception, noting that "With respect to free space analysts' claim that dense and isolated networks facilitate protest, it is just as likely that, depending on the circumstances, such networks may impede protest" (Polletta 1999b: 20).

4   Futrell and Simi (2004) are the sole exception we have found here.

cannot be reduced to the movement itself or to the organizations within it. And where scenes *are* connected to a movement, the relationship between the two is not always beneficial for the movement.

We define a scene as *simultaneously a network of people* who share a common identity and a common set of subcultural or countercultural beliefs, values, norms, and convictions *as well as a network of physical spaces* where members of that group are known to congregate. Put differently, it is a network of free spaces that encompasses one or more subcultures and/or countercultures. Where movement and scene are tightly interconnected, one may speak of a movement scene. Countercultural scenes are necessarily engaged in a political struggle in the sense that they actively oppose and want to change the dominant culture. Subcultural scenes are sometimes political and sometimes purely lifestyle oriented.[5] Based on the orientation of their core, then, we can identify three main types of scenes: subcultural non-movement scenes, subcultural movement scenes, and countercultural movement scenes. Any kind of subculture may develop a scene, but only some subcultures develop a political agenda, leading the scene to attach itself to a movement. For example, Irish expatriates living in Boston today would probably be classified as an apolitical subculture, whereas a century ago, that same social network would be better classified as a political subculture, formed in response to active repression. In both cases, there was a scene comprised of a network of clubs, pubs, and periodic gatherings that were more or less geographically concentrated (more then, less now) in certain parts of the city.

There are three characteristics of scenes we want to emphasize. First, a scene has its own culture. In addition to shared convictions, participants in a scene share distinctive dress codes, aesthetic tastes, social norms, linguistic patterns, signs and symbols, and specialized knowledge that set them apart. Yet, being part of a scene is more than just an expressive act or a question of style. Even though expressive forms play a central role, scenes cannot be reduced to "sign-communities" (Hebdige 1979). They are more an attempt at experimenting with a culture than they are an expression of it.

Second, the boundaries of scenes are constantly in flux. The transition between core members and those less integrally involved is fluid, as is the transition between members and non-members. Neither the boundaries of a scene nor its membership criteria can be determined from the outside,

---

5   Until now, it is only the subcultural aspect of the scene as an alternative lifestyle that has garnered scholarly attention. In the only systematic study of scenes to date, Hitzler, Bucher, and Niederbacher (2001) analyze twelve different lifestyle groups in Germany, including among others "skaters," Turkish street gangs, "ravers," "free-climbers," and young anti-fascists. They categorize seven of these lifestyle groups as scenes, using the following criteria: the participants shared a common and acquired knowledge, identified with the scene, acted in a value-oriented way, felt that engagement in the scene was important for their lives, and had their own meeting points, events, and internal media.

because a scene is ultimately constituted through a face-to-face process of self-identification and mutual recognition. In establishing the boundaries of membership this process also marks social territory, lending distinction to scene members and differentiating them from other social groups. As informal structures with fluid boundaries, scenes are somewhat fragile entities. Membership is generally based on cultural markers that are not difficult to shed, making it relatively easy to leave a scene. In principle, one is free to come and go as they please, although the scene can exert substantial pressure on a person to either join or leave.

Third, perhaps the most distinctive feature of a scene is that it refers simultaneously to an integrated network of both people and specific locales. The geographic aspect of scenes is expressed in the fact that they form around recognized scene locations—meeting places like bars, clubs, parks, street corners, and so on, in recognized parts of town—where being part of the scene can be physically experienced and the signifiers of membership can be enacted and validated. Knowing the location of such places is often itself a badge of membership.

Studying scenes as rooted in physical space rather than merely being symbolic communities has three important implications: that understanding scenes requires a focus on concrete collective *practices*, not just the discursive meanings and frames conveyed by those practices; that those practices shape and are shaped by the physical spaces in which they occur; and that the presence of a scene suggests a physical struggle for control over territory. Indeed, the ability to determine how scene spaces will be used and by whom is often violently contested. This struggle may take place between factions of a subculture or competing subcultures within a non-movement scene; between a subculture and a counterculture within a movement scene; or between a movement scene and the police or a countermovement.

As social networks, scenes also share traits with Melucci's notion of "submerged networks" and with what Taylor and Whittier call "social movement communities." Melucci refers to submerged networks as "movement areas" that "take the form of networks composed of a multiplicity of groups that are dispersed, fragmented, and submerged in everyday life, and which act as cultural laboratories [for] the experimentation and practice of new cultural models, forms of relationships and alternative perceptions and meanings of the world" (Melucci 1989: 60). These social networks become visible when they become engaged in overt political conflict, but during phases of less obvious political activity, they operate as a latent movement infrastructure, under the radar of most non-participants. In a similar vein, Taylor and Whittier define social movement communities as "a network of individuals and groups loosely linked through an institutional base, multiple goals and actions, and a collective identity that affirms members' common interests in opposition to dominant groups" (Taylor and Whittier 1992: 107).

Movement scenes, submerged networks, and social movement communities all share a high degree of autonomy from dominant groups, all refer to networks of persons, groups, and places, and are all prefigurative spaces created in the movement's image rather than indigenous premobilization groups. Where they differ is that both of the other two concepts are seen as necessarily connected to and beneficial for social movements, and the concept of a scene more explicitly addresses the importance of physical space as it relates to social movement action. By investigating both the social and spatial aspects of scene networks and by distinguishing scenes analytically both from the movement itself and from the mainstream communities in which scenes are embedded, we hope to better capture the various relationships that may obtain between scenes and movements and the conditions that determine whether and how that relationship develops.

The Scene in the German Autonomous Movement

To elaborate how the scenes concept contributes to our understanding of movement behavior, we will draw some examples from the autonomous movement in Germany, focusing on the scenes in Berlin and Hamburg that have grown up around this movement over the last several decades. This analysis is based on our own experiences as activists in this movement between 1995 and 2005 and on extensive fieldwork conducted for separate projects, including a year of participant observation in an autonomous antinuclear group (2000–2001), the evaluation of movement newspapers over a period of thirteen years, as well as online sources, and other movement documents, and in-depth interviews with thirty-two movement participants in six Autonomen-style groups from various German cities.

The German autonomous movement developed out of remnant strands of the post 1968 New Left. Activists from Frankfurt's "Spontis" who rejected the parliamentary path of leading figures like Joschka Fischer and Daniel Cohn Bendit, and radicals in the antinuclear movement who did not want to reduce their political agenda to ecological issues were the first to call themselves "Autonome" (Geronimo 2002). Influenced by the Italian "autonomia operaia," they developed their oppositional politics around a militant anti-authoritarian subjectivism and opposition to what they perceived as the dogmatism of both the old and new left. As Katsiaficas (1997) has noted, however, in contrast to the Italian movement, where autonomy was primarily seen as a form of working-class organization, free from the control of trade unions and political parties, in the German context the term connotes a rejection of all forms of hierarchical organization. The Autonomen have been a continuous presence in the German left since the late 1970s, playing a significant role in a range of movements and campaigns, from the antifascist, women's, and antiwar movements, to the current global justice movement.

The politics of the Autonomen is often called a "politics of the first person." In part, this expresses a rejection of representative politics of any stripe. They are equally antagonistic toward capitalist and state-socialist economic systems, and they reject the structural hierarchy and ideological dogmatism they see as inherent in old-leftist strategies for social change that call for an intellectual vanguard to lead "the people" in revolution. As a group in 1981 put it in their "Theses on the Autonomous Movement":

> We fight for ourselves, others fight for themselves, and together we are stronger. We are not leading any representative struggle. It works through personal participation— politics of the first person. We are not fighting for any ideology, not for the proletariat or for "the people," but for a self-determined life, well knowing that we can only be free when all others are free as well! (Anonymous 1981)

On a deeper level, though, a politics of the first person refers to a commitment to a prefigurative praxis that aligns means and ends, expressed in the slogan *der Weg ist das Ziel*, or "the way is the goal." If the way is the goal, and autonomy is their central value, then being autonomous is both the end they seek and the means by which they work to accomplish it. In practice this means that both among themselves and in their interactions with the rest of society they strive to create practices and structures in which they not only refuse to be subservient to others, but also refuse to dominate others. It is this prefigurative principle that underlies their experimentation with non-hierarchical collectivist forms of organization, and makes the scene a critical factor in the movement's development.

The Autonomen first became visible in the mid to late 1970s as a militant faction within the antinuclear and squatters movements. The importance of militancy, however, reaches far beyond the question of the use of violence as a tactic. In autonomous politics, militancy additionally signifies a radically oppositional standpoint—a refusal to be co-opted or to let one's behavior be dictated by the laws and norms of the dominant society. With the rise of the squatter's movement in 1980 in many larger European cities, the Autonomen became part of a growing alternative scene, characterized by a local infrastructure of bars, cinemas, info shops, book stores, squatted cultural and youth centers, living projects, and media groups. In the 1980s a potent Autonomen identity began to emerge, containing the following core elements: a dual emphasis on self-determination and collective responsibility, an antiauthoritarian leftist political orientation, the devaluation of paid work, a distinctive clothing style, and preferences for punk and "hardcore" music, collective living, non-hierarchical organization, and participatory democratic decision making.[6]

---

6   While this is a good general description of the movement identity in Germany, it should not be taken as either complete or conclusive, as one distinctive feature of the

The Scene in Berlin

With a population of 3.3 million, Berlin hosts the largest concentration of radical leftists in Germany and also has the largest and most active autonomous scene.[7] The four most common access points for tapping into the information channels of the scene and keeping abreast of leftist politics in Berlin are the streets, scene publications, Indymedia, and scene locales.

As in most German university towns and larger cities, to find out what is "really" going on in Berlin, one does not read the newspapers, one reads the streets. Those arriving in Berlin for the first time, even if they do not know a single person, can find entry into the political scene simply by reading the posters and graffiti that cover the building walls, overpasses, and telephone poles all over town. Posters especially convey all kinds of political information—about protest actions, meetings, informational events, the formation of new groups, and social events like street festivals, parties, and concerts.

As second source of this information are movement newspapers like the *Interim* or a monthly calendar called *Stressfaktor*. The *Interim* is a participatory biweekly newsletter, which has a strong focus on Berlin, but is available and read nationwide. Since its founding in 1988 it has been the most important national discussion forum for the autonomous movement. The *Stressfaktor* is a monthly events calendar specifically targeted at the radical leftist scene in Berlin. It is available on-line and is also distributed gratis in hard copy at scene locations throughout the city. It includes a calendar of leftist events and actions, a list of standing dates with the addresses of relevant scene locations (numbering one hundred and forty-four at last count, including fourteen leftist bookstores/"info-shops"),[8] and a "Vokü-Fahrplan," which lists all of the places where one can find "Vokü" (*Volkxküche,* or people's kitchen) each night.

As a means of social and informational integration into the movement, the Vokü is itself an important scene institution. A number of scene bars and living projects open their doors once or twice a week to offer a hot homemade meal for €2–3 a plate (roughly $3 or $4). At this writing, the *Stressfaktor* lists an average of eleven different scene locations offering Vokü on any given weeknight; five on Fridays and Saturdays. Vokü offers activists on a budget an affordable opportunity to eat out in a way that corresponds to their political principles (generally: organic, vegan or vegetarian, inexpensive, and social), and in a place where they can "come as they are" and socialize with other radical

---

autonomous movement is its tendency to resist the development of any stable collective identity or ideology (Leach forthcoming).

7   The scenes relevant for the autonomous movement are variably described as "radical leftist," "leftist," "autonomous," or "alternative." Most people involved in scenes refer to them simply as "the scene" without any modifier.

8   Aside from books, infoshops sell a whole range of movement-made political goods, including pamplets, posters, t-shirts, videos, records, patches, and buttons.

leftists. As a way of drawing people from the scene into the movement, many venues schedule Voküt right before a more political activity such as a plenary meeting or panel discussion.

A third point of access in Berlin for information about the autonomous movement and leftist politics in general is the website of the German Independent Media Center (IMC).[9] Intended as a grassroots corrective to the mainstream bias of commercial media, "Indymedia's" participatory, interactive concept of activist-reporting gives activists and others a chance to read first-hand accounts of protest events from the perspective of the participants themselves, as well as position papers, announcements, and calls to action. The sites are also structured for readers to contribute to a running commentary in response to each article. There is a filter that screens out postings with overtly racist, sexist, and fascist content, but otherwise everything gets posted, even if it ends up in the "postings not offering any new content" section. Beyond just disseminating information, this interactive structure pulls the reader into the fray, making it easy to get involved.

Whatever the point of departure, however, all roads to leftist political engagement eventually run through the scene itself. With information gathered from the streets, *Interim*, *Stressfaktor*, or Indymedia, people might first go to an action or festival where they would meet others who might then take them to a scene location—maybe to attend a political meeting, have an affordable drink or meal, pick up flyers or buy a book, go to a movie, see a panel discussion, or maybe find a locally produced video of last month's protest action. Or people may go on their own directly to an event in one of the scene locales. Once there, they soon realize that not only are they tapped into a social network in a safe space with like-minded people and similar tastes, but they also have stable access in these places to all kinds of current political information via the posters, flyers, brochures, pamphlets, and movement periodicals that are regularly laid out there. One could stay *informed* without hanging out at scene locations, but it is more difficult, and it is almost impossible to stay *involved* without having some contact with the scene.

The scene in Berlin is geographically concentrated, though as we will see, not as concentrated as the Hamburg scene. Scene establishments can be found in almost any part of town, but they are most visible and concentrated in the districts of Kreuzberg, Prenzlauer Berg, Mitte, and Friedrichshain. That the latter three districts are in what was formerly East Berlin is no coincidence.

---

9   See http://germany.indymedia.org/. Since the first IMC was formed in Seattle in preparation for the protests against the WTO in 1999, one hundred and seventy-seven IMC collectives have been founded around the world, one hundred and sixteen of them outside of the US. Each autonomous collective must agree with the general IMC concept and structure. The mission statement on the German site reads (translated): "Indymedia is an international network of media initiatives and activists for independent and noncommercial news coverage from below—on location and worldwide. It sees itself as part of the worldwide resistance against capitalist globalization."

Kreuzberg has been the heart of the scene for several decades, but when the wall came down, the Autonomen and others took advantage of the situation and squatted a large number of empty houses in East Berlin. Though most squatters were eventually forced to sign leases, the projects that were founded in these squats nevertheless successfully extended a strong radical leftist presence into a much wider area. There is also a territorial possessiveness that develops in the parts of town where the scene is most entrenched. One sees this reflected in action campaigns mounted to defend individual "leftist structures" against evictions and rent increases, often coordinated by the "Pi-rat" (Projects and Initiatives Council). Identification with particular parts of town is also manifested in the physical defense of the territory itself against incursions by opposing groups, such as the Autonomen's efforts to keep Kreuzberg a "Nazi-free zone."

The Hamburg Scene

Hamburg is Germany's second largest city with a population of about 1.8 million people. Despite extensive damage in WWII its densely populated core still contains large tracts of old multistory buildings. Urban flight during the 1960s and 1970s and the poor conditions in many of these houses made spacious and relatively cheap inner-city housing in Hamburg accessible to the less privileged—especially immigrants and students. Here, as in other German cities, the availability of cheap housing that allows low-income young people to live together in shared apartments (*Wohngemeinschaften*) was the first building block for Hamburg's scene. In the 1980s these conditions existed in the neighborhood known as the "Schanzenviertel," and since that time this part of town has been the center of the autonomous scene in Hamburg. Citing the scene as an indicator of the success of ten years of struggle against urban renewal projects in this part of town, one "old Autonomer" comments:

> Moreover, there is the veritable service network of the scene, from bars, cafes, book and record stores, and taxi collectives to clothing stores and several social facilities, that guarantees bread and wages to activists in the area. On top of that there's an array of implemented living projects and the Rote Flora, the autonomous community center that's been squatted and self-managed without paid staff from November 1989 until today. (Blechschmidt 1998: 83–4)

The visible epicenter of the Hamburg scene is still the "Rote Flora," located on the main shopping street in the Schanzenviertel. The building offers space for a range of groups and activities: political groups meet there, there are practice rooms for local musicians, an archive of movement documents, a motorcycle repair shop, and a silk screen print shop, and several days a week the bar offers Vokü. During the 1990s, the Flora was the default location for larger political meetings, and it still puts out the local autonomous movement newspaper. For the majority of its visitors, however, the Rote Flora is primarily a venue that hosts concerts and parties almost every night, with various styles of music that often have broad appeal but are not culturally mainstream.

Most of Hamburg's scene infrastructure is located in the immediate vicinity of the Rote Flora. The "Schwarzmarkt," a volunteer-run autonomous infoshop located in a formerly squatted house, serves as the main distribution point for political flyers, brochures, books and posters. More political in character than the Rote Flora, it is frequented almost exclusively by committed movement activists. A non-profit bar in the same building attracts a much wider public and reaches out especially into the alternative gay subculture. Also close by is the "B5" (shorthand for its location in the Brigittenstraße 5) another community center in a formerly squatted building that houses a community-run café/bar, a community kitchen, and a non-profit alternative cinema. With a varied daily program, the B5 attracts people from a range of cultural and political backgrounds, from cultural hedonists to anarchists, Maoists, and Stalinists. It functions as well as a bridge to a number of radical leftist Turkish and Kurdish organizations that hold their weekly meetings there. Other scene locations in the immediate vicinity of the Rote Flora include an alternative bookshop, an anarchist center, an alternative radio station, alternative projects, and a number of bars that have been founded by former movement activists or fellow travelers.

Hamburg's autonomous scene is smaller and geographically more centralized than Berlin's. As in Berlin, the scene's boundaries are also visibly marked by political posters, which are abundant on walls, fences, and any other suitable surfaces in certain areas of the city but virtually non-existent everywhere else. These areas coincide with the neighborhoods that contain the bars and venues of the autonomous and/or alternative scene, and are at the same time the neighborhoods in which most movement activists live. Certainly, people who identify with the scene also live in other neighborhoods in Hamburg, but the concentration is nowhere near as dense as it is in and around the Schanzenviertel.

To further illustrate the character and scope of the Berlin and Hamburg scenes, we have collected data from the online leftist calendars for the two cities, *Stressfaktor* and *Bewegungsmelder*, for the months of April, July, and October in each of three years, 2003, 2005, and 2007. Table 10.1 shows the number and type of various kinds of events per month. We see a relatively stable number of demonstrations, and a sizable number of political and cultural events announced each month. The total number of events is always significantly higher in Berlin, reflecting in part the larger size of the leftist scene there, but also the more established readership of the *Stressfaktor*.

Table 11.1   Scene events in Berlin (B) and Hamburg (HH) 2003–2007

Scene events	April 2003		July 2003		October 2003		April 2005		July 2005		October 2005		April 2007		July 2007		October 2007	
	B	HH	B	HH	B	HH	B	HH	B	HH	B	HH	B	HH	B	HH	B	HH
Demonstrations	9	10	7	7	13	3	14	5	7	5	12	2	13	4	13	9	13	21
Topical events	38	9	41	13	53	12	83	19	65	8	60	7	109	46	52	27	62	34
Film showings	45	2	75	10	95	8	126	5	98	0	102	3	116	18	94	17	132	22
Solidarity parties	20	1	11	2	20	2	35	5	19	5	35	10	45	9	27	7	38	11
Other parties	19	14	24	13	26	17	52	8	40	7	50	26	41	42	40	40	30	30
Concerts	33	22	25	19	36	33	103	20	77	13	124	56	98	112	66	70	89	122
Other events	5	10	15	4	13	9	24	4	28	33	19	6	24	15	10	8	31	21
Total	183	68	208	68	266	84	451	66	342	71	419	110	452	246	313	178	406	261

In Figure 11.1 we have collapsed this data into categories of cultural and political events for each city.[10] The figure shows that for the most part cultural and political activities followed a parallel pattern. The data therefore show fluctuations in the level of overall scene activity but no shift in focus over time from political to cultural or vice versa. The peak in April 2005 in Berlin was caused mainly by the mobilization around the annual demonstration on May 1 (Rucht 2003), which that year involved a concerted attempt to "re-politicize" the event. The peak in April 2007 that is visible in both cities reflects the big mobilization push leading up to the G8 meetings held in June in Heiligendamm.

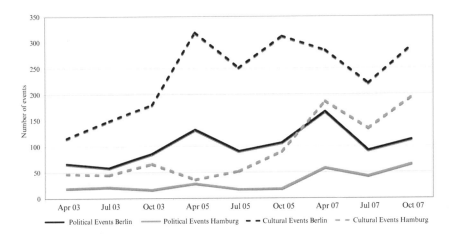

Figure 11.1   Cultural and political activities in the Berlin and Hamburg scenes

Scenes and Social Movements

Not all movements require or develop scenes, which raises the question: Under what conditions would we expect movements to become attached to scenes? Based on the Autonomen, we would expect scenes to develop in new social movements whose political ideals are intimately bound up with their day-to-day personal behaviors, and for whom defending, creating and/or promoting a marginalized, repressed, or countercultural way of life is an essential aspect of their political praxis. Others have referred to movements in this category as

---

10   In the category of political events we included demonstrations, topical events, and solidarity parties/concerts; under cultural events counted films, parties, concerts, and other events. Because solidarity parties serve an explicitly political purpose, we counted them in the political events category, and parties that were not explicitly political as cultural events.

"left-libertarian" (della Porta and Rucht 1995), "expressive" (Rucht 1990), and "nonviolent direct action" (Epstein 1991) movements. Specific examples might include the radical wings of the women's, peace, and environmental movements, the lesbian-feminist movement, and the gay movement—at least in the US and Germany—and on the other side of the political spectrum, neo-Nazi, nationalist, and fundamentalist religious movements. Whatever their orientation, *countercultural* movements striving for a fundamental reorganization of society and trying to live in a way that prefigures their desired social arrangements and *subcultural* movements seeking to defend and preserve a stigmatized and/or repressed subcultural lifestyle are the most likely to develop a scene. Thus, we offer two general propositions about scene-movement linkages.

1 Scenes are likely to develop around movements that operate according to a prefigurative, value-rational logic and are concerned with creating, promoting, and/or preserving a particular subcultural or countercultural lifestyle.
2 The more a subcultural lifestyle is stigmatized and repressed, the more likely it is to take on a political-orientation characteristic of a movement scene, usually in defense of its right to freely exist, unmolested by the dominant culture.

European autonomous scenes have benefited from a number of structural and historical conditions that facilitated their emergence. Because of their embeddedness in physical space, several factors related to the rise of a widespread squatters' movement are relevant. Primary among them are a legal environment favoring squatters' rights and widespread housing shortages (aided in the German case by reunification, which spurred rampant speculation and ambiguity about who could lay legitimate claim to previously state-owned properties in the East). Also key in the Autonomen case was the existence of an advanced welfare system with unemployment insurance and a universal health-care system in which benefits were not tied to employment status. These combined to guarantee a minimum standard of living, reducing the urgency of finding full-time employment and making it possible for the underemployed and unemployed to engage full-time in radical politics. Also relevant here are the *Kindergeld* entitlement program (which pays a fixed monthly amount to parents for each child until s/he either finishes college or reaches the age of twenty-six), a university system with only nominal tuition fees (by US standards), and government loans that make it possible for a large proportion of students to finance their education without having to find paid employment. Last, more relaxed regulations and/or enforcement about such things as the sale and public consumption of alcohol, the sale of home cooked food, and public film showings make it much easier for groups to subsidize their activities through such mainstays of the scene as Vokü, cocktail hours, and solidarity parties, rather than being dependent upon foundation grants. Thus, we suggest the following propositions about scenes and the structural environment.

3   Scenes are more likely to develop where conditions are conducive to squatting and/or where rents are low enough to support non-commercial initiatives.

4   Scenes are more likely to develop in more advanced welfare states which are more conducive to full-time political engagement and where social regulation facilitates independent, socially based fundraising methods.

Scenes and Mobilization

The most straightforward way in which the scene enhances mobilization is by providing a ready pool of potential recruits. The German Minister of the Interior's Federal Office for the Protection of the Constitution estimates that while there are only about 5,500 Autonomen in the country, the movement has a mobilization potential of closer to 10,000 within the scene (Bundesministerium des Innern 2006). Because a scene offers a sense of community at a low social cost, it attracts more people than the movement does. Subcultural activities in the scene, like concerts and parties, attract people and continuously expose them to the movement's political lifestyle and ideology in a low-pressure context. And while the scene attracts people to the movement, the edgy/dangerous image of the movement also attracts people to the scene. Because engagement in the movement requires a greater commitment and often a willingness to engage in high-risk activity, one advantage of the scene is that it provides a way of "easing into" the movement, with the first step being subcultural identification with the scene. The next step can be left open for a relatively long period of time, but once people begin to feel connected to the scene, they are much more likely to increase their level of commitment, due to the "foot-in-the-door" principle whereby people feel compelled to act in a way that is consistent with an initial (if unintentional) commitment. This means that as long as the scene remains culturally attractive, the movement need do little more to mobilize people for an action than simply to publicize the event within the scene.

5   Movement scenes serve as a gateway to active engagement in the movement—a low-pressure context in which people are exposed to movement norms and then feel drawn to make a greater commitment due to consistency pressures.

The relationship between scene and movement is not always mutually reinforcing, however, as developments in the Hamburg scene illustrate. While concerts and parties at the Rote Flora bring people into contact with the autonomous movement who otherwise would have little interest in its political claims, this function of the scene also challenges the movement to deal with positions and lifestyles that conflict with those claims. A review of the local movement newspaper shows that the relationship between (sub)culture and politics—between scene and movement—in the Rote Flora has always been conflictual, especially since the advent of techno music in the mid-1990s, when the more hedonistic lifestyle of the techno subculture came into conflict with the more ascetic and anti-consumerist ideals of the movement counterculture. Over time, however, the techno subculture has *de facto* opened up the spectrum of "allowable" lifestyle choices in the movement. On the one hand, this has been positive, as the movement has become accessible to a larger potential constituency, but it has also had negative consequences, as the movement's principles and its everyday radical practices have been diluted.

6   In countercultural movements, tensions between movement and scene are often rooted in the trade-off between openness and purity – between the need to reach a broader public and the danger that this will undermine the movement's adherence to a prefigurative praxis.

Certain spatial and discursive characteristics of scenes may also influence mobilization by structuring the flow of information. In the autonomous movement, the scene tends to be the target audience to which almost all movement communications are addressed. Geographic concentration, as exemplified by the Hamburg scene, amplifies this tendency. The general public is virtually ignored, severely limiting the movement's reach. In Hamburg, this concentration positively affects the movement's ability to mobilize quickly in response to political challenges, because information distributed through the dense network of bars and shops in the scene reaches a large number of likely supporters with little effort. It also fosters a tight-knit cultural matrix in which verbal communication is the primary means of information exchange, with all of the advantages and disadvantages that brings. On the positive side, there is an increased sense of commitment through the development of insider linguistic codes and dense social ties. On the downside, this verbal, self-referential infrastructure makes the movement virtually invisible to those who do not regularly frequent the right bars, parties and events, and who are thus easily cut off from the movement's information flows. Although some of this information is publicly available in the indymedia websites, political posters, and newspapers, it is not likely to be understood by anyone who is not conversant in the scene's vernacular or who does not at least share/understand its underlying assumptions.

Granovetter's (1983) theory of the strength of weak ties may help to unravel these contradictory tendencies. When scenes have a relatively greater number of weak ties with the broader society, they should have more access to the resources, information, and ideas that would enhance mobilization. On the other hand, effective mobilization (measured as successful turnout of those asked) depends most directly on the density of the network—on the existence of strong ties.

So the movement's vitality over time should depend on there being a sufficient number of weak ties between groups within the scene and between members of the scene and the rest of society, but the mobilization potential of the movement at any given time will depend on the overall density of the scene's network.

7 Due to the greater density of social ties, geographically concentrated scenes should have more success mobilizing within the scene, but they are also likely to generate more insular norms of interaction and discourse, limiting their scope of influence.

8 The tendency toward insularity may be offset to the degree that weak ties between local scenes in different locations facilitate exposure to a broader population and increase access to resources, diverse ideas, and information.

Collective Identity and the Politics of Everyday Life

Scenes play a central role in the construction and maintenance of alternative identities, lifestyles, and modes of interaction. An important connotation of the Autonomen principle of a "politics of the first person" is that activists should organize around their personal experiences and interests while simultaneously working to minimize the degree to which their own behaviors contribute to the oppression of others (Leach 2006). In the autonomous movement, the scene facilitates this process of integrating the personal and the political by providing the space in which to (a) construct an oppositional ideology and collective identity, and (b) create and implement associational forms and norms of interaction that embody their anti-authoritarian values. Collective movement identities are not only constructed during the meetings and actions of social movement organizations, but also through the performance and negotiation of what it means to be a member of the movement in their everyday lives. These processes can take place in any social space where it is relatively safe to be different. For movements that generate scenes, constructing a collective identity is about more than self-expression or affirmation; it is itself a component of the change being sought, a form of subjectivity understood to prefigure the kind of world for which they are fighting. For these movements, the scene is the primary location for identity work.

Parallel to the construction of new identities are the processes by which such movements construct alternative norms and forms of organization as a part of their strategy for social change. For the Autonomen, whose ideal is a "dominance-free society" (*herrschaftslose Gesellschaft*), the scene is a cultural laboratory for experimenting with non-hierarchical ways of structuring daily life. They seek spaces that are free of any pre-existing rules that would inhibit their efforts, and then work to create sustainable non-hierarchical forms of organization characterized by radically democratic decision-making processes and non-oppressive modes of social interaction. While it is not true across the board, scene locales in Berlin and Hamburg are generally organized as collectives that operate either by consensus or some other form of direct democracy (see della Porta, Chapter 8 in this volume). This non-hierarchical ideal is evident in every kind of movement group and gathering, from the open plenaries, affinity groups, regional delegate meetings, national conferences, and action camps of the movement itself, to the bars, info shops, theaters, media projects, squats, finance collectives, and community and youth centers of the scene, to transmovement collectives that provide cooking, training, legal aid, and street-medic services for activists, and those offering support for newly forming collectives.

However, this close integration of politics and everyday practices can also generate deep conflicts about how best to implement the movement's principles, for example over what constitutes sexist behavior, or criticisms of consumerist lifestyle practices in the scene. Alongside traditional struggles over organization and decision making, these lifestyle conflicts prominently influence the viability of the movement.

9   In movements that stress the integration of politics and everyday life, processes related to identity and cultural construction are likely to be centered in the scene, rather than in official movement organizations and activities, and conflicts between movement and scene are likely to be focused on these processes.

Scenes and Movement Longevity

The final issue in which scenes seem to be deeply implicated has to do with the movement's ability to sustain itself over time and/or rebound after periods of inactivity. In a study of three German locales where movement activity was particularly robust, Roth (1994) found that social movements avoided becoming institutionalized by becoming institutionalized *as movements*. That is, they sustained a heightened level of extraparliamentary activity, because extraparliamentary engagement had become the normative form of interest representation. Roth attributes this to "stable local movement networks" in each place, consisting of "communications centers, media, and alternative living forms and projects" (Roth 1994: 413). These networks facilitate sustained mobilization, cushion against defeat, and encourage self-reflection and learning.

Based on Roth's study and others, we would posit three general ways in which scenes are likely to contribute to movement longevity. The first is as "abeyance structures" for the whole movement during periods of low activity. As others have pointed out, free spaces can provide a way for activists to maintain their movement identity, when it has once again become stigmatized or marginalized without the strength of the movement behind it (Taylor 1989; Taylor and Whittier 1992, 1995; Taylor and Rupp 1993). Because the autonomous movement in Germany has never had a sustained period of inactivity, it is difficult to say to what degree the scene has contributed in this way, but it is clear that the scene has continued to flourish even when the movement has not been highly active.

Second, generalizing from the Hamburg and Berlin cases, we suggest that scenes serve as a kind of living archive that helps preserve movement identity and cultural practices. Tactical innovations, organizational forms, decision-making practices, strategic lessons, movement history, symbols, frames, theoretical analyses, and movement identities are all preserved and transmitted to subsequent waves of activists through the scene. In a movement with no central organization and little if any formal organization, this is an especially important (and difficult) task. Activists themselves have documented and preserved the movement's history and ideology through a variety of media, including self-published books (Geronimo 1997, 2002; HSK 13 1999; AG Grauwacke 2003; Haunss 2004), documentations of important protest events, and self-managed movement archives such as the Papier Tiger in Berlin, the archives at the Rote Flora, and many others. Websites like the one put together by AG Grauwacke[11] also have worked to make movement documents more accessible and encourage participation in writing the movement's history.

Third, scenes may serve as "retreat structures"—to coin a term—for individual activists during phases of high activity, a function not typically attributed to abeyance structures. In the autonomous movement this has been especially important in response to repression or as activists get older and the requirements and demands of constant mobilization lead to burn out. In both cases, they always have the option to use the scene as "a retreat place" (Rückzugsort) where they can stay in touch with the movement but reduce the overall amount of time and energy they invest, leaving them available for later mobilizations. This effect has been most obvious when central movement institutions have come under threat. For example, when underground movement newspapers have been targeted by state repression, the subsequent solidarity campaigns often involved unusual numbers of older activists who often had not been active in the movement for some time. We therefore offer the following proposition, recognizing that the Autonomen case is only suggestive.

10 Scenes support longevity in different ways during different phases of the movement, providing individuals with a means of "laying low" and/or recharging during periods of peak activity, and preserving movement identities and culture during periods of decline.

---

11   http://autox.nadir.org/archiv/auto/index.html.

Conclusion: Scenes and Social Movement Research

Based on our analysis of two scenes attached to the German autonomous movement, we have argued that scenes can play a vital role in movement processes related to mobilization, the construction and maintenance of collective identities, practices and organizational forms, and movement longevity. For value-rational movements, whose lifestyles are severely marginalized or whose interests stand in opposition to those of dominant elites, acquiring support from mainstream institutions may require too great a compromise in their interests or ideological principles. Such movements will more likely rely on scenes to facilitate mobilization, sustain commitment, connect politics and everyday life, construct alternative collective identities, and preserve their traditions, innovations, and ideologies over time—even if these activities may hamper their chances to advance their political goals or attract support.

We have offered our propositions as a first step in thinking about scenes as a different type of free-space configuration. Based on the Berlin and Hamburg scenes, we have distilled several basic relationships that are directly implicated in movement dynamics, but are not captured by current theorizing about free spaces. Still, there are a number of important topics that remain to be considered, such as the relationship between state repression and the vitality of movement scenes, the role of subcultural scenes that are not attached to movements and the conditions under which they become political, and the impact of countermovements on movement scenes. In Germany, for example, there is a long-standing conflict between Autonomen and neo-Nazi groups including violent confrontations and attempts to shut down each others' scene locations, but space limitations have not allowed us to pursue this topic.

In choosing new cases to refine the scenes concept, two questions should be central in guiding future inquiry. First, we need to understand more about the conditions under which scenes take root and thrive. For example, even though the collectivist-democratic structure used in the German autonomous scene can in part be traced back to the US anti-nuclear movement in the mid-1970s, and even though there have been a few examples of countercultural movements scenes in the US, like the one that developed in the Haight-Ashbury district in San Francisco, neither the structure nor the scene has proved sustainable in the US context. In contrast, both have taken root in much of Western Europe and have prospered in Germany for nearly three decades now, to the point of becoming taken-for-granted features of extraparliamentary politics (Leach 2006). How can we explain these patterns of diffusion?

Second, for comparisons, it would be useful to know more about the negative effects scenes may have on a movement. We have argued that movement scenes play an important role in collective identity processes by providing an infrastructure for bridging politics and everyday life. The effectiveness of scenes as mobilization pools, movement abeyance structures, and individual retreat structures lays in the fact that they act as a cultural buffer, blurring the boundaries of the movement and making it easy for people to move in and out of active engagement. But their role as lifestyle communities can also negatively affect a movement by alienating people with more mainstream lifestyles. In his comparative study of collective identity processes, for example, Haunss (2004) has shown that the second German gay movement was not only founded in explicit opposition to the gay scene, but also coexisted in a conflictual relationship with it. Also, the geographical concentration of scenes in a few neighborhoods can lead activists to be ignorant of or even act condescendingly toward other neighborhoods, thereby limiting the movement's reach.

As a community of meaning in which oppositional ideologies and alternative cultural forms are constructed and performed, scenes occupy an intermediate location between the movement and broader political contexts and serve as a cultural lens that mediates the way political opportunities are interpreted at the local level. As such, the performances that occur in scenes may be thought of as bridging the gap between cultural and structural approaches to movement dynamics (Goodwin and Jasper 2004). In its duality as both a social network and a network of spatial settings, a scene is a cultural laboratory where macro-level opportunities are discussed and evaluated in terms of personal politics and political ideals. The influence these processes have on movement trajectories points to the pivotal role of social movement scenes.

Works Cited

Abbot, Andrew. 1995. "Sequence Analysis: New Methods for Old Ideas." *Annual Review of Sociology* 21: 93–113.

Ableson, Robert P. 1981. "The Psychological Status of the Script Concept." *American Psychologist.* 36: 715–29.

AG Grauwacke. 2003. *Autonome in Bewegung: aus den ersten 23 Jahren.* Berlin: Assoziation A.

Agrikolianski, Eric, and Dominique Cardon, 2005, "Un programme en débats: forum, formes et formats." Pp. 45–74, in *Radiographie du mouvement altermondialiste*, Eric Agrikolianski and Isabell Sommier, eds. Paris: La Dispute.

Alexander, Jeffrey. 1990. "Analytic Debates: Understanding the Autonomy of Culture." Pp. 1–27 in *Culture and Society: Contemporary Debates,* Jeffrey Alexander and Steven Seidman, eds. New York: Cambridge University Press.

Alexander, Jeffrey. 2006. "Cultural Pragmatics: Social Performance between Ritual and Strategy." Pp. 29–90 in *Social Performance: Symbolic Action, Cultural Pragmatics and Ritual*, Jeffrey Alexander, Bernhard Giesen, and Jason L. Mast, eds. New York: Cambridge University Press.

Alexander, Jeffrey C., and Jason L. Mast 2006. "Introduction: Symbolic Action In Theory and Practice: The Cultural Pragmantics of Symbolic Action." Pp. 1–28 in *Social Performance*, Jeffrey C. Alexander, Bernhard Giesen, and Jason L. Mast, eds. New York: Cambridge University Press.

Alexander, Jeffery, Bernhard Giesen, and Jason L. Mast. 2006. *Social Performance: Symbolic Action, Cultural Pragmatics and Ritual.* New York: Cambridge.

Almond, Gabriel, and Sidney Verba. 1963. *The Civic Culture.* Princeton, NJ: Princeton University Press.

———. 1989. *The Civic Culture Revisited.* Newbury Park, CA: Sage.

Alsop, Joseph, and Robert Kintner. 1941. "Ways and Means of the Opposition." *Washington Post* (May 28): 11.

Amenta, Edwin, and Michael P. Young. 1999. "Making an Impact: Conceptual and Methodological Implications of the Collective Goods Criterion." Pp. 22–41 in *How Movements Matter: Theoretical and Comparative Studies on the Consequences of Social Movements*, Marco Giugni, Doug McAdam, and Charles Tilly, eds. Minneapolis, MN: University of Minnesota Press.

Amenta, Edwin, Kathleen Dunleavy, and Mary Bernstein. 1994. "Stolen Thunder: Huey Long's Share our Wealth, Political Mediation, and the Second New Deal." *American Sociological Review* 59: 678–702.

Amenta, Edwin. 1998. *Bold Relief: Institutional Politics and the Origins of Modern American Social Policy*. Princeton, NJ: Princeton University Press.

Andretta, Massimiliano, Donatella della Porta, Lorenzo Mosca, and Herbert Reiter. 2002. *Global, noglobal, new global. La protesta contro il G8 a Genova*. Bari-Roma: Laterza.

———. 2003. *Global, new global. Identität und Strategien der Antiglobalisierungsbewegung*. Frankfurt am Main: Campus Verlag.

Andrews, Molly. 1991. *Lifetimes of Commitment*. New York: Cambridge University Press.

Anonymous. 1981. " Thesen zur Autonomen Bewegung." On-line archives of German autonomous movement. Webpage: http://autox.nadir.org/archiv/auto/81_1.html. Accessed on April 5, 2004.

Archer, Margaret S. 1996. *Culture and Agency: The Place of Culture in Social Theory*. New York: Cambridge University Press.

Arkin, William M. 2003. "The Dividends of Delay." *Los Angeles Times*. February 23.

Aronowitz, Stanley. 1974. *False Promises: The Shaping of American Working Class Consciousness*. New York: McGraw-Hill.

Austin, John. 1962. How to Do Things With Words: The William James Lectures Delivered at Harvard University in 1955. Oxford: Clarendon Press.

Bakhtin, M.M. 1984 [1929]. *Problems of Dostoevsky's Poetics*. Manchester, UK: Manchester University Press.

———. 1986. *Speech Genres and Other Late essays*. Austin, TX: University of Texas Press.

Baldwin, John R., Sandra L. Faulkner, Michael L. Hecht, and Sheryl L. Lindsey. 2006. *Redefining Culture*. Mahwah, NJ: Lawrence Erlbaum Associates.

Barker, Colin. 2006. "Ideology, Discourse and Moral Economy: Consulting the People of North Manchester." *Atlantic Journal of Communication* 14(1/2): 7–27.

Barker, Colin, and Michael Lavalette. 2002. "Strategizing and the Sense of Context: Reflections on the First Two Weeks of the Liverpool Docks Dispute, September-October 1995 " Pp. 140–56 in *Social Movements: Identity, Culture and the State*, David S. Meyer, Nancy Whittier, and Belinda Robnett, eds. New York: Oxford University Press.

Barthes, Roland. 1977. "Introduction to the Structural Analysis of Narratives." Pp. 79–124 in *Image, Music, Text*. New York: Hill and Wang

Bauman, Richard. 1986. Story, *Performance and Event: Contextual Studies in Oral Narrative*. New York: Cambridge University Press.

BBC. December 3, 1972. "'It's Your Line' with Jimmy Reid and Robin Day."

Becucci, Stefano. 2003. "Disobbedienti e centri sociali fra democrazia diretta e rappresentanza." Pp. 75–94 in *La democrazia dei movimenti*, Paolo Ceri, ed. Soveria Mannelli: Rubettino.

Benford, Robert A. 1993a. "Frame Disputes within the Nuclear Disarmament Movement." *Social Forces* 71: 677–701.

———. 1993b. "'You Could be the Hundredth Monkey': Collective Action Frames and Vocabularies of Motive Within the Nuclear Disarmament Movement." *Sociological Quarterly* 34: 195–216.

———. 1997. "An Insider's Critique of the Social Movement Framing Perspective." *Sociological Inquiry* 67(4): 409–30.

———. 2002. "Controlling Narratives and Narratives as Control within Social Movements." Pp. 53–75 in *Stories of Change: Narrative and Social Movements*, Joseph E. Edwards, ed. Albany, NY: State University of New York.

Benford, Robert D., and Scott A. Hunt. 1994. "Dramaturgy and Social Movements: The Social Construction and Communication of Power." *Sociological Inquiry* 62: 36–55.

———. 2003. "Interactional Dynamics in Public Problems Marketplaces: Movements and the Counterframing and Reframing of Public Problems." Pp. 153–86 in *Challenges and Choices: Constructionist Perspectives on Social Problems*. James A. Holstein and Gale Miller, eds. Hawthorne, NY: Aldine de Gruyter.

Benford, Robert A., and David A. Snow. 2000. "Framing Processes and Social Movements: An Overview and Assessment." *Annual Review of Sociology*. 26: 611–39.

Bennett, W. Lance. 1996. *The Politics of Illusion*, 3rd ed. White Plains, NY: Longman.

Bennigsen, Alexandre, and S. Enders Wimbush. 1985a. *Muslims of the Soviet Empire: A Guide.* London: C. Hurst & Company.

———. 1985b. *Mystics and Commissars.* Berkeley, CA: University of California Press.

Berg, A. Scott. 1998. *Lindbergh.* New York: G.P. Putnam's Sons.

Berlet, Chip, and Matthew N. Lyons 2000. *Right-Wing Populism in America: Too Close for Comfort.* New York: Guilford.

Berrigan, Daniel, and Robert Coles. 1971. The *Geography of Faith.* Boston: Beacon.

Bertaux, Daniel. 1981. *Biography and Society.* Beverly Hills, CA: Sage.

Best, Joel, ed. 1995. *Images of Issues.* 2nd ed. Hawthorne, NY: Aldine de Gruyter.

———. 2003. "But Seriously Folks: The Limitations of the Strict Constructionist Interpretation of Social Problems." Pp. 51–69 in *Challenges and Choices: Constructionist Perspectives on Social Problems.* James A. Holstein and Gale Miller, eds. Hawthorne, NY: Aldine de Gruyter.

Blechschmidt, Andreas. 1998. "Vom 'Gleichgewicht des Schreckens': Autonomer Kampf gegen Unstrukturierung in Hamburger Schanzenviertel." In *Umkämpfte Räume.* Hamburg: Verlag Libertäre Assoziation und Verlag der Buchläden Schwarze Risse-Rote Strasse.

Blee, Kathleen M., and Verta Taylor. 2002. "Semi-Structured Interviewing in Social Movement Research." Pp. 92–117 in *Methods of Social Movement Research*, Bert Klandermans and Suzanne Staggenborg, eds, Minneapolis: University of Minnesota Press.

Bildungswerk für Demokratie und Umweltschutz, ed. 1990. *Genau Hingesehen. Nie Geschwiegen. Sofort Widersprochen. Gleich Gehandelt.* Dokumente aus dem Gewebe der Heuchelei 1982–1989. Berlin: Widerstand autonomer Frauen in Berlin Ost und West.

Billig, Michael. 1991. *Ideology and Opinions: Studies in Rhetorical Psychology.* London: Sage.

———. 1992. *Talking of the Royal Family.* London: Routledge.

———. 1995. "Rhetorical Psychology, Ideological Thinking, and Imagining Nationhood." Pp. 64–81 in *Social Movements and Culture*, Hank Johnston and Bert Klandermans, eds. Minneapolis, MN : University of Minnesota Press.

Billig, Michael, Susan Condon, Derek Edwards, Mike Gane, David Middleton, and Alan Radley. 1988. *Ideological Dilemmas: A Social Psychology of Everyday Thinking.* London: Sage.

Bloor, Michael, Jane Frankland, Michelle Thomas and Kate Robson. 2001. *Focus Groups in Social Research.* London: Sage.

Bohman, James. 1997. "Deliberative Democracy and Effective Social Freedom: Capabilities, Resources, and Opportunities." Pp. 321–48 in James Bohman and William Rehg, eds. *Deliberative Democracy: Essays on Reason and Politics.* Cambridge, MA: MIT Press.

Bohnsack, Ralf. 1993. *Rekonstruktive Sozialforschung. Einführung in Methodologie und Praxis qualitativer Forschung.* Opladen: Leske + Budrich.

———. 1997. "Youth Violence and the 'Episodal Community of Fate': A Case Analysis of Hooligan Groups in Berlin." *Sociologicus* 46(2).

Bosman, Jan. 1987. "Persuasive Effects of Political Metaphors." *Metaphor and Symbolic Activity* 2: 97–113.

Bourdieu, Pierre. 1990. *The Logic of Practice.* Cambridge, UK: Polity.

Breines, Wini. 1989. *Community and Organization in the New Left. 1962–1968: The Great Refusal.* New Brunswick, NJ: Rutgers University Press.

Brinkley, Alan. 2004. "The End of an Elite." *The New Republic* (June 7 and 14): 36–40.

Bromberg, Minna, and Gary Alan Fine. 2002. "Resurrecting the Red: Pete Seeger and the Purification of Difficult Reputations." *American Sociological Review* 80: 1135–55.

Bromley, David G., and Anson D. Shupe Jr. 1979. *"Moonies" in America: Cult, Church, and Crusade.* Beverly Hills, CA: Sage.

Buchanan, Patrick. 1999. *A Republic, Not an Empire: Reclaiming America's Destiny.* Washington, DC: Regnery.

Buechler, Steven M. 1990. *Women's Movements in the United States.* New Brunswick, NJ: Rutgers University Press.

Bundesministerium des Innern. 2006. "Verfassungsschutzbericht." Berlin.

Bumiller, Kristin. 1988. *The Civil Rights Society: The Social Construction of Victims.* Baltimore, MD: Johns Hopkins University Press.

Burstein, Paul. 1999. "Social Movements and Public Policy." Pp. 3–21 in *How Movements Matter: Theoretical and Comparative Studies on the Consequences of Social Movements,* Marco Giugni, Doug McAdam, and Charles Tilly, eds. Minneapolis, MN: University of Minnesota Press.

Carlson, John Roy. 1943. *Under Cover.* New York: E.P. Dutton.

Carroll, William K., and R.S. Ratner. 1996. "Master Framing and Cross Movement Net-working in Contemporary Social Movements." *Sociological Quarterly* 37: 601–25

Carson, Clayborne. 1995. *In Struggle. SNCC and the Black Awakening of the 1960s,* 2nd ed. Cambridge, MA: Harvard University Press,

Cerullo, Karen. 2002.*Culture in Mind.* New York: Routledge.

Chamberlayne, Prue, Joanna Bornat and Tom Wengraf, eds. 2000. *The Turn to Biographical Methods in Social Science.* London: Routledge.

Chatwin, Mark Lincoln. 1968. *The Hawks of World War II.* Chapel Hill, NC: University of North Carolina Press.

Chiantera-Stutte, Patricia. 2003. *Anarchici globali e Black Bloc: due diverse espressioni dell'anarchismo o due movimenti?* Pp. 133–68 in *La democrazia dei movimenti,* Paolo Ceri, ed. Soveria Mannelli: Rubettino.

Chicago Tribune. 1941. "America First Fights threat to Muzzle It." (September 3): 1.

———. 1941. "America First Welcomes Dies Committee Quiz." (November 14): n.p.

———. 1941. "New Move to Gag Lindbergh: Brooklyn Ball Park Denied to America First." (June 14): 1, 6.

Cialdini, Robert, Richard Petty, and John Cacioppo. 1981. "Attitude and Attitude Change." *Annual Review of Sociology* 32: 357–404.

Clark, John. 2003. "Introduction: Civil Society and Transnational Action." Pp. 1–28 in *Globalizing Civic Engagement,* John Clark, ed. London, Earthscan.

Clark, John, and Nuno Themundo. 2003. "The Age of Protest: Internet-Based 'Dot Causes' and the 'Anti-Globalization' Movement." Pp. 109–27 in *Globalizing Civic Engagement,* John Clark, ed.. London: Earthscan.

Clemens, Elisabeth S., and Debra C. Minkoff. 2003. "Beyond Iron Law: Rethinking the Place of Organizations in Social Movement Research." Pp. 201–30 in *Methods of Social Movement Research,* Bert Klandermans and Suzanne Staggenborg, eds. Minneapolis: University of Minnesota Press.

Cloward, Richard A., and Lloyd E. Ohlin. 1960. *Delinquency and Opportunity.* New York: Free Press.

Cohen, Cathy. 2000. "Contesting Membership: Black Gay Identities and the Politics of AIDS." Pp. 382–406 in *Creating Change: Sexuality, Public Policy, and Civil Rights*, John D'Emilio, William B. Turner, and Urvashi Vaid, eds. New York: St Martin's.

Cohen, Jean L. 1985. "Strategy and Identity: New Theoretical Paradigms in Contem-porary Social Movements." *Social Research* 52: 663–716.

Cohen, Joshua. 1989. "Deliberation and Democratic Legitimacy." Pp.17–34 in *The Good Polity*, Alan Hamlin and Philip Pettit, eds, Oxford: Blackwell.

Cole, Wayne S. 1953. *America First: The Battle Against Intervention*. Madison, WI: University of Wisconsin Press.

———. 1962. *Gerald P. Nye and American Foreign Relations*. Minneapolis, MN: University of Minnesota Press.

———. 1974. *Charles A. Lindbergh and the Battle Against American Intervention in World War II*. New York: Harcourt Brace Jovanovich.

Collins, Chik.1996. "To Concede or to Contest? Language and Class Struggle." In *To Make Another World: Studies in Protest and Collective Action*, Colin Barker and Paul Kennedy, eds. Burlington, VT: Ashgate Publishers.

———. 1999. *Language, Ideology and Social Consciousness: Developing a Socio-historical Approach*. Aldershot, UK: Ashgate Publishers.

Conley, John M. and William M. O'Barr. 1990. *Rules versus Relationships: The Ethnography of Legal Discourse*. Chicago, IL: University of Chicago Press.

Cooper, Alice H. 1996. "Public-Good Movements and the Dimensions of Political Process: Postwar German Peace Movements." *Comparative Political Studies* 29: 267–89.

Cortright, David. 1993. *Peace Works: The Citizen's Role in Ending the Cold War*. Boulder, CO: Westview.

Couto, Richard A. 1993. "Narrative, Free Space, and Political Leadership in Social Movements." *The Journal of Politics* 55: 57–79.

D'Andrade, Roy. 1995. *The Development of Cognitive Anthropology*. New York: Cambridge.

Dalton, Russell. 1994. *The Green Rainbow. Environmental Groups in Western Europe*. New Haven, CT: Yale University Press.

Davis, Joseph E. 2002. *Stories of Change: Narrative and Social Movements*. Albany, NY: SUNY Press.

———. 2005. *Accounts of Innocence: Sexual Abuse, Trauma, and the Self*. Chicago, IL: University of Chicago Press.

Del Giorgio, Elena. 2002. *I social forum*. University of Bologna: Tesi di laurea (BA thesis).

de Saussure, Ferdinand. 1972 [1909]. *Course in General Linguistics*. Bally, Charles, and Sechehaye, Albert, eds. Paris: Duckworth.

della Porta, Donatella. 1992. "Life Histories in the Analysis of Social Movement Activists." Pp. 168–93 in Mario Diani and Ron Eyermann eds. *Studying Social Movements*. Newbury Park, CA: Sage.

————. 1999. "Protest, Protesters, and Protest Policing: Public Discourse in Italy and Germany from the 1960s to the 1980s." Pp. 66–96 in *How Movements Matter: Theoretical and Comparative Studies on the Consequences of Social Movements*, Marco Giugni, Doug McAdam, and Charles Tilly, eds. Minneapolis, MN: University of Minnesota Press.

————. 2003. "Social Movements and Democracy at the Turn of the Millennium." Pp. 105–36 in *Social Movements and Democracy*, Pedro Ibarra, ed. New York: Palgrave.

————. 2004. "Multiple Belongings, Flexible Identities and the Construction of 'Another Politics': Between the European Social Forum and the Local Social Fora." Pp. 175–202 in *Transnational Movements and Global Activism*, Donatella della Porta and Sidney Tarrow, eds. Rowman and Littlefield.

della Porta, Donatella, and Mario Diani. 1999. *Social Movements: An Introduction*. Oxford: Blackwell.

della Porta, Donatella, and Mario Diani. 2005. *Social Movement*, 2nd ed. Malden, MA: Blackwell.

della Porta, Donatella, and Lorenzo Mosca, eds. 2003. *Globalizzazione e movimenti sociali*. Roma: Manifestolibri.

della Porta, Donatella, and Dieter Rucht. 1995. "Left-Libertarian Movements in Context: A Comparison of Italy and West Germany, 1965–1990." In *The Politics of Social Protest*, Bert Klandermans and J. Craig Jenkins, eds. Minneapolis, MN: University of Minnesota Press.

della Porta, Donatella, Massimiliano Andretta, Lorenzo Mosca, and Herbert Reiter. 2004. *Global Movement and Transnational Protest*. Minneapolis: University of Minnesota Press.

D'Emilio, John. 1992. *Making Trouble: Essays on Gay History, Politics, and the University*. New York, NY: Routledge.

Denisoff, R. Serge, and Richard Peterson. 1973. *The Sounds of Social Change*. New York: Rand McNally

Denzin, Norman K., Yvonna S. Lincoln. 1994. *Handbook of Qualitative Research.* Thousand Oaks, CA: Sage.

Derluguian, Georgi M. 2005. *Bourdieu's Secret Admirer in the Caucasus.* Chicago, IL: University of Chicago Press.

Derrida, Jacques. 1978. "Structure, Sign, and Play in the Discourse of the Human Sciences." Pp. 287–93 in *Writing and Difference*, translated by Alan Bass. Chicago, IL: University of Chicago Press.

Diani, Mario. 1992. "The Concept of Social Movement," *Sociological Review* 40: 1–25

————. 1995. *Green Networks. A Structural Analysis of the Italian Environmental Movement*. Edinburgh: Edinburgh University Press.

————. 1996. "Social Movements and Social Capital: A Network Perspective on Movement Outcomes." *Mobilization* 1: 129–47.

DiMaggio, Paul J. 1997. "Culture and Cognition." *Annual Review of Sociology* 23: 263–287.

————. 2002. "Why Cognitive (and Cultural) Sociology Needs Cognitive Psychology." Pp. 274–281 in *Culture in Mind*, Karen Cerullo, ed. New York: Routledge.

Doenecke, Justus D. 1977. "Non-Interventionism of the Left: The Keep America Out of War Congress, 1938–1941." *Journal of Contemporary History* 12: 221–36.

————. 1979. "Beyond Polemics; An Historiographical Re-Appraisal of American Entry into World War II." *The History Teacher* 12: 237–51.

————. 1990. *In Danger Undaunted: The Anti-Interventionist Movement of 1940–1941 as Revealed in the Papers of the America First Committee.* Stanford, CA: Hoover Institution Press.

Doenecke, Justus D., and John E. Wilz. 1991. *From Isolation to War 1931–1941.* Second ed. Arlington Heights, IL: Harlan Davidson.

Donati, Paolo R. 1992. "Political Discourse Analysis." Pp. 136–67 in *Studying Collective Action*, Mario Diani and Ron Eyerman, eds. London: Sage.

Dryzek, John S. 2000. *Deliberative Democracy and Beyond.* New York: Oxford University Press.

————. 2004. "Handle with Care: The Deadly Hermeneutics of Deliberative Democracy." A paper presented at the conference on empirical approaches to deliberative politics, European University Institute, Florence, 22–23 May.

Dubet, Françios, and Michel Wieviorka. 1996. "Touraine and the Method of Sociological Intervention." Pp. 55–75 in *Social Movements in a Comparative Perspective: Situating Alain Touraine*, John Clark and Mario Diani, eds. London: Falmer Press.

Dudziak, Mary L. 2000. *Cold War Civil Rights: Race and the Image of American Democracy.* Princeton, NJ: Princeton University Press.

Duncombe, Stephen. 1997. *Notes from the Underground: Zines and the Political of Alternative Culture.* New York: Verso.

Dunlop, John B. 1998. *Russia Confronts Chechnya.* Cambridge, UK: Cambridge University Press.

Dunn, Jennifer L. 2005. "'Victims' and 'Survivors': Emerging Vocabularies of Motive for 'Battered Women Who Stay.'" *Sociological Inquiry* 75: 1–30.

Durkheim, Emile. 1933. *The Division of Labor in Society.* New York: Free Press.

————. 1965 [1915]. *The Elementary Forms of the Religious Life.* Translated by Joseph Ward Swain. New York: Free Press.

Dutton, Jane, and Janet Dukerich. 1991. "Keeping an Eye on the Mirror: Image and Iden-tity in Organizational Adaptation." *Academy of Management Journal* 34: 517–54.

Dwyer, Lynn E. 1983. "Structure and Strategy in the Antinuclear Movement." Pp. 148–61 in *Social Movements of the Sixties and Seventies*, Jo Freeman, ed. New York: Longman.

Easterbrook, Gregg. 1995. *A Moment on the Earth: The Coming Age of Environmental Optimism.* New York: Viking.

Echols, Alice. 1989. *Daring to Be Bad: Radical Feminism in America, 1967–1975.* Minneapolis, MN: University of Minnesota Press.

Edelman, Murray J. 1988. *Constructing the Political Spectacle.* Chicago, IL: University of Chicago Press.

Edwards, Bob, and Sam Marullo. 1995. "Organizational Mortality in a Declining Social Movement: The Demise of Peace Movement Organizations in the End of the Cold War Era." *American Sociological Review* 60: 908–27.

Elsbach, Kimberly, and Robert I. Sutton. 1992. "Acquiring Organizational Legitimacy Through Illegitimate Actions: A Marriage of Institutional and Impression Management Theory." *Academy of Management Journal* 35: 699–738.

Elster, Jon. 1998. "Deliberation and Constitution Making." Pp. 97–122 in *Deliberative Democracy*, Jon Elster, ed. Cambridge: Cambridge University Press.

Engeström, Yrjö. 1987. *Learning by Expanding: An Activity-Theoretical Approach to Developmental Research.* Helsinki Orienta-Konsulit (available online at http://communication.ucsd.edu/MCA/Paper/Engestrom/expanding/toc.htm).

Epstein, Barbara Leslie. 1991. *Political Protest and Cultural Revolution: Nonviolent Direct Action in the 1970s and 1980s.* Berkeley, CA: University of California Press.

Epstein, Barbara. 2000. "Not Your Parents' Protest." *Dissent*, Spring: 8–11.

Epstein, Steven. 1996. *Impure Science: AIDS, Activism, and the Politics of Knowledge.* Berkeley, CA: University of California Press.

Evangelista, Matthew. 1999. *Unarmed Forces: The Transnational Movement to End the Cold War.* Ithaca, NY: Cornell University Press.

Evans, Sara M. and Harry C. Boyte. 1992. *Free Spaces: the Sources of Democratic Change in America*, 2nd ed. Chicago, IL: University of Chicago Press.

Ewick, Patricia, and Susan Silbey. 2003. "Narrating Social Structure: Stories of Resistance to Legal Authority." *American Journal of Sociology* 108: 1328–72.

Eyerman, Ron, and Andrew Jamison. 1991. *Social Movements: A Cognitive Approach.* University Park, PN: Pennsylvania State University Press.

———. 1998. *Music and Social Movements.* New York: Cambridge University Press.

Fantasia. Rick. 1988. *Cultures of Solidarity.* Berkeley, CA: University of California Press.

Fantasia, Rick and Eric Hirsch. 1995. "Culture in Rebellion: The Appropriation and Transformation of the Veil in the Algerian Revolution." Pp. 144–59 in *Repression and Mobilization*, Christian Davenport, Hank Johnston, and Carol Mueller, eds. Minneapolis, MN: University of Minnesota Press.

Fauconnier, Gilles, and Eve Sweeter, eds. 1996. *Spaces, Worlds, and Grammar.* Chicago, IL: University of Chicago Press.

Fernandez, James W., ed. 1991. *Beyond Metaphor: The Theory of Tropes in Anthropology*. Stanford, CA: Stanford University Press.

Ferree, Myra Marx. 2003. "Resonance and Radicalism: Feminist Framing in the Abortion Debates of the United States and Germany." *American Journal of Sociology* 109: 304–44.

Ferree, Myra Marx, William Anthony Gamson, Jürgen Gerhards, Dieter Rucht. 2002. *Shaping Abortion Discourse: Democracy and the Public Sphere in Germany and the United States*. New York: Cambridge University Press.

Ferree, Myra Marx, and David A. Merrill. 2004. "Hot Movements, Cold Cognition: Thinking About Social Movements in Gendered Frames." Pp. 247–62 in *Rethinking Social Movements*, Jeff Goodwin and James A. Jasper, eds. Lanham, MD: Rowman and Littlefield.

Ferree, Myra Marx and Silke Roth. 1998. "Gender, Class, and the Interaction between Social Movements. A Strike of West Berlin Day Care Workers." *Gender and Society* 12(6): 626–48.

Fine, Gary Alan. 1979. "Small Groups and Culture Creation: The Idioculture of Little League Baseball Teams." *American Sociological Review* 44: 733–45.

———. 1982. "The Manson Family as a Folk Group: Small Groups and Folklore." *Journal of the Folklore Institute* 19: 47–60.

———. 1985. "Can the Circle be Unbroken?: Small Groups and Social Movements." In *Advances in Group Processes*. Vol. 2. Edward Lawler, ed. Greenwich, CN: JAI Press.

———. 1995. "Public Narration and Group Culture: Discerning Discourse in Social Movements." Pp. 127–43 in *Social Movements and Culture*, Hank Johnston and Bert Klandermans, eds. Minneapolis, MN : University of Minnesota Press.

———. 1996. "Reputational Entrepreneurs and the Memory of Incompetence: Melting Supporters, Partisan Warriors, and Images of President Harding." *American Journal of Sociology* 101: 1159–93.

———. 1999. "John Brown's Body: Elites, Heroic Embodiment, and the Legitimation of Political Violence." *Social Problems* 46: 225–49.

———. 2001. *Difficult Reputations: Collective Memories of the Evil, Inept and Controversial*. Chicago, IL: University of Chicago Press.

Fine, Gary Alan, and Terry McDonnell. 2007. "Erasing the Brown Scare: Referential Afterlife and the Power of Memory Templates." *Social Problems* 54(2): 170–87.

Fine, Gary Alan, and Rashida Z. Shaw. 2006. "An Isolationist Blacklist?: Lillian Gish and the America First Committee." *Theatre Survey* 47: 283–88.

Fine, Gary Alan, and Patricia Turner. 2001. *Whispers on the Color Line: Rumor and Race in America*. Berkeley, CA: University of California Press.

Finelli, Pietro. 2003. *"Un'idea partecipativa della politica". Strutture organizzzative e modelli di democrazia in Attac Italia*, Pp. 31–56 in *La democrazia dei movimenti*, Paolo Ceri, ed. Soveria Mannelli: Rubettino.

Fineman, Martha Albertson. 1995. "Masking Dependency: The Political Role of Family Rhetoric." *University of Virginia Law Review* 81: 2181–216.

Fischer-Rosenthal, Wolfram, and Gabriele Rosenthal. 1997. Daniel Bertaux's Complaints or Against False Dichotomies in Biographical Research." *Biography and Society* (Research Committee 38 of the ISA), December 1997: 5–11.

Flam, Helena. 1998. *Mosaic of Fear. Poland and East Germany Before 1989.* Boulder, CO: Eastern European Monographs.

Fleck, Ludwig. 1979 [1935]. *Genesis and Development of a Scientific Fact.* Chicago, IL: University of Chicago Press.

Foster, John and Charles Woolfson. 1986. *The Politics of the UCS Work-In: Class Alliances and the Right to Work.* London: Lawrence and Wishart

Frake, Charles O. "How to Ask for a Drink In Subanun." *American Anthropologist* 66(2): 127–32.

Franzosi, Roberto, 1999. "The Return of the Actor: Interaction Networks Among Actors During Periods of High Mobilization (Italy, 1919–1922)." *Mobilization* 4: 131–50.

———. 2004. *From Words to Numbers: Narrative, Data, and Social Science.* New York: Cambridge University Press.

Freeman, Jo. 1974. "The Tyranny of the Structureless." In *Women in Politics*, Jane Jaquette, ed. New York: Wiley.

Freeman, Jo. 1983. "Introduction." Pp. 1–7 in *Social Movements of the Sixties and Seventies*, Jo Freeman, ed. New York: Longman.

Fried, Albert. 1999. *FDR and His Enemies.* New York: St Martin's.

Friends of Democracy. 1941. *The America First Committee: The Nazi Transmission Belt.* Kansas City, MO: Friends of Democracy.

Fruci, Gian Luca. 2003, *La nuova agorà. I social forum tra spazio pubblico e dinamiche organizzative.* Pp. 169–200 in *La democrazia dei movimenti*, Paolo Ceri, ed. Soveria Mannelli: Rubettino.

Fuller, Sylvia. 2003. "Creating and Contesting Boundaries: Exploring the Dynamics of Conflict and Classification." *Sociological Forum* 18: 3–30.

Fung, Archon. 2003. "Associations and Democracy: Between Theories, Hopes, and Realities." *Annual Review of Sociology* 29: 515–39.

Futrell, Robert and Pete Simi. 2004. "Free Spaces, Collective Identity, and the Persistence of US White Power Activism." *Social Problems* 51: 16–42.

Gall, Carlota, and Thomas. de Waal. 1998. *Chechnya: Calamity in the Caucasus.* New York: New York University Press.

Gamson, Joshua. 1995. "Must Identity Movements Self-Destruct? A Queer Dilemma." *Social Problems* 42(3): 390–407.

———. 1997. "Messages of Exclusion: Gender, Movements, and Symbolic Boundaries." *Gender and Society* 11: 178–99.

Gamson, William A. 1988. "Political Discourse and Collective Action." Pp. 219–44 in *International Social Movement Research*, Vol. 1, B. Klandermans, H. Kriesi and S. Tarrow, eds. Greenwich, CT: JAI. Press.

————. 1990 [1975]. *The Strategy of Social Protest*, 2nd ed. Belmont, CA: Wadsworth.

————. 1992. "The Social Psychology of Collective Action." Pp. 53–76 in *Frontiers of Social Movement Theory.* Aldon D. Morris and Carol McClurg Mueller, eds. New Haven: Yale University Press.

————. 1992. *Talking Politics.* Cambridge, MA: Harvard University Press.

————. 1995. "Constructing Social Protest." Pp. 85–106 in *Social Movements and Culture*, Hank Johnston and Bert Klandermans, eds. Minneapolis, MN: University of Minnesota Press.

————. 1996. "Safe Spaces and Social Movements." *Perspectives on Social Problems* 8: 27–38.

————. 2001. "How Storytelling Can Be Empowering." Pp. 187–99 in *Culture in Mind: Toward a Sociology of Culture and Cognition*, Karen Cerulo, ed. New York, NY: Routledge.

Gamson, William, Bruce Fireman, and Steven Rytina. 1982. *Encounters with Unjust Authority.* Homewood, IL: Dorsey

Gamson, William A., and David S. Meyer. 1996. "Framing Political Opportunity." Pp. 275–90 in *Comparative Perspectives on Social Movements: Political Opportunities, Mobilizing Structures, and Cultural Framings*, Doug McAdam, John D. McCarthy, and Mayer N. Zald, eds. New York: Cambridge University Press.

Ganz, Marshall. 2000. "Resources and Resourcefulness: Strategic Capacity in the Unionization of California Agriculture, 1959–1966." *American Journal of Sociology* 105: 1003–62.

————. 2004. "Why David Sometimes Wins: Strategic Capacity in Social Movements." Pp. 177–98 in *Rethinking Social Movements: Structure, Meaning and Emotion*, Jeff Goodwin and James M Jasper, eds. Lanham, Maryland: Rowman and Littlefield.

Geertz, Clifford. 1973. "Thick Description: Toward an Interpretive Theory of Culture." In *The Interpretation of Cultures.* New York: Basic Books.

Gentner, Dedre, and Donald R. Gentner. 1983. "Flowing Waters or Teaming Crowds: Mental Models of Electricity." Pp. 99–129 in *Mental Models*, Dedre Gentner and Albert L. Stevens, eds. Hillsdale, NJ: Lawrence Erlbaum Associates.

Gerhards, Juergen, and Dieter Rucht. 1992. "Mesomobilization: Organizing and Framing in Two Protest Campaigns in West Germany." *American Journal of Sociology* 98: 555–95.

Gerlach, Luther. 1976. "La struttura dei nuovi movimenti di rivolta." Pp. 218–32 in *Movimenti di Rivolta.* Alberto Melucci, ed. Milan: Etas.

Gerlach, Luther, and Virginia Hine. 1970. *People, Power, and Change.* Indianapolis, IN: Bobbs-Merrill.

German, Tracey. C. 2003. *Russia's Chechen War.* New York: Routledge Curzon.

Geronimo. 1997. *Glut und Asche: Reflexionen zur Politik der autonomen Bewegung.* Munster: Unrast Verlag.

———. 2002. *Feuer und Flamme: zur Geschichte der Autonomen,* 2nd ed. Berlin: ID Verlag.

Gibbs, Raymond W., Jr. 1994. *The Poetics of Mind: Figurative Thought, Language, and Understanding.* Cambridge, UK: Cambridge University Press.

Giddens, Anthony. 1987. "Structuralism, Post-structuralism, and the Production of Culture." Pp. 195–223 in *Social Theory Today,* Anthony Giddens and Jonathan H. Turner, eds. Stanford, CA: Stanford University Press.

Gitlin, Todd. 1980. *The Whole World is Watching: Mass Media in the Making and Unmaking of the New Left.* Berkeley, CA: University of California Press.

Giugni, Marco. 1998. "'Was It Worth the Effort?' The Outcomes and Consequences of Social Movements." *Annual Review of Sociology* 98: 171–93.

Glaser, Barney, and Anselm Strauss. 1967. *The Discovery of Grounded Theory.* Chicago, IL: University of Chicago Press.

Godwin, R. Keith, and Helen M. Ingram. 1980. "Single Issues: Their Impact on Politics." Pp. 279–99 in *Why Policies Succeed or Fail,* Helen M. Ingram and Dean E. Mann, eds. Beverly Hills, CA: Sage.

Goffman, Erving. 1956. *The Presentation of Self in Everyday Life.* New York: Doubleday

———. 1963. *Stigma: Notes on the Management of Spoiled Identity.* Englewood Cliffs, NJ: Prentice-Hall.

———. 1974. *Frame Analysis.* Cambridge: Harvard University Press.

Goldberg, Adele E. 1998. "Patterns of Experience in Patterns of Language." Pp. 203–20 in *The New Psychology of Language: Cognitive and Functional Approaches to Language Structure,* Michael Tomasello, ed. Mahwah, NJ: Lawrence Erlbaum.

Goldfarb, Jeffery. 1980 *The Persistence of Freedom.* Boulder, CO: Westview Press.

Goldfield, Michael. 1987. *The Decline of Organized Labor in the United States.* Chicago, IL: University of Chicago Press.

Goodenough, Ward H. 1964. "Cultural Anthropology and Linguistics." Pp. 36–9 in *Language in Culture and Society,* Dell Hymes, ed. New York: Harper and Row.

Goodwin, Jeff, and James M. Jasper. 2004. *Rethinking Social Movement.* Lanham, MD: Rowman and Littlefield

Gornick, Janet C., and David S. Meyer. 1998. "Changing Political Opportunity: The Anti-Rape Movement and Public Policy." *Journal of Policy History* 10: 367–98.

Graham, Katharine. 1941. "Propaganda Groups Seek to Mold Public Opinion on US Foreign Policy." *Washington Post* (January 5): B1–B2.

Gramsci, Antonio. 1971. *Selections from the Prison Notebooks*. London: Lawrence and Wishart.

Granovetter, Mark. 1983. "The Strength of Weak Ties: A Network Theory Revisited." *Sociological Theory* 1: 201–33.

Green, Melanie E. and Timothy C. Brock. 2000. "The Role of Transportation in the Persuasiveness of Public Narratives." *Journal of Personality and Social Psychology* 79: 701–21.

Greenhouse, Steven. 1999. "Vowing to Go From Scandal to Strength, City Union Looks for a Fight." *New York Times*, 12 July.

Grenier, Paola. 2003. "Jubelee 2000: Laying the Foundations for a Social Movement." Pp. 86–108 in *Globalizing Civic Engagement*, John Clark, ed. London: Earthscan.

Groch, Sharon. 2001. "Free Spaces: Creating Oppositional Consciousness in the Disability Rights Movement." In *Oppositional Consciousness: the Subjective Roots of Social Protest*, Jane Mansbridge and Aldon Morris, eds. Chicago, IL: University of Chicago Press.

Griffin, Larry J. 1993. "Narrative, Event-Structure Analysis, and Causal Interpretation in Historical Sociology." *American Journal of Sociology* 98: 1094–33.

Gubrium, Jaber F., and James M. Holstein. 1998. *The New Language of Qualitative Methods*. New York: Oxford University Press.

Habermas, Jürgen. 1981. *Theorie des kommunikativen Hendeln*. Frankfurt am Main: Suhrkamp.

Habermas, Jürgen. 1984. *Theory of Communicative Action. Vol. 1. Reason and the Rationalization of Society*. Boston: Beacon.

———. 1987. *The Theory of Communicative Action*, Vol. 2, *Lifeworld and System: A Critique of Functionalist Reason*. Translated by T. McCarthy. Boston: Beacon.

———. 1996. *Between Facts and Norms: Contribution to a Discursive Theory of Law and Democracy*. Cambridge, MA: MIT Press.

Haenfler, Ross. 2006. *Straight Edge: Clean-Living Youth, Hardcore Punk, and Social Change*. New Brunswick, NJ: Rutgers University Press.

Haines, Herbert H. 1988. *Black Radicals and the Civil Rights Mainstream, 1954–1970*. Knoxville, TN: University of Tennessee Press.

Halker, Clark D. 1991. *For Democracy, Workers, and God: Labor Song-Poems and Labor Protest 1865–95*. Urbana, IL: University of Illinois Press.

Harcave, Sidney. 1965. *First Blood: The Russian Revolution of 1905*. London: The Bodley Head.

Harris, Zelig S. 1952. "Discourse Analysis." *Language* 28: 1–30.

Haunss, Sebastian. 2004. *Identität in Bewegung. Prozesse kollektiver Identität bei den Autonomen und in der Schwulenbewegung*. Wiesbaden: VS Verlag für Sozialwissenschaften.

———. 2006. "Commitment Frames: Movement Strategies to Secure Persistence Over Time." Unpublished manuscript.

Hay, Roy. 1972. "Interview with Jimmy Reid." *Glasgow News.*

Haynes, John E. 1996. *Red Scare or Red Menace?: American Communism and Anticommunism in the Cold War Era.* Chicago, IL: Ivan R. Dee.

Hebdige, Dick. 1979. *Subculture: The Meaning of Style.* London and New York: Routledge.

Henze, Paul. 1995. "Islam in the North Caucasus: The Example of Chechenya." P-7935. Santa Monica: Rand Corporation.

Hewitt, John P., and Randall Stokes. 1975. "Disclaimers." *American Sociological Review* 40: 1–11.

Hewitt, Lyndi, and Holly J. McCammon. 2005. "Explaining Suffrage Mobilization: Balance, Neutralization and Range in Colletive Action Frames" Pp. 33–52 in *Frames of Protest: Social Movements and the Framing Perspective*, Hank Johnston and John A. Noakes, eds. Lanham, MD: Rowman and Littlefield.

Hilgartner, Stephen and Charles L. Bosk. 1988. "The Rise and Fall of Social Problems: A Public Arenas Model." *American Journal of Sociology* 94: 53–78.

Hill-Collins, Patricia. 2000. *Black Feminist Thought: Knowledge, Consciousness, and the Politics of Empowerment*, 2nd ed. New York: Routledge.

Hirsch, Eric. 1990. *Urban Revolt.* Berkeley, CA: University of California Press.

Hitzler, Ronald, Thomas Bucher, and Arne Niederbacher. 2001. *Leben in Szenen. Formen jugendlicher Vergemeinschaftung heute.* Opladen: Leske + Budrich.

Hobsbawm, Eric. 1963. *Primitive Rebels.* New York: Praeger.

Holland, Dorothy, and Naomi Quinn. 1987. *Cultural Models in Language and Thought.* Cambridge, UK: Cambridge University Press.

Holstein, James A., and Jaber F. Gubrium. 2002. "Active Interviewing." Pp. 112-126 in, *Qualitative Research Methods*, D. Wenberg, ed. Oxford: Blackwell.

Holstein, James A., and Gale Miller, eds. 2003. *Challenges and Choices: Constructionist Perspectives on Social Problems.* Hawthorne, New York: Aldine de Gruyter.

Holstein, James A., and Gale Miller. 2003. "Social Constructionism and Social Problems Work." Pp. 70–91 in *Challenges and Choices: Constructionist Perspectives on Social Problems.* James A Holstein and Gale Miller, eds. Hawthorne, NY: Aldine de Gruyter.

HSK 13. 1999. *hoch die kampf dem. 20 Jahre Plakate autonomer Bewegungen.* Berlin: Assoziation A.

Hug, Simon. 1999. "Nonunitary Actors in Spatial Models: How Far is Far in Foreign Policy?" *Journal of Conflict Resolution* 43(4): 479–500.

Hunt, Scott A., Robert D. Benford, and David A. Snow. 1994. "Identity Fields: Framing Processes and the Social Construction of Movement Identities." Pp. 185–208 in *New Social Movements: From Ideology to Identity*, Enrique

Laraña, Hank Johnston, and Joseph R. Gusfield, eds. Philadelphia, PA: Temple University Press.

Hymes, Dell. 1964. *Language in Culture and Society.* New York: Harper and Row.

Ignatow, Gabriel. 2007. *Transnational Identity Politics and the Environment.* Lanham, MD: Lexington Books.

Inglehart, Ronald. 1990. *Culture Shift in Advanced Industrial Society*. Princeton, NJ: Princeton University Press.

———. 1997. *Modernization and Postmodernization: Cultural Economic, and Political Change in 43 Societies*. Princeton, NJ: Princeton University Press.

Iser, Wolfgang. 1972. "The Reading Process: A Phenomenological Approach." *New Literary History* 3: 279–99.

Jankofsky, Michael. 2005. "Demonstrators Revel in Opposition on Big Day for President." *New York Times*, January 21.

Jasper, James M. 1990. *Nuclear Politics: Energy and the State in the United States, Sweden, and France.* Princeton, NJ: Princeton University Press.

———. *The Art of Moral Protest. Culture, Biography and Creativity in Social Movements.* Chicago. The University of Chicago Press.

———. 2004. "A Strategic Approach to Collective Action: Looking for Agency in Social-Movement Choices." *Mobilization* 9: 1–16.

———. 2006. *Getting Your Way: Strategic Dilemmas in the Real World*. Chicago, IL: Chicago University Press.

Jenkins, Philip. 1997. *Hoods and Shirts: The Extreme Right in Pennsylvania, 1925–1950.* Chapel Hill, NC: University of North Carolina Press.

Johnson, Joel T., and Shelley E. Taylor. 1981. "The Effect of Metaphor on Political Attitudes." *Basic and Applied Social Psychology* 24: 305–16.

Johnson, Walter. 1944. *The Battle Against Isolation*. Chicago, IL: University of Chicago Press.

Johnston, Hank 1991. *Tales of Nationalism: Catalonia, 1939–1979*. New Brunswick, NJ: Rutgers University Press.

———. 1993. "Religion and Nationalist Subcultures under the Communists." *Sociology of Religion* 54(3): 337–55.

———. 1995. "A Methodology for Frame Analysis: From Discourse to Cognitive Schemata." Pp. 217–46 in *Social Movements and Culture*, Hank Johnston and Bert Klandermans, eds. Minneapolis, MN: University of Minnesota Press.

———. "Verification and Proof in Frame and Discourse Analaysis." Pp. 62–91 in *Methods of Social Movement Research*, Bert Klandermans and Suzanne Staggenborg, eds, Minneapolis, MN: the University of Minnesota Press.

———. 2005. "Comparative Frame Analysis". Pp. 237–260 in *Frames of Protest. Social Movements and the Framing Perspective*, Hank Johnston and John A. Noakes, eds. Lanham, MD: Rowman and Littlefield Publishers.

————. 2005. "Talking the Walk: Speech Acts and Resistance in Authoritarian Regimes." Pp. 108–37 in *Repression and Mobilization*, Christian Davenport, Hank Johnston, and Carol Mueller, eds. Minneapolis, MN: University of Minnesota Press.

————. 2006. "Let's Get Small: The Dynamics of (Small) Contention in Repressive States." *Mobilization* 11(2): 195–212.

Johnston, Hank, and Bert Klandermans. 1995 *Social Movements and Culture*. Minneapolis, MN: University of Minnesota Press.

Johnston, Hank, Enrique Laraña, and Joseph R. Gusfield. 1994. "Identities, Grievances, and New Social Movements." Pp. 3–35 in *New Social Movements: From Ideology to Identity*. Philadelphia, PA: Temple University Press.

Johnston, Hank, and Carol Mueller. 2001 "Unobtrusive Contention in Leninist Regimes." *Sociological Perspectives* 44: 351–75.

Johnston, Hank, and John A. Noakes. 2005. *Frames of Protest: A Roadmap to a Perspective*. Lanham, MD. Rowman and Littlefield.

Johnston, Hank, and Pamela E. Oliver. 2000. "Breaking the Frame." *Mobilization* 5: 61–4.

Johnston, Hank, and Pamela Oliver. 2005. "Breaking the Frame." Pp. 213–16 in *Frames of Protest*, Hank Johnston and John A. Noakes, eds. Lanham, MD: Rowman & Littlefield.

Johnston, Hank, and David A. Snow. 1998. "Subcultures of Opposition and Social Movements." *Sociological Perspectives* 41: 473–97.

Joppke, Christian. 1993. *Mobilizing against Nuclear Energy: A Comparison of Germany and the United States*. Berkeley, CA: University of California Press.

Kamenitsa, Lynn. 1998. "The Complexity of Decline: Explaining the Marginalization of the East German Women's Movement." *Mobilization* 3: 245–63.

Kaminer, Wendy. 1993. *I'm Dysfunctional, You're Dysfunctional: The Recovery Movement and Other Self-Help Fashions*. New York, NY: Vintage.

Kann, Mark E. 1986. *Middle Class Radicalism in Santa Monica*. Philadelphia, PA: Temple University Press.

Katsiaficas, George N. 1997. *The Subversion of Politics: European Autonomous Social Movements and the Decolonization of Everyday Life, Revolutionary studies*. Atlantic Heights, NJ: Humanities Press.

Katznelson, Ira. 1981. *City Trenches: Urban Politics and the Patterning of Class in the United States*. Chicago, IL: University of Chicago Press.

Kauffman, Bill. 1995. *America First!: Its History, Culture, and Politics*. Amherst, NY: Prometheus.

Kempton, Willett. 1987. "Two Theories of Home Heat Control." In *Cultural Models in Language and Thought*, Dorothy Holland and Naomi Quinn, eds. New York: Cambridge University Press.

Kenawi, Samirah, ed. 1995. *Frauengruppen in der DDR. Eine Dokumentation*. Berlin: Redaktion Weibblick.

Kenney, Padraic. 2005. "Framing, Political Opportunities, and Eastern Eruopean Mobilization." Pp. 143–62 in *Frames of Protest*, Hank Johnston and John A. Noakes, eds. Lanham, MD: Rowman and Littlefield.

King, Adam, and Gary Alan Fine. 2000. "Ford on the Line: Business Leader Reputation and the Multiple Audience Problem." *Journal of Management Inquiry* 9: 71–86.

Klandermans, Bert. 1997. *The Social Psychology of Protest*. Oxford: Blackwell.

Klandermans, Bert, and Jackie Smith. 2002. "Survey Research: A Case for Comparative Designs." Pp. 3–31 in *Methods of social Movement Research*, Bert Klandermans and Suzanne Staggenborg, eds. Minneapolis, MN: Univeristy of Minnesota Press.

Klatch, Rebecca E. 1999. *A Generation Divided: The New Left, the New Right, and the 1960s*. Berkeley, CA: University of California Press.

Knopf, Jeffrey W. 1998. *Domestic Society and International Cooperation: The Impact of Protest on US Arms Control Policy*. New York: Cambridge University Press.

Koopmans, Ruud. 2004. "Movements and Media: Selected Processes and Evolutionary Dynamics in the Public Sphere." *Theory and Society* 33: 367–91.

Kriesi, Hanspeter. 1996. "The Organizational Structure of New Social Movements in a Political Context." Pp. 152–84 in *Comparative Perspective on Social Movements. Political Opportunities, Mobilizing Structures, and Cultural Framings*, Doug McAdam, John McCarthy and Mayer N. Zald, eds. New York: Cambridge University Press.

Kriesi, Hanspeter, Ruud Koopmans, Jan-Willem Duvendak, and Marco Giugni. 1995. *New Social Movements in Western Europe*. Minneapolis, MN: University of Minnesota Press.

Krinsky, John. 2007. *Free Labor: Workfare and the Contested Language of Neoliberalism*. Chicago, IL: University of Chicago Press.

Kubal, Timothy J. 1998. "The Presentation of Political Self: Cultural Resonance and The Construction of Collective Action Frames." *Sociological Quarterly* 39: 539–54.

Kukutz, Irena. 1995. "Die Bewegung 'Frauen für den Frieden' als Teil der unabhängigen Friedensbewegung der DDR." Pp. 1285–1408 in Materialien zur Enquete-Kommision "Aufarbeitung von Geschichte und Folgen der SED-Diktatur in Deutschland," vol. 4. Berlin: Deutscher Bundestag.

abov, William. 1972. *Language in the Inner City*. Philadelphia, PA: University of Pennsylvania Press.

Kupisch, Karl. 1966. *Deutschen Landeskirchen Im 19. und 20. Jahrhundert*. Gottingen: Vandenhoeck u. Ruprecht.

Labov, William. 1972. *Language in the Inner City*. Philadelphia: University of Pennsylvania Press.

Labov, William, and Joshua Waletsky. 1967. "Narrative Analysis: Oral Versions of Personal Experience." Pp. 12–44 in *Essays on the Verbal and Visual Arts*, June Helm, ed. Seattle, WA: University of Washington Press.

Lahusen, Christian. 1993. "The Aesthetic of Radicalism: Between Punk and the Patriotic Nationalist Movement of the Basque Country." *Popular Music* 12: 263–80.

Lakoff, George. 1987. *Women, Fire, and Dangerous Things: What Categories Reveal about the Mind.* Chicago, IL: Univerrsity of Chicago Press

———. 1996. *Moral Politics: What Conservatives Know and Liberals Don't.* Chicago, IL: University of Chicago Press

Lakoff, George, and Johnson, Mark. 1980. *Metaphors We Live By.* Chicago, IL: University of Chicago Press.

Lakoff, George, and Mark Johnson. 1999. *Philosophy in the Flesh.* New York: Basic Books.

Lang, Gladys Engel, and Kurt Lang. 1988. "Recognition and Renown: The Survival of Artistic Reputation." *American Journal of Sociology* 94: 79–109.

Langacker, Ronald W. 1991. *Foundations of Cognitive Grammar 2*. Stanford, CA: Stanford University Press.

Latour, Burno. 1988. "Mixing Human and Nonhumans Together." *Social Problems* 35: 298–310.

Leach, Darcy K. 2006. "The Way is the Goal: Ideology and the Practice of Collectivist Democracy in German New Social Movements." Doctoral Thesis, Department of Sociology, University of Michigan.

Leach, Darcy K. in press. "An Elusive 'We': Anti-Dogmatism, Democratic Practice, and the Contradictory Identity of the German Autonomen." *American Behavioral Scientist.*

Lehmann, Susan Goodrich. 1995. "Islam Commands Intense Devotion among the Chechens." Opinion Analysis: USIA. Washington DC: USIA. July 27, 1995.

Leitch, Thomas M. 1986. *What Stories Are: Narrative Theory and Interpretation.* University Park: Pennsylvania State University Press.

Leontiev, Alexsei N. 1978. *Activity, Consciousness, and Personality.* http://www. marxists. org/archive/leontev/works/1978/index.htm.

———. 1981. *Problems of the Development of the Mind.* Moscow: Progress Publishers.

Leviero, Anthony. 1953. "Spearhead of Isolation." *New York Times* (September 27): 364.

Levi-Strauss, Claude. 1963. "The Structural Analysis of Myth." In *Structural Anthropology*, translated by Claire Jacobson and Brooke Grundfest Schoepf. New York, NY: Basic Books.

———. 1963. *Structural Anthropology.* Garden City, NY: Doubleday.

———. 1966. *The Savage Mind.* Chicago, IL: University of Chicago Press.

Lewin, Tamar. 1991a. "More States Study Clemency for Women Who Killed Abusers." *New York Times*, February 21, sec. A.

———. 1991b. "Criticism of Clemency May Affect Efforts to Free Battered Women." *New York Times*, April 2, 1, sec. A.

Lichterman, Paul. 1996. *The Search for Political Community*. New York: Cambridge University Press.

———. 1999. "Talking Identities in the Public Sphere: Broad Visions and Small Spaces in Sexual Identity Politics." *Theory and Society* 28: 101–41.

Lieven, Anatol. 1998. *Chechenya. Tombstone of Russian Power.* New Haven, CT: Yale University Press.

Lippmann, Walter. 1925. *The Phantom Public.* New York: Harcourt Brace.

Lofland, John. 1996. *Social Movement Organizations: Guide to Research on Insurgent Realities.* New York: Aldine de Gruyter.

Loseke, Donileen. 2000. "Ethos, Pathos, and Social Problems: Reflections on Formula Narratives." *Perspectives on Social Problems* 12: 41–54.

MacDonnell, Francis. 1995. *Insidious Foes: The Axis Fifth Column and the American Home Front.* New York: Oxford University Press.

MacLean, Paul D. 1998. "A Frame Analysis of Favor Seeking in the Renaissance: Agency, Networks, and Political Culture." *American Journal of Sociology* 104: 51–91.

Maguigan, Holly. 1991. "Battered Women and Self-Defense: Myths and Misconceptions in Current Reform Proposals." *University of Pennsylvania Law Review* 140: 379–486.

Mahoney, Martha R. 1994. "Victimization or Oppression? Women's Lives, Violence, and Agency." Pp. 59–92 in *The Public Nature of Private Violence: The Discovery of Domestic Abuse*, Martha Albertson Fineman and Roxanne Mykitiuk, eds. New York: Routledge.

Mansbridge, Jane. 1985. *Beyond Adversary Democracy.* Chicago: University of Chicago Press.

———. 1986. *Why We Lost the ERA*. Chicago, IL: University of Chicago Press.

———. 1996. "Using Power/Fighting Power: The Polity." Pp. 46–66 in *Democracy and Difference: Contesting the Boundaries of the Political*, Seyla Benhabib, ed. Princeton, NJ: Princeton University Press.

Martin, Joanne, and Melanie Powers. 1983. "Organizational Stories: More Vivid and Persuasive Than Quantitative Data." Pp. 161–8 in *Psychological Foundations of Organizational Behavior*, 2nd ed. Barry Staw, ed. Glenview, IL: Scott, Foresman.

Mayring, Phillipp. 2000. "Qualitative Content Analysis." *FQS* 1(2) http://www.qualitative-research.net/fqs/fqs-eng.htm.

McAdam, Doug 1982. *Political Process and the Development of Black Insurgency, 1930–1970*. Chicago, IL: University of Chicago Press.

———. 1988. *Freedom Summer*. New York: Oxford University Press.

————. 1989. "The Biographical Consequences of Activism." *American Sociological Review* 54: 744–60.

McAdam, Doug, John D. McCarthy and Mayer N. Zald, eds. 1996. *Comparative Perspectives on Social Movements. Political Opportunities, Mobilizing Stuctures, and Cultural Framings*. New York: Cambridge University Press.

McAdam, Doug, and Yang Su. 2002. "The War at Home: Antiwar Protests and Congressional Voting, 1965 to 1973." *American Sociological Review* 67: 696–721.

McAdam, Doug, Sidney Tarrow, and Charles Tilly. 2001. *Dynamics of Contention*. New York: Cambridge University Press.

McCammon, Holly J., Karen E. Campbell, Ellen M. Granberg, and Christine Mowery. 2001. "How MovementsWin: Gendered Opportunity Structures and US Women's Suffrange Movements, 1866–1916." *American Sociological Review* 66: 49–70.

McCarthy, John D., and Mayer N. Zald. 1987. *Resource Mobilization and Social Movements: A Partial Theory*. Pp. 337–91 in *Social Movements in an Organizational Society*, Mayer N. Zald and John D. McCarthy, New Brunswick, NJ: Transaction

McEnaney, Laura. 1994. "He-men and Christian Mothers: The America First Movement and the Gendered Meanings of Patriotism and Isolationism." *Diplomatic History* 18: 47–57.

Melucci, Alberto. 1985. The Symbolic Challenge of Contemporary Movements." *Social Research* 52: 789–816.

————. 1989. *Nomads of the Present*. Philadelphia, PA: Temple University Press.

————. 1994 "A Strange Kind of Newness: What's 'New' in New Social Movements." Pp. 101–30 in *New Social Movements: From Ideology to Identity*, Enrique Laraña, Hank Johnston, and Joseph Gusfield, eds. Philadephia, PA: Temple University Press.

————. 1995. "The Process of Collective Identity." Pp 41–63 in *Social Movements and Culture*, Hank Johnston and Bert Klandermans, eds. Minneapolis, MN: University of Minnesota Press.

Merelman, Richard M. 1998. "The Mundane Experience of Political Culture." *Political Communication* 15: 515–35.

Meyer, David S. 2007. *The Politics of Protest: Social Movements in America*. New York: Oxford University Press.

Meyer, David S., and Catherine Corrigall-Brown. 2005. "Coalitions and Political Context: US Movements against Wars in Iraq." *Mobilization* 10: 327–44.

Meyer, David S., and Sam Marullo. 1992. "Grassroots Mobilization and International Change." *Research in Social Movements, Conflict and Change* 14: 99–147.

Meyer, David S. and Suzanne Staggenborg. 1996. "Movements, Counter-movements, and the Structure of Political Opportunity." *American Journal of Sociology* 101: 1628–60.

Meyer, David S., and Sidney Tarrow. 1998. "A Movement Society: Contentious Politics for the New Century," Pp. 1–28 in *The Social Movement Society: Contentious Politics for the New Century*, David S. Meyer and Sidney Tarrow. eds. Lanham, MD: Rowman and Littlefield.

Meyer, David S., and Nancy Whittier. 1994. "Social Movement Spillover." *Social Problems* 41: 277–98.

Middleton, David, and Derek Edwards. 1990. "Conversational Remembering: A Social Psychological Approach." Pp. 23–45 in *Collective Remembering*, David Middleton and Derek Edwards, eds. London: Sage.

Miethe, Ingrid. 1999a. *Frauen in der DDR-Opposition. Lebens- und kollektivgeschichtliche Verläufe in einer Frauenfriedensgruppe*. Opladen: Leske + Budrich.

———. 1999b. "From 'Mother of Revolution' to 'Fathers of Unification': Concepts of Politics among Women Activist Following German Unification." *Social Politics* 6(1): 1–22.

———. 2000. "Changes in Spaces of Political Activism: Transforming East Germany." Pp. 315–34 in *Biographies and the Division of Europe. Experience, Action and Change on the 'Eastern Side'*, Roswitha Breckner, Devorah Kalekin-Fishman and Ingrid Miethe eds. Opladen: Leske+Budrich.

———. 2002. "East German Dissident Biographies in the Context of Family History: Interdependence of Methodological Approach and Empirical Results." *The History of the Family*. Special Issue "Family History-Life Story" 7: 207–24.

Miethe, Ingrid, and Anne Ulrich-Hampele. 2001. "Preference for Informal Democracy. The East(ern) German case." Pp. 23–32 in *Pink, Purple, Green. Women`s, Religious, Environmental and Gay/Lesbian Movements in Central Europe Today*, Helena Flam, ed. New York: Columbia University Press.

Miller, David. 1993. *Deliberative Democracy and Social Choice*, Pp. 74–92 in *Prospects for Democracy*. David Held, ed. Cambridge: Polity Press.

———. 2003. "Deliberative Democracy and Social Choice." Pp. 182–99 in *Debating Deliberative Democracy*. James S. Fishkin and Peter Laslett, eds. Oxford: Blackwell.

Miller, J. Hillis. 1990. "Narrative." In *Critical Terms for Literary Study*, Frank Lentricchia and Tom McLaughlin, eds. Chicago, IL: University of Chicago Press.

Minieri, Joan, and Paul Getsos. 2007. *Tools for Radical Democracy*. San Francisco: Jossey-Bass.

Minow, Martha. 1993. "Surviving Victim Talk." *UCLA Law Review* 40: 1441–5.

Mische, Ann. 2003. "Cross-Talk in Movements: Reconceiving the Culture-Nework Link." Pp. 258–80 in *Social Movements and Networks*, Mario Diani and Doug McAdam, eds. New York: Oxford University Press.

Mische, Ann, and Phillippa Pattison. 2000. "Composing a Civic Arena: Publics, Projects and Social Settings." *Poetics* 27: 163–94.

Mitroff, Ian I., and Ralph H. Kilmann. 1984. *Corporate Tragedies: Product Tampering, Sabotage, and Other Catastrophes*. New York: Praeger.

Moore, Kelly. 1996. "Organizing Integrity: American Science and the Creation of Public Interest Organizations, 1955–1975." *American Journal of Sociology* 101: 1592–627.

Moore, Ryan, and Michael Roberts. 2007. "Do-It-Yourself Mobilization: Punk as a Social Movement." Unpublished manuscript, San Diego State University.

Morgan, D.L. 1997. *Focus Groups as Qualitative Research*. London: Sage.

Morgan, Ted. 2003. *Reds: McCarthyism in Twentieth-Century America*. New York: Random House.

Morris, Aldon D. 1984. *The Origins of the Civil Rights Movement: Black Communities Organizing for Change*. New York: Free Press.

Moscovici, Serge. 1961. *La Psychoanalyse Son Image et Son Public*. Paris: Presses Universitaires de France.

Mouchard, Daniel. 2003. "Le difficoltà di un'alternativa. Dinamiche organizzative in 'Agir ensamble contre le chomage.'" Pp. 57-74 in *La democrazia dei movimenti*, Paolo Ceri, ed. Soveria Mannelli: Rubettino.

Mowjee, Tasneem. 2003a. "Consumers United Internationally." Pp. 29–44 in *Globalizing Civic Engagement*. John Clark, ed. London, Earthscan.

———. 2003b. "Campaign to Increase Access to HIV/AIDS Drugs." Pp. 66–85 in *Globalizing Civic Engagement*. John Clark, ed. London: Earthscan,.

Mueller, Carol. 1994. "Conflict Networks and the Origins of the Women's Movement." Pp. 234–63 in *New Social Movements: From Ideology to Identity*, Enrique Laraña, Hank Johnston, and Joseph R. Gusfield, eds. Philadelphia, PA: Temple University Press.

Munck, Geraldo L. 2001. "Game Theory and Comparative Politics: New Perspectives on Old Concerns." *World Politics* 53: 173–204.

New Republic. 1941. "Smoke Out 'America First.'" (October 6): 422–3.

———. 1941. "60% at Garden Rally Pro-Nazi, Morris Says." (May 25): 3.

———. 1941. "9 Disclaim Attack on Flynn Group." (March 15): 6.

———. 1941. "Anti-War Group Spurns Bund Aid." (May 9): 12.

———. 1941. "Hitler Front Laid to 'America First." (August 29): 18.

———. 1941. "Lindbergh Joins in Wheeler Plea to US to Shun War." (May 24): 1, 6.

———. 1941. "Miami Bars LaFollette Rally." (May 4): 9.

———. 1941. "New Rochelle Voters' Unit Head Quits in Favor of America First." (October 8): 18.

———. 1941. "Wheeler Makes Denial: Calls Kingdon-Swope Un-American Charge 'Deliberate Lie.'" (February 23): 24.

Muro, Diego and Nuno Themundo. 2003, "Trade Unions in a Changing World: Challenges and Opportunities of Transnationalization." Pp. 45–65 in *Globalizing Civic Engagement*, John Clark ed. London, Earthscan.

Noakes, John A. and Hank Johnston. 2005. "Frames of Protest. A Road Map to a Persective." Pp. 1–29 in *Frames of Protest. Social Movements and the Framing Perspective*, Hank Johnston and John A. Noakes, eds. Lanham, MD: Rowman and Littlefield.

Noonan, Rita K. 1995. "Women Against the State: Political Opportunities and Collective Action Frames in Chile's Transition to Democracy." *Sociological Forum* 10(1): 81–101.

Norton, Ann. 2004. *Ninety-Five Theses on Politics, Culture, and Method.* New Haven, CT: Yale University Press.

Novick, Peter. 1999. *The Holocaust in American Life.* Boston: Houghton Mifflin.

Oevermann, Ulrich. 1979. "Die Methodologie einer 'Objektiven Hermeneutik' und ihre allgemeine forschungslogische Bedeutung in den Sozialwissenschaften." Pp. 352–434 in *Interpretative Verfahren in den Sozial- und Textwissenschaften*, H.-G. Soeffner, ed. Stuttgart: Metzler.

Offe, Claus, 1985. "New Social Movements: Changing Boundaries of the Political." *Social Research* 52: 817–68.

———. 1997. "Microaspects of Democratic Theory: What Makes for the Deliberative Competence of Citizens?" Pp. 81–104 in *Democracy's Victory and Crisis.* Axel Hadenius, ed. New York: Cambridge University Press.

———. 2005. "What a Good Idea! Ideologies and Frames in Social Movement Research." Pp. 185–203 in *Frames of Protest*, Hank Johnston and John A. Noakes, eds. Lanham, MD: Rowman and Littlefield.

Oliver, Pamela E., and Hank Johnston. 2005. "What a Good Idea! Ideologies and Frames in Social Movement Research." Pp. 185–203 in *Frames of Protest*, Hank Johnston and John A. Noakes, eds. Lanham, MD: Rowman & Littlefield.

Orem, Anthony M., Joe R. Feagin, and Gideon Sjoberg. 1991. "The Nature of the Case Study." Pp. 1–26 in *The Case for the Case Study*, Joe R. Feagin, Anthony M. Orum, and Gideon Sjoberg, eds. Chapel Hill, NC: University of North Carolina Press.

Ormrod, Jane. 1997. "The North Caucasus: Confederation in Conflict." In *New States, New Politics: Building the Post-Soviet Nations,* Ian Bremmer and Ray Taras, eds. New York: Cambridge University Press.

Oslzly, Petr. 1990. "On Stage with the Velvet Revolution." *Drama Review* 34: 88–96.

Pareles, Jon. 2007. "Rock 'n' Revolution." *New York Times* November 11, AR: 1–32.

Parkin, Frank. 1968. *Middle Class Radicalism: The Social Bases of the British Campaign for Nuclear Disarmament.* New York: Praeger.

Payne, Charles M. 1995. *I've Got the Light of Freedom: The Organizing Tradition and the Mississippi Freedom Struggles.* Berkeley, CA: University of California Press.

Peirce, Charles S. 1991. *Peirce on Signs.* James Hoopes, ed. Chapel Hill, NC: University of North Carolina Press.

Perry, Charles. 2005. *The Haight-Ashbury: A History.* New York: Wenner Books.

Petersen, Trond. 1994. "On the Promise of Game Theory in Sociology." *Contemporary Sociology* 23: 498–502.

Phelan, Shane. 1997. "The Shape of Queer: Assimilation and Articulation." *Women and Politics* 18: 55–73.

Piazza, Gianni, and Marco Barbagallo. 2003. Tra globale e locale. L'articolazione territoriale del movimento per una globalizzazione dal basso: i social forum in Sicilia, paper presented at the annual congress of the Società Italiana di Scienza Politica, Trento, September.

Pinckney, Alphonso. 1968. *The Committed: White Activists in the Civil Rights Movement.* New Haven, CT: College and University Press.

Piven, Frances Fox, and Richard A. Cloward. 1977. *Poor People's Movements: How they Succeed, Why They Fail.* New York: Vintage.

Plummer, Kenneth. 1995. *Telling Sexual Stories: Power, Change, and Social Worlds.* New York, NY: Routledge.

Polkinghorne, D.E. 1988. *Narrative Knowing and the Human Sciences.* Albany: State University of New York.

Polletta, Francesca. 1997. "Culture and Its Discontents: Recent Theorizing on the Cultural Dimensions of Protest." *Sociological Quarterly*, 67(4): 431–50.

———. 1998a. "It Was Like a Fever ... Narrative and Identity in Social Protest." *Social Problems* 45: 137–59.

———. 1998b. "Legacies and Liabilities of an Insurgent Past: Remembering Martin Luther King on the House and Senate Floor." *Social Science History* 22(4): 479–512.

———. 1999a. "Snarls, Quacks, and Quarrels: Culture and Structure in Political Process Theory." *Sociological Forum* 14(1): 63–70.

———. 1999b. "'Free Spaces' in Collective Action." *Theory and Society* 28: 1–38.

———. 2002. *Freedom Is an Endless Meeting: Democracy in American Social Movements.* Chicago, IL: University of Chicago Press.

———. 2005. "How Participatory Democracy Became White: Culture and Organizational Choice." *Mobilization* 10(2): 271–88.

———. 2006. *It Was Like a Fever: Storytelling in Protest and Politics.* Chicago, IL: University Chicago Press.

Powers. Richard Gid. 1998. *Not Without Honor: The History of American Anticommunism.* New Haven, CT: Yale University Press.

Public Justice Center. 1990. *A Plea for Justice* [Video]. Group Two Productions.

Raeburn, Nicole C. 2004. *Changing Corporate America from Inside Out.* Minneapolis, MN: University of Minnesota Press.

Ragin, Charles C. 1992. "Cases of 'What is a Case?'" Pp. 1–17 in *What is a Case? Exploring the Foundations of Social Inquiry*, Charles C. Ragin and Howard S. Becker, eds. New York: Cambridge University Press.

Read, Stephen J., Ian L. Cesa, David K. Jones, and Nancy L. Collins. 1990. "When is the Federal Budget Like a Baby? Metaphor in Political Rhetoric." *Metaphor and Symbolic Activity* 53: 125–49.

Reilly, William K., Philip Shabecoff, and Devra Lee Davis. 1995. "Is There Cause for 'Environmental Optimism'"? *Environmental Science and Technology* 29 (August 8) 8: 366A+.

Ricoeur, Paul. 1979. "The Model of the Text: Meaningful Action Considered as a Text." Pp. 73–101 in *Interpretative Social Sciences: A Reader*, Paul Rabinow and William Sullivan, eds. Berkeley, CA: University of California Press.

———. 1981. *Hermeneutics and Human Sciences: Essays on Language, Action, and Interpretation*. Edited and translated by John B. Thompson. Cambridge: Cambridge University Press.

Risse-Kappen, Thomas. 1994. "Ideas Do Not Float Freely: Transnational Coalitions, Domestic Structures, and the End of the Cold War." *International Organization* 48: 185–214.

Robnett, Belinda. 1997. *How Long? How Long? African-American Women in the Struggle for Civil Rights*. New York: Oxford University Press.

Rochford, Jr, E. Burke. 1985. *Hare Krishna in America*. New Brunswick, NJ: Rutgers University Press.

Rochon, Thomas R. 1998. *Culture Moves: Ideas, Activism, and Changing Values*. Princeton, NJ: Princeton University Press.

Rochon, Thomas R., and David S. Meyer, eds. 1997. *Coalitions and Political Movements: The Lessons of the Nuclear Freeze*. Boulder, CO: Lynne Rienner.

Roiphe, Katie. 1993. *The Morning After: Sex, Fear, and Feminism on Campus*. Boston: Little Brown.

Rosenthal, Gabriele. 1993. "Reconstruction of Life Stories. Principles of Selection in Generating Stories for Narrative Biographical Interviews." *Narrative Study of Lives* 1: 59–91.

———. 2004. "Biographical Research." In *Qualitative Research Practice*, Clive Seale, David Silverman, Jay Gubrium, and Gobo Giampetro, eds. London: Sage.

Rosi, Marco. 2003. *Decidere tra politica ed economia: il movimento del Commercio Equo e Solidale in Italia*. Pp. 95–132 in *La democrazia dei movimenti*, Paolo Ceri, ed. Soveria Mannelli: Rubettino.

Rosigno, Vincent J., and William F. Danaher 2004. *The Voice of Southern Labor*. Minneapolis, MN: University of Minnesota Press.

Roth, Philip. 2004. *The Plot Against America*. Boston: Houghton Mifflin.

Roth, Roland. 1994. "Lokale Bewegungsnetzwerke und die Institutionalisierung von neuen sozialen Bewegungen." In *Öffentlichkeit, öffentliche Meinung, soziale Bewegungen, KZfSS, Sonderhelft 34/1994*, Friedrik Niedhard, ed. Berlin: Opladen.

Roth, Silke. 1997. "Political Socialization, Bridging Organization, Social Movement Interaction. The Coalition of Labor Union Women, 1974–1996." Doctoral Dissertation, University of Connecticut.

———. 2000. "Developing Working-Class Feminism: A Biographical Approach to Social Movement Participation." Pp. 300–23 in *Identity and Social Movements*, S. Stryker, J. Timothy, T. Owens and W. White, eds. Minneapolis, MN: University of Minnesota Press.

———. 2002. *Building Movement Bridges: The Coalition of Labor Union Women.* Westport, CT: Greenwood.

Rothman, Franklin Daniel, and Pamela Oliver. 2002. "From Local to Global: the Anti-Dam Movement in Southern Brazil, 1979–1992." Pp. 115–32 in *Globalization and Resistance*, Jackie Smith and Hank Johnston, eds. Lanham, MD: Rowman and Littlefield,

Routledge, Paul. 2003. "Convergence Space: Process Geographies of Grass-Roots Globalization Networks." *Transactions of the Institute of British Geographers* 28 (3), 333–49.

Rucht, Dieter. 1990. "The Strategies and Action Repertoires of New Movements." Pp. 156–75 in *Challenging the Political Order: New Social and Political Movements in Western Democracies*, Robert. J. Dalton and Manfred. Keuchler, eds. Cambridge: Polity Press.

———. 1999. "The Impact of Environmental Movements in Western Societies." Pp. 204–24 in *How Movements Matter: Theoretical and Comparative Studies on the Consequences of Social Movements*, Marco Giugni, Doug McAdam, and Charles Tilly, eds. Minneapolis, MN: University of Minnesota Press.

———, ed. 2003. *Berlin, 1. Mai 2002 – Politische Demonstrationsrituale.* Leverkusen: Leske + Budrich.

———. 2005, "Un movimento di movimenti? Unità e diversità fra le organizzazioni per una giustizia globale." *Rassegna Italiana di sociologia* 46(2): 275–306.

———. 1996. "The Impact of National Contexts on Social Movements Structure." Pp. 185–205 in *Comparative Perspective on Social Movements. Political Opportunities, Mobilizing Structures, and Cultural Framings*, Doug McAdam, John McCarthy, and Mayer N. Zald, eds. New York: Cambridge University Press.

Rupp, Leila, and Verta Taylor. 1987. *Survival in the Doldrums: The American Women's Rights Movement, 1945 to the 1960s.* New York: Oxford University Press.

———. 2005. "Un movimento di movimenti? Unità e diversità fra le organizzazioni per una giustizia globale." *Rassegna Italiana di sociologia* 46(2): 275–306.

Ryan, Barbara. 1989. "Ideological Purity and Feminism: The US Women's Movement from 1966 to 1975." *Gender and Society* 3: 239–57.

Ryan, Charlotte. 1991. *Prime Time Activism: Media Strategies for Grassroots Organizing.* Boston: South End Press.

Sawyers, Traci M., and David S. Meyer. 1999. "Missed Opportunities: Social Movement Abeyance and Public Policy," *Social Problems* 46: 187–206.

Sayers, Michael, and Albert E. Kahn. 1942. *Sabotage!: The Secret War Against America.* New York: Harper and Brothers.

Scheppele, Kim Lane. 1992. "Just the Facts, Ma'am: Sexualized Violence, Evidentiary Habits, and the Revision of Truth." *New York Law School Law Review* 37: 123–72.

Schneider, Anne Larason, and Helen Ingram. 1997. *Policy Design for Democracy.* Lawrence: University Press of Kansas.

Schneider, Elizabeth M. 2000. *Battered Women and Feminist Lawmaking.* New Haven, CT: Yale University Press.

Schön, Donald A. 1979. "Generative Metaphor and Social policy: A Perspective on Problem-setting in Social Policy." In *Metaphor and Thought,* Andrew Ortony, ed. Cambridge, UK: Cambridge University Press.

Schönleitner, Günther. 2003. "World Social Forum: Making Another World Possible?" Pp. 127–49 in *Globalizing Civic Engagement*, John Clark, ed. London: Earthscan.

Schultz, Vicki. 1990. "Telling Stories About Women and Work: Judicial Interpretations of Sex Segregation in the Workplace in Title VII Cases Raising the Lack of Interest Argument." *Harvard University Law Review* 103: 1749–843.

Schuman, Howard, and Jacqueline Scott. 1989. "Generations and Collective Memories." *American Sociological Review* 54: 359–81.

Schwartz, Barry. 1996. "Memory as a Cultural System: Abraham Lincoln in World War II." *American Sociological Review* 61: 908–27.

Scott, James C. 1990. *Domination and the Arts of Resistance.* New Haven, CT: Yale University Press.

Scott, Joan W. 1994. "Deconstructing Equality-versus-Difference: Or, the Uses of Poststructuralist Theory for Feminism." Pp. 282–98 in *The Postmodern Turn: New Perspectives on Social Theory*, Steven Seidman, ed. New York, NY: Cambridge University Press.

Scott, Marvin, and Stanford Lyman. 1968. "Accounts." *American Sociological Review* 33: 46–62.

Searle, John. 1979. *Expression and Meaning: Studies in the Theory of Speech Acts.* Cambridge: Cambridge University Press.

Searle, John R. 2002. *Consciousness and Language.* New York: Cambridge University Press.

Searles, Ruth. 2003. *A Story of America First: The Men and Women Who Opposed US Intervention in World War II.* Westport, CT: Praeger.

Selznick, Philip. 1952. *The Organizational Weapon: A Study of Bolshevik Strategy and Tactics.* New York: McGraw-Hill.

Sewell, William H., Jr. 1999. "The Concept(s) of Culture." Pp. 35–61 in *Beyond the Cultural Turn*. Victoria E. Bonnell and Lynn Hunt, eds. Berkeley, CA: University of California Press.

Shepard, Roger N., and Cooper, Lynn A. 1982. *Mental Images and Their Transformations*. Cambridge, MA: MIT Press.

Silverstein, Michael. 1993. "Metapragmatic Discourse and Metapragmatic Function." In *Reflexive Language: Reported Speech and Metapragmatics*. John A. Lucy, ed. Cambridge, UK: Cambridge University Press.

Simon, Herbert W. 1990. *The Rhetorical Turn: Invention and Persuasion in the Conduct of Inquiry*. Chicago, IL: University of Chicago Press.

Slater, Michael D., and Donna Rouner. 2002. "Entertainment-Education and Elaboration Likelihood: Understanding the Processing of Narrative Persuasion." *Communication Theory* 12: 173–91.

Small, Melvin. 1988. *Johnson, Nixon, and the Doves*. New Brunswick, NJ: Rutgers University Press.

Smelser, Neil J. 1992. "Culture: Coherent or Incoherent." Pp. 3–28 in *Theory of Culture*. Richard Munch and Neil J. Smelser, eds. Berkeley, CA: University of California Press.

Smith, Christian. 1996. *Resisting Reagan: The US Central America Peace Movement*. Chicago, IL: University of Chicago Press.

Smith, Geoffrey S. 1973. *To Save a Nation: American Countersubversives, the New Deal, and the Coming of World War II*. New York: Basic Books.

Smith, Kimberly. 1998. "Storytelling, Sympathy, and Moral Judgment in American Abolitionism." *Journal of Political Philosophy* 6: 356–77.

Smith, Sebastian. 2001. *Allah's Mountains: The Battle for Chechnya*. London: I.B. Taurus.

Snow, David A. 1979. "A Dramaturgical Analysis of Movement Accommodation: Building Idiosyncrasy Credit as a Movement Mobilization Strategy." *Symbolic Interaction* 2: 23–44.

———. 2004. "Framing Processes, Ideology, and Discursive Fields." Pp. 380–412 in *The Blackwell Companion to Social Movements*, David A. Snow, Sarah A. Soule, and Hanspeter Kriesi, eds. Malden, MA: Blackwell.

Snow, David A., and Leon Anderson. 1987. "Identity Work Among the Homeless: The Verbal Construction and Avowal of Personal Identities." *American Journal of Sociology* 92: 1336–71.

Snow, David A., and Robert D. Benford. 1988. "Ideology, Frame Resonance, and Participant Mobilization." Pp. 197–217 in *International Social Movement Research,* Bert Klandermans, Hanspeter Kriesi, and Sidney Tarrow, eds. Greenwich, CT: JAI Press.

———. 1992. "Master Frames and Cycles of Protest." Pp. 133–55 in *Frontiers of Social Movement Theory*. Aldon D. Morris and Carol McClurg Mueller, eds. New Haven, London: Yale University Press.

Snow, David A., and Scott C. Byrd. 2007. "Ideology, Framing Processes, and Islamic Terrorist Movements." *Mobilization: An International Quarterly.* 12: 119–36.

Snow, David A. and Pamela W. Oliver. 1995. "Social Movements and Collective Behavior. Social Psychological Dimensions and Considerations." Pp. 571–99 in *Sociological Perspectives on Social Psychology*, Karen S. Cook, Gary Alan Fine and James S. House, eds. Boston: Allyn and Bacon.

Snow, David A., E. Burke Rochford Jr, Steven K. Worden and Robert D. Benford. 1986. "Frame Alignment Processes, Micromobilization, and Movement Participation." *American Sociological Review* 51: 464–81.

Snow, David A., and Danny Trom. 2002. "The Case Study and the Study of Social Movements." Pp. 146–72 in *Methods of Social Movement Research*, Bert Klandermans and Suzanne Staggenborg, eds. Minneapolis, MN: University of Minnesota Press.

Somers, Margaret. 1992. "Narrativity, Narrative Identity and Social Action: Rethinking English Working-Class Formation." *Social Science History* 16: 591–630.

Sommier, Isabelle. 2005. "Produire l'événement: logiques de coopération et conflits feutrés." Pp. 19–43 *Radiographie du mouvement altermondialiste*, Eric Agrikoliansky and Isabelle Sommier, eds. Paris: La Dispute.

Soule, Sara, and Jennifer Earl. 2005. "A Social Movement Society Evaluated: Collective Protest in the United States 1960–1985." *Mobilization* 10: 345–64.

Spector, Malcolm, and John I. Kitsuse. 2001. *Constructing Social Problems.* New Brunswick, NJ: Transaction Books.

Spelman, Elizabeth V. 1988. *Inessential Woman: Problems of Exclusion in Feminist Thought.* Boston, MA: Beacon Press.

Steinberg, Marc W. 1998. "Tilting the Frame: Considerations on Collective Action Framing from a Discursive Turn." *Theory and Society* 27(6): 845–72.

———. 1999. *Fighting Words: Working-Class Formation, Collective Action, and Discourse in Early Nineteenth Century England.* Ithaca, NY: Cornell University Press.

———. 2000. "The Talk and Back Talk of Collective Action: A Dialogic Analysis of Repertoires of Discourse among Nineteenth-Century English Cotton Spinners." *American Journal of Sociology* 10: 736–80.

———. 2002. "Toward a More Dialogic Analysis of Social Movement Culture." in *Social Movements: Identity, Culture, and the State*, David S. Meyer, Nancy Whittier, and Belinda Robnett, eds. New York: Oxford University Press.

Stoecker, Randy. 1995, "Community, Movement, Organization: The Problem of Identity Convergence in Collective Action." *The Sociological Quarterly* 36: 111–30.

Stone, Deborah. 1997. *Policy Paradox: The Art of Political Decision Making.* New York: Norton.

Stryker, Sheldon, Owens, Timothy J. and White, Robert W. eds. 2000. *Self, Identity and Social Movements*. Minneapolis: University of Minnesota Press.

Swart, William. 1995. "The League of Nations and the Irish Question: Master Frames, Cycles of Protest, and 'Master Frame Alignment'." *The Sociological Quarterly* 36: 111–30.

Swidler, Ann. 1986. "Culture in Action: Symbols and Strategies." *American Sociological Review* 51: 273–86.

———. 1995. "Cultural Power and Social Movements." Pp. 25–40 in *Social Movements and Culture*, Hank Johnston and Bert Klandermans, eds. Minneapolis, MN: University of Minnesota Press.

———. 1997. *Talk of Love. How Americans Use Their Culture*. Chicago, IL: University of Chicago Press.

Tajfel, Henri. 1981. *Human Groups and Social Categories*. London: Cambridge University Press.

Tarrow, Sidney. 1992. "Mentalities, Political Cultures and Collective Action Frames: Constructing Meanings through Action". Pp. 174–202 in *Frontiers in Social Movement Theory*, Aldon Morris and Carol MClurg Mueller, eds. New Haven, CT and London: Yale University Press.

———. 1994. *Power in Movement: Social Movements, Collective Action and Politics*. New York: Cambridge University Press.

———. 1998. *Power in Movement*, 2nd ed. New York: Cambridge University Press.

Taylor, Verta A. 1989. "Social Movement Continuity: The Women's Movement in Abeyance." *American Sociological Review* 54: 761–75.

Taylor, Verta and Leila J. Rupp. 1993. "Women's Culture and Lesbian Feminist Activism: A Reconsideration of Cultural Feminism." *Signs* 19: 32–61.

Taylor, Verta, and Nancy E. Whittier. 1992. "Collective Identity in Social Movement Communities." Pp. 104–29 in *Frontiers in Social Movement Theory*, Aldon Morris and Carol McClurg Mueller, eds. New Haven, CT: Yale University Press.

———. 1995. "Analytical Approaches to Social Movement Culture: the Culture of the Women's Movement." Pp. 163–87 in *Social Movements and Culture*, edited by H. Johnston and B. Klandermans. Minneapolis, MN: University of Minnesota Press.

Tilly, Charles. 1978. *From Mobilization to Revolution*. New York: Random House.

———. 1995. *Popular Contention in Great Britain, 1758–1834*. Cambridge, MA: Harvard University Press.

———. 2003. *Stories, Identities, and Political Change*. Lanham, MD: Rowman and Littlefield.

Touraine, Alain. 1981. *The Voice and the Eye. An Analysis of Social Movements*. Cambridge: Cambridge University Press.

Trafford, Abigail. 1991. "Why Battered Women Kill: Self-Defense, Not Revenge, is Often the Motive." *Washington Post*, February 26.

Tsebelis, George. 1999. *Nested Games: Rational Choice in Comparative Politics.* Berkeley, CA: University of California Press.

Turner, John C. 1987. *Rediscovering the Social Group. A Self-Categorization Theory.* New York: Basil Blackwell.

Turner, Jonathan. 1996. "The Evolution of Emotions in Humans: A Darwinian-Durkheimian Approach." *Journal for the Theory of Social Behaviour* 26: 1–33.

Turner, Ralph H. 1996. "The Moral Issue in Collective Behavior and Collective Action." *Mobilization*: 1: 1–15

Turner, Ralph, and Lewis Killian. 1987. *Collective Behavior*, 3rd ed. Englewood Cliffs, NJ: Prentice-Hall.

UCS transcripts of tape recordings of the meeting and discussions of shop-stewards and workers of the Upper Clyde Shipbuilders during the period of their "work-in" in 1971–1972. Vol. I. Charles A. Woolfson, ed.

Uncensored Poland News Bulletin. 1988. "More on the Orange Alternative." No. 12/88: 22–23. London: Information Centre for Polish Affairs.

Valocchi, Stephen. 2005. "Collective Action Frames In the Gay Liberation Movememnt , 1969–1973." Pp. 53–68 in *Frames of Protest*, Hank Johnston and John A. Noakes, eds. Lanham, MD: Rowman and Littlefield.

Veltri, Francesca. 2003. *"Non si chiama delega, si chiama fiducia." La sfida organizzativa della Rete di Lilliput*, Pp. 3–30 in *La democrazia dei movimenti*, Paolo Ceri, ed. Soveria Mannelli: Rubettino.

Vološinov, V.N. 1986. *Marxism and the Theory of Language*. Cambridge, MA: Harvard University Press.

Voss, Kim. 1996. "The Collapse of a Social Movement: The Interplay of Mobilizing Structures, Framing, and Political Opportunities in the Knights of Labor." Pp. 227–58 in *Comparative Perspectives on Social Movements: Political Opportunities, Mobilizing Structures, and Cultural Meanings*, Doug McAdam John D McCarthy and Mayer N Zald, eds. New York: Cambridge University Press.

———. 1998. "Claim Making and the Framing of Defeats: The Interpretation of Losses by American British Labor Activists, 1886–1895." Pp. 136–48 in *Challenging Authority: The Historical Study of Contentious Politics*, Michael P. Hanagan, Leslie Page Moch, and Wayne Ph. te Brake, eds. Minneapolis, MN: University of Minnesota Press.

Vygotsky, Lev. 1978. *Mind in Society The Development of Higher Psychological Processes*. Cambridge, MA: Harvard University Press.

———. 1986. *Thought and Language*. Cambridge, MA: MIT Press.

Wagner, Wolfgang, Fran Elejabarrieta, and Ingrid Lahnsteiner. 1995. "How the Sperm Dominates the Ovum: Objectification by Metaphor in the Social Representation of Conception." *European Journal of Social Psychology* 13: 175–91.

Waite, Lori. 2001. "Divided Consciousness: The Impact of Black Elite Consciousness on the 1966 Chicago Freedom Movement." Pp. 170–203 in *Oppositional Consciousness: The Subjective Roots of Social Protest*, Jane Mansbridge and Aldon Morris, eds. Chicago, IL: University of Chicago Press.

Wallace, Max. 2003. *The American Axis: Henry Ford, Charles Lindbergh, and the Rise of the Third Reich*. New York: St Martin's Press.

Washington Post. 1941. "Ickes Brands Lindbergh No. 1 Nazi Dupe." (April 14): 24.

———. 1941. "Riot at Rally: Crowd Beats Lindbergh's Detractors." (April 24): 1, 4.

———. 1941. No title. (January 5): B1.

Weber, Max. 1946 [1922–23]. "The Social Psychology of the World Religions." In *From Max Weber*, Hans H. Gerth and C. Wright Mills, eds. New York: Oxford University Press.

———. 1968. *Economy and Society: An Outline of Interpretive Sociology*. Translated by E. Fischhoff. New York: Bedminster Press.

Wernick, Laura, John Krinsky, and Paul Getsos. 2000. *The Work Experience Program, New York City's Public Sector Sweatshop Economy*. New York: Community Voices Heard. Online at www.cvhaction.org.

White, Hayden. 1980. "The Value of Narrativity in the Representation of Reality." *Critical Inquiry* 7: 5–27.

Whittier, Nancy. 1995. *Feminist Generations: The Persistence of the Radical Women's Movement*. Philadelphia, PA: Temple University Press.

———. 2001 "Emotional Strategies: The Collective Reconstruction and Display of Oppositional Emotions in the Movement against Child Sexual Abuse." Pp. 233–50 in *Passionate Politics: Emotions and Social Movements*, Jeff Goodwin, James M. Jasper, and Francesca Polletta, eds. Chicago, IL: University of Chicago Press.

Wildavsky, Aaron. 2006. *Cultural Analsysis*. edited by Brendon Swedlow. New Burnswick, NJ: Transaction Publishers.

Wilhelmsen, Julie. 2005. "Between a Rock and a Hard Place: The Islamization of the Chechen Separatist Movement." *Europe-Asia Studies* 57: 35–59

Wilkins, L.T. 1965. *Social Deviance: Social Policy, Action, and Research*. Englewood Cliffs, NJ: Prentice-Hall.

Williams, Rhys. 1995. "Constructing the Public Good: Social Movements and Cultural Resoruces." *Social Problems*: 42: 124–44.

Williams, Rhys, and Timothy J. Kubal. 1999. "Movement Frames and their Cultural Environment: Resonance, Failure and the Boundaries of the Legitimate." *Research in Social Movements, Conflict, and Change* 21: 225–48.

Wilson, James Q. 1995. *Political Organizations*, 2nd ed. Princeton, NJ: Princeton University Press.

Wittgenstein, Ludwig. 1953. *Philosophical Investigations.* Translated by G.E.M. Anscombe. New York: Macmillian

Wixman, Ronald. 1980. *Language Aspects of Ethnic Patterns and Processes in the North Caucasus*, Chicago, IL: University of Chicago Press.

Wolf, Naomi. 1993. *Fire with Fire: New Female Power and How It Will Change the Twenty-First Century.* New York: Random House.

Wolfson, Nessa 1979. "Conversational Historical Present Alternation." *Language* 55: 168–82.

Woolfson, Charles A. 1976. "The Semiotics of Working Class Speech." *Working Papers in Cultural Studies* 9: 163–97.

Wuthnow, Robert. 1984. "Introduction." Pp. 1–20 in *Cultural Analysis: The Work of Peter L. Berger, Mary Douglas, Michel Foucault, and Jurgen Habermas*, Robert Wuthnow, James Davison Hunter, Albert Bergesen, and Edith Kurzweil, eds. Boston: Routledge and Kegan Paul.

———. 1989. *Communities of Discourse.* Cambridge, MA: Harvard University Press.

Wuthnow, Robert, and Witten, Marsha. 1988. "New Directions in the Study of Culture." *Annual Review of Sociology* 14: 49–67.

Wuthnow, Robert, James Davison Hunter, Albert Bergesen, and Edith Kurzweil, eds. 1984. *Cultural Analysis: The Work of Peter L. Berger, Mary Douglas, Michel Foucault, and Jurgen Habermas.* Boston: Routledge and Kegan Paul.

Young, Iris Marion. 1996. "Communication and The Other: Beyond Deliberative Democracy." Pp. 120–35 in *Democracy and Difference: Contesting the Boundaries of the Political*, Seyla Benhabib, ed. Princeton, NJ: Princeton University Press.

———. 2003. "Activist Challenges to Deliberative Democracy." Pp. 102–20 in *Debating Deliberative Democracy.* James S. Fishkin and Peter Laslett, eds. Oxford: Blackwell.

Young, Michael. 2002. "Confessional Protest: The Religious Birth of US National Social Movements." *American Sociological Review* 67: 660–688.

Zald, Mayer N. 1996. "Culture, Ideology and Strategic Framing." In *Comparative Perspectives on Social Movements: Political Opportunities, Mobilizing Structures and Cultural Framings*, Douglas McAdam, John D. McCarthy, and Mayer N. Zald, eds. Cambridge, UK: Cambridge University Press.

Zerubavel, Eviatar. 1997. *Social Mindscapes: An Invitation to Cognitive Sociology.* Cambridge, MA: Harvard University Press.

Zillmann, Dolf, and Hans-Bernd Brosius. 2000. *Exemplification in Communication: The Influence of Case Reports on the Perception of Issues.* Mahwah, NJ: Erlbaum.

Index